DATE DUE

APR 1 3			
NOV 1 0 1999			

Amazing Grace

Evangelicalism in Australia, Britain, Canada, and the United States

Edited by
George A. Rawlyk
and Mark A. Noll

Baker Books
A Division of Baker Book House Co
Grand Rapids, Michigan 49516

Published by Baker Books,
a division of Baker Book House Company
PO Box 6287, Grand Rapids, Michigan 49516–6287

Printed in the United States of America

Library of Congress Cataloging-in-Publication Data

Amazing grace : Evangelicalism in Australia, Britain, Canada, and the United States /
    edited by George A. Rawlyk and Mark A. Noll.
       p.   cm.
       "Ten of the chapters in this book were presented in earlier versions at a
    conference, 'Evangelicalism in Trans-Atlantic Perspective,' held on April 8–11, 1992,
    at Wheaton College, Illinois"—Acknowledgments
       Includes bibliographical references and index.
       ISBN 0-8010-7772-9
       1. Evangelicalism—Great Britain—History—Congresses. 2. Evangelicalism—
United States—History—Congresses. 3. Evangelicalism—Canada—History—
Congresses. 4. Evangelicalism—Australia—History—Congresses. 5. Great Britain—
Church history—Congresses. 6. United States—Church history—Congresses. 7.
Canada—Church history—Congresses. 8. Australia—Church history—Congresses.
I. Rawlyk, George A. II. Noll, Mark A., 1946– .
BR1642.G7A53   1993
270.8—dc20   923-31996

To John R. W. Stott,
international evangelical

Contents

Part 1   The Origins of Evangelicalism

Part 2   The United States and Britain: Modern History

Acknowledgments

Ten of the chapters in this book were presented in earlier versions at a conference, "Evangelicalism in Transatlantic Perspective," held on 8–11 April 1992, at Wheaton College, Illinois. The editors are grateful to the others who presented papers at this conference, to those who commented upon them publicly or privately, and to all who, simply by attending, showed their concern for the subject of this book. Other papers from this conference appear in *Evangelicalism: Comparative Studies of Popular Protestantism in North America, the British Isles and Beyond, 1700–1990*, edited by Mark Noll, David Bebbington, and George Rawlyk, published by Oxford University Press in 1994. The conference was sponsored by Wheaton's Institute for the Study of American Evangelicals; the institute's staff—Darryl Hart, Edith Blumhofer, Katherine Tinlan-Vaughan, and especially Larry Eskridge—were diligent beyond expectation in managing the complex details of the meeting. The editors are also eager to thank the Pew Charitable Trusts, which provided the funding to make the conference possible.

Essays by David Bebbington, David Hempton, Larry Eskridge, and the editors were written, or revised, expressly for this volume.

We would also like to thank Mrs. Beatrice Horne, Gina Lombardo, Mary Noll, Kristal Otto, and Lori Wellemsen for efficient typing.

The book is dedicated, with deep appreciation, to an individual who has, in our own day, perceived the international potential of evangelical Christianity every bit as clearly as George Whitefield, John Newton, D. L. Moody, and F. B. Meyer did in theirs.

9

Contributors

David W. Bebbington, who is reader in history at the University of Stirling in Scotland, is the author of *Evangelicalism in Modern Britain: A History from the 1730s to the 1980s* (London, 1989; Grand Rapids, 1992) and *William Ewart Gladstone: Faith and Politics in Victorian Britain* (Grand Rapids, 1993).

Robert K. Burkinshaw, whose dissertation at the University of British Columbia dealt with Protestant conservatism in the Canadian West during the early decades of the twentieth century, teaches history at Trinity Western University, Langley, British Columbia.

Ted A. Campbell, who teaches modern church history at Wesley Theological Seminary, is the author of *The Religion of the Heart: A Study of European Religious Life in the Seventeenth and Eighteenth Centuries* (Columbia, SC, 1991).

James C. Deming, who teaches at Princeton Theological Seminary, recently received the Ph.D. in history from the University of Notre Dame, where his dissertation concerned the origins and early decades of Methodism in France.

Brian Dickey studied at Sydney and Cambridge universities before completing a Ph.D. in history at the Australian National University. He is the author of five books on Australian history, including a critical study of the oldest Anglican congregation in Adelaide. Currently Dr. Dickey edits a newsletter for the International Association for the Study of Christianity and History.

David R. Elliott, who teaches history at St. Francis Xavier University, Antigonish, Nova Scotia, is coauthor of a biography on Wil-

11

liam Aberhart and editor of *Aberhart: Outpourings and Replies* (Edmonton, Alberta, 1991).

Larry Eskridge is a graduate student in history at the University of Notre Dame and administrator of Wheaton College's Institute for the Study of American Evangelicals. He has published essays on the early use of radio by American evangelists.

Michael S. Hamilton is completing a Ph.D. in history at the University of Notre Dame, where his dissertation concerns the twentieth-century history of an evangelical institution of higher learning, Wheaton College. He is the program coordinator of the Evangelical Scholarship Initiative at Notre Dame.

David Hempton is a professor of modern history, the Queen's University of Belfast. He is the author of *Methodism and Politics in British Society, 1750–1850* (Stanford, CA, 1984) and coauthor of *Evangelical Protestantism in Ulster Society, 1740-1890* (London, 1992).

D. Bruce Hindmarsh, whose Oxford D.Phil. concerns the evangelical hymn writer, correspondent, and minister, John Newton, teaches at Briercrest Seminary in Saskatchewan.

Mark Hutchinson, whose dissertation at the University of New South Wales dealt with trends in Australian history writing before 1900, is administrator of the Centre for the Study of Australian Christianity, Robert Menzies College, Macquarie University, New South Wales. His research deals with the international connections of Pentecostalism, the InterVarsity Christian Fellowship, and other facets of modern evangelicalism.

Barry Mack, who recently completed a Ph.D. in history at Queen's University in Ontario on the influential nineteenth-century Canadian Presbyterian George Monro Grant, is minister of St. Andrews Presbyterian Church in St. Lambert, Quebec.

Mark A. Noll, McManis Professor of Christian Thought at Wheaton College, Illinois, is the author of *Princeton and the Republic, 1768–1822* (Princeton, 1989) and *A History of Christianity in the United States and Canada* (Grand Rapids, 1992).

Ian Randall is a Baptist lay minister who, after working with various British utility companies for a number of years, has recently become a tutor at Spurgeon's College, London. He has studied at St.

Andrews University in theology, with distinction, and has recently completed an external program of research from Stirling University, Scotland, on the career of F. B. Meyer.

George A. Rawlyk edits a series on religion for McGill-Queen's University Press, is coordinating a multi-year research project on evangelicalism in Canada, edited *The Canadian Protestant Experience* (Burlington, Ont., 1990), and has authored several books on the revival tradition in Canada, including *Ravished by the Spirit* (Montreal and Kingston, 1984). He is a professor of history at Queen's University, Kingston, Ontario.

John G. Stackhouse, Jr., is associate professor of religion at the University of Manitoba in Winnipeg. He is the author of *Canadian Evangelicism in the Twentieth Century* (Toronto, 1993).

Introduction

George A. Rawlyk and Mark A. Noll

During the first half of the eighteenth century, English-speaking Protestantism was profoundly affected by a series of revivals, or religious awakenings, that helped to define an emerging evangelical impulse. "Amazing Grace," a hymn published in 1779 by John Newton, a slave trader turned Anglican cleric who himself underwent a moving conversion, evocatively expresses the character of that impulse.

> Amazing grace! how sweet the sound
> That saved a wretch like me!
> I once was lost, but now am found,
> Was blind, but now I see.[1]

Its title is therefore fitting as the title for a book that attempts to describe both the evangelical impulse and some of the institutions, re-

1. John Newton, "Olney Hymns," in *A Burning and a Shining Light: English Spirituality in the Age of Wesley*, ed. David Lyle Jeffrey (Grand Rapids, 1987), 451. This anthology is a well-edited, accessible resource for the spirituality of the eighteenth-century Evangelical Revival in Britain. Recent works that are especially useful for grasping the religious or spiritual character of the evangelical movement include James M. Gordon, *Evangelical Spirituality: From the Wesleys to John Stott* (London, 1991); and Ulrich Gäbler, *Auferstehungszeit: Erweckungsprediger des 19. Jahrhunderts* (Munich, 1991). Gäbler's book is especially important for comparative purposes, since his nineteenth-century evangelical preachers include representatives from the United States, Scotland, France, Holland, and Germany.

gions, personalities, turmoils, social actions, political instincts, and religious goals of the multinational movement that arose from that eighteenth-century evangelical experience.

The most visible human agents in these pulsating religious movements were larger-than-life figures—men like George Whitefield, the remarkable transatlantic itinerant; John Wesley, the saintly founder of Methodism; and Jonathan Edwards, the extraordinarily gifted New England theologian and preacher. But for every Whitefield in the eighteenth century, there were hundreds of lesser-known evangelists—men *and* women—who felt themselves to be the special conduits of the Holy Spirit in bringing about the defining evangelical moment, "the New Birth." This "regeneration" or "conversion" (many of the evangelicals were little concerned about precision concerning the word) was often a sudden, transforming experience involving all the sensory perceptions and permanently branding Christ's salvation upon "the redeemed of the Lord."

In his published journal, John Wesley described what took place on Wednesday, 24 May 1738, at a religious gathering on Aldersgate Street, London, when "one was reading Luther's preface to the *Epistle to the Romans.* About a quarter before nine, while he was describing the change which God works in the heart, through faith in Christ, I felt my heart strangely warmed. I felt I did trust in Christ, Christ alone for salvation; and an assurance was given me that He had taken away *my* sins, even *mine*, and saved *me* from the law of sin and death."[2] In the spring of 1779, William Black, a nineteen-year-old emigrant from Yorkshire who later became a well-known Methodist itinerant, experienced the New Birth in Nova Scotia. In his journal, Black observed:

> We tarried . . . singing and praying for about two hours when it pleased the Lord to reveal his free grace; his fulness and his suitableness, as a Saviour: his ability and willingness to save *me*. So that I was enabled to venture on the sure mercies of *David*, and claim my interest in his blood, with "I am thine and thou art mine": while our friends were singing

2. *The Journal of John Wesley*, ed. Nehemiah Curnock, 8 vols. (London, 1938), 1:475–76.

My pardon I claim,
For sinner I am,
A sinner believing in Jesus' name.

Now I could lay hold of him, as the hope set before me: *The Lord my righteousness*. My burden dropped off: my guilt was removed: condemnation gave place to mercy: and a sweet peace and gladness were diffused through my soul. My mourning was turned into joy, and my countenance, like *Hannah's* was no more heavy. After tarrying some time, and returning public thanks, I went home with my heart full of love, and my mouth full of praise.[3]

Other eighteenth-century evangelicals would describe their conversions as being "ravished with a divine ecstasy . . . as if I were wrapped up in God,"[4] or as being overwhelmed by "a lively sense of the excellency of Christ,"[5] or as being ecstatically redeemed "by God's mercy—that my sins had crucified Christ; and now the Lord took away my distress."[6]

During its formative stages in the eighteenth and early nineteenth centuries, conversionism and revivalism largely defined the inner core of the evangelicalism that is the subject of this book.[7] Along with that stress on conversion, these evangelicals also were marked by biblicism (a reliance on the Bible as ultimate religious authority), activism (a concern for sharing the faith), and crucicenticism (a focus on Christ's redeeming work on the cross).[8] But in the first genera-

---

3. *Arminian Magazine* (London, 1791), 68–70.

4. Henry Alline, *The Life and Journal* (Boston, 1806), 35.

5. *The Works of Jonathan Edwards*, vol. 4: *The Great Awakening*, ed. C. C. Goen (New Haven, Conn., 1972), 193.

6. "An Account of the Life of Mr. David George," in *From Slavery to Freedom: The Life of David George, Pioneer Baptist Minister*, ed. Grant Gordon (Hantsport, Nova Scotia, 1992), 171–72.

7. The term "evangelical" is used in many other legitimate ways—for example, as a general description of Christianity's message of redemption or as an adjective for the Protestant (especially Lutheran) churches descending from the sixteenth century. Our concentration on the evangelicalism descending from the eighteenth-century British and American revivals is not meant to deny these and other legitimate uses of the word.

8. For a convincing rationale concerning the centrality of these four characteristics in the entire history of evangelicalism, see David W. Bebbington, *Evangelicalism in Modern Britain: A History from the 1730s to the 1980s* (London, 1989; Grand Rapids, 1992), 2–17.

tions of the evangelical movement, the immediate experience of God's grace came first.

By the late nineteenth century, conversion, or the immediate experience of God, may have become less important in the evangelical tradition than was the case a century before.[9] By that time, it was functioning as one of the several characteristics that had come to be regarded, in the phrases of a modern social scientist, as the "set of 'minimalist' criteria for evangelical membership."[10] As the twentieth century unfolded, some groups tracing their origins to the eighteenth-century evangelical revivals came to lay more emphasis on an inerrant and inspired Bible, the divinity of Christ, the role of Christ as the only way of salvation, or a commitment to the missionary spread of the gospel rather than on the earlier, more exclusive focus on the new birth. Late in the twentieth century, many—perhaps even a majority—of those who in North and South America are regarded as evangelicals are Pentecostals or charismatics and hence stress the immediate presence of the Holy Spirit in their lives. If the New Birth defined the essence of evangelicalism during the first century of its history, the emphases of Pentecostalism may well be the defining characteristic of evangelicals in the twenty-first century.

This brief recital of shifting religious emphases suggests that Anglo-American evangelicalism has undergone significant, even revolutionary, change since the mid-eighteenth century. In addition, the very power and complexity of the movement has made it extraordinarily adaptable to the forces of change. At the same time, however, Anglo-American evangelicalism is also a movement undergirded by powerful pillars of continuity. It has been especially consistent in defending its fourfold characteristics by appealing to traditions of biblical orthodoxy and New Testament primitivism.

Evangelicalism has also come to expression differently in different parts of the Anglo-American world because of its relative dominance or marginality in a culture. Evangelicalism was never a majority movement within Protestantism in Great Britain or in Australia, but

9. A basic guide to literature on the history of Anglo-American evangelicalism is found below in the Bibliographic Afterword.

10. Lyman A. Kellstedt, "The Meaning and Measurement of Evangelicalism: Problems and Prospects," in *Religion and Political Behavior in the United States*, ed. T. G. Jelen (New York, 1989), 5.

especially in the nineteenth century, it certainly was the dominant religion in both the United States and English Canada. The Canadian historian Michael Gauvreau has justifiably described the nineteenth century as Canada's evangelical century, and similar claims have been persuasively made by many scholars about the United States.[11] In all of the major English-speaking regions of the world, even in North America, evangelicalism was put on the defensive at the start of the twentieth century. Evangelical hegemony in these two regions gave way in the face of a varied combination of forces—a new biblical scholarship, Darwinism, the growth of comparative religion, the new psychology, rampant consumerism, and the new industrial/commercial order. Evangelical loss of cultural dominance may also have been hastened by a loss of nerve, especially among evangelical leaders who themselves supported, often with considerable ambiguity, the forces of "progress" that were undermining evangelical influence.

In recent decades, the decline of evangelicalism in Canada has been far more precipitous than in the United States—a decline from which traditional Canadian evangelicalism will probably never recover. In Canada, where evangelicals were once every bit as influential as in the United States, evangelical strength—now approximately 15 per cent of the total population—is somewhat greater than the relatively low level of evangelical strength in contemporary Great Britain and about the same level as that in Australia.[12] By contrast, evangelicalism in the United States remains the most powerful force within American Protestantism, whether measured simply by the number of adherents or gauged by the energetic creativity of its leaders.[13]

These preliminary comments about the history and present character of evangelicalism are meant to suggest the richly textured international character of evangelicalism from its very beginning. What is

11. Michael Gauvreau, *The Evangelical Century: College and Creed in English Canada from the Great Revival to the Great Depression* (Montreal and Kingston, 1991). For the United States, see Sydney E. Ahlstrom's depiction of the first half of the nineteenth century as "the golden day of democratic evangelicalism" (*A Religious History of the American People* [New Haven, Conn., 1972], 385).

12. Canadian information from Angus Reid Survey, January 1993; data in the possession of George Rawlyk.

13. Nathan O. Hatch and Michael S. Hamilton, "Can Evangelicalism Survive Its Success?" *Christianity Today* 5 (October 1992): 22–31.

so obviously true of evangelicalism in Canada—that it can be understood only through comparative study that embraces Britain as well as the United States—is in fact true of evangelicalism in all the major English-speaking regions of the world. That truth is hardest to see for the history of evangelicalism in the United States and Britain, since both regions have had such large and powerful evangelical movements. But as most of the essays in this book demonstrate, the international character of evangelicalism has shaped every period of evangelical history in both the United States and Great Britain.

This volume of essays underscores the crucial importance of the comparative dimension in evangelical history and highlights the virtues of comparative study itself. Each of the essays has something of the comparative dimension; some more, others less, but present nonetheless in each. Each essay is based upon research in primary sources, and each tries to break new research ground. Each takes religious belief seriously, yet each is written in a way that also takes seriously the contexts of religious faith as these contexts have been explored in general historical literature on the Anglo-American world.

The essays that follow—with their highlighting of comparisons and contrasts between regions, movements, and individuals—are possible only because of three or more decades of exemplary scholarship on evangelicals. Much of that scholarship is recognized in the notes to the various essays or in the Bibliographic Afterword. Comparative history of the sort attempted in this book is not possible without the kind of sophisticated historical scholarship that has been building for the United States, Great Britain, Canada, and Australia over the last several decades.

The essays in this book are not strewn randomly but possess coherence in several ways. First, they feature a limited number of chronological periods. Several of them examine the revolutionary period from roughly 1760 to 1830, when evangelicalism became prominent in several North Atlantic regions. Another cluster describes evangelicalism in the century that has just passed, when the center of worldwide evangelicalism shifted from Great Britain to the United States.

Second, several regions receive sustained attention. The two essays on Australia are pioneering works that show how evangelical developments in that country participated in global evangelical networks. Most of the essays on the early period, and several of those on later developments, treat important features of British evangelicalism (Irish and Scottish as well as English) during the period when Great Britain was still the most influential center of worldwide evangelicalism. These essays are especially informative for those who are familiar with evangelical developments in the United States, since they offer fascinating opportunities to compare characteristics of evangelical life in the United States (where those characteristics often defined central cultural values for American civilization) with similar expressions in Britain or Australia (where those characteristics were often pushed to the margins by the dominant state church or, later, by the forces of secularism). The flourishing scholarship on evangelicalism that now prevails in the United States justifies the relatively light coverage of that region in this book. At the same time, however, many of the chapters focused on developments in Canada, Australia, and (for later periods, as in David Bebbington's chapter) Great Britain are also, in fact, histories-from-a-distance of events, personalities, disputes, techniques, strategies, successes, and failures in the United States that have had a ripple impact in other parts of the world.

A notable feature of the book is the six essays concentrating on evangelicalism in Canada. This collection by itself represents the most significant concentration of scholarly work to date on Canadian evangelicalism, especially for the period after Confederation (1867). In these chapters an evangelicalism appears that is somewhat more populist in its orientation than British evangelicalism but that is also more accommodationist or open-minded than the relatively hard-edged evangelicalism and fundamentalism of the United States at comparable periods. These Canadian essays tell us a great deal not only about Protestantism in Canada but also about parallel developments among evangelicals in the United States. A similar point can be made about Canadian-British or Canadian-Australian comparisons. Yet the comparisons between Canadian and American evangelicals reveal so much that is held in common (e.g., a common reliance on voluntary agencies for the work of evangelistic outreach and social ministry) as well as so much that reflects important differences (e.g, the willingness of Canadian evangelicals to seek funding for various purposes from the state) that a fuller academic exploration of these comparisons will be especially illuminating.

Finally, almost all of the essays come back to many of the same general themes—for example, on how different strands of evangelicalism (conservative or liberal, socially engaged or socially disengaged) have flourished better in some regions than in others; on how evangelicals have adapted a substantially similar set of Christian concerns in the face of a widely differing set of regional conditions, and how the results have been a singular combination of shared values and strikingly different local expression of those values; on how centers of influence (e.g., the British and Foreign Bible Society in the early nineteenth century, the work of Billy Graham in the twentieth century) have affected attitudes in peripheral regions, even as the peripheries continue to shape influences from the center; and on how large-scale new movements (e.g., eighteenth-century revival or the twentieth-century Pentecostal movement) have traveled by speedy osmosis through preexisting evangelical networks.

A brief comment on the chapters will indicate how each contributes to these larger themes. Bruce Hindmarsh's study of John Newton rescues this evangelical patriarch from undue historical neglect. (He was better known in his own day as a mediator among evangelicals than as the author of "Amazing Grace," "How Sweet the Name of Jesus Sounds," and other hymns that later helped define the evangelical movement.) The essay also explores one of the perennial tensions of evangelicalism—how to maintain loyalty both to a denominational tradition (in Newton's case, the Church of England) and to the evangelical voluntary networks that so regularly deprecate the traditional denominations. David Hempton's sensitive study of evangelicalism in eighteenth-century Ireland performs a similar function by showing how both English-speaking Methodists and pietist refugees from the Continent came to influence a broad network of intra-evangelical connections. Mark Noll's examination of the common cultural framework in which contrasting theological developments took place in Scotland and America illustrates how adaptable the theological concerns of evangelicals have always been. Ted Campbell's study of popular religious literature suggests how the Atlantic Ocean may have filtered out certain kinds of "disreputable" works while remaining a wide-open conduit for literature coming from socially approved sources. The last of the essays on the early period, by

James Deming and Michael Hamilton, explores the reasons why Methodism did not flourish in France and also why it flourished differently in Canada and the United States.

Two essays follow that compare directly the major powers in the evangelical empire—the United States and Great Britain. Ian Randall performs this task by focusing on the career of only one individual. Since that individual, F. B. Meyer, was widely appreciated on both sides of the Atlantic, the single career reveals much about the similarities that joined and the differences that divided evangelicals in the two regions during the early twentieth century. David Bebbington's sweeping essay is to the forest what Randall's is to a significant tree. His broadly based comparison is both an overview of a complicated history as well as an agenda for further research on the multiple connections that bind (but also sometimes divide) British evangelicals and their American cousins.

The next two essays are as far removed geographically from the North Atlantic axis as it is possible to be. Yet the chapters by Brian Dickey and Mark Hutchinson on Australian matters testify to the power of evangelical practices and beliefs to travel literally around the world. Dickey's essay on Anglican evangelicals features the oldest bonds drawing Australia into worldwide evangelicalism, while Hutchinson's concentration on Pentecostals of Italian origin suggests something of the complicated international ties linking twentieth-century evangelicals in an era dominated by newer, nonestablished, or even sectarian churches.

From the start in the mid-eighteenth century, evangelicalism in Canada was intimately related to parallel movements in the colonies that became the United States, as well as in all regions of Great Britain (Ireland, Wales, and Scotland, as well as England).[14] The path-breaking essays that follow (along with the study by Deming and Hamilton) are therefore critical for achieving the major purpose of this volume—that is, to show the ebb and flow across national boundaries of almost all significant theological, religious, and spiri-

---

14. See especially Nancy Christie, "'In These Times of Democratic Rage and Delusion': Popular Religion and the Challenge to the Established Order, 1760–1815," and Michael Gauvreau, "Protestantism Transformed: Personal Piety and the Evangelical Social Vision, 1815–1867," both in *The Canadian Protestant Experience, 1760–1990*, ed. George A. Rawlyk (Burlington, Ontario, 1990).

tual aspects of evangelicalism. At the same time, they reveal much about the singular character of evangelicalism in Canada itself. Barry Mack's chapter features George Munro Grant, a late nineteenth-century Presbyterian who pursued a course different from both American Presbyterian conservatives and British Reformed liberals. Mack thus clarifies one of the reasons why a tradition of liberal evangelicalism remained stronger in Canada than in the United States. George Rawlyk's monograph on two relatively small denominations in the Canadian Maritimes shows that questions of doctrine have remained critical for almost all evangelical groups, but it also shows how influences from abroad (in this case the United States) are always modified by local religious and social conditions. Robert Burkinshaw moves us to western Canada by providing an analysis for why similar evangelical impulses resulted in a self-conscious fundamentalism south of the Canadian-American border but not to the north. Pursuing the theme of fundamentalism in Canada and the United States further, David Elliott provides little-known information about the Canadian origins of the surprisingly large number of evangelicals who made their mark as fundamentalists in the United States. Finally, John Stackhouse's examination of twentieth-century Canadian evangelicalism assesses the quality and quantity of influences from both Britain and the United States and, by so doing, analyzes some of the more general opportunities and perils that have confronted evangelicals in all English-speaking regions since World War II.

With such a broad-ranging scope, Stackhouse's essay exemplifies the larger purposes of *Amazing Grace*. As Bruce Hindmarsh's essay shows so clearly, John Newton, who corresponded with evangelicals throughout the English-speaking world of his day and whose hymns have been sung everywhere that English-speaking evangelicals have gone around the globe, would certainly have endorsed enthusiastically the effort to understand the international dimensions of the evangelical movement.

Much the same thing can be said about the other founders of evangelicalism—George Whitefield, who spent almost as much time on board ship crossing the Atlantic as he did in the American colonies, Ireland, Scotland, or his native England; John Wesley, whose success in Ireland and Scotland may have matched his original goals for the Methodist movement more closely than his results in England and whose abject failure in America prepared him for the experience of the New Birth in his own country; Henry Alline, who exerted his greatest influence in Nova Scotia but who died in the effort to bring a similar renewal to back-country New England; or, to cite only one more of the many who could be mentioned, David George, who promoted an evangelical faith among African-Americans in South Carolina, Nova Scotia, and Sierra Leone.

All of these "first evangelicals" were eager internationalists who took it for granted that the conversionist, activistic, and Bible- and cross-centered faith they embraced (or, as each would have said in slightly different ways, embraced them) was a faith that did not respect national boundaries. It is the hope of those who have contributed to this volume that their historical work may measure up to the deeply ingrained internationalism of the founding evangelicals themselves.

Part 1

The Origins of
Evangelicalism

1

"I Am a Sort of Middle-Man"

The Politically Correct Evangelicalism of John Newton

D. Bruce Hindmarsh

Once a profligate slave trader, John Newton (1725–1807) later became one of the leading evangelicals in the Church of England in the second generation of the Evangelical Revival. While Jonathan Edwards's congregation at Northampton, Massachusetts, was moving in a cloud of revival wonders, Newton was a ten-year-old boy at a boarding school near London who was already neglecting most of what his late, pious mother had earlier taught him; while John Wesley's heart was being strangely warmed, twelve-year-old Newton was suffering repeated struggles between sin and conscience; and while Whitefield was stirring the crowds at Cambuslang in Scotland, Newton at sixteen had taken up and laid aside his religious profession three or four different times. The course of Newton's moral and spiritual declension over the next several years to its nadir on the Guinea coast in 1747 is well known from his dramatic account of it in his *Authentic Narrative* (1764). From his muttered prayer for mercy on the high seas in March 1748 to his slow return to more serious religious profession, he proceeded in large measure in ignorance of the wider revival movement. Not until 1754 did a fellow ship captain lead him to conceptions "clearer and more evangelical" and inform him of the state of religion and "the errors and controversies of the times." From this late introduction to contemporary evangelicalism he quickly went on to make the acquaintance of many prominent gospel ministers, including Wesley and Whitefield, to study divinity for himself, and to take advantage of every opportunity for religious betterment. In 1758 he began to contemplate entering the ministry himself and was at length ordained in the Church of England in 1764. He exercised a ministry of sixteen years at the small market town of Olney in the south Midlands and another of twenty-seven years at a fashionable church across the street from the Bank of England in the heart of London. He is remembered today chiefly for the story of his conversion, his hymnody (especially "Amazing Grace"), his letters of spiritual counsel, and his personal influence on contemporaries such as the poet William Cowper or the political reformer William Wilberforce.[1]

Newton's conversion and introduction to evangelical religion took place during the halcyon days of the revival in England, between the Calvinistic controversies of the 1740s and 1770s and before the controversial outbreaks of perfectionism among the followers of Wesley during 1758–63. It was also a time when relations between church and chapel were their most amicable, between the church-in-danger crises of the beginning and end of the century. Newton's own parentage—his mother a Congregationalist, his father an Anglican—may be taken as a symbol of the spirit of religious tolerance, which reached its high-water mark in the middle of the century and which found so strong a champion in Newton. For Newton was the original of the "circulating evangelical," running freely along the interstices of church and Dissent, happily cooperating with all the partisans of the revival. Like Janus, the Roman god of gates, he faced more than one direction. And because he developed his evangelical theology in this

1. The most important biographies of John Newton are Richard Cecil, *Memoirs of the Rev. John Newton* (London, 1808); Josiah Bull, *John Newton of Olney and St. Mary Woolnoth* (London, 1868); and Bernard Martin, *John Newton* (London, 1950). The principal primary sources are collected in *The Works of John Newton*, 6 vols. (London, 1808–9). References to this edition of Newton's *Works* appear in parentheses in the text, showing volume and page number.

in-between situation without merely equivocating between factions, his writings uniquely demonstrate the limits of evangelical consensus in England during the formative period between the conversions of Wesley and Wilberforce. Symbolically, his is much of the territory between Aldersgate Street and Clapham Common.

Newton's genius was not as an original theologian like Jonathan Edwards, a spectacular preacher like George Whitefield, or a theological synthesizer and organizational leader like John Wesley. His achievement was rather as a broker of consensus who preached and wrote in a "politically correct" theological style in the service of evangelical solidarity. John Wesley once wrote to Newton: "You appear to be designed by Divine Providence for an healer of breaches, a reconciler of honest but prejudiced men, and an uniter (happy work!) of the children of God."[2] Because of this, his writings still stand as a register of evangelicalism in one of its most catholic forms in the last half of the eighteenth century.

In what follows, Newton is used as a representative site in which to explore the limits of this evangelical consciousness along first a religious and then a theological axis, paying close attention to the cultural envelope in which his evangelicalism was sent successfully to various denominational and doctrinal addresses. In each case, a document from Newton's *Works* is examined together with the local controversy to which it was related, and then a short analysis draws out implications for a wider understanding of evangelical religion during the period. Understanding how Newton reconciled opposing parties and opinions illumines his own theology, defines more sharply contemporary transdenominational evangelical awareness, and suggests a general model for the adaptability of evangelicalism to cultural change.

It is important to add, moreover, that this consciousness included for Newton a tacit recognition of all true believers on both sides of the Atlantic. Coming to maturity during a period of increasing English prosperity and cultural self-confidence, and having traversed the Atlantic along the triangular slave-trading route five times over, he was well aware of England as a preeminent North Atlantic colonial power. Rumors of war with France gave him cause to reflect in

2. *The Letters of the Rev. John Wesley*, ed. John Telford (London, 1931), 4:293.

1756 upon the superior privileges, both civic and religious, enjoyed by the English-speaking peoples in the eighteenth-century: "From all the history I have read I can find no country [or] age since the appearance of our Lord in the flesh, so highly distinguished with spiritual and temporal blessings as the dominions of Great Britain since the year 1715."[3] In the manner of a Puritan jeremiad, he commented also, however, upon the urgent need for national repentance in England in order to avert the impending judgment of God. If it came to war with France, Newton hoped that English soldiers would learn to pray as well as fight like their New England counterparts. He was aware of the evangelistic labors of Whitefield in the American colonies and prayed that the gospel would continue to spread likewise at home so that "Happy England" would not find its peace and plenty destroyed through invasion and war.[4]

Indeed, Whitefield was the key figure linking Newton to the wider transatlantic context of the revival. Whitefield's own sense of evangelical religion as something transcending confessional distinctives and church order had developed several years before Newton's conversion, but the two men arrived at similar convictions for many of the same reasons. At several key points Newton's evangelical self-understanding was shaped by Whitefield, and at Liverpool he was even tagged with the epithet "Little Whitefield" for his constant attendance upon the evangelist. Thus, Whitefield's evangelical consciousness was both parallel to, and a significant influence upon, Newton's own religious sensibilities and helps to establish the elements of evangelical consensus observed in Newton in England as representative of the wider North Atlantic revival.

Evangelical Consciousness: The Religious Axis

Because he claimed not to wear the full color of any sect or party, Newton liked to call himself a speckled bird. He wrote in 1778, "It is impossible I should be all of a colour, when I have been debtor to all sorts, and, like the jay in the fable, have been beholden to most of the birds in the air for a feather or two. Church and Meeting, Methodist

3. John Newton, diary entry for 10 February 1756, MS diary vol. 1 [1751–56], Firestone Library, Princeton University, Princeton, N.J.
    4. Ibid., entries for 4 November 1755 and 2 March 1756.

and Moravian, may all perceive something in my coat taken from them."[5]

Newton did not overstate his case, for his biography reveals how varied were his religious debts. He imbibed the piety of Old Dissent with his mother's milk but passed through his adolescence under the eye of an Anglican father and stepmother. When after his five misspent years at sea he was provoked by near shipwreck to take religion more seriously, his first recourse was to an Anglican High Church style of piety, but then shortly thereafter he sought his late mother's Independent pastor to help him in his faith. A few years later he consorted with some younger Independents in London who had links with Whitefield, and through them he was introduced to Calvinistic Methodism. In 1755 he moved to Liverpool to take up a civil service job, and while there his religious acquaintance broadened even further as he circulated between Wesley's Methodists, two Baptist meetings, and the Church of England. He also ventured at least half a dozen journeys into Yorkshire to see the progress of the revival there, preaching alike for Inghamites, Independents, and Anglicans. One of the Anglicans led Newton to cherish hopes of ordination in the Established Church, but he was checked by repeated refusals. Continuing to move widely among all parties, he considered ordination as an Independent, even serving a locum nearby for several months. When the story of his dramatic conversion brought him to the attention of the Earl of Dartmouth, however, he found an advocate who could at last provide him a living in the Establishment and achieve his episcopal ordination as he had originally wished. Once settled as curate of Olney, Newton immediately threw the door of friendship and cooperation wide open with the Baptist and Independent ministers in town and established his most intimate spiritual friendships with a neighboring Independent minister and a Moravian layman. As Newton became more widely known through his writings, his links with evangelicals of all varieties continued to grow in

5. *One Hundred and Twenty Nine Letters from the Rev. John Newton . . . to the Rev. William Bull*, ed. Thomas Palmer Bull (London, 1847), 25. See further, Bernard Martin, "Some Dissenting Friends of John Newton," *Congregationalist Quarterly* 29 (1951): 133–44, 236–45; R. W. Thomson, "John Newton and His Baptist Friends," *Baptist Quarterly* 9 (1939): 368–71; Geoffrey F. Nuttall, "Baptists and Independents in Olney to the Time of John Newton," *Baptist Quarterly* 30 (1983): 26–37.

number and intimacy. To list all of his religious acquaintances and correspondents during his ministry at Olney and London would be tantamount, as Dr. Walsh once commented, to writing a *Who's Who* of eighteenth-century evangelicalism.[6]

Notwithstanding his lifelong liberality toward all evangelicals, Newton was, however, at various times more closely linked to some groups than others. For several years after his conversion his connections were chiefly among Dissenters, but by the end of his life he was, if still not very high in his churchmanship, very satisfied as a minister of the Church of England. When some Dissenters accused him of prevarication for remaining in the Establishment, Newton published his *Apologia* (1784) to defend his principles, and in so doing shed light on the basis of his catholic approach to evangelicalism. Although the tract was published in 1784, Newton had begun it several years earlier; its occasion reflected the growing tension between church and chapel during the American War of Independence. The subsequent response to it among Dissenters varied from acerbic criticism to warm endorsement.[7] Its contents may be summarized as follows.

Newton claimed that with the demise of the old persecuting High Church principles in the Establishment, nothing remained to inhibit reciprocal goodwill between parties, for the gospel ought to be a much stronger bond between Christians than church order. Although a national religious establishment was not of express divine appointment, it was nonetheless expedient, serving to preserve at least a minimal Christian influence in many regions that would otherwise be entirely spiritually destitute. His personal reason for conformity was, he added provocatively, the regard he owed to Christ alone as the head of the church. This was a principle widely acknowledged but

6. John Walsh, "The Yorkshire Evangelicals" (Ph.D. diss., Cambridge University, 1956), 175. A cross-section of Newton's wide acquaintance may be observed in *Letters by the Rev. John Newton . . . with Biographical Sketches*, ed. Josiah Bull (London, 1869).

7. The varied response to Newton's *Apologia* may be traced in Dr. Henry Mayo's line-by-line rebuttal, *An Apology and a Shield, In these Times of Instability and Misrepresentation. Four Letters to the Rev. Mr. John Newton . . . by a Dissenting Minister* (London, 1784); in the vitriolic anonymous satire *Apologia Secunda; or, a Supplementary Apology for Conformity: Two Epistles, humbly addressed to the Awakened Clergy by a Layman* (London, 1785); and in Samuel Palmer's letters of friendship in *Correspondence of the Late Rev. John Newton with a Dissenting Minister* (London, 1809).

wrongly construed by the people of God, resulting in many unhappy divisions. Because the visible church comprised all professing Christians, it was necessarily a *mixed* body of both regenerated persons and nominal Christians. But as Christ could not be governor of merely nominal Christians ("for his kingdom is a spiritual kingdom, which none can understand . . . until born from above" [5:24]), he must be understood as head of the church only in its more limited and proper sense as his mystical body, composed of all those who by faith were united to him. There were hidden ones who belonged to him among every body of professing Christians—even among the Roman and Greek churches. Sadly, people equally eminent in piety and learning—whether from the Church of England, the Church of Scotland, the Independent churches, or the Baptists—disagreed widely over which system of church order was of divine right. Because in the essentials of the gospel he agreed with them all, in the disputed matters of church order he would himself honor the headship of Christ over his entire mystical body by refusing to call any party or subdivision of God's people the true church to the exclusion of the others. He would maintain friendly relations with all but allow none to be master of his conscience. As his conscience concurred happily with the articles, liturgy, and rubric of the Establishment; as he saw the probability of greater usefulness there; and as he felt he had been specifically led by Providence to a suitable situation on that side, so he was satisfied that he had done well to seek episcopal ordination. He claimed not to have regretted the decision since.

What are the implications of the ecclesiological compromise here worked out by Newton? To begin with, it is remarkable to what extent his experience of religious pluralism marked his exposition. Indeed, his acceptance of a range of religious diversity must be seen as one of the most basic assumptions underlying his writings.[8] That he rejected the ideal of a confessional state and monopolistic national church—the two sides of the traditional Anglican church-state con-

8. This is well illustrated in Newton's correspondence with the Congregationalist John Campbell in the 1790s, in which, for example, he remarked that he regularly entertained a wide variety of Dissenters in his home, that he supported many of the proposed measures for Catholic Emancipation, and that he heartily endorsed the rising tide of missionary activity by Dissenters at home and abroad (*Letters and Conversational Remarks of the Rev. John Newton*, ed. John Campbell [London, 1808], 14–107 passim).

stitution—was at the same time both a simple recognition of the contemporary reality and an act of theological commitment. For, by basing his defense of religious establishments upon their instrumental value, he was acknowledging the de facto status of the Church of England as a voluntary, if privileged, society that people would join or not as a matter of private judgment. He also knew that his primary theological concern with true belief over nominal profession would not in any case be advanced by state-coerced, religious uniformity. He thought it simply made good sense, as a matter of expediency, for the state to make wide provision for religious services. This was a markedly different position from the magisterial reformers, who assumed the ideal of a confessional state, or again of the nonseparatist Puritans, who fought for their particular version of it. Newton's position reflects the attitudes of a very different generation that had grown up after the Hanoverian succession was secure and had entrenched the revolutionary settlement of 1689. The constitutional status of the church had been significantly lowered by the official recognition given to all Trinitarian Protestant denominations, and the passage of time lent this pluralism an added sense of legitimacy. Newton grew up with some measure of pluralism as part of the world-as-given, and if pluralism, then also voluntarism, for diversity implied the freedom to choose (even if this was still officially understood in the establishmentarian sense of freedom to dissent).[9]

From the beginning, therefore, Newton's understanding of evangelicalism was rooted in a religious landscape of acceptable diversity. The force of this assumption can be seen in the central irony that in Newton's *Apologia*, not only did a minister of the Establishment feel he had to justify himself for having dissented from Dissent, but also he used classic separatist apologetics to do so. Newton turned the argument that Christ, not the king, is the only true head of the church and that Christ alone is the Lord of a person's conscience into a peculiar defense for remaining *in* the Establishment—out-dissenting the Dissenters. No wonder that some Dissenters complained bit-

9. See further Michael R. Watts, *The Dissenters* (Oxford, 1978), 263–393; Alan D. Gilbert, *Religion and Society in Industrial England* (London, 1976), 1–48. As Newton's case illustrates, however, Gilbert's phenomenological interpretation does not give adequate weight to the ideological continuities between evangelicals within and without the Establishment.

terly at this reasoning, for Newton could be seen as cutting out from under them their whole *raison d'être*.[10]

That pluralism was a simple fact underlying evangelical consciousness relates to a second point implicit in Newton's text, namely, the inevitable tension that acceptable diversity creates between inclusive and exclusive types of evangelicalism. This can be seen even more clearly in the case of Whitefield, whose wide travels across two continents exposed him to more of the varieties of Protestantism within the dominions of Great Britain than probably any of his contemporaries. Whitefield uniquely experienced an "advanced pluralism" as time and again he crossed the threshold of religious communities whose loyalties had much to do with a local or even national history that he himself largely transcended simply by virtue of his extensive itinerancy. As a consequence, very early in Whitefield's career he encountered the problem of separatism. In 1741 in Scotland the Associate Presbytery of the Erskine brothers asked him to preach only for them, as it was they who were truly the Lord's people. Famously, Whitefield rejected separatism in favor of transdenominationalism, saying, "If the Pope himself would lend me his pulpit, I would gladly proclaim the righteousness of Jesus Christ therein."[11]

Newton resolved the problem of evangelical diversity in a similar way, recognizing that evangelicalism could be transdenominational only insofar as it subordinated denominational distinctives on matters of church-state constitutionality, church order, and sacramental discipline to the overriding concern for the simple gospel. Thus he wrote in 1778 to an Antiburgher Secessionist in Scotland who, unlike those whom Whitefield had earlier met, was more disposed to recognize other varieties of evangelicalism: "My heart is . . . more especially with those who, like you, can look over the pales of an enclo-

10. See Mayo, *Apology and a Shield* and *Apologia Secunda*, cited in n. 7 above. If it were not for Newton's slender acknowledgment of the visible church as a mixed body, his position would look very much like an application of the gathered-church model to those local churches within the Establishment that had evangelical ministers. His comments to Scottish secessionist William Barlass go far in this direction: "At Olney, (and it is much the same in all the parishes where the Lord has placed awakened ministers) we are Ecclesia intra Ecclesium. I preach to many, but those whose hearts the Lord touches are the people of my peculiar charge" (*Original Letters from the Reverend John Newton, A.M.* [*sic*: Newton did not have a degree]*to the Rev. W. Barlass* [New York, 1819], 52).

11. *The Works of . . . the Revd. George Whitefield*, ed. John Gillies (London, 1771), 1:308.

sure, and rejoice in the Lord's work where he is pleased to carry it on, under some difference of forms."[12]

But by abandoning the Puritan-Reformed question "What constitutes a true church?" for the evangelical-pietistic question "What constitutes a true Christian?" Newton effectively committed himself to a Low Church ecclesiology.[13] This was the price that an inclusive evangelical was willing to pay to maintain maximum evangelical solidarity. And this was the route that Whitefield had taken earlier when he wrote to a Presbyterian minister: "My one sole question is *Are you a christian?* . . . If so, you are my brother, my sister, and mother."[14] Among those who held a higher position on church order were many who still recognized a spiritual bond with other evangelicals. But the implication that one's fellow evangelical was schismatic, belonging only to a religious organization, not to the true church, could only act to restrain a fully transdenominational evangelical consciousness. While inclusive evangelicals inhabited the ecclesiastical valleys, exclusive evangelicals dwelt further up the mountain of their own High Churchmanship and were therefore at a further remove from their spiritual fellows on the slopes or peaks of other ecclesiologies. The inference is that evangelical consciousness, while not incompatible with either a developed ecclesiology or denominational insularity, was of itself essentially *not* ecclesiological. To talk of an evangelical ecclesiology is an oxymoron.

Newton's *Apologia* suggests that the evangelical disregard for ecclesiology was, at least in his case, based on a deeper assumption in evangelical consciousness that the spirit was opposed to the flesh. Newton's discussion of the church as visible and invisible was drawn almost verbatim from Calvin *(Institutes* 4.1.7), but he used it to very different effect. Whereas Calvin was concerned in page after page of the *Institutes* to uphold strongly the divinely ordered authority of the visible church, Newton's concern was principally with the

12. *Letters from Newton to Barlass*, 49.
13. Likewise, in 1788 and again in 1798 the members of the Eclectic Society agreed in affirming that there is no express form of church order binding upon the consciences of all. See John Newton, "Minutes of the Eclectic Society (1787–89)," MS notebook, Firestone Library; and *The Thought of the Evangelical Leaders*, ed. John H. Pratt (London, 1856; reprint, Edinburgh, 1978), 3–6.
14. *Works of Whitefield*, 1:126. Punctuation and capitalization Whitefield's.

church under its invisible, eschatological aspect, stressing that
Christ's kingdom was not of this world and did not consist in "meats
and drinks" or "forms and parties" (5:41). In his familiar correspondence he would often, in discussing the differences that separated
devout Christians in his own day, conclude his case for mutual for-
bearance with a pietistic appeal to that future day when all divisions
would be at an end.[15] For Newton, the distinction between the
church under its visible and mystical aspects gave way to what
seemed a much more important distinction *within* the visible
church, however constituted—namely, that between nominal and
true Christians. Here was the focus of evangelical, proselytizing ardor. The dialectic between visible and invisible was subtly ex-
changed for one between nature and grace. Whereas nominal profession of faith was linked with the merely physical aspects of church
life and discipline, true belief was equated with the wholly spiritual
experience of regeneration. That the Christian life was an affair of
the spirit was an underlying emphasis in Reformed theology that
Newton elevated in his own understanding of the church. In this he
was abetted by the Enlightenment prejudices of his own age, which
perpetuated the so-called dissociated sensibility of Cartesian dualism and Newtonian mechanism, in which the relation of the spiritual
and material was construed in largely isomorphic terms.[16] Newton's
use of the word "spirituality" itself was always in this sense of something spiritual in contrast with something corporeal. From his perspective, evangelicalism was essentially a form of this kind of spirituality. A different generation of evangelicals would return to the
ideal of a direct sensuous apprehension of the spiritual world. If to

15. See in Newton's *Works*, for example, his letter to Miss Delafield (2:210–11) or his plan
for a nonpartisan ministerial academy in "Utopia" (5:59–100). The elevation of the mystical
body of Christ over external forms of religion could also be seen in Whitefield. In Whitefield's
Works, see the letter quoted above in which Whitefield, after stressing the invisible over the visible aspect of the church, exclaimed, "Blessed be GOD that his love is so far shed abroad in our
hearts, as to cause us to love one another, though we differ a little as to externals. . . . Yet a little
while, and we shall sit down together in the kingdom of our Father" (1:126–27).

16. On this element in the Reformed tradition, see Brooks Holifield, *The Covenant Sealed*
(New Haven, 1974), 1–2. On Enlightenment dualism, see John Hoyles, *The Waning of the Renaissance*, International Archives of the History of Ideas, no. 39 (The Hague, 1971); idem, *The
Edges of Augustanism*, International Archives of the History of Ideas, no. 53 (The Hague,
1972).

talk of an evangelical ecclesiology constitutes an oxymoron, to speak of evangelical spirituality is a tautology.

In summary, a number of related characteristics of evangelical consciousness, implicit in Whitefield's earlier career, can be observed from Newton's treatment of ecclesiology in the *Apologia:* the tacit acceptance of some degree of religious pluralism and therefore also of voluntarism, the subordination of ecclesiology to the simple gospel, and the presupposition that the spiritual is opposed to the material. The picture emerges of a spontaneous spiritual brotherhood, diverse and uncoerced, little concerned with cult or with sensuous worship but universally preoccupied with real belief versus a nominal profession. Not surprisingly, therefore, the locus of this evangelicalism was largely outside of authorized parochial or denominational structures in the activity of itinerant preachers and the intimacy of society meetings, where hymn singing, extemporaneous prayer, and personal testimony were given broad scope. As Gordon Rupp commented, "The cell, the *koinonia*, the society, was at the heart of the Revival."[17]

Yet the ideal of catholic evangelicalism for which Newton stood was manifestly an ideal under siege during his own lifetime, for these close-knit fellowships were often seen to harden along connectional and denominational lines. Partisanship could not forever be eschewed in the name of spiritual union, for as long as there was something to be done (for example, celebrating the Lord's Supper), it would have to be done one way rather than another. It was one of the central paradoxes of evangelicalism that while standing for an ideal of spiritual catholicity based upon the New Birth, cooperative action was in practice continually under threat from separatist tendencies. Still, the ideal of a deeper evangelical solidarity continued always, if at times only quietly, to be expressed across denominational and factional boundaries through simple friendship between clergy and laity alike, sustained by mutual visits and conversation and through familiar correspondence. Indeed, this was the broad foundation upon

17. Gordon Rupp, *Religion in England, 1688–1791*, Oxford History of the Christian Church (Oxford, 1986), 330. See further, John Walsh, "Religious Societies: Methodist and Evangelical, 1738–1800," in *Voluntary Religion*, Studies in Church History, 23, ed. W. J. Shiels and Diana Wood (Oxford, 1986).

which Newton and three other friends originally established the Eclectic Society in London in 1783.[18]

Evangelical Consciousness: The Theological Axis

Having examined the religious axis of Newton's evangelicalism, we now turn to explore the limits of his evangelical identity along a theological axis. Nurtured in the bosom of Old Dissent, Newton was baptized by the Independent minister David Jennings (1691–1762), lecturer under the conservative Calvinistic Coward Trust, and he was taught the hymns and catechisms of Isaac Watts by his mother.[19] Years later, when his spiritual and moral waywardness was arrested by a near-death encounter at sea, it was to this early Calvinistic matrix he returned to interpret his experience. His dramatic deliverance provided a strong prima facie credibility to the notion that God was mysteriously at work in his life prior to his conversion. Likewise, when despite renewing his religious vows he continued to be tormented by a bad conscience, he readily cast himself upon the hope proffered by his Calvinistic acquaintances that God's grace was indefectible. Newton spent most of the winter of 1754–55 in London, making up for lost time at sea by immersing himself in the life of religious societies and listening to sermons whenever he could. This first taste of spiritual camaraderie was had largely among Calvinists of one sort or another and fortified his nascent predestinarian convictions.[20] His diary and his correspondence over the next two years reveal that he passed through the classic experience of Puritan interior piety, asking himself whether his life afforded sufficient evidence of his election, struggling slowly to a hard-won if yet uneasy assurance of his

18. *Letters and Conversational Remarks of Newton*, 64–65; *Letters of Newton to Bull*, 167–69. The problems created by the transdenominational impulse of the revival for later evangelicals who wished to remain loyal churchmen is treated in Charles Smyth, *Simeon and Church Order* (Cambridge, 1940).

19. On Jennings, see further the *Dictionary of National Biography* and also Joshua Toulmin, "A Review of the Life and Writings of the Rev. David Jennings, D.D.," *Protestant Dissenters Magazine* (1798): 81–89, 121–27.

20. Especially important were the Congregationalists Alexander Clunie and Samuel Brewer. See *The Christian Correspondent; . . . John Newton . . . to Captain Alexr. Clunie* (Hull, 1790); "Life of the Rev. Samuel Brewer," *Evangelical Magazine* 5 (1797): 5–18.

final salvation. As he developed more intimacy with George Whitefield, with Calvinistic Methodists, and with Independent ministers in
the revival milieu, a forward-looking, evangelistic optimism was
grafted onto this interior piety.[21] Then, for about six years prior to his
ordination, he undertook a vigorous program of self-study in divinity
and became convinced that, despite fashionable prejudices to the
contrary, Calvinism could be defended as scripturally sound, intellec-
tually respectable, and socially constructive.

By the early 1760s Newton's theological formation was complete,
and there would be few significant realignments of his essential beliefs. He was a five-point Calvinist. Yet, while the substance of his theology had been acquired, its elasticity remained to be tested by two
controversies. The first related to the perfectionist outbreaks among
the followers of Wesley in 1758–63; the second, to the shift away from
high Calvinism among Particular Baptists in Northamptonshire in the
1770s.[22] The middle ground Newton carved out for himself between
these two extremes may be seen in his comment to Richard Cecil: "I
find that I am considered as an Arminian among the high Calvinists,
and as a Calvinist among the strenuous Arminians."[23]

Newton first met Wesley in 1757 while residing at Liverpool, and
they struck up a warm acquaintance, despite their acknowledged
theological differences. He soon accounted Wesley a spiritual father
and brother, wrote to him for guidance in his faith, attended his
preaching, and entertained him at his home whenever possible. Then,
sometime around 1762, Newton dropped the correspondence entirely, until Wesley wrote to him at Olney in 1765, setting off a short

21. The Puritan antecedents to this piety are described in John von Rohr, "Covenant and
Assurance," in *The Covenant of Grace in Puritan Thought*, American Academy of Religion
Studies in Religion, no. 45, ed. Charley Hardwick and James O. Duke (Atlanta, 1986), 155–91;
cf. David Bebbington on evangelicals and assurance in *Evangelicalism in Modern Britain: A
History from the 1730s to the 1980s* (London, 1989; Grand Rapids, 1992), 42–50.

22. The eighteenth-century designation "high Calvinism" is used here, rather than "hyper-
Calvinism," to avoid anachronism ("hyper-Calvinist" did not come into currency until the nineteenth century), though in the current secondary literature "high Calvinism" is used variously
to describe the confessional orthodoxy of the seventeenth century or the supralapsarian
scheme of Theodore Beza reproduced in England by William Perkins. When Newton and his
contemporaries used the term, however, they were referring to the specifically eighteenth-century development that is more commonly described today as hyper-Calvinism.

23. Cecil, *Memoirs of Newton*, 227–28.

controversial exchange of letters.[24] Newton's estrangement from Wesley related to a spectacular perfectionist revival in the vicinity of Liverpool in 1762. Fifty-one Methodists claimed instantaneous and entire sanctification at Liverpool, and at nearby Bolton, where Newton had significant links with Calvinistic seceders from Wesley's connection, several Methodists reported having been justified and sanctified together within the space of a few days and some even within a few minutes.[25] While Newton had been able to suppress his differences with Wesley over predestination, the extent of the atonement, and final perseverance, he was not able to accept the behavior of Wesley's followers in the wake of the perfectionism revival. The claim to perfection, however hedged about by talk of grace, seemed in many cases no more than an enthusiastic self-righteousness that belied trusting wholly in the merits of Christ for redemption.[26] Newton had earlier worked out a formula that would maintain evangelical solidarity with Arminians by saying, "Though a man does not accord with my view of election, yet if he gives me good evidence, that *he* is *effectually called of God*, he is my brother" (6:199). He could not, however, make any rapprochement with Wesley's growing stress upon perfectionism. The behavior of his followers raised the specter of a Pelagianism that lay outside his understanding of evangelical theology, unduly stressing human agency in salvation.

The dealings of Newton with high Calvinists during his curacy at Olney marks the extent of his theology in the opposite direction of divine agency. Newton's many and close links with Calvinistic Baptists brought him into contact with John Collett Ryland of Northampton in 1765, and shortly thereafter Newton began a lasting friendship with his son John Ryland, Jr. (1753–1825).[27] For fifty years the powerful influence of John Gill and John Brine had held sway in much of

24. The course of the controversy between Newton and Wesley may be followed in the cryptic references in the *Letters of Wesley*, 4:292–93, 296–300; and Bull, *John Newton*, 146–47. Of particular importance is the MS letter Newton to Wesley, 18 April 1765, Southern Methodist University, Dallas, Tex. I am indebted to Prof. Frank Baker for helping me to locate this letter.

25. *The Journal of John Wesley*, ed. Nehemiah Curnock (London, 1913), 4:523.

26. Cf. Newton's complaint to John Thornton about an allegedly perfected Methodist in Martin, "Some Dissenting Friends," 237.

27. See L. G. Champion, "The Letters of John Newton to John Ryland," *Baptist Quarterly* 27 (1977): 157–63; Michael A. G. Haykin, "Anglican and Baptist: A View from the Eighteenth Century," *Prolegomena* 2 (1990): 21–28.

the denomination to which the Rylands belonged, perpetuating a heightened version of predestinarian theology. This theology popularized the view that preachers ought not to use moral suasion in presenting the claims of the gospel, for because none but the elect have the power to repent and believe, none but they have the duty to do so. While Gill and Brine were not themselves doctrinal antinomians, some of their followers were, and their theology acted to deter evangelism and to sustain an introspective separatistic piety among some groups of Baptists for many years.[28] The junior Ryland was raised in this milieu but later joined with important contemporaries such as Andrew Fuller and William Carey to effect a momentous theological shift away from Gill and Brine that in turn stimulated a burst of activity among the Baptists at the end of the century in education, associational life, prayer for the unconverted, and foreign missions. Newton played an important part—through private discussions and correspondence, and by recommending books—in helping Ryland toward his later more evangelical opinions.[29] The distinction between natural and moral ability that Ryland discovered in Jonathan Edwards was reinforced by Newton and was the fulcrum upon which his necessitarian beliefs were accommodated to a measure of free will. Newton's position was plain. He declared, "What is by some called high Calvinism, I dread" (6:278). Several issues placed high Calvinism outside of his evangelical theology. He felt that it tended to antinomianism, that it constrained the free offer of the gospel, that it failed adequately to insist upon the duty of the unconverted to believe, and that it too often drifted into merely noetic speculation.

Thus, between John Wesley's *Plain Account of Christian Perfection* and John Gill's *Doctrines of God's Everlasting Love to His Elect,*

28. See further Geoffrey F. Nuttall, "Northamptonshire and *The Modern Question:* A Turning-Point in Eighteenth-Century Dissent," *Journal of Theological Studies,* n.s., 16 (1965): 101–23; Raymond Brown, *English Baptists of the Eighteenth Century,* History of the English Baptists, 2 (London, 1986), 71–95; Olin C. Robison, "The Particular Baptists in England" (D.Phil. diss., Oxford University, 1963); Peter Toon, *The Emergence of Hyper-Calvinism in English Non-Conformity* (London, 1967). The high Calvinist milieu in which the younger Ryland was raised may be observed in his MS diary, entitled "The Experience of Jo/n R.l..d junr as wrote by himself in a letter to Thos. R..t dated Feby: 1770," Angus Library, Regent's Park College, Oxford.

29. See particularly John Ryland, Jr., *Life of the Rev. Andrew Fuller,* 2d ed. (London, 1818), 6n; idem, *Serious Remarks on the Different Representations of Evangelical Doctrine* (Bristol, 1817); Newton, *Works,* 2:112–32.

Newton's own evangelical theology strove to steer a middle course, maintaining an even equipoise between predestinarian grace and responsible voluntarism. A similar balance, forged under similar conditions, was struck earlier by Whitefield. In 1739 he had returned from New England fortified in his Calvinistic orthodoxy and resolved to be more explicit about the doctrine of election. But over the next six years, in a process parallel to that observed in Newton, Whitefield sought to moderate his theological tone to accommodate the bipolar tension in evangelical theology between the principles of high Calvinist separatists such as he had encountered in Scotland and New England and those of Methodist or Establishment Arminians such as he had met in England and the American colonies.[30] When in 1754–55 Newton experienced a "foretaste of the business of heaven" upon hearing Whitefield preach and becoming intimate friends with him, he discovered a model for his own theological formation. Whitefield had gone before, blazing a trail that Newton would follow over the next several years.

The catholic middle ground thus sought by Newton may be seen, for example, in his sermon "The Lamb of God, the Great Atonement," preached in 1785 and printed the following year as part of a very topical series based on the libretto of Handel's *Messiah* and timed to coincide with the commemoration at Westminster Abbey (4:184–97).[31] The text, which opens the second part of the oratorio, was John 1:29: "Behold the Lamb of God, which taketh away the sin of the world!" Upon the announcement of such a text, the ears of every evangelical hearer would have been pricked, for this verse, like 1 John 2:2, was a hermeneutical test case for the doctrine of the limited atonement. And the limited atonement was in turn a test case for strict Calvinistic orthodoxy.

30. See further Harry S. Stout, *The Divine Dramatist: George Whitefield and the Rise of Modern Evangelicalism* (Grand Rapids, 1991), 135–39, 174–200.

31. Alan C. Clifford, in his recent study *Atonement and Justification: English Evangelical Theology, 1640–1790, an Evaluation* (Oxford, 1990), 80–81, uses this sermon to argue that Newton was one of the eighteenth-century moderate Calvinists who "shared Wesley's view of the extent of the atonement." In the exposition and analysis of the sermon that follows above, it is maintained, on the contrary, that Newton did adhere to an orthodox position on the limited atonement but that he consciously subordinated this doctrine to evangelical priorities.

Newton's sermon may be summarized as follows. The splendid works of God in creation, everywhere observable, ought to be enough to incite all persons to adore their creator. That they do not is signal proof of their depravity. In order to soften such obdurate creatures, God appointed an even greater wonder by offering a suffering savior in the person of his own Son. As the Lamb of God, Christ superseded the sacrificial system, dying as the one voluntary substitute for death-deserving sinners. This way of redemption satisfied the rights of God's justice, the demands of his law, and the honor of his government, providing an atonement that was fully efficacious to deliver a believer from the guilt and penalty of sin. With its sin removed, the soul is open to Christ, whose grace is richly imparted for a life of continuing obedience.

What of the extent of the atonement? Newton continued that the atonement is, indeed, plainly spoken of in the Scriptures in a large and indefinite manner as taking away the sins of the *world*. Yet it is equally certain from Scripture that all people will not be saved in the end. Moreover, the Bible speaks of those finally redeemed in peculiar language, such as when it says that Christ laid down his life for *his sheep*. They are spoken of not in the language of conjecture or hypothesis but in the definite language of predestination. Is this not the experience of all those who are truly spiritual and enlightened—not that they first sought God but that he first sought them? Having said this, those who would explain away the text by saying that Christ died for the whole world merely in the sense of having died for only some people of all nations are not following the scriptural manner of expression, for Scripture speaks of Christ's having died for *sinners*. Herein is warrant for all to seek him for forgiveness. The atonement was not a substitution in the sense of a precise calculation of so much suffering for so many sins. God is always more magnanimous than that. Rather, his atonement was sufficient for the sins of all the world and more. Again, this is warrant for the gospel to be extended to all. God commands all people everywhere to repent and believe. That some do not is a moral defect on their part, not a natural one, and they themselves are culpable for it. It is wrong for God's sovereign grace to be so exalted that sinners begin to think themselves as unable to comply with God's requirements and therefore not responsible for their own disobedience. No, salvation is wholly of grace, but those who reject the Lamb of God have their blood on their own head.

Several elements of theological moderation and consensus building may be seen in this sermon. By beginning with the predicament of depraved creatures in a glorious creation, Newton characteristically started with an existential point upon which all evangelicals could agree. As he proceeded to discuss God's provision of redemption, he freely drew on several traditional theories of the atonement, and his language variously reflected emphases that were Abelardian (moral incitement), Anselmic (satisfaction), Reformation (penal substitution), and Grotian (governmental). Although he stressed the penal concept of the atonement most strongly, he did not use the rhetoric of precise imputation or of Christ's active and passive righteousness, which, while dear to some high Calvinists, would have alienated him from many of the followers of Wesley. Rather, he related penal substitution to the simple experience of justification by faith, another point upon which his audience could agree. When Newton dealt with the extent of the atonement, he likewise picked his footing deftly along a path between a hypothetical and a commercial view of the atonement, respectively characteristic of Richard Baxter and Philip Doddridge on the one hand and John Owen and his followers on the other. Newton alluded to both positions only to reject them both insofar as they pretended to be comprehensive theories of the atonement. Effectively, he supplanted the whole question of the extent of the atonement in favor of evangelical priorities and acceptable biblical paradox, however much he knew he would be upbraided by some Calvinists for a failure of nerve or by some Arminians for vestiges of particularistic diffidence. For him it was enough that Christ died for sinners, for who was not a sinner? Of supreme importance was simply the free offer of the gospel, graciously extended to all.

This was more, however, to shift the ground of the debate than it was to solve the theological problem. For the question could still be asked whether Christ died for *all* sinners or just for *some*. Acutely aware of partisans to the right and to the left on this issue, Newton sought not so much to resolve the logical tensions inherent in relating divine and human agency as to live with them. Along the theological axis, the evangelical consciousness that Newton represented was held together by belief in a simple gospel that was to be addressed to the conscience and will of the unconverted sinner but the efficacy of which depended wholly upon the free and mysterious grace of God. Wesley had once tried to rally the evangelical clergy around a three-fold platform of belief in original sin, justification by faith, and that holiness without which no one shall see God.[32] This was a clear enough statement of evangelical essentials. That only three ministers responded to his call reflected more on their distrust of his Arminianism and perfectionism than on his grasp of an evangelical theological consensus with which Newton could readily have concurred.

In evaluating Newton's evangelical theology, we observe first its marked continuity with Reformed theology. The dialectic between predestination and piety, between the covenant as absolute and conditional, has been demonstrated as a central feature of Puritan theology in the seventeenth century. The concern to relate grace and law in a way that avoided the polar extremes of antinomianism and legalism was perennial.[33] While the Calvinistic tradition had been driven underground in the Church of England during the decades before the revival, it was sustained among Dissenters; Newton's case shows how many ways there were for the old inheritance to be transmitted to the new evangelical leaders. Indeed, during the Evangelical Revival, the entire spectrum of seventeenth-century Reformed theology from the Arminianism of John Goodwin to the antinomianism of Tobias Crisp was reconstituted under the new cultural conditions of the eighteenth century. Just as Wesley's Arminianism was the odd one out in the theological matrix of the revival, so too had Arminianism among the Puritans been in ambiguous relationship with the Calvinist tradition. Still, the Arminian-Calvinist tension was in both cases *within* a broad tradition of English evangelical theology. Inevitably, after six generations in England, the Reformed tradition had by Newton's time feathered out in increasing complexity. But Newton pointed to the continuity of the revival with the old inheritance when he claimed that those who maintained an evangeli-

32. *Journals of Wesley*, 5:61.
33. See von Rohr, *Covenant of Grace;* Dewey D. Wallace, Jr., *Puritans and Predestination: Grace in English Protestant Theology, 1525–1695* (Chapel Hill, N.C., 1982); Isabel Rivers, *Reason, Grace, and Sentiment: A Study of the Language of Religion and Ethics in England, 1660–1780*, vol. 1: *Whichcote to Wesley* (Cambridge, 1991).

cal strain of doctrine were in his own day called Methodists but earlier had been variously described as Lollard and Gospeller, or Puritan and Pietist (6:571).[34]

Conversely, however, Newton's evangelical theology also demonstrates in several ways a sharp break with seventeenth-century cultural traditions. Against the popular notion that the Evangelical Revival was wholly at odds with the culture created in England by the Enlightenment—a reactionary movement of the heart against the head—there has been advanced in recent years a thesis of significant contemporary cultural accommodation. In different ways Haddon Willmer, Reginald Ward, and David Bebbington have all stressed the kinship of the revival with the dominant ideological currents of the period.[35] This may be seen in Newton's case in his exploitation of latitudinarian principles to evangelical ends, and in his conformity to Augustan and pre-Romantic aesthetic standards.

Newton's correspondence with ministers of other denominations often involved him in a careful rhetoric of toleration. To John Campbell at Edinburgh, Newton wrote, "I congratulate you and myself on the progress of what some may call latitudinarianism in Scotland," adding that he thought the prayer in Ephesians 6:24 was a very latitudinarian prayer.[36] While there may not have been a direct transmission of ideas from the Cambridge Platonists and Archbishop Tillot-

34. On the continuity in piety, see F. Ernest Stoeffler, *The Rise of Evangelical Pietism*, Studies in the History of Religions, no. 9 (Leiden, 1971). Stoeffler's argument that all experiential Protestantism after the Reformation can be treated as an essential unity—defined as experiential, perfectionistic, biblical, and oppositive—while convincing in the main, cuts a swath a little too wide to be finally definite, leaving out, as it does, ideological factors. The theological continuity is treated by Bebbington, *Evangelicalism in Modern Britain*, 34–35; and John Walsh, "The Origins of the Evangelical Revival," in *Essays in Modern English Church History*, ed. G. V. Bennet and John Walsh (London, 1966), 154–60.

35. In 1962 Willmer set forth the thesis that the evangelicalism of the eighteenth-century Church of England was expressed precisely in the basic pattern provided by the certainties of the age; in 1979 Ward argued that pietism, religious revival, and the Enlightenment were most often linked in a kinship of opposition to allegedly dead confessional orthodoxies; and in 1989 Bebbington put it most strongly, saying, "The Evangelical version of Protestantism was created by the Enlightenment" (Haddon Willmer, "Evangelicalism, 1785–1835," Hulsean Prize Essay, Cambridge, 1962; Reginald Ward, "The Relations of Enlightenment and Religious Revival in Central Europe and in the English-Speaking World," in *Reform and Reformation: England and the Continent, c. 1500–c. 1750*, Studies in Church History, Subsidia, no. 2 [Oxford, 1979], 281–305; Bebbington, *Evangelicalism in Modern Britain*, 74).

36. *Letters and Conversational Remarks of Newton*, 107.

son to Newton, he nevertheless appropriated the principle that religious experience itself is a more profound bond between Christians than the form of words in which it is expressed.[37] This was noted earlier when it was observed that Newton gave evangelical Arminians the credit of actually being elect even if they did not maintain his particular doctrine of election. His reading of the Earl of Shaftesbury's *Characteristics* and of the *Spectator* and the *Tatler* as a young man may have instilled in him an ideal of refined toleration—polite culture certainly disdained bigotry and deplored "party rage," at least in name—but it was most likely his contact with Whitefield and Wesley that convinced him of the possibility of an evangelical latitudinarianism. Two years before Whitefield met Newton, Whitefield was writing in a chastened tone to his friends at the Tabernacle, "Let us not dispute, but love. . . . Let us look above names and parties."[38] Likewise, for all Wesley's controversial wrangles, he too was, as Jean Orcibal has commented, "the exponent of a toleration which was mystical rather than doctrinal, such as he had seen John Byrom champion from the time of his youth."[39] Wesley once wrote to Newton in exactly this vein when, acknowledging that they differed on some things, he added, "Notwithstanding this, we tasted each other's spirits, and often took sweet counsel together."[40] Newton used the same rhetoric when writing to John Ryland about a disagreement over eternal justification, saying in 1772, "If we hold the head and love the Lord, we agree in him, and I should think my time ill employed in disputing the point with you" (2:111). As always with this formula, the problem came when parties could no longer agree over which principles were essential and which were nonessential. Still, Newton was arguably one of the most successful evangelicals of his century in cultivating a wide religious acquaintance upon just such a basis.

Latitude implies a reduced creed of essential beliefs, a reduction that was in harmony with the Augustan aesthetic preference for sim-

---

37. Cf. Willmer, "Evangelicalism," 80–81.

38. *Works of Whitefield*, 2:428.

39. Jean Orcibal, "The Theological Originality of John Wesley and Continental Spirituality," trans. R. J. A. Sharp, in *A History of the Methodist Church in Great Britain*, ed. Rupert Davies and Gordon Rupp, vol. 1 (London, 1965), 110.

40. *Letters of Wesley*, 4:292.

plicity over discursiveness. This aesthetic may be seen, waning into
a pre-Romantic focus on sentiment, in the style of Newton's evangelical theology. Thus, while John Owen was one of his favorite authors,
Owen's digressive prose style was rejected, Newton feeling that scholastic theology was in his own refined age "now exploded as uncouth
and obsolete" (4:523). The bias was to pare down the gospel to its essentials rather than to exhaust its implications. Sources for this new
preference were various. The insistence of the Royal Society at the
turn of the century upon a clear and plain style of English compatible
with scientific exposition and the call for clarity and distinctness in
Cartesian ideology were, for example, inextricably bound up with the
neoclassical canons in literature that prevailed during the early part
of Newton's life. Isaac Watts has been identified as one of the finest
representatives of this aesthetic. His "art of sinking" poetry to the
level of a whole congregation reflected a conscious ideal of restrained sensual pleasure that drew equally on the Enlightenment
and on the Calvinistic values of simplicity, sobriety, and measure.[41]
While the hegemony of these classical ideals waned toward the end
of the century as sentiment became more idealized and the forces of
democracy gathered momentum, Newton's theology reflected a simplicity that owed much to his education in the old Dissent of Watts
and to his early efforts to acquire entrance to polite society through
a program of reading based on Addison and Steele. Newton later gave
up the ideal of politeness for one of sincerity, and sought purity of
sentiment more than purity of diction and syntax, but his evangelical
theology was throughout cast in a lean form that was entirely consistent with his period and very unlike that of his Puritan predecessors.[42] The style he adopted was consonant with Wesley's dictum

41. Hoyles, *Waning of the Renaissance*, 143–251; Donald Davie, *A Gathered Church*, 1976
Clark Lectures (London, 1978), 24–28.

42. Evangelical camaraderie in many ways relieved Newton of the burden of aspiring up
the social ladder and achieving a polite refinement of manners. His letters to his wife from
1750–57 illustrate the transition from affected *politesse* to pietistic sentiment that accompanied his conversion. Observe the disclaimer with which he began a letter to his wife on her
birthday in 1757: "You will not expect me to address you in the strain of modern politeness, but
I am persuaded that you will favourably accept what I may write, because you approve of my
motive and my sincerity" (5:515). Newton here points to the important way in which evangelical pietism could hasten the shift from Augustan ideals of propriety to sentimental ideals of
"the man of feeling."

about offering plain truth for plain people and Whitefield's expressed desire in preaching to emphasize the simplicity of the gospel.

The twin ideals of latitude and simplicity, together with a preoccupation to edify, resolved Newton's confessional orthodoxy into a christocentric form acceptable to most of his evangelical contemporaries. He could have echoed Whitefield's earlier words to his followers, "Let Jesus, the ever-loving, the ever-lovely Jesus, be our all in all."[43] Moreover, for Newton, as for many of his evangelical fellows, experience bulked large in his theological method, and reason was understood to function more along Lockean (or Edwardsean) than Aristotelian lines. For though Newton's Calvinism was strict, predestination was in no way the leading speculative principle from which he derived an entire religious system; neither did the motif of covenant or the *ordo salutis* provide a central structure around which his thought was organized. On the contrary, he admitted to sublimating his Calvinism deliberately in order to reach the widest possible audience. William Jay recalled Newton saying once, "'I am more of a Calvinist than anything else; but I use my Calvinism in my writings and my preaching as I use this sugar'—taking a lump, and putting it into his tea-cup, and stirring it, adding, 'I do not give it alone, and whole; but mixed and diluted.'"[44] This reticence to trumpet Calvinistic orthodoxy derived in part from his ambiguous ecclesiastical position as a minister in the Church of England who still had links with orthodox Dissent, and it derived from his marginal theological position between high and low predestinarians. It also derived from cultural norms relating to toleration and taste. Seeking the widest possible evangelical solidarity, he carried on a theological discourse that was "politically correct," offending as few partisans of the revival as possible. It is not surprising, therefore, that he wrote principally biographies, sermons, letters, and hymnody—not treatises or polemical tracts, much less a "body of divinity."

It was observed above that by eschewing the physical and organizational side of ecclesiology, Newton's ideal of the spiritual solidarity of evangelicals, expressed through ingenuous friendship, foundered

43. *Works of Whitefield*, 2:428.
44. *The Autobiography of William Jay*, ed. George Redford and John Angell James (London, 1854; reprint, Edinburgh, 1974), 272.

on the rock of separatism. So too, here again, by neglecting rigorous intellectual and cultural discourse, Newton's simple evangelical theology suffered by assimilating culture uncritically. Haddon Willmer has shown how the rejection of vigorous intellectual theology by evangelicals like Newton during this period, and the link they so often assumed between providence and prudence, led in practice to an easy acceptance of the social order and the certainties of the age.[45] Critical thought was inhibited by a too facile rejection of culture as worldly. What was sent out the front door merely returned through the back. Doreen Rosman captures this paradox in her discussion of evangelicalism during the period at the close of Newton's life. She argues that "evangelicals shared in the tastes and interests of the more cultured of their contemporaries to a far greater extent than is always recognised, but were unable to justify their enjoyment within the terms of their world-denying theology."[46]

Likewise, by renouncing system in favor of sentiment and simplicity, there was danger that evangelical diction would deteriorate into bathos and threadbare clichés. This can be seen in the way the very word "evangelical" lost some of its theological freshness and became more of a merely partisan label at the close of the eighteenth century. Newton's most vigorous intellectual period was from 1758 to 1764. After that, he grew increasingly satisfied with a "pass-the-buck" approach to theology, typically referring inquirers to Jonathan Edwards, for example, on the knotty problem of moral and natural inability, or to John Owen on the propriety of the free offer of the gospel, rather than working out these arguments afresh himself. While it is no disgrace that Newton was more a pastor than a theologian, it is one of the most serious indictments of the English Evangelical Revival that it produced so few theologians of stature.

Conclusion

Placing the religious and theological axes at right angles, a matrix of transdenominational evangelical consciousness emerges from John Newton's life and writings. Such a consciousness first appeared

45. Willmer, "Evangelicalism," 81–109.
46. Doreen Rosman, *Evangelicals and Culture* (London, 1984), 43.

in George Whitefield and had much to do with his unique exposure to the many local varieties of evangelical religion across the dominions of Great Britain on both sides of the Atlantic. Where Whitefield pioneered, Newton followed. The tacit acceptance of religious pluralism formed the critical infrastructure for evangelical thought in Newton's period, preparing the way for the accommodation of a degree of theological dissent within a larger structure of evangelical consensus. As Reformed theology was refracted under these conditions into a similar spectrum to that observed in seventeenth-century Puritanism, there was inevitably greater scope for voluntarism, since officially sanctioned diversity implied an elevated role for private judgment. But because pluralism made a *de jure divino* position on church order seem invidious, the ideal of a Protestant solidarity that cut across the lines of territorial churches and religious denominations was achieved by subordinating the empirical reality of the church as a *corpus permixtum* with a physical cultus to its mystical reality as the community of the spiritually regenerate. Hence, a union of spirituality could be advanced through friendship and the voluntary fellowship meeting, and sometimes through cooperative action in evangelism, if not through denominational union or exact theological agreement. Wider cultural developments abetted this process. The Augustan aesthetic of simplicity encouraged the gospel message to be stripped down to its most basic rather than festooned to its most elaborate, and the ideal of latitude favored the practice of accepting all who had experienced the same spiritual reality, while making allowance for differences in mode of expression.

The central paradox of this evangelicalism remained, however, that while eschewing church order, it was dogged by separatism; and that while stressing the importance of real belief, its neglect of intellectual theology created a stereotyped diction for a new kind of nominalism. Nonetheless, the late eighteenth-century evangelical consensus bore a necessary witness to the surpassing importance of personal belief in a simple gospel for all people and to the priority of the eschatological reality of the church over all temporal concerns. John Newton was testimony to the way in which such a consciousness of what it meant to be evangelical extended across a variety of social and religious boundaries. The qualities of evangelicalism that thus allowed the development of loyalties that transcended denominational distinctives of creed and church order may even help to account for the manifest sense of solidarity that even today links various Canadian, American, and British evangelicals, who are separated by the very North Atlantic seas upon which Newton first cried out to God for mercy in 1748.

2

Noisy Methodists and Pious Protestants

Evangelical Revival and Religious Minorities in Eighteenth-Century Ireland

David Hempton

The roots of the great religious revivals of the eighteenth century—from eastern and central Europe to the Middle Colonies of America—are to be found, according to Professor Ward, in the resistance of confessional minorities to the real or perceived threat of assimilation by powerful states and established churches.[1] Such a perspective inevitably shifts the center of gravity away from the Anglo-American preoccupation of much revival scholarship to the displaced and persecuted Protestant minorities of Habsburg-dominated central Europe.[2]

1. I am grateful to Mark Noll and John Walsh for comments made on earlier drafts of this essay.
2. See William R. Ward, "Power and Piety: The Origins of Religious Revival in the Early Eighteenth Century," *Bulletin of the John Rylands University Library of Manchester* 63 (1980): 231–52; and idem, "The Relations of Enlightenment to Religious Revival in Central Europe and in the English-Speaking World," *Studies in Church History*, Subsidia 2 (1979): 281–305.

In his important book *The Protestant Evangelical Awakening*, Ward invites his readers to penetrate a tangled web of circulating literature, itinerant revivalists, and folk migrations that combine to show that the Great Awakening of the eighteenth century was more a truly international event than some have imagined and cannot be reduced to the social and economic peculiarities of specific places, however much they may have shaped the distinctive local expression of revival enthusiasm.[3] Instead, he suggests that the seeds of future revivals in the eighteenth century are to be found within a worldwide Protestant frame of mind that was a compound of low morale, fear of confessional conflict, eschatological neuroses, and pious devotion, all of which was serviced by an astonishing array of post Reforma tion devotional publications. The spiritual life of Europe was quite simply breaking free from confessional control at precisely the time when such control was being pursued with renewed vigor by early modern states. As a result the pietism of Halle and Herrnhut was fanned into revivals in various Protestant corners of the Habsburg Empire and was then carried to the British Isles and North America by sweeping population movements and by a remarkable collection of revivalists who knew of each other's labors and who believed themselves to be part of a worldwide evangelical movement.

The theological spark that ignited this spiritually combustible material was the pietist emphasis on the New Birth and the priesthood of all believers, teachings that were translated into actuality by itinerant preaching and the *collegia pietatis*, or class meetings. Added urgency was provided by the orthodox unwillingness to extend legal toleration to the pietists and by vigorous policies of recatholicization, which often led to forced migrations. Little wonder, then, that many of the heirs of this tradition had little time for unaccommodating established churches or for the Roman Catholic Church in particular.

Ward's assessment of the importance of Continental pietist influences on the early history of the Great Awakening unfortunately, because of editorial constraints, excludes Ireland, though he is well aware that his general thesis applies there even more clearly than in some other parts of the British Isles. Indeed he states that in the late seventeenth-century and early eighteenth-century Protestant di-

3. William R. Ward, *The Protestant Evangelical Awakening* (Cambridge, 1992).

aspora, "thousands of Protestants fetched up in Ireland." Of the myriad of Protestant refugees (the word itself was first used of the seventeenth-century French Calvinists) who made their way across Europe and even into the New World in this period, representatives of two groups—the Huguenots and the Palatines—made their way to Ireland. Huguenots were not new to Ireland in the late seventeenth century, but the most important wave of settlers (about ten thousand) came in the wake of the Revocation of the Edict of Nantes in 1685, when Huguenots lost their legal protection.[4] France's loss was Ireland's gain, for the Huguenots brought with them military expertise, liquid capital, mercantile networks, and a range of skills from linen manufacturing to sail making.[5] In particular they made a telling, if sometimes exaggerated, contribution to William of Orange's Irish campaigns and to the development of the Irish linen industry. Moreover, Huguenot descendants played a significant role in the development of Irish commerce and banking, literature and architecture, and map-making and surveying, but in the well-known lists of contributors and contributions it is sometimes forgotten that the real reason for Huguenot migration was to obtain freedom of worship. Here too they were successful, but at a price.

Huguenots were welcomed by the Protestant Ascendancy in early eighteenth-century Ireland for their industry and their Protestantism. Conformity to the Church of Ireland was made profitable, nonconformity relatively easy, and access to the social elite was kept open. As a result the Huguenots, despite sharing a common language, culture, and theology, and despite widely practiced intermarriage and controlled apprenticeships, were slowly assimilated into a wider Irish Protestantism. Ironically perhaps, far more Huguenot descendants passed through the doors of the Church of Ireland than ever joined the ranks of the other Calvinistic settlers—the Ulster-Scots Presbyterians. Not all Huguenot congregations conformed to the Church of

4. C. E. J. Caldicott, H. Gough, and J.-P. Pittion, *The Huguenots and Ireland: Anatomy of an Emigration* (Dun Laoghaire, Ireland, 1987); Robin D. Gwynn, *Huguenot Heritage: The History and Contribution of the Huguenots in Britain* (London, 1985); G. L. Lee, *The Huguenot Settlements in Ireland* (London, 1936); James Camlin Beckett, *Protestant Dissent in Ireland, 1687–1780* (London, 1948).

5. William A. Maguire et al., *The Huguenots and Ulster, 1685–1985* (Lisburn, Ireland, 1985).

Ireland, however, but those that did were allowed to retain important elements of their French Presbyterian past. Nevertheless, Irish Huguenots, in common with other Huguenot communities in western Europe, were either unwilling or unable to sustain a distinctively French culture beyond the third or fourth generation. The last of the French churches closed their doors in the early nineteenth century.[6] Only the graveyards remained as the last gesture of the unassimilated.

It is clear from John Wesley's *Journal* that despite the theological gulf between French Calvinism and English evangelical Arminianism, Huguenot communities played an important part in the early dissemination of Methodism in London and Bristol, and it was here that French preaching was most useful. The same is true in Ireland, where the Huguenot banker William Lunell opened up facilities for early evangelical itinerants in Dublin,[7] and the Huguenot community of Portarlington was visited by Wesley and religious revivalism in 1749.[8] Perhaps of more long-term significance for the evangelical cause in Ireland, descendants of Huguenot and Flemish families turn up with monotonous regularity in the records of early Episcopalian and Presbyterian evangelicalism in Dublin. The Maturins, La Touches, Lefroys, and others played a vital role, both as spiritual leaders and as fund-raisers, in the great explosion of evangelical societies in early nineteenth-century Ireland.[9]

An even smaller confessional minority, equally the victim of the Sun King's brutality, was the German Palatine community that arrived in Ireland in 1709.[10] After suffering successive devastations of the Palatinate through war and economic dislocation, 821 families arrived in Dublin via London and were settled in estates in Limerick, Kerry, and Tipperary. These humble German farmers were given land

6. S. J. Knox, *Ireland's Debt to the Huguenots* (Dublin, 1959).

7. John Wesley, *Journal*, standard ed. (London, 1909–16), 3:312, 313, 463.

8. Ibid., 407–8.

9. Alan R. Acheson, "The Evangelicals in the Church of Ireland, 1784–1859" (Ph.D. diss., Queen's University, Belfast, 1967); Joseph Liechty, "Irish Evangelicalism, Trinity College Dublin, and the Mission of the Church of Ireland at the End of the Eighteenth Century" (Ph.D. diss., St. Patrick's College, 1987).

10. Dwight Lloyd Savory, "The Huguenot-Palatine Settlements in the Counties of Limerick, Kerry, and Tipperary," *Proceedings of the Huguenot Society of London* 18 (1948): 111–33 and 215–31; Helmut Blume, "Some Geographical Aspects of the Palatine Settlement in Ireland," *Irish Geography* 2, no. 4 (1952): 172–79.

under decidedly favorable terms, much to the chagrin of their Catholic Irish neighbors. To a greater degree than other ethnic and confessional minorities in Ireland, the Palatines lived as a distinct people, separated from the indigenous population by language, culture, religion, folk memories, farming methods, and relative prosperity. Aided by their general rural seclusion and fervent Protestantism, which was spectacularly revived by John Wesley and the Methodists, the Palatines resisted assimilation by practicing strict intermarriage and by regulating their own affairs through an appointed burgomaster. Even when their native language disappeared around 1800 and they experienced greater economic integration in the period after the famine, the Palatines still retained subtle elements of their late seventeenth-century Germanic origins until well into the twentieth century.

There are two important postscripts to the Palatine encounter with Irish Methodism. The first is that when the campaign for Catholic Emancipation reached a climax in 1828, it was the Methodists of Palatine descent who most vigorously opposed any concession, in the process severely testing the no-politics resolve of Jabez Bunting and his Irish associates.[11] Second, and far more important, the majority of Palatine settlers left Ireland for North America when their favorable leases ran out in 1760. Among those who set out from Limerick harbor in 1760 were Philip Embury and Barbara Heck, who have been credited with the formation of the first permanent Methodist society in North America, established in the city of New York in 1766. Contemporaneously, another Irish Methodist exile, Robert Strawbridge of County Leitrim, was establishing the Methodist system on Sam's Creek in the backwoods of Maryland.[12] In the folk migrations of displaced Protestant minorities, Ireland, as Europe's last off-shore island and as an unrivaled exporter of humanity, certainly played a strategic role.[13]

While Palatine migrants from Ireland made an important contribution to religious life in North America, an encounter between John

11. Matthew Tobias to Jabez Bunting, 17 March 1829, Irish Wesleyan Historical Society Manuscripts, Northern Ireland Public Record Office.

12. W. J. Townsend, H. B. Workman, and George Eayrs, eds., *A New History of Methodism* (London, 1909), 2:36–37 and 56–61; Emory Stevens Bucke, *The History of American Methodism* (Nashville, 1964), 74–78.

13. Norman W. Taggart, *The Irish in World Methodism* (London, 1986).

Wesley and another German confessional minority, the Moravians, on a ship bound for American was to have profound implications for religious life in Ireland.[14] Wesley, after his Moravian-inspired "conversion," looked upon the world as his parish, and he made twenty-one preaching visits to Ireland between 1747 and 1789.[15] The early history of Methodist- and Moravian-inspired revivalism in Ireland, as in England, proved to be exceptionally turbulent and is worth studying in some detail for what it reveals about the later history of popular evangelicalism on the island.[16]

John Cennick, a Wiltshire itinerant preacher of Bohemian descent and early Methodist associations, arrived in Ireland in 1746 largely as a result of invitations from the Dublin Baptists, who allowed him to make use of their meetinghouse in Skinner's Alley.[17] By the mid-1740s Dublin already had an informal network of religious societies, some Established Church, some Presbyterian, some Bradilonian, and some Baptist. They formed a colorful, argumentative, eclectic, and messy subculture, full of disputes about the nature of grace, the efficacy of the sacraments, and the ownership of buildings. Allowing for the risk of reproducing Cennick's own evangelical hyperbole, it seems that he quickly achieved a preeminent position among Dublin's popular Protestants owing to his preaching ability and his connections with the English and Continental Moravian communities. His journal is a mine of information about the state of metropolitan Protestantism on the eve of Wesley's first visit.

> He [Mr. Edwards, a Baptist pastor] proffer'd me their great meeting in Swift's Alley if I would preach there, but as I knew there were parties there who adher'd to Arianism or New-Light, and others of Orthodox schemes, and fearing my preaching there would incense the opposite party I declin'd it which prov'd best, for not long after they met with sad confusions in that congregation.

14. Clifford W. Towlson, *Moravian and Methodist: Relationships and Influences in the Eighteenth Century* (London, 1957).

15. Robert Haire, *Wesley's One-and-Twenty Visits to Ireland* (London, 1947).

16. C. H. Crookshank, *History of Methodism in Ireland*, 3 vols. (London, 1885–88); David Hempton and Myrtle Hill, *Evangelical Protestantism in Ulster Society, 1740–1890* (London, 1992), 1–44.

17. Frank Baker, ed., *The Works of John Wesley*, vol. 26: *Letters II, 1740–1755* (Oxford, 1982), 281–98.

About this time many pamphlets were printed and handed about Dublin. One was wrote by some of the chief of the Dissenters—a Poem in a pretty good stile ridiculing me and my Doctrine, manner of preaching etc. . . . Opposition increas'd on all sides, the Catholic Priests threaten'd their people under pain of excommunication to come to hear me, and one Father Lyons told one who lov'd us that I was a Devil in human shape, and no real man.[18]

To ecclesiastical opposition was added serious mob violence throughout 1746 and 1747, which in turn elicited feeble action from the civil, ecclesiastical, and legal authorities, who, not unreasonably, began to associate revival preaching with serious social disorder.[19] Such excitement nevertheless attracted record crowds to Cennick's Moravian sermons, but internecine disputes between Methodists and Moravians, on the one hand, and between new revivalists and old Baptists, on the other, restricted evangelical potential at a crucial stage in its development. The disputes between the Baptists and the Methodists were particularly unfortunate, for the net result was that the revival made little headway among the old Puritan Dissenters of Ireland until well into the nineteenth century, by which stage it was too late to make much difference. The roots of the quarrel are well captured by the author of the Cork Baptist Church Book.

As this people [the Methodists] have made considerable noise in the world and particularly in this city, but more especially as we apprehend, the Baptists have been much injured by them, we think we ought to take some notice of them by producing such facts as have come under our knowledge.

From their first appearance the novelty of preaching in the fields, their seeming zeal and disinterestedness gained them a multitude of hearers. What gave them countenance at first and warded off resentment of the Protestants was that they constantly declared they were not come to form any new party among Christians, that they only desired to win souls to Christ. The multitudes of all ranks of people that

18. John Cennick, "An Account of the Most Remarkable Passages Relating to the Awakening in Dublin in Ireland from the Beginning of the Settlement of the Congregation," Transcript of his Journal, Moravian Church House, London.

19. David N. Hempton, "Methodism and the Law, 1740–1820," *Bulletin of the John Rylands University Library of Manchester* 70, no. 3 (1988): 93–107.

resorted to the fields to hear them gave rage to the magistrates and 'tis not improbable but the mob were countenanced in disturbing their assemblies, 'tis certain that such kind of assemblies are subject to tumults and therefore tho' our government is the most indulgent in the world to everything that has the appearance of religion, yet the laws do not protect such wild promiscuous assemblies. Besides there was some reason to think that the working people were interrupted from their labour and while out of pretense of religion they ran after such preachers their families at home were left destitute.[20]

In addition to this Irish version of Puritan sobriety, the author, in a formidable list of charges, accused the Methodists of empire building, moncy grabbing, family splitting, heiress hunting, and "sheep" stealing.[21] Baptist sensibilities about congregational independence and adult baptism were also offended by Wesley's connectional authoritarianism and devotion to Anglican sacraments. Finally, with logic that would not have been out of place in seventeenth-century Reformed councils, the author stated that Methodist claims to be loyal and enthusiastic Anglicans were almost certainly a cunning deception; if true, however, then Baptists had an even greater duty to shun them, as "the same reasons which are given for our dissenting from the established church will hold good against them."[22]

Such sentiments revealed that Protestant religious minorities in eighteenth-century Ireland, despite being surrounded by a Roman Catholic populace and despite being ruled by an Anglican minority, felt themselves to be beneficiaries of a relatively tolerant state apparatus in which the right to dissent was protected by law. Hence, the threat of assimilation by powerful states and established churches, which fanned the flames of religious revivalism in central Europe, simply did not operate with the required urgency in eighteenth-century Ireland. Of rather more danger to the future well-being of the Baptists in Ireland was their stubborn adherence to a form of church polity and religious tradition that afforded little opportunity for

20. Cork Baptist Church Book (1653–1875), which is still in the possession of the Cork Baptist Church.

21. These accusations are similar to those encountered by English Methodists in the same period. See John Walsh, "Methodism and the Mob in the Eighteenth Century," *Studies in Church History* 8 (1972): 213–27.

22. Cork Baptist Church Book, 42.

growth and development. Rooted firmly in congregational independence and autonomy, and surviving in an uncongenial religious landscape, the Irish Baptists were unable to match the eighteenth-century
growth rates of their Welsh and North American counterparts.[23] Even
the writer of the Cork Church book was sensitive to the fact that Protestantism of the Baptist variety was unlikely to convert much of Ireland, and that if that task was to be accomplished, something approaching Methodist zeal was mandatory.

> After all we think there may be something worthy of imitation among
> the Methodists . . . they are more frequent in assembling together than
> any other people. Their classes serve as nurseries to exercise their
> members in prayer and admonishing. From these they can call out
> such as are likely to be popular men for preachers. . . . It cannot be de-
> nied but the Methodist preachers are generally well chosen—of free
> utterance, good memory, warm and vehement. . . . The frequent ex-
> changing of their preachers affords constant variety to the people as
> well as a kind of breathing to the preacher. Their preachers are inde-
> fatigable not only in preaching but inquiring into the progress of the
> classes, visiting the people, encouraging them, directing to proper
> books, warning them when they in the least deviate from Wesley's doc-
> trine and entertaining them both in public and private with marvellous
> accounts of the success of the Gospel as they call it, extraordinary con-
> versions and the like for which they are well furnished by that constant
> correspondence which they keep up with each other through the sev-
> eral parts of the British dominions.[24]

There could be no clearer delineation of the chief components of
the eighteenth-century international awakening—class meetings,
itinerant preaching, "extraordinary conversions," enthusiastic leadership, and a remarkable circulating medium of revival news and
preaching personalities.

The most influential of the early evangelical itinerants in Ireland
was John Wesley, who made his first visit in 1747. Wesley professed a
genuine love for the Irish, but they did not always love him or his trav-

23. Kevin Herlihy, "The Irish Baptists, 1650–1780" (Ph.D. diss., Trinity College, University
of Dublin, 1992).
24. Cork Baptist Church Book, 44–45.

eling band of itinerant preachers, who were disparagingly nicknamed Black Caps, Swaddlers, and cavalry preachers. The old Methodist class ticket motto "everywhere spoken against" was particularly appropriate in Ireland, where, initially at any rate, unsympathetic authorities abandoned early Methodists to the license of the crowd. License became mayhem in Cork between 1749 and 1751, when Nicholas Butler, an eccentric ballad-singer, mock preacher, and rabble-rouser who was allegedly in the pay of the corporation, led the city mobs in repeated anti-Methodist forays.[25] The mobs were virtually indemnified by the lack of restraining authority: the mayor and sheriffs refused to take action; the bishop and the clergy were publicly opposed to the Methodists; the assize courts sided repeatedly with the rioters; and the local gentry and merchants wanted an end to Methodism.[26] Wesley was thus confounded to find his societies the victims of both Ascendancy hostility and "popish" mobs: "Upon the whole one question readily occurs, whether, setting aside both Christianity and common humanity, it be *prudent* thus to encourage a popish mob to tear Protestants in pieces. And such Protestants as are essentially and remarkably attached to the present government! Nay, and on that very account peculiarly odious both to Papists and Jacobites."[27]

What these sentiments show is that a combination of the '45 rebellion and his encounters with Irish Catholics had helped nudge Wesley away from the crypto-Jacobite and country Tory associations of early Methodist opposition to Walpolean corruption.[28] Of more lasting consequence for the future of evangelicalism in Ireland was the way in which early Methodist encounters with "popish mobs" confirmed Wesley's deep-seated fear of Catholic illiberality and increasingly directed his mission to the revival of Ireland's "slumbering" Protestants.

When Wesley died in 1791, there were about fifteen thousand men and women enrolled in Methodist societies, with twice as many again coming under the influence of Methodist preaching. Such growth had taken place largely in southern cities and market towns, but increas-

25. Crookshank, *History of Methodism in Ireland*, 1:43–72; Baker, *Works of John Wesley*, 26:361–73, 427–29.
26. See Secker Papers, 8 folios, 73-74, Lambeth Palace Library MSS.
27. Baker, *Works of John Wesley*, 26:372.
28. Ward, *Protestant Evangelical Awakening*, 332–35.

ingly from the 1780s, Methodism grew most rapidly within the traditionally Anglican populations of the Fermanagh lake lands and the "linen triangle" of southern Ulster.[29] Such growth reached revivalistic proportions in the turbulent conditions at the turn of the century, when Gaelic-speaking Methodist missionaries, to use their own words, "denounced the judgements of heaven against the crimes of a guilty nation."[30] So successful was Methodist recruitment in the frontier counties of Ulster in this period that the future history of Methodist expansion in Ireland is largely a northern story. The concentration of Protestantism in the northern part of the island is therefore a feature not only of Presbyterian history, as is conventionally assumed; it also, as recent demographic surveys have shown, is of much wider application in pre-famine Ireland.

Methodism introduced into Ireland a new kind of associational, voluntaristic, and noncreedal religion that had obvious roots in both Continental pietism and early British evangelicalism. Wesley's network of religious societies, serviced by itinerant preachers and committed to the spiritual disciplines of self-examination, worship, fellowship, and education, brought a new dimension to the Irish religious landscape, which until then had been dominated by churches ministering to preassigned communities.[31] Although early Methodists were generally speaking more concerned with "saving the lost" than in poaching from the other churches, their conversionist message inevitably introduced a new competitiveness to Irish religion. It is, however, one of the paradoxes of Irish history that early evangelical enthusiasts, by preaching in Irish, were better conservators of Gaelic culture than the representatives of the three main churches—Roman Catholic, Anglican, and Presbyterian.[32]

29. David N. Hempton, "Methodism in Irish Society, 1770–1830," *Transactions of the Royal Historical Society*, 5th ser., 36 (1986): 117–42.

30. Charles Graham and Gideon Ouseley to Dr. Coke, 6 January 1800, Ouseley Collection, Northern Ireland Public Record Office; Dr. Coke, *Copies of Letters from the Missionaries who are employed in Ireland, for the Instruction in their Own Language, and for the Conversion of the Native Irish* (London, 1801); the best collections of Irish Methodist missionary letters are held by the University of London School of Oriental and African Studies and the John Rylands University Library of Manchester.

31. David Miller, "Presbyterianism and 'Modernization' in Ulster," *Past and Present* 80 (1978): 66–90.

32. Desmond Bowen, *The Protestant Crusade in Ireland, 1800–1870* (Dublin, 1978).

Early Methodism in Ireland also threw up a host of engaging and controversial itinerant preachers who collectively bear eloquent testimony to the internationalism of the Great Awakening. Connections are easily traced to European pietist minorities, the Welsh revivalism surrounding Howell Harris, the Middle Colonies of North America, and the Scottish revivals at Kilsyth and Cambuslang.[33] Two of the most interesting figures in terms of what they reveal about the social and political dynamics operating on early revivalists are Gideon Ouseley and Lorenzo Dow. Ouseley was an Irish-speaking itinerant preacher of minor gentry origins who, between his conversion in 1791 and his death in 1839, had an ambition to preach in every human settlement in Ireland.[34] In 1799 Ouseley was invited by the Methodist conference to be part of a team of Irish-speaking evangelists with a specific mission to the Irish Catholic poor in the wake of the Rebellion of the United Irishmen. Ouseley was thereby taken under the umbrella of Irish Methodism without ever being taken into full connection as a regular preacher. He refused to sign Wesley's Large Minutes as mere human compositions and jealously defended his right of independence and private judgment. His instincts were unashamedly populist and anticlerical, and he was frequently the victim of both mob attacks and establishment hostility. Except for his vigorous anti-Catholicism, Ouseley could easily have become a religious and political radical after the fashion of Joseph Rayner Stephens. After a lifetime spent in trying to overturn the religion of the people, Ouseley was rewarded with the approval of evangelical Anglo-Irish aristocrats and even joined the Orange Order. Though committed to the value of cheap religious literature, much of Ouseley's prodigious output was dominated by schemes to lessen the influence of the Roman Catholic priesthood in Ireland.[35]

33. This is true not only of the well-documented lives of international personalities such as John Wesley and George Whitefield but also of more minor figures. See, for example, A. H. Williams, "Thomas Williams (1720–1787): Pioneer of Irish Methodism," *Bulletin of the Wesley Historical Society* (Irish Branch) 2, no. 3 (1992): 15–30.
34. David Hempton, "Gideon Ouseley: Rural Revivalist, 1791–1839," *Studies in Church History* 25 (1989): 203–14; William Arthur, *The Life of Gideon Ouseley* (London, 1876); R. H. Gallagher, *Pioneer Preachers of Irish Methodism* (Belfast, 1965), 144–47.
35. See three works by Gideon Ouseley: *Old Christianity Defended* (Dublin, 1820), *An Easy Mode of Securing Ireland's Peace* (Dublin, 1833), and *A Dreadful Conspiracy against the Church of Christ Developed* (Dublin, 1837).

In his early preaching career Ouseley forged a close relationship
with the American frontier revivalist Lorenzo Dow, who was also an
independent spirit of populist anticlerical convictions. Both were
committed to vernacular preaching, both were captivating public
performers, both had deep-seated aversions to traditional authority,
both were avid publishers, and both were associated with religious
revivals wherever they went. Yet the striking difference between the
two is that whereas Ouseley came to be patronized by the Irish Protestant gentry, Dow was "a radical Jeffersonian who could begin a sermon by quoting Tom Paine" and who "sought the conversion of sinners at the same time as he railed at tyranny and priest-craft and the
professions of law and medicine."[36] Dow's advocacy of "popular sovereignty and the responsibility of independent persons to throw off
the shackles of ignorance and oppression" marked him out as a Jeffersonian republican of a particularly populist kind, whereas Ouseley's commitment to similar values led him into a lifelong campaign
against priestcraft and the baleful influence of the Roman Catholic
Church in Ireland. Ironically, the Irish Methodist elite, whose nerves
had been set on edge by Dow's antiestablishment rhetoric in Ireland,
used his republicanism as a stick with which to beat Ouseley for his
association with him.[37] The politics of revivalism, in its different social and cultural settings, are engagingly unpredictable.

Methodism's association with anti-Catholicism in Ireland, for
whatever motivation, probably limited its potential for growth. Unless the Irish Catholic poor could be convinced that their sorry plight
was caused more by the rapaciousness of their own church than by
the careless indifference of the British government, the outlook
seemed bleak. Early nineteenth-century Irish evangelicals left no
stone unturned to propagate that opinion, but by the 1820s events
were turning against them, and from then on their increasingly controversial methods, by and large, produced the reverse of what they
intended. The exception was the province of Ulster, where religio-
political configurations worked in favor of the evangelicals in the tur-

36. Nathan Hatch, *The Democratization of American Christianity* (New Haven, 1989),
36–40, 185–86.
37. Ouseley Collection, XI fol. 5; XII fol. 13; XV fol. 24; XXVIII fol. 43, Northern Ireland Public Record Office. See also Lorenzo Dow, *Works: Providential Experience of Lorenzo Dow in
Europe and America*, 3d ed. (Dublin, 1806).

bulent century after the Rebellion of the United Irishmen. The Methodist branch of the revival movement was therefore unable to reap the same kind of harvest in Ireland as it managed in England, Wales, and North America.[38]

Another revival strand, also dating back to Dublin in the 1740s, fared even worse. John Cennick, who had been drawn into the inner circle of Moravianism before he arrived in Dublin in 1746, quickly built up a strong following initially in the Dublin area and then in Ulster. By the early 1750s some thirty to forty Moravian preachers were itinerating in Ulster, servicing ten chapels and over two hundred societies.[39] The voluminous surviving records of this early Moravian expansion not only testify to the Moravian belief that divine purposes are more discernible in the living experiences and past histories of "God's people" than in confessions of faith, but also show the importance to them of the Reformation belief in the priesthood of all believers. Moravian sources also betray a distrust of Irish Catholicism based on a mixture of Enlightenment hostility to priestcraft and superstition, circulating stories of Catholic persecutions in Europe, and more conventional bigotry. Unfortunately for the long-term future of Moravianism in Ireland, Cennick and other early Moravian leaders were not as successful in organizing their societies as they had been in creating them.

As in other parts of the world, Moravianism in Ireland fell victim to its inner ideological uncertainty about whether it was an episcopally organized ancient church, an eclectic new sect, or pious "tropuses" within the Lutheran, Reformed, and Anglican churches.[40] As a result the one substantial survival of early Moravian enthusiasm in Ireland was the Gracehill Community, which was built after the Herrnhut model with Dutch and German help. The aim was to establish a self-regulating Christian village with a chapel, a school, an inn for travel-

38. Hempton and Hill, *Evangelical Protestantism in Ulster*, 32–39.

39. Samuel George Hanna, "The Origin and Nature of the Gracehill Moravian Settlement, 1764–1855, with Special Reference to the Work of John Cennick in Ireland, 1746–1755" (M.A. thesis, Queen's University Belfast, 1964); R. H. Hutton, *A History of the Moravian Church* (London, 1909).

40. William R. Ward, "The Renewed Unity of the Brethren: Ancient Church, New Sect, or Interconfessional Movement?" *Bulletin of the John Rylands University Library of Manchester* 70, no. 3 (1988): 77–92.

ers, and accommodation and workshops for single men and women. In early Moravian communities the separation of the sexes was strictly enforced, and all decisions were made by the whole group, however inconvenient the result. The Moravian approach to evangelism envisaged the creation of numerous quasi-monastic settlements that would not only be inward looking in the sense that the inhabitants would seek to live out a disciplined and charitable Christianity but also be outward looking to work for the conversion of the world. To a remarkable extent for such a tiny religious community, the Moravians spearheaded the first phase of the international Protestant missionary movement of the eighteenth century. In Ireland, Gracehill, for all its utopian idealism, never attracted more than five hundred to its community, and by 1850 non-Moravians were permitted to settle in its neat little squares. Although Moravians established many such communities throughout the world, Gracehill in County Antrim bears a striking resemblance to the settlement at Salem in North Carolina, which was built two years later in 1766. The building records of these settlements reveal a great deal about the theological motivation, international finances, and remarkable architectural preoccupations of Moravian communities in the middle of the eighteenth century. Scarcely in the history of the Christian church can faith and practice have been given such precise spatial expression than in the detailed plans of such settlements.

What conclusions, then, can we draw from this rapid tour of Ireland's Protestant minorities? In the first place, there is a need for perspective. The eighteenth-century religious minorities were small groups of relatively powerless people drawn together by religious and/or ethnic identity. Never forming more than a tiny percentage of the Irish population, they settled initially on the eastern part of the island and in seaports. As is true of all immigration, the pace and pattern of assimilation depended on a range of factors including social and geographic mobility, language, intermarriage, prosperity, religion, native resistance, and the pace of social change. The Palatines, for example, assimilated slowly because they were distinctive in race, religion, and culture and experienced little social and geographic mobility, at least until many of them decided to move on to North America. The Huguenots, through conformity to the Established Church and access to commercial wealth, combined a fierce pride in their own tradition with a relatively easy penetration of the host culture. Some, like the Methodists and the Quakers, owed their origins to outside influences but soon generated their own energy and created their own indigenous communities. Those minorities based primarily on religious allegiances thus had a greater ability to adapt and survive than those based on ethnicity alone.

Second, it must be said that many of these religious minorities, either through a history of persecution or through the ideological dynamics of evangelical theology, or both, carried with them a strong antipathy to Roman Catholicism and state-enforced religion. In the nineteenth century it was not uncommon to find such people at the forefront of opposition to Catholic Emancipation and other attempts to dismantle the Protestant Ascendancy. Folk memories of old injustices linger long in migrant communities.

Perhaps most important of all for the history of popular Protestantism in Ireland is the way in which the Great Awakening, itself an international event, was in Ireland largely filtered through the remnants of a surprisingly international and diverse Protestant tradition. It is noteworthy that even in this off-shore island of an off-shore island, the early history of evangelicalism is incomprehensible outside a genuinely international context and that the relative failure of evangelicalism in Ireland is inextricably bound up with its mid-eighteenth-century roots. The unusual combination of a relatively tolerant state church catering for a small minority, a regionally and ethnically distinct Presbyterian Church preoccupied by its own discipline, and a ramshackle Roman Catholic Church maintaining some kind of influence over the great majority of the population was not fertile ground for evangelical enthusiasm in eighteenth-century Ireland. Only in Ulster, and at a much later date, was evangelical religion able to exercise the kind of cultural dominance that crowned its efforts in Wales, the highlands of Scotland, and parts of North America, and that was because evangelicalism had ceased to be the preserve of powerless minorities and had made substantial inroads into the Established and Presbyterian churches.[41] But perhaps the early enthusiasts had the last laugh when Ulster was convulsed in 1859 by the kind of revival-

41. Myrtle Hill, "Evangelicalism and the Churches in Ulster Society, 1770–1850" (Ph.D. diss., Queen's University, Belfast, 1987).

ism that would not have been out of place a century before.[42] It is surely one of the ironies of history that that revival, as with the early history of the Great Awakening, was occasioned as much by wider British and North American stimuli as by local circumstances and that the mainstream churches were as much embarrassed by it all as they were participators in it.

42. Hempton and Hill, *Evangelical Protestantism in Ulster*, 145–60.

Revival, Enlightenment, Civic Humanism, and the Evolution of Calvinism in Scotland and America, 1735–1843

Mark A. Noll

In 1846 one of America's most representative religious thinkers, Charles Grandison Finney, published his *Lectures on Systematic Theology*. A central theme of this work was Finney's rejection of the dominant theology of previous generations, a rejection nowhere more explicit than in his comments on Jonathan Edwards. According to Finney, Edwards had erred particularly in drawing false distinctions between the moral and natural abilities of human beings before God. "Men have been told," wrote Finney,

> that they are as really unable to will as God directs, as they were to create themselves. . . . Ridiculous! Edwards I revere; his blunders I deplore. I speak thus of this Treatise on the Will, because . . . it abounds with unwarrantable assumptions, distinctions without a difference,

and metaphysical subtleties. ... It has bewildered the head, and greatly embarrassed the heart and the action of the church of God. It is time, high time, that its errors should be exposed, and so exploded, that such phraseology should be laid aside, and the ideas which these words represent should cease to be entertained.[1]

Less than three years before the publication of Finney's *Lectures*, Scotland's most influential clergyman of the period, Thomas Chalmers, expressed an entirely different opinion on the same subject: "There is no European Divine to whom I make such frequent appeals in my class rooms as I do to [Jonathan] Edwards. No book of human composition which I more strenuously recommend than his *Treatise on the Will*—read by me forty-seven years ago, with a conviction that has never since faltered, and which has helped me more than any other uninspired book, to find my way through all that might otherwise have proved baffling and transcendental and mysterious in the peculiarities of Calvinism."[2]

The contrast between Finney and Chalmers on Edwards's *Freedom of the Will* illustrates nicely a larger contrast in Scottish and American ecclesiastical history from the 1730s to the 1840s. During this period the Scottish and American churches passed through a similar set of circumstances. Each absorbed the impact of revival, each experienced extensive ecclesiastical controversy, each confronted a growing pluralism in religious allegiance, each faced the challenge of the Enlightenment, and each advanced along a path from aristocratic to democratic conceptions of social order. At the same time, though they shared much, the Scottish and American churches did not share a common course of theological development. At the beginning of the period, both embraced—with, to be sure, varying levels of specificity—a largely Calvinistic theology. By the end of the period, however, the center of American theology, as represented by Finney, had moved considerably beyond Calvinism,

1. Charles Finney, *Lectures on Systematic Theology* (New York, 1876; orig. 1846), 333. On the predominance of theologies like Finney's in the antebellum United States, see Timothy L. Smith, *Revivalism and Social Reform: American Protestantism on the Eve of the Civil War* (Baltimore, 1980; orig. 1957), 15–33.
2. Chalmers to William B. Sprague, in Sprague, *Annals of the American Pulpit* (New York, 1859), 1:334.

while the center of theology in Scotland had become, if anything, more thoroughly Calvinistic than it had been a century before.[3]

In comparing the course of theological development in Scotland and America over this period, it will be seen that relationships between formal religious thought and its social, political, and intellectual contexts help greatly in explaining why theology developed differently in the two regions during this period.[4] The argument is not that such relationships provide the only, or even the best, explanation for the development of theological convictions but only that they offer one potentially plausible version.

Theological parallels between Scotland and America in the 1730s and 1740s were indeed striking. In both regions a hereditary Calvinism provided the dominant theological perspective. In both, this "people's Calvinism" included a cherished view of a heroic past. New England's veneration of its Puritan ancestors who braved the elements, Archbishop Laud, and the ravages of the wilderness to establish a godly commonwealth was matched by the Scottish veneration for Presbyterian ancestors who braved the pope, Archbishop Laud, and the troops of Charles II to preserve their nation in covenant with God.[5] Both areas were also conscious that they upheld their religion as people on a periphery, colonists susceptible to the dominance of London and the imperialistic aspirations of the English.[6]

3. "American theology" in this chapter means primarily elite, formal theology, though many of the trends noted for the learned clergy were paralleled in more populist movements. "America" is also used synonymously with what became the United States; a fuller look at North America as a whole would reveal that common sense philosophy, civic humanist republican theory, and Baconian theology combined with evangelical religion differently in Canada than in either the United States or Scotland. See especially Michael Gauvreau, *The Evangelical Century: College and Creed in English Canada from the Great Revival to the Great Depression* (Kingston and Montreal, 1991).

4. In these terms, the article is an effort to expand upon a promising essay by Daniel Walker Howe entitled "The Decline of Calvinism: An Approach to Its Study," *Comparative Studies in Society and History* 14 (June 1972): 306–27, which traces the passing of Calvinism to the successes of capitalism.

5. Compare Cotton Mather, *Magnalia Christi America; or, The Ecclesiastical History of New England* (London, 1702), with Ebenezer Erskine's reverence for the past, as described in Hugh Watt, "Ebenezer Erskine, 1680–1754," in *Fathers of the Kirk: Some Leaders of the Church in Scotland from the Reformation to the Reunion,* ed. Ronald Selby Wright (London, 1960), 113–18.

6. See John Clive and Bernard Bailyn, "England's Cultural Provinces: Scotland and America," *William and Mary Quarterly,* 3d ser., 11 (April 1954): 179–99.

The similarities went much further, for the dominant Calvinism of the two regions contained a strikingly similar range of theological subpositions. Both areas contained a group of determinedly scholastic Calvinists—in Scotland especially the proponents of the strict covenanting tradition, and in America especially the Dutch, Scottish, and Scotch-Irish confessionalists of the Middle Colonies.[7]

Both regions also contained large numbers of evangelical Calvinists, promoters of revivalistic piety who nonetheless often wanted to explain their religion in contemporary intellectual terms. In America this subgroup was strongest in New England and would come to follow Jonathan Edwards. In Scotland it included active promoters of revival such as William McCulloch of Cambuslang, and also several leaders like John McLaurin, who, with Edwards, used the new thinking of the Enlightenment for traditional Christian purposes.[8]

Both regions also contained a substantial group of mediating figures, ministers, and lay leaders who were theological traditionalists (and so remained faithful to the confessions) but who were also social conservatives (and so distrusted the enthusiasm of revival, even as they opposed doctrinal precisionism as a threat to peace). In America, this group has been called Old Calvinists, and in Scotland Old Moderates.[9]

Within the established churches, each region contained a fourth subgrouping—rationalistic Calvinists who exalted reason at the expense of the hereditary Reformed convictions. In America, this group was largely confined to Boston and the close associates of Jonathan Mayhew and Charles Chauncy; in Scotland, it may have been slightly larger because of the principles that had come to dominate theologi-

7. See Leonard J. Trinterud, *The Forming of an American Tradition: A Re-examination of Colonial Presbyterianism* (Philadelphia, 1949), 42–52; Randall Balmer, *A Perfect Babel of Confusion: Dutch Religion and English Culture in the Middle Colonies* (New York, 1989); and Stewart Mechie, "The Theological Climate in Early Eighteenth Century Scotland," in *Reformation and Revolution*, ed. Duncan Shaw (Edinburgh, 1967), 267–68.

8. For a fine overview, see the chapter on the eighteenth century in David Bebbington, *Evangelicalism in Modern Britain: A History from the 1730s to the 1980s* (London, 1989; Grand Rapids, 1992).

9. See Mechie, "Theological Climate in Early Eighteenth Century Scotland," 268–71; and on one of the leading Old Calvinists, see Edmund S. Morgan, *The Gentle Puritan: A Life of Ezra Stiles* (Chapel Hill, N.C., 1962).

cal and philosophical instruction at the Universities of Edinburgh and Glasgow from early in the eighteenth century.[10]

Finally, a surprisingly dense network of personal relationships joined the Calvinists of the New World to their counterparts in Scotland. Much of the dynamic of Calvinism in the American Middle Colonies came from Scottish or Ulster immigrants. The Tennent family, leaders of evangelical Calvinism in Pennsylvania and New Jersey throughout the whole eighteenth century, represented only one of many ties between Calvinists in the two regions.[11] Contacts between New England and Scottish Calvinists were almost as close. Once word began to circulate about the revivals of 1734 and 1735 in Jonathan Edwards's Northampton, Massachusetts, an extensive correspondence developed between the two regions that drew its evangelical leaders closely together. Jonathan Edwards became a name to be reckoned with in Scotland perhaps even more than in New England, and Scottish evangelical Calvinists led by John Erskine paid close attention to the religious (and also political) life of the colonies.[12]

Differences of course existed in the formulation and expression of Reformed theology in the two regions. In America, looser social structures allowed more room for practical variations within the Calvinistic norm. In Scotland, the weight of influential teachers who were less than enthusiastic about Westminster orthodoxy had a similar effect. In the main, however, it would be difficult to exaggerate the resemblances between the two regions in their adherence to Calvinistic faith and practice at the middle of the eighteenth century. If a differ-

10. See John Corrigan, *The Hidden Balance: Religion and the Social Theories of Charles Chauncy and Jonathan Mayhew* (New York, 1987); and Mechie, "Theological Climate in Early Eighteenth Century Scotland," 271–72.

11. Trinterud, *Forming an American Tradition*, 35; Marilyn J. Westerkamp, *Triumph of the Laity: Scots-Irish Piety and the Great Awakening, 1625–1760* (New York, 1988), 155, 167–68; and Ned C. Landsman, *Scotland and Its First American Colony, 1683–1765* (Princeton, N.J., 1985), esp. chap. 8, "The Uses of Revivalism: Religion and National Identity in Scotland and America."

12. Harold P. Simonson, "Jonathan Edwards and His Scottish Connections," *Journal of American Studies* 21 (December 1987): 353–76; G. D. Henderson, "Jonathan Edwards and Scotland," in *The Burning Bush: Studies in Scottish Church History* (Edinburgh, 1957), 151–62; and more generally, Susan O'Brien, "A Transatlantic Community of Saints: The Great Awakening and the First Evangelical Network, 1735–1755," *American Historical Review* 91 (October 1986): 811–32; and Michael J. Crawford, *Seasons of Grace: Colonial New England's Revival Tradition in Its British Context* (New York, 1991).

ence could be noted, it was that Scotland seemed to be moving away from its ancestral Calvinism more rapidly than America from its own.

To be sure, in the 1740s the Scottish church was still officially Calvinistic, and no serious challenge had arisen to the traditions of subscription in either the Establishment or the Secession churches. Yet a number of circumstances suggested the weakness of traditional Reformed theology.[13] The zeal of Seceders who had left the Established Church bestowed the taint of enthusiasm upon ardent confessionalism. Compared with the situation in America and particularly the work of Jonathan Edwards, Scotland's theological conservatives were not as successful at mastering modern learning. Again compared with America, Scotland's "infidels" (especially David Hume) mounted a stronger intellectual challenge to orthodoxy. In addition, since early in the century a series of effective teachers had been moving Scotland's formal religious thought away from ardent confessionalism toward a faith more in keeping with the conventions of the Enlightenment. These included John Simson, divinity professor at Glasgow until 1729, Francis Hutcheson (at Glasgow 1730–46), and divinity professors William Hamilton at Edinburgh and Archibald Campbell at St. Andrews.

The result by the 1740s was a situation in which, as one historian summarizes it, "the Church's most acute thinkers, by challenging the dogmatism of a previous age, prompted by the attacks of the opponents of the Christian religion as well as stimulated by the new departures in philosophy and science, were . . . helping to create a liberalising atmosphere in which the spirit of enlightenment could thrive."[14]

Scotland was still formally Calvinistic, but the drift seemed to be away from a rigid adherence to the doctrines of the Westminster Confession. In America, by contrast, although ecclesiastical structures were more pluralistic, theological convictions were more thoroughly Reformed.

---

13. For this general picture, I am indebted to James K. Cameron, "Theological Controversy: A Factor in the Origins of the Scottish Enlightenment," in *The Origin and Nature of the Scottish Enlightenment*, ed. R. H. Campbell and A. S. Skinner (Edinburgh, 1982), 116–30; Andrew L. Drummond and James Bulloch, *The Scottish Church, 1688–1843: The Age of the Moderates* (Edinburgh, 1973), 31–34, 47–48; Mechie, "Theological Climate in Early Eighteenth Century Scotland," 258–72; and Henry Sefton, "'New Lights and Preachers Legall': Some Observations on the Beginnings of Moderatism in the Church of Scotland," in *Church, Politics, and Society: Scotland, 1408–1929*, ed. Norman MacDouglasc (Edinburgh, 1983), 186–96.

14. Cameron, "Theological Controversy," 128.

The mainstream theology of the American colonies in the 1720s and 1730s testified to the weight of Puritan influence. Although the Puritan tradition by this time was being modified by an increasingly active pietism and a greater reliance upon natural reason, the center of colonial theology as late as the 1740s retained the major Calvinistic emphases defined early in the seventeenth century by the Puritans. In particular, the heart of formal religious thought retained a fundamental commitment to the centrality of God's grace for the salvation of individuals, their incorporation into the church, and their orientation to society. Significant varieties existed, but the Augustinian-Calvinist picture of the fallen human condition, of merciful divine sovereignty in redemption, and of the self-authenticating dignity of the divine law prevailed without serious opposition.[15]

These themes established the leitmotifs of New England's most prominent theological voices in the first half of the century, including Samuel Willard, Cotton Mather, Benjamin Colman, Jonathan Edwards, and even for a time the Anglican Samuel Johnson.[16] Outside of New England, the principal spokesmen for the Presbyterian interest in the Middle Colonies during the first three decades of the century—Jonathan Dickinson and the Tennent family—were, if anything, more forthrightly Calvinistic than the Congregationalists of New England.[17] The colonies' foremost Anglicans in the first decades of the new century could not be considered Calvinists, but they were still more pietistic modifiers of the Puritan strand than proponents of Enlightenment religion.[18]

It is a testimony to the continuing power of Calvinism in America that the most important religious events of the period, the great colo-

15. For an overview, see Sydney E. Ahlstrom, "Theology in America: A Historical Survey," in *The Shaping of American Religion*, ed. J. W. Smith and A. L. Jamison (Princeton, N.J., 1961), 236–51.

16. See Ernest Benson Lowrie, *The Shape of the Puritan Mind: The Thought of Samuel Willard* (New Haven, 1974); Richard F. Lovelace, *The American Pietism of Cotton Mather: Origins of American Evangelicalism* (Grand Rapids, 1979); Perry Miller, *The New England Mind: From Colony to Province* (Cambridge, Mass., 1953), 272–73 (on Colman); Conrad Cherry, *The Theology of Jonathan Edwards* (Garden City, N.Y., 1966); and Joseph Ellis, *The New England Mind in Transition: Samuel Johnson of Connecticut, 1696–1772* (New Haven, Conn., 1973), 56.

17. See Milton J. Coalter, Jr., *Gilbert Tennent, Son of Thunder* (Westport, Conn., 1986).

18. J. F. Woolverton, *Colonial Anglicanism in North America* (Detroit, 1984), 184.

nial revivals, were promoted by men—Theodore Frelinghuysen, Gilbert Tennent, and especially George Whitefield—who affirmed this theology; that the presence of what Ruth Bloch calls a "vast reservoir of ethnic immigrant Calvinism" aided their rapid spread;[19] and that the revivals became the occasion for the century's greatest theologian, Jonathan Edwards, to restate the precepts of Calvinism with subtle force. To be sure, some colonists by 1740 were questioning Calvinistic certainties, and Protestant theology had certainly moved in the direction of activism, moralism, and, to some extent, individualism. At the same time, covenantal Calvinism still defined the mainstream.

From that fairly secure Calvinistic base, however, the center of gravity of American theology shifted dramatically during the course of the next century. In Scotland, by contrast, a relatively less secure Calvinism became more sharply defined over the same period. The question is why the development of doctrine took place in contrasting ways in the two areas.

In America the evolution beyond Calvinism began not with developments in theology but in the life of the church and in the relationship of church to society. The most important of the ecclesiastical developments was the Great Awakening. The key event in the church's relation to society was the alliance between Puritan theology and the radical Whig tradition of civic humanism at the time of the American Revolution. The two developments, moreover, were intimately related.

The Great Awakening, representing more an upsurge of revivalistic piety throughout the colonies than a discrete set of events, was extremely important for both churches and American society. From the beginnings of New England, a theology of integrated covenants had provided a foundation for individual religion, church structure, and social order. The individual believer closed with Christ in a covenant of grace; believers as a group covenanted with each other and with God in the establishment of Congregational Churches; members of the Congregational Churches and their leaders then provided the di-

19. Ruth Bloch, *Visionary Republic: Millennial Themes in American Thought, 1756–1800* (New York, 1985), 14.

rection for society as whole.[20] The effect of the Great Awakening was to disrupt the integrating power of the covenant. In New England especially, the resulting parties were separated by social allegiance as well as theological persuasion. Each, in fact, appropriated a different aspect of the covenantal tradition. Separates and Baptists followed out Edwardsean themes to what they considered logical conclusions and applied the covenant mostly to themselves and their gathered churches. New Light nonseparates such as Edwards maintained formal allegiance to an integrated system of covenants but came to deny that membership in the social covenant conferred ecclesiastical privileges under the covenant of grace. Old Calvinist traditionalists, unwilling to choose between the covenant for individuals and the covenant for New England, defended the standing order as an adequate protection for the health of both religion and society. Rationalistic Congregationalists and latitudinarian Anglicans opted for the social covenant at the expense of the personal covenant of grace and sought to create a heaven from the revival's religious and social strife.[21] The covenant had become all things to all people, and so nothing to them all. With the covenant in disarray, new languages, defined by the needs of the mid-eighteenth century instead of the early seventeenth, would reestablish different bonds between private faith and public life.

The point of importance for theological development is that, in the wake of the revival, New England's religious leaders did not propose a religious alternative to the Puritan theology of society. Rather, they accepted the notion that a healthy society was possible if Christians simply adopted as their own social theory the civic humanism of the republican tradition that was becoming increasingly important in America.

The awakening did not bring theological innovation, at least in a strictly dogmatic sense. In fact, as the occasion for the most affecting (with Whitefield) and the most brilliant (with Edwards) statement of Calvinism in American history, it was just the reverse. Yet in ideolog-

20. See Peter Y. De Jong, *The Covenant Idea in New England Theology* (Grand Rapids, 1945); and Perry Miller, *The New England Mind: The Seventeenth Century* (New York, 1939), 365–491.

21. For overviews, see Edwin Scott Gaustad, *The Great Awakening in New England* (New York, 1957); and C. C. Goen, *Revivalism and Separatism in New England, 1740–1800* (New Haven, Conn., 1962).

ical terms the consequences of this theologically conservative movement were curious. The modes of its propagation brought it closer to
the humanist assumptions of the "Real Whigs." As Perry Miller once
phrased it, "From the time of Calvin, the focus of Calvinist and of
most Protestant thinking had been the will of God; the great divide
that we call the Awakening forced both American parties, whether
proponents or opponents, to shift the focus of analysis to the nature
of man."[22] The curiosity is compounded by noting that it was the essentially conservative thrust of the revival (to preserve the reality of
individual salvation and the purity of the church) that detached the
social sense of covenant from its organic connections with person
and church. It was then precisely the loss of an indigenously theological definition of society that allowed religious leaders to endorse, as
from God, first the republicanism of civic humanism and then the individualism of laissez-faire liberalism, two ideologies that would
exert anything but a conservative influence on theology itself.

The French and Indian War became the occasion for the first full
rehearsal of a distinctly Christian republicanism, as religious leaders,
frightened by the menace of France and mesmerized by the evils of
Rome, linked together liberty, property, and true Christianity as the
colonies' bulwarks against slavery, corruption, and the "Whore of
Babylon."[23] But the final stage in the creation of pietistic, covenantal
civic humanism took place as tensions grew between the colonies
and the mother country after 1763. Disputes over the Stamp Act, the
Townshend Duties, and the Coercive Acts of 1774 set the scene for a
simple, but important ideological transition. The great enemy of true
religion, and of the liberty with which it was so tightly bound, turned
out to be not Continental, papal tyranny but tyranny itself. During the
crisis of independence, Americans of many sorts—clerical and lay,
representing all regions of the country—made the language of Christian republicanism their own.[24] Ministers and some laypeople regu-

22. Perry Miller, "The Great Awakening from 1740 to 1750," in *Nature's Nation* (Cambridge, Mass., 1967), 86.

23. See Nathan O. Hatch, "The Origins of Civil Millennialism in America: New England Clergymen, War with France, and the Revolution," *William and Mary Quarterly*, 3d ser., 31 (July
1974): 407–30.

24. See Bloch, *Visionary Republic*; Nathan O. Hatch, *The Sacred Cause of Liberty: Republican Thought and the Millennium in Revolutionary New England* (New Haven, Conn., 1977);

larly transformed the conflict into a harbinger of the End. In 1776, for example, the theological liberal Samuel West of Dartmouth, Massachusetts, and the theological conservative Samuel Sherwood of Weston, Connecticut, both used the imagery of the beast from Revelation 13 to describe British oppression.[25] Such examples could be multiplied nearly without number, as could the practice of rendering the conflict in more specific biblical terms, like the frequent use of the Curse of Meroz from Judges 5:23 to rally support for colonial liberty.[26] Through the time of the Constitutional Convention and beyond, clergymen especially took for granted the congruence of political ideology and Christian theology. The unprecedented torrent of memorial sermons after the death of Washington in late 1799—a torrent united by the common conviction that Washington's republican dignity had been an antitype fulfilling biblical typology for a godly ruler—showed the ongoing strength of the convergence.[27]

And what of formal theology in the half-century from the outbreak of revival in Jonathan Edwards's Northampton to the meeting of the Constitutional Convention? To first appearances, there were only slight changes. The most articulate New England theologians were still the most visible theologians in the new nation, and they were still staunchly Reformed. The Presbyterians, broadening out as an intellectual force in the middle and southern states, were, as defenders of the Westminster Confession, even more creedal in their Calvinism. Isaac Backus of Massachusetts, probably the best-known Baptist toward the close of the century, had his differences with New Light Congregationalists on questions of church order, but he proudly proclaimed his solidarity with "our excellent Edwards" on questions of fallen human nature, the sovereign grace of God, and

---

John F. Berens, *Providence and Patriotism in Early America, 1640–1815* (Charlottesville, Va., 1978); and Mark A. Noll, *Christians in the American Revolution* (Grand Rapids, 1977).

25. Samuel Sherwood, *The Church's Flight into the Wilderness* (New York, 1776), 14–15; and Samuel West, *A Sermon Preached before the Honorable Council* (Boston, 1776), 63.

26. See Alan Heimert, *Religion and the American Mind from the Great Awakening to the Revolution* (Cambridge, Mass., 1966), 332–34, 500–9.

27. See Robert P. Hay, "George Washington: American Moses," *American Quarterly* 21 (Winter 1969): 780–91; James H. Smylie, "The President as Republican Prophet and King: Clerical Reflections on the Death of Washington," *Journal of Church and State* 18 (Spring 1976): 233–52; and Mark A. Noll, "The Image of the United States as a Biblical Nation, 1776–1865," in *The Bible in America*, ed. N. O. Hatch and M. A. Noll (New York, 1982), 41.

the supernatural means of salvation.[28] Non-Calvinist or rationalist theological opinions were possible in the colonies, but quite often they were discussed in private or, if written down, filed in a drawer, as Charles Chauncy did with his manuscript defending universal salvation. Other theological alternatives, like the Methodism of Francis Asbury or the Lutheranism of Henry Melchoir Muhlenberg, were still marginalized in scattered communities or ones that did not use English. In sum, religious thinkers were aware of rumblings beneath the surface, but the edifices of Calvinism still stood firm.

The apparent stability of the mainstream theology in 1789 was, however, deceptive. Once yoked with political ideology and enlisted fully as a servant of the national purpose, American theology was destined to reflect changes in the country's political ideology and to be shaped by efforts at creating the new American civilization. In the early years of the republic, political ideology was in fact evolving. In addition, fresh intellectual resources were being called into service for the effort to stabilize the new nation and subdue the frontier. The evolution of political ideology involved the shift from civic humanism (with ideals of disinterested public virtue and freedom as liberation from tyranny) toward political liberalism (with ideals of individualized private virtue and freedom as self-determination). It also comprehended an upsurge of popular democracy. The fresh intellectual resources involved an increasing reliance on the methodology of Newtonian scientism and the reasoning of Scottish moral philosophy. Each of these national developments became important for American theology precisely because in the half-century between the Great Awakening and the Constitution, America's religious leaders had identified themselves so thoroughly with the ebb and flow of American civilization.

The liberal ideology that became increasingly important in early America constituted, as Gordon Wood has put it, "the self-interested pursuit of happiness" pointing to an emerging "world of business, money-making, and the open promotion of interests."[29] In theology

28. See Bruce Kuklick, *Churchmen and Philosophers from Jonathan Edwards to John Dewey* (New Haven, Conn., 1985), 43–79; and on Backus's respect for Edwards, see William G. McLoughlin, "Introduction," in *Isaac Backus on Church, State, and Calvinism: Pamphlets, 1754–1789* (Cambridge, Mass., 1968), 16.

29. Gordon S. Wood, "Ideology and the Origins of Liberal America," *William and Mary Quarterly*, 3d ser., 44 (July 1987): 635.

the liberal influence had at least something to do with a series of delicate maneuvers in New England designed to insulate the inherited Calvinist God from charges of arbitrarily affronting natural human rights or undervaluing human happiness. As early as 1750, Joseph Bellamy, one of Edwards's closest students, gently modified earlier Calvinistic conceptions of the atonement along lines suggested by current political concerns. The work of Christ, for Bellamy, became not the placation of divine wrath (as had been traditional) but the restoration of moral order in the universe.[30] Because Christ's death met the divine requirement for a perfect fulfilling of the law, God as "the supreme governor of the world" could be approached by all who would trust in him. Bellamy's proposal was something of an innovation, for he came close to saying that the work of Christ merely established the conditions for salvation, a transaction now dependent upon human exertion to complete. The restatement of divine sovereignty from an old language of deferential hierarchy to a newer language of egalitarian contractualism had begun. The same sort of changes could also be viewed in the theology of Samuel Hopkins, Bellamy's friend and fellow student of Edwards, who likewise came to stress more God's kindly designs for the world than the world's calling to worship the glory of God.[31]

Bellamy and Hopkins had seen their mentor employ modern conceptions—Locke's sensationalism and Hutcheson's moral philosophy—to restate the traditional faith, but their own efforts to the same end, using this time the imperatives of human happiness and individual rights, were not as successful. The difference was that Edwards had translated the new language back into the old dogma, while Bellamy and Hopkins had begun the process of translating the old dogma into the new language.

Another language that gained great force in the wake of independence was the language of popular sovereignty. It was a broadened sense of popular sovereignty, for example, that led the writers of the

30. For a good discussion of Bellamy's theology, including the phrases quoted in the next sentence, see Glenn Paul Anderson, "Joseph Bellamy (1719–1790): The Man and His Work" (Ph.D. diss., Boston University, 1971), 437–45. A forthcoming book by Mark Valeri on the social and intellectual contexts of Bellamy's theology will be the definitive study on such connections.

31. See Joseph A. Conforti, *Samuel Hopkins and the New Divinity Movement* (Grand Rapids, 1981).

Constitution to substitute the idea of balanced powers, with each part of government representing the people, for the British ideal of mixed government, where the rights of the people in the House of Commons were balanced by the authority of lords and monarch. Among the lower orders, aggressive actions against hierarchy, like those of Daniel Shays in western Massachusetts, were part of a growing revolt against inherited authority of whatever sort.[32] In theology the influence of popular sovereignty in the 1780s was not yet as widespread as it was in politics. But among the most vibrant religious movements of that decade were revivals in backcountry New England and the Canadian Maritimes triggered by Free Will Congregationalists, Free Will Baptists, Shakers, and Universalists. Their message placed a high priority, not only on the role of the individual in the salvation process, but also on the assertion of popular rights against hereditary efforts at defining religion from on high.[33]

Newtonian scientism and Scottish moral philosophy also became influential conceptual languages in the 1780s, probably because they represented means of asserting public authority that did not depend upon the sanction of tradition or the habits of deference. By the late eighteenth century, most Americans had abandoned both tradition and deference as means of ordering society. To take their place emerged "philosophical" proof, meaning procedures of both physical and mental sciences supposedly accessible to all people. Neither mathematical demonstration nor the moral philosophy of common sense required the imprimatur of tradition. Rather, both strategies were widely held to convey a self-authenticating authority. The avidity with which Madison, Hamilton, Tom Paine, and other articulate leaders pursued the "science of politics" testified to the new power of the "language of science."[34] Among the common people the vogue of

32. See Nathan O. Hatch, *The Democratization of American Christianity* (New Haven, Conn., 1989); and Edmund S. Morgan, *Inventing the People: The Rise of Popular Sovereignty in England and America* (New York, 1988).

33. For the Maritimes, see the introductions by George A. Rawlyk to *New Light Letters and Songs* (Hantsport, N.S., 1983); *The Sermons of Henry Alline* (Hantsport, Nova Scotia, 1986); and *Henry Alline: Selected Writings* (New York, 1987). For backcountry New England, see Stephen A. Marini, *Radical Sects of Revolutionary New England* (Cambridge, Mass., 1982).

34. For the use of this phrase, see Alexander Hamilton, *The Federalist*, no. 9, and James Madison, *The Federalist*, no. 47, conveniently available in Michale Kammen, ed., *The Origins of the American Constitution: A Documentary History* (New York, 1986), 141, 187; on Paine,

numeracy (a fascination with numbers and numerical calculations) spoke of the same respect for this sort of authority.[35]

In theology, the second half of the eighteenth century witnessed a corresponding fascination with demonstration through science. John Witherspoon's lectures in moral philosophy at Princeton, substantially completed by the early 1770s, admitted that "the evidence which attends moral disquisitions is of a different kind from that which attends mathematics and natural philosophy." But he also held that this kind of evidence could be every bit as certain as the raw material of the physical scientists, and he hoped that "perhaps a time may come when men, treating moral philosophy as Newton and his successors have done natural, may arrive at greater precision."[36]

The Scottish philosophy of common sense proved to be the most useful way of establishing authoritative discourse in a society marked by a suspicion of tradition.[37] Witherspoon's student and eventual successor, Samuel Stanhope Smith, already in 1787 had indicated something of the authority being ascribed to the language of common sense reasoning. In that year, Smith spoke out against recent proposals from Europe suggesting that humanity consisted of several different species. Against such views, Smith argued that climate and geography were enough to explain differences of skin color and bodily form. Smith's overarching concern, however, was more comprehensive. He needed to save the unity of humanity in order to preserve the universality of philosophy. "If there really were a plurality of human types," Smith argued, "the science of morals would be absurd . . . no general principles of human conduct, of religion, or of policy could be framed; for, human nature . . . could not be comprehended in any

---

see Isaac Kramnick, "Religion and Radicalism: English Political Theory in the Age of Revolution," *Political Theory* 5 (November 1977): 526–30.

35. See Patricia Cline Cohen, *A Calculating People: The Spread of Numeracy in Early America* (Chicago, 1982).

36. Witherspoon, "Lectures on Moral Philosophy," in *The Works of the Rev. John Witherspoon* (Philadelphia, 1802), 3:470.

37. An overstatement is Garry Wills, *Inventing America: Jefferson's Declaration of Independence* (Garden City, N.Y., 1978). For examples of better balance, see Douglas Adair, *Fame and the Founding Fathers*, ed. Trevor Colbourn (New York, 1974); and Daniel Walker Howe, "The Political Psychology of *The Federalist*," *William and Mary Quarterly*, 3d ser., 44 (July 1987): 485–509.

system."[38] Within a few years of Smith's address, Unitarian Harvard and Congregationalist Yale joined Presbyterian Princeton by adopting a system of thought that set aside the prerogatives of traditional intellectual authority in favor of the common sense of the people.[39]

The early republic was a period when practical needs of great moment—including the need to create a national government ex nihilo, the need to reorganize denominations on a voluntary footing, the need to rescue the frontier from barbarism—called for creative use of old vocabularies and the transformation of inherited ideologies. Ideologically, the late 1780s marked a break with the past in the fragmenting last gasp of spent worldviews: classical republicanism in public ideology and Puritan Calvinism in theology.

Between the ratification of the Constitution and the election of William Henry Harrison to the American presidency in 1840, the assumptions of the nation's public philosophy evolved from a basic republicanism to a basic, if not exclusive, liberalism. Throughout the period, roughly the same assumptions were at work in the public philosophy and in the mainstream theology. In the public sphere, the language of liberalism, emphasizing the freedom of individuals from hierarchical restraint and the formation of community upon the unfettered choices of free individuals joined by contract, became increasingly the language of politics and the economy. The American system, the rise of market capitalism, and, as Gordon Wood puts it, "the scrambling, individualistic, acquisitive society that suddenly emerged in the early nineteenth century" all underscore the importance of these conceptions.[40]

Liberalism also seems to have shaped salient characteristics of the period's religious life—of revival (where conversion was defined as an unmediated choice made by individuals), voluntary organization (where individuals joined together of their free will to move others

38. Samuel Stanhope Smith, *An Essay on the Causes of the Variety of Complexion and Figure in the Human Species* (Philadelphia, 1787), 109.

39. See Daniel Walker Howe, *The Unitarian Conscience: Harvard Moral Philosophy, 1805–1861* (Cambridge, Mass., 1970); and for Yale, John R. Fitzmier, "The Godly Federalism of Timothy Dwight, 1752–1817" (Ph.D. diss., Princeton University, 1986), chap. 3, "The New Divinity Movement."

40. Wood, "Ideology and the Origins of Liberal America," 635.

toward the good), and the triumph of the believer's church (defined as the sum of its members, whose own choices brought it into existence).[41] If the language of popular sovereignty became the unquestioned argot of Jacksonian America, it was no less so for popular theology. The denominations that grew rapidly in the early republic—Methodists, Baptists, Disciples, Mormons, and Millerites—all spoke the language of the people more distinctly than did the largest denominations from the colonial era, namely, the Congregationalists, Episcopalians, and Presbyterians.[42] If in politics the Scottish moral philosophy provided a faculty psychology from which to draw analogies for the body politic and a moral sense intuition upon which to ground formal political theory, no less in religious thought did faculty psychology provide the starting point for theological anthropology and its moral sense intuitionism the foundation for soteriology.[43] If a Newtonian scientism running into Baconianism offered the public a convincing model of inductive certainty, a similar scientism infused the rage for natural theology among the elite and, as has been already pointed out, for biblical numerology among the population at large.[44] Substantial qualifications are appropriate for these parallels, but even a rudimentary sketch is enough to show considerable congruence between the language of the public philosophy and the language of the mainstream theology.

After the turn of the century explicit employment of the language of liberalism for religious purposes seems to have been concentrated

41. I know of no study making these points directly. My conclusions rest on an incomplete reading of the immense current literature on the place of republicanism and liberalism in the early United States. For summaries, see Lance Banning, "Jeffersonian Ideology Revisited: Liberal and Classical Ideas in the New American Republic," *William and Mary Quarterly*, 3d ser., 43 (Jan. 1986): 3–19, and Joyce Appleby, *Liberalism and Republicanism in the Historical Imagination* (Cambridge, Mass., 1992).

42. See especially Hatch, *Democratization of American Christianity*.

43. See Howe, "Political Philosophy of *The Federalist*"; D. H. Meyer, *The Instructed Conscience: The Shaping of the American National Ethic* (Philadelphia, 1972); and David L. Weddle, *The Law as Gospel: Revival and Reform in the Theology of Charles G. Finney* (Metuchen, N.J., 1985), chap. 6, "The Plan of Salvation."

44. See William Smith, "William Paley's Theological Utilitarianism in America," *William and Mary Quarterly*, 3d ser., 11 (1954): 402–24; Theodore Dwight Bozeman, *Protestants in an Age of Science: The Baconian Ideal and Antebellum American Religious Thought* (Chapel Hill, N.C., 1977); and on popular biblical numerology, *The Disappointed: Millerism and Millenarianism in the Nineteenth Century*, ed. R. L. Numbers and J. M. Butler (Bloomington, Ind., 1987).

among leaders of the newer sects. In 1830, Alexander Campbell, the leading spirit in the Disciples of Christ, proclaimed that 4 July 1776 was "a day to be remembered as was the Jewish Passover. . . . This revolution, taken in all its influences, will make men free indeed." Everywhere among "Christians," "Disciples," and similar indigenous American denominations, the great goal was "gospel liberty."[45] The application of warrants from the public philosophy was often more subtle among elite groups, but it was no less a defining characteristic of the period. Of Timothy Dwight's theology, for example, a recent historian has written, "God was sovereign but his sovereignty was such as befitted republican conceptions of government." According to Dwight, God's rule "is a government by motives, addressed to the understanding and affections of rational subjects, and operating on their minds, as inducements to voluntary obedience. No other government is worthy of God: there being, indeed, no other, beside that of mere force and coercion."[46]

In sum, America's religious leaders in the early national period were busy adjusting the mainstream theology in order to meet the spiritual needs of the new nation, needs that were themselves defined in considerable part by the conceptual structure of the new nation's public philosophy. If the most salient characteristic of American ideology in the 1770s was the bond between a pious Puritanism and classical republicanism, the most salient characteristic of American ideology in the 1840s was the bond between democratic evangelicalism and democratic liberalism.

A clear indication of that bond is the shift in theological conceptions between the mid-eighteenth and mid-nineteenth centuries, a shift displaying a remarkable resemblance to the shifts of meaning in the public philosophy. Jonathan Edwards was not entirely representative of theology in the mid-eighteenth century, nor were Nathaniel W. Taylor and Charles Finney in the mid-nineteenth. But their works were still notable landmarks from which we can measure the changes taking place.

45. Quoted from Nathan O. Hatch, "The Christian Movement and the Demand for a Theology of the People," *Journal of American History* 67 (December 1980): 551, 555.
46. Marie Caskey, *Chariot of Fire: Religion and the Beecher Family* (New Haven, Conn., 1978), 39, includes quotation.

The most obvious change in the period between 1735 and 1843 concerned notions of *freedom*. To republicans, liberty meant "the right of the people to share in the government." In liberal America it had become "unrestrained competition and equality, an absence of built-in handicap."[47] The parallel development in theology was just as abrupt. In Edwards's *Freedom of Will*, liberty meant "power, opportunity, or advantage, that anyone has, to do as he pleases. Or in other words, his being free from hindrance or impediment in the way of doing, or conducting in any respect, as he wills."[48] A century later, for N. W. Taylor freedom meant "power to the contrary" in all moral choices; a person was "a Free Agent without the Aids of Divine Grace." Finney was even more direct: "The moral government of God everywhere assumes and implies the liberty of the human will, and the natural ability to obey God. Every command, every threatening, every expostulation and denunciation in the Bible implies and assumes this. Nor does the Bible do violence to the human intelligence in this assumption; for . . . the human mind necessarily assumes the freedom of the human will as a first truth."[49] In 1740 "freedom" was something about which to reason, a quality of human life to be considered in relation to other aspects of existence, and a positive value that nevertheless needed to be fenced in by other, weightier considerations. In 1840 it had become axiomatic, the fundamental defining trait of humanity, and a value than which nothing was greater.

The movement from a theology consonant with republican language to one at home with liberalism was not as rapid or as thorough as the shift from republicanism to liberalism in political and economic life. Yet little doubt can exist that the dynamic ideological transformation in American public philosophy after the American Revolution stimulated, and to a lesser extent was stimulated by, a similar transformation of similar dynamism in the nation's mainstream theology. Nor can there be much doubt that the circumstances that made possible this interconnected ideological evolution

47. Gordon S. Wood, *The Creation of the America Republic, 1776–1787* (Chapel Hill, N.C., 1969), 609; Kramnick, "Religion and Radicalism," 514.

48. Jonathan Edwards, *Freedom of the Will*, ed. Paul Ramsay (orig. 1754; New Haven, 1957), 163.

49. Taylor quoted in George M. Marsden, *The Evangelical Mind and the New School Presbyterian Experience* (New Haven, Conn., 1970), 49; Finney, *Systematic Theology*, 335.

were themselves the last stage in a history stretching back well before the onset of the War for Independence.

The key to understanding changes in the mainstream theology—before, during, and after the century under consideration here—is to realize that a persistent motive of its expounders was to preserve the vocabulary of Christianity as an essential part of the American language. Thus, by taking as their own the concepts of republicanism, religious thinkers ensured that Christian concerns would color the ideology of the Revolution. By later taking on the overtones of liberalism, they guaranteed that theology would be heard, and that it would exert a powerful influence, in liberal America.

America's Christian theologians in 1840 wanted very much to see the population converted, to make their society godly, and to show citizens of the world how the unique blend of Protestant evangelicalism and liberal democracy could open the way to the millennium. To each of these goals it was necessary to speak persuasively, to witness with power. For their appeal, the theologians needed a language that could be understood, a language that could persuade their fellow Americans. Because of the long tradition of interconceptual borrowing between the language of theology and the language of public philosophy—a major feature of the ideological landscape since the 1730s and an important part of New England's influential history before then—it was natural to make these appeals in the language of the then-dominant public philosophy. But since ideologies embedded in cultures—words in flesh—have a historical logic of their own, there is scant surprise that as Christian theologians learned the language of political and economic liberalism, such liberalism transformed the language of Christian theology.

The history of Christian doctrine in Scotland during the century from the Cambuslang revival of 1742 to the Disruption of 1843, which split the Presbyterian state church into warring camps, is quite different from the history of doctrine in America during the same period. Only in the decades immediately preceding the Disruption does the Scottish scene begin to resemble the American. As a result, the movement beyond traditional Calvinism that was substantially complete in America before the Civil War did not take place in Scotland until the second half of the nineteenth century.

The century from Cambuslang to the Disruption can be divided into two clearly defined segments of unequal length, separated by a less sharply focused period of transition. The Moderate ascendancy, when leaders of the Established Church solidified an alliance between orderly, polite religion and scientific, polite learning, extended from the 1740s for the next fifty years.[50] In the two decades from 1790 to 1810, a weakening Moderate grip coincided with evangelical renewal.[51] In the wake of the French Revolution, evangelical energies mounted dramatically, both inside and outside the Established Church. This evangelical energy was marked by an outpouring of new publications, a plethora of new voluntary agencies for missions and reform, a concentrated effort to found new schools, a diligent application to the spiritual life, and the rise of important evangelical leaders such as Thomas Chalmers. The election of Chalmers as moderator of the General Assembly in 1832, and the success of evangelicals two years later in putting the Established Church on record against the arbitrary exercise of patronage, testified to the dominance that evangelicals enjoyed from the first decades of the new century.

With their American contemporaries, Scottish churchmen also accommodated themselves to new forms of piety, especially revivalism. They also worked in an intellectual milieu defined by the tenets of common sense moral philosophy, Scotland's own contribution to the domestication of the Enlightenment. And they too faced a political situation defined by the language of civic humanism. In the face of these developments, however, Scottish religious thinkers did not follow the American pattern.

To put matters negatively first: In Scotland, revival reinforced the organic strength of the covenant rather than undermining it. In Scotland, the Christian version of the Enlightenment functioned as a sup-

50. For a learned account of the Moderates, see Richard B. Sher, *Church and University in the Scottish Enlightenment: The Moderate Literati of Edinburgh* (Princeton, N.J., 1985). John R. McIntosh, "The Popular Party in the Church of Scotland, 1740–1800" (Ph.D. diss., University of Glasgow, 1989), modifies Sher and all other earlier historians on the non- or anti-Moderates of the period.

51. See especially David Alan Currie, "The Growth of Evangelicalism in the Church of Scotland, 1793–1843" (Ph.D. diss., University of St. Andrews, 1990); and Stewart J. Brown, *Thomas Chalmers and the Godly Commonwealth in Scotland* (New York, 1982).

plement to tradition and history rather than as their replacement. In
Scotland, civic humanism did not lead on to popular sovereignty or
political liberalism but was enlisted on the side of hierarchy and deference. The result was that, although Scottish church life felt the impact of revival, the Enlightenment, and civic humanism, these influences did not reduce the comprehensive intellectual vision of
theologians as they had in America. Put positively, since Scottish
Christians maintained the struggle to control institutions and ideas,
Scottish theology was freer to follow internal impulses, and from the
1770s and 1780s one of these impulses was an upsurge of Calvinism.

Revival, the Enlightenment, and civic humanism transformed theology in America much more dramatically than in Scotland, because
in each case the context was different. Revivalism, in the first instance, was never as pervasive in Scotland as in America, nor did revivalism shape religious culture as thoroughly as in America. John
Erskine, Scotland's most influential evangelical in the eighteenth century, seems to have been won for the ministry in the Kirk by his participation at Cambuslang. But he went out of his way to disassociate
himself not only from the theology of John Wesley but also from revivalism as a way of church life.[52]

A comparison between Cambuslang and the First Great Awakening reveals important differences.[53] Both featured the ministry of
George Whitefield, both witnessed a number of dramatic conversions, both were fueled by significant lay involvement, and both were
attended by crowds of unprecedented size. The critical difference,
however, was that the Scottish revivals acted as agents of communal
cohesion instead of fragmentation. The Scottish revivals worked to
solidify and evangelize the Established Church rather than split it
apart. The end result of New England's Great Awakening was the
fourfold division of its established church. In Scotland, the revivals

52. John Macleod, *Scottish Theology in Relation to Church History* (orig. 1946; Edinburgh, 1974), 215.

53. For Cambuslang, I have depended on Arthur Fawcett, *The Cambuslang Revival: The
Scottish Evangelical Revival of the Eighteenth Century* (London, 1971); T. C. Smout, "Born
Again at Cambuslang: New Evidence on Popular Religion and Literacy in Eighteenth-Century
Scotland," *Past and Present* 97 (1982): 114–27; and Ned Landsman, "Evangelists and Their
Hearers: Popular Interpretations of Revivalists' Preaching in Eighteenth-Century Scotland,"
Journal of British Studies 28 (1989): 120–49.

associated with Cambuslang led to a strengthened Established Church. The Scottish revival drew young evangelicals such as John Erskine *into* the church; the American often pushed evangelicals *out of* the church.

Socially, theologically, and culturally, it is of the greatest importance that the focus of revival in New England was the preached word of an itinerant outsider, whereas in Scotland it was the celebration of Communion under the general oversight of the parish minister.[54] To be sure, George Whitefield also appeared at Cambuslang, and preaching accompanied the Scottish celebration of the Lord's Supper, but the form was essentially different. Moreover, the Scottish revivals did not lead to a socially disruptive promotion of the "pure church," as they did for Jonathan Edwards, but rather to the evangelical strengthening of an establishment that maintained its comprehensive aspirations for Scottish society. On the eve of the Disruption, a century after Cambuslang, a further wave of revivals similarly meshed with the comprehensive, Calvinistic goals of the leading evangelicals rather than working at cross purposes against them.[55] Once again, revival was functioning *in* rather than *over* the church.

As revival strengthened traditional institutions in Scotland, so also did the Enlightenment. A process of accommodation that in America led to the decline of Calvinism did not have that result in Scotland. Religious thinkers in both venues admired Jonathan Edwards for having put categories of the Enlightenment to work for Calvinism. In both regions a moral philosophy of common sense, developed first for ethics by Francis Hutcheson and then for general epistemological purposes against Hume by Thomas Reid, contributed to the shape of theology.[56] In addition, theologians in both coun-

54. Leigh Eric Schmidt, *Holy Fairs: Scottish Communions and American Revivals in the Early Modern Period* (Princeton, N.J., 1989). On how forms of revivals affect the substance of religion more generally, see Harry S. Stout, *The New England Soul: Preaching and Religious Culture in Colonial New England* (New York, 1986), sec. 4, "Delivery, 1731–1763"; and Stout, "Puritanism Considered as a Profane Movement," *Christian Scholar's Review* 10 (1980): 3–19.

55. Iain Murray, "Biographical Introduction," in *Historical Theology by William Cunningham* (London, 1960), xiv, xix.

56. For a philosopher's introduction, see S. A. Grace, *The Scottish Philosophy of Common Sense* (Oxford, 1960); and for a still-useful summary paying more attention to theology, James McCosh, *The Scottish Philosophy: Biographical, Expository, Critical, from Hutcheson to Hamilton* (New York, 1875).

tries linked an exalted opinion of Newtonian scientific method to their use of the Scottish moral philosophy. Both Americans and Scots believed that it was impossible not to presuppose the existence of an external world and normal connections of cause and effect, and that moral intuitions could be treated as axioms for a comprehensive ethics applicable in all situations.[57] Yet despite these real similarities in the use of Scottish moral philosophy, the results for theology were quite different.

Environment, moreover, seems to be the key factor for the difference. In Scotland, evangelicals such as John Witherspoon, John Erskine, Charles Nesbit, and Thomas Chalmers—as well as William Robertson's circle of Moderates and their successors such as George Hill of St. Andrews—used common sense moral philosophy primarily to repudiate the skepticism of David Hume and in order to reconcile religious faith and the deliverances of reason. Common sense intuitions provided Moderates with building blocks for theistic proofs, and they offered evangelicals a vocabulary for describing the quickened spirituality of revival.[58] A common sense alliance with Newtonianism also refurbished the argument from design for both Moderates and evangelicals.[59] Unlike the situation in America, however, Scottish theologians did not look to common sense moral philosophy as the principal means of creating public order in the face of frontier chaos or to erect an apologetic for Christianity in the face of a barbaric rejection of tradition. In Scotland the common sense philosophy worked its greatest effect in the domain of formal academic thought. To sustain orthodoxy, the Scots looked much more to the Westminster Confession than to the argument from design. At times of crisis like the French Revolution and the threat of Napoleon, they tended to rely, not on "the science of politics," but on the institutions of the Established Church and traditional society.

57. An effort to distinguish ethical from epistemological aspects of the Scottish philosophy is found in Mark A. Noll, "Common Sense Traditions and American Evangelical Thought," *American Quarterly* 37 (Summer 1985): 220–25.

58. On the Moderates' concern for design, see Drummond and Bulloch, *Scottish Church*, 112; on evangelical spirituality, see Jonathan Edwards, *A Treatise concerning Religious Affections*, ed. John E. Smith (orig. 1746; New Haven, Conn., 1959).

59. See J. David Hoeveler, Jr., *James McCosh and the Scottish Intellectual Tradition from Glasgow to Princeton* (Princeton, N.J., 1981), 21–22 and chap. 5, "Protestant Scholasticism."

The career of John Witherspoon in Scotland and America illustrates the divergent course of the Enlightenment in the two regions. Witherspoon was a leading minister in the Kirk's antipatronage party from the mid-1740s to 1768, when he migrated to America to become the president of Princeton College, where he served with great impact on church and nation until his death in 1794.[60] In Scotland, Witherspoon had written articles affirming the reliability of the senses, a theme prominent among more famous proponents of the Scottish philosophy. But he was best known for his satiric attacks on the Moderates, including their theological mentor Francis Hutcheson. Particularly galling to Witherspoon was the habit of the Moderates, following the example of Hutcheson, "to give such views of Christianity, as will render it palatable to a corrupt worldly mind: and instead of abasing, will soothe and gratify the pride of man. Hence the unnatural mixture often to be seen of modern philosophy with ancient Christianity."[61] As a Scottish evangelical, in other words, Witherspoon employed the common sense philosophy of his Moderate contemporaries for narrow philosophical purposes but denounced the Moderate effort to give polite philosophy a dominant role in shaping the theology of the church or in governing the social order. For those purposes, Witherspoon relied on the ancient confessions. While in Scotland his most notable effort at protecting public order was to defend the rights of lairds and male heads of households to control local congregations.[62]

In America, Witherspoon's theological convictions as such did not change. He was still an evangelical Calvinist who believed in the value of the Westminster Confession for the church and the usefulness of common sense moral philosophy for the academy. But with

60. A substantial biography is Varnum Lansing Collings, *President Witherspoon* (Princeton, N.J., 1925). The best study of the apparent contradictions between Witherspoon the Scot and Witherspoon the American, which finds significant continuity in Witherspoon's consistent attention to wider worlds of revivalism and learning, is Ned Landsman, "Witherspoon and the Problem of Provincial Identity in Scottish Evangelical Culture," in *Scotland and America in the Age of the Enlightenment*, ed. R. B. Sher and J. R. Smitten (Princeton, N.J., 1990). For Witherspoon's importance for the evolution of Calvinism in America, see Mark A. Noll, *Princeton and the Republic, 1768–1822* (Princeton, N.J., 1989).

61. Witherspoon, "Salvation through Christ," in *Works*, 2:340.

62. See Richard Sher and Alexander Murdoch, "Patronage and Party in the Church of Scotland, 1750–1800," in *Church, Politics, and Society: Scotland, 1408–1929*, ed. Norman MacDouglass (Edinburgh, 1983), 208–11.

the absence of a settled social structure, in a situation where Presbyterians had to compete against other denominations and exert great efforts at bringing more of the vast unchurched population under its influence, and at a time when radical social ideas seemed to threaten both social order and the future of religion, Witherspoon's philosophical convictions moved from the periphery to the center. It was no great matter for Witherspoon, when lecturing on moral philosophy and divinity at the College of New Jersey, to exploit, almost to the point of plagiarism, the best texts of his native land, even if they had been written by his onetime *bête noir*, Francis Hutcheson.[63]

The noteworthy change in America was that now Hutcheson's moral philosophy provided also a social vision and, to some extent, a perspective on theology. Early in his lectures in moral philosophy, for example, Witherspoon affirmed that "the principles of duty and obligation" in all social and political relationship "must be drawn from the nature of man." The "internal sensation"—that which "Mr. Hutchinson [*sic*] calls the finer powers of perception," including "a sense of moral good and evil"—shows humans their duties.[64] In America, that is, the moral philosophy of Francis Hutcheson was being asked to secure the social ordering that in Scotland had been provided by the traditional hegemony of the Established Church. Similarly, Witherspoon's Princeton *Lectures on Divinity* devotes much more attention to proving the truthfulness of Christianity (by miracles, fulfilled prophecy, and religious experience) than to any other topic.[65] Again, Witherspoon seems to have turned to the philosophy of the Enlightenment for props to uphold the faith, whereas in the Old World he had turned to the Westminster Confession, the Established Church, and its courts. The American Witherspoon, though he remained doctrinally a Calvinist, relied upon a moral philosophy of reason and human nature to provide the foundations for the Reformed theology and social order that for the Scottish Witherspoon were rooted in the Old World institutions that themselves embodied Calvinist confession and social ordering. In other words, the common sense moral

63. For the extent of Witherspoon's borrowing, see Jack Scott, "Introduction," in *An Annotated Edition of Lectures on Moral Philosophy by John Witherspoon* (Newark, Del., 1982).

64. Witherspoon, *Works*, 3:369, 378, 379.

65. Such matters are treated in ibid., 4:32–62. The divinity lectures as a whole contain only 115 pages.

philosophy that had functioned within the casing of Calvinist institutions and thought while in Scotland had in the open American environment itself became the casing for convictions about theology and social order.

A third major difference between America and Scotland in this period concerns the appropriation of civic humanist ideology. The picture is simpler than for revivalism and common sense moral philosophy, since revivalism and common sense reasoning became integral, albeit in different ways, in both regions. Civic humanism, in contrast, did not play as central a role in Scotland as in America. The bonds among revivalism, evangelical practice, and democratic republicanism that were so important in America simply did not exist in Scotland. During the reign of the Moderates, the antipatronage party of Witherspoon and John Erskine was more democratic than William Robertson and his Moderate colleagues. But as Richard Sher and Alexander Murdoch have shown, the eighteenth-century evangelicals were "Popular" only in their resistance to patronage and their support for the ecclesiastical authority of heritors and elders.[66] They were always far from egalitarian. During the 1770s John Erskine and his evangelical colleague Charles Nesbit did speak out for the American patriots against the British attempt to subdue the colonies. But the burden of Erskine's widely noticed tract *Shall I Go to War with My American Brethren?* (1769, 1776), betrayed more concern about the advance of Roman Catholicism in the New World than it did about the political rights of the colonists.[67]

Charles Nesbit, who preached courageously against the British government during the War for Independence, eventually migrated to America because of his admiration for America's stand.[68] But it took only a very few months on the Pennsylvania frontier, as the president of the struggling Dickinson College, to turn Nisbet into an embittered

66. Sher and Murdoch, "Patronage and Party," 208–11, 215; see also Sher, *Church and University in the Socttish Enlightenment*, 262–76.

67. Dolphy I. Fagerstrom, "Scottish Opinion and the America Revolution," *William and Mary Quarterly*, 3d ser., 11 (April 1954): 265–66.

68. Documents testifying to Nisbet's early fascination with America are found in Whitfield J. Bell, Jr., "Scottish Emigration to America: A Letter of Dr. Charles Nisbet to Dr. John Witherspoon, 1784," *William and Mary Quarterly*, 3d ser., 11 (April 1954): 276–89; and Michael Kraus, "Charles Nisbet and Samuel Stanhope Smith—Two Eighteenth Century Educators," *Princeton University Library Chronicle* 6 (November 1944): 17–36.

cynic about the virtues of the American experiment. When he left Montrose in 1785, Nisbet told his friends that America was a land of "Liberty and Plenty" where people were free "from the shackles of authority" and open to the persuasion of reason. Before long he had his fill of such liberty. By 1800 he was telling Scottish correspondents about how Americans construed the Bible: "In the Beginning the Sovereign People created Heaven & the Earth." And he bemoaned "the Political Errors of our Citizens" and "their Errors in Religion," both of which rise from "an over-weaning Conceit of themselves, or an extravagant opinion of their own wisdom."[69] Although Nisbet's evangelicalism and his sympathy for American independence had made him a dangerously "advanced" thinker in Scotland, his political views—though in the abstract similar to the republican ideals of the American Revolution—did not drive his theology toward greater concern for the "unalienable rights" of individuals.

Principles of public virtue, freedom from tyranny, and mixed government remained important for Scottish churchmen in the half century after the American Revolution. But these principles continued to support the status quo in politics and, by implication, theology.[70] The French Revolution and Tom Paine especially discouraged political radicalism and gave a great boost to orthodoxy of every kind.[71] When in the 1830s the rising evangelical power in the Kirk established an alliance with the Whig Parliament and its Scottish managers, the Whig ideology was still moderate and progovernment, most unlike the suspicious and antihierarchical "Real Whiggery" that loomed so large in America. Across the Atlantic, the democratization of theology came about through the revolution and the application of radical Whig ideology to religion. In Scotland, democratic language did reenter the religious sphere in the early decades of the nineteenth century. But it was to be most found among the Congregational and Baptist associ-

69. Quoted in James H. Smylie, "Charles Nisbet: Second Thoughts on a Revolutionary Generation," *Pennsylvania Magazine of History and Biography* 98 (April 1974): 191, 195, 200.

70. Sher, *Church and University in the Scottish Enlightenment*, 187–212.

71. G. D. Henderson, "Religion and Democracy in Scottish History," in *The Burning Bush: Studies in Scottish Church History* (Edinburgh, 1957), 131–32; T. C. Smout, *A History of the Socttish People, 1560–1830* (London, 1969), 220; V. Kiernan, "Evangelicalism and the French Revolution," *Past and Present* 1 (1952): 44–56; and A. C. Cheyne, *The Transforming of the Kirk: Victorian Scotland's Religious Revolution* (Edinburgh, 1983), 11.

ates of James and Robert Haldane, and not in the still-dominant Established Church.[72] When democratic ideology surfaced in the Kirk, it was often a by-product of the most intensely traditional aspects of the Scottish tradition. In the words of a Scottish observer from around 1815, "Our popular struggles have been struggles for the right of worshipping God according to the dictates of our conscience and under the guidance of ministers of our own choice, and . . . when anxiously employed in finding arguments by which rights so dear to us might be rationally defended, our discovery of the principles of civil liberty was merely a sort of chance-consequence of the search."[73] Liberty in Christ was every bit as important in Scotland as in America. But once again, the discourse of liberty was contained by the traditions of theology and church instead of containing them.

At the Disruption of 1843, theology in Scotland still belonged to the church and was still self-consciously dependent upon ancient religious traditions. Much had changed from the age of Knox and the later era of the national covenant, but an indication of how much had not changed is provided by the fact that after nearly one and a half centuries of rule from London, the Kirk still administered the Poor Law and still ran the nation's schools, in which the Bible remained the central text.[74] In 1843 the overwhelming majority of Scotland's church-going population still adhered to churches committed to an ideal of national religious comprehension. To be sure, the significant number of voluntarists in the United Secession Church and the Relief Church, in dissenting bodies, and among those with secular convictions provided growing competition for the notion of such an establishment. But both major factions in the Established Church, along with the tiny minority of Reformed Presbyterians and Antiburgher Presbyterians, still contended for the notion of *a nation* in covenant with God. That sentiment was probably strongest among evangeli-

72. Deryck W. Lovegrove, "Unity and Separation: Contrasting Elements in the Thought and Practice of Robert and James Alexander Haldance," in *Protestant Evangelicalism: Britain, Ireland, Germany, and America, c. 1750–c. 1950*, ed. Keith Robbins (Oxford, 1990).

73. Hugh Miller to Lord Brougham, quoted in Henderson, "Religion and Democracy in Scottish History," 133–34.

74. Smout, *Scottish People, 1560–1830*, 457; and Christopher Smout, "Centre and Periphery in History, with Some Thoughts on Scotland as a Case Study," *Journal of Common Market Studies* 18 (March 1980): 264.

cals who became leaders of the Free Church after the Disruption. Thomas Chalmers led the battle against voluntarism throughout the 1830s.[75] Shortly after 1843 his pupil William Cunningham labored to "establish [the Free Church] claim to be regarded as the true Church of Scotland,—the inheritors and possessors both of the principle and the rights of those by whom that church was reformed, first from Popery, and then from Prelacy, and the ecclesiastical supremacy of the Crown."[76] It is of telling significance that the great goal in the life of Thomas Chalmers, who "was acclaimed in a manner seldom accorded to any Scot in his own lifetime," was to solve the crisis of urban Scotland by promoting a comprehensive *national* plan of parish paternalism.[77] The point here is not whether he failed or succeeded but that such a goal was prominent at such a time. Taken as an exemplar, the experience of Chalmers shows that Scottish churchmen aspired to a comprehensive institutional control of their own affairs, including their theology, almost unimaginable in America at the same time.

Such structural differences between America and Scotland do not by themselves explain the development of theology in the two regions. They do suggest, however, that in Scotland the story of the development of doctrine is a story primarily *within* the church. Much more than in America, it is still ecclesiastical history that explains the relative strength of traditional Calvinism in Scotland on the eve of the Disruption.

The relatively undiluted Calvinism of mid-century Scotland had been reinforced by three developments since the late eighteenth century. First, the theology of the Moderates remained moderate; if anything, it drifted back toward a more precise Calvinism after the turn of the century. For reasons that may extend well beyond theology, leaders of the Moderate party in the eighteenth century proved to be remarkably faithful to their confessional subscription. Thomas Chalmers's theological instruction at St. Andrews in the 1790s from

75. Brown, *Thomas Chalmers*, 220–36.
76. Cunningham, *Historical Theology*, 587.
77. Quotation from T. C. Smout, *A Century of the Scottish People, 1830–1950* (New Haven, 1986), 181; a full portrayal of that effort can be found in Brown, *Thomas Chalmers*.

the Moderate George Hill was formally, if not fervently, Calvinistic. Moreover, Hill's *Lectures in Divinity* had more than a few appreciative words for precise Calvinistic authors like Jonathan Edwards.[78] Somewhat later, descendants of the Moderates would contribute significantly to the middle party of "evangelical Erastians," who welcomed renewed evangelical (and Calvinistic) emphases in the Kirk, but who rested content with patronage in its eighteenth-century form.[79] The theological left on the Scottish scene, perhaps because it was also the social right, remained a truly Moderate influence almost as prone to move toward evangelical and Calvinistic positions as in the opposite direction.

Second, throughout the period of Moderate dominance, Scotland's evangelicals retained a large measure of doctrinal Calvinism, which then came to more public expression at their own rise to power in the Kirk. John Witherspoon and John Erskine in the eighteenth century and the circle around Thomas Chalmers in the nineteenth pursued their practical labors within a framework established by their Calvinist confession.

To be sure, the leader of the evangelicals in the early nineteenth century, Sir Henry Moncrieff Wellwood, came to doubt rigid Calvinist notions of predestination.[80] And some have perceived in Chalmers's mature theology "a mind struggling against doubts about some of the harsher doctrines of scholastic Calvinism and seeking a more personal form of Christianity."[81] At the same time, however, Wellwood and especially Chalmers retained more than formal allegiance to the inherited faith. Chalmers in particular was an enthusiastic proponent of an active Calvinism. The contrast with America is sharp at this point, for while the American descendants of Jonathan Edwards had begun to sift the gold from what they considered the dross of his legacy, Chalmers's admiration remained unbounded. "The American di-

78. Henderson, "Jonathan Edwards and Scotland," 161; and Brown, *Thomas Chalmers*, 7.

79. Drummond and Bulloch, *Scottish Church*, 240; the quoted phrase is from Macleod, *Scottish Theology*, 197.

80. Henry Moncrieff Wellwood, *Account of the Life and Writings of John Erskine* (Edinburgh, 1818), 200, 205, 217–20.

81. Brown, *Thomas Chalmers*, 377; and more generally with the same opinion, John Roxborogh, "Chalmers' Theology of Mission," in *The Practical and the Pious: Essays on Thomas Chalmers (1780–1847)*, ed. A. C. Cheyne (Edinburgh, 1985), 174–85.

vine affords, perhaps, the most wondrous example in modern times of one who stood richly gifted both in natural and spiritual discernment: and we know not what most to admire in him, whether the deep philosophy that issued from his pen, or the humble and childlike piety that issued from his pulpit."[82] Although the evangelical party may have blurred some of the sharp edges of its doctrinal Calvinism in the century after Cambuslang, its leading figures continued to embrace the main outlines of that system and showed very little tendency to modify or repudiate that heritage as many of their evangelical contemporaries were doing at the same time in America.

Third, in the early decades of the nineteenth century, the religious life of Scotland experienced a significant infusion of more militant Calvinism from Covenanters and from the newly evangelized Highlands. Although the Antiburghers and the Reformed Presbyterians were still no more than a tiny minority in the early nineteenth century, their determined defense of the national covenant in tandem with rigorous Calvinism gave them an unusual public influence among a people still swayed by history and tradition. The nature of that influence is well illustrated by the biographies of John Knox and Andrew Melville published in 1811 and 1819 by Thomas McCrie, a leader of the Antiburghers. These books show, in the words of an unfriendly commentator, "an intransigence worthy of their subject." But they also, as a friendly historian put it, "aroused a holy ambition in many to follow the noble example of these two spiritual giants."[83]

Probably even more important than the impact of these histories for the continuation of a rigorous Calvinism was the conversion of the Highlands. During the breakup of the clans after the defeat of Charles Stuart in 1746 and the disastrous economic and social shocks suffered by the region over the next century, the christianizing work of the Scottish Society for the Propagation of Christian Knowledge and the indigenous labors of the Highland "Men"—lay elders of the church— exerted a tremendous impact. The result was that by the early nineteenth century a Presbyterianism both vigorous in its evangelical zeal

---

82. Thomas Chalmers, *The Christian and Civic Economy of Large Towns* (Glasgow, 1821), 1:318. For the same sentiments at the end of his career, see idem, *Institutes of Theology*, 2 vols., in *Posthumous Works of the Rev. Thomas Chalmers*, ed. Wm. Hanna (Edinburgh, 1849), 2:292–355.

83. Drummond and Bulloch, *Scottish Church*, 213; Murray, "Introduction," vi.

and rigorous in its Calvinistic profession had come to dominate that area.[84] At the Disruption, the Highlands, with its more militant Calvinism, went almost en bloc into the Free Church. For an entire region, even if declining in population, to embrace such a strenuous faith meant a great deal for the renewal of Calvinism precisely at a time when it was fading away in other regions of the North Atlantic world.

By the 1830s Scotland was rapidly modernizing. It had enjoyed two generations of an Enlightenment that was frequently the envy of educated Europe. By some reckonings this social and intellectual climate would make Scotland a prime candidate for the decline of Calvinism and the rise of more human-centered faith. Yet at that very time Calvinism in both doctrinal and practical forms had not been stronger in Scotland for a least a century. Sabbatarianism and a religiously inspired anti-Catholicism were on the rise.[85] The evangelicalism of the church in the Lowlands and of the SSPCK in the Highlands decisively shaped the public ethos of the nation.

To be sure, the stricter Calvinists by no means had things to themselves. By the 1830s significant challenges had been issued to hereditary formulations of the faith—from John McLeod Campbell's denial of the penal atonement,[86] Edward Irving's promotion of a charismatic message,[87] James Morison's importation of Finney's revival methods into the New Light United Secession Church,[88] and Thomas Erskine of Linlathen's attack on the divine decrees of the hereditary confession.[89]

84. See John MacInnes, *The Evangelical Movement in the Highlands of Scotland, 1688–1800* (Aberdeen, 1951); Smout, *Scottish People, 1560–1830*, 358, 463, 498; Smout, *Scottish People, 1830–1950*, 198; Smout, "Centre and Periphery," 268; and Drummond and Bulloch, *Scottish Church*, 215.

85. Drummond and Bulloch, *Scottish Church*, 214.

86. B. A. Gerrish, "The Protest of Grace: John McLeod Campbell on the Atonement," in *Tradition and the Modern World: Reformed Theology in the Nineteenth Century* (Chicago, 1978), 71–98; and George M. Tuttle, *So Rich a Soil: John McLeod Campbell on Christian Atonement* (Edinburgh, 1986).

87. Bebbington, *Evangelicalism in Modern Britain*, 76–96.

88. Richard Carwardine, *Trans-atlantic Revivalism: Popular Evangelicalism in Britain and America, 1790–1865* (Westport, Conn., 1978), 98–100; Drummond and Bulloch, *Scottish Church*, 219; and Macleod, *Scottish Theology*, 242–43.

89. Nicholas R. Needham, *Thomas Erskine of Linlathen: His Life and Theology, 1788–1837* (Edinburgh, 1990).

The central historical circumstance of the 1830s, however, was the unqualified rejection of such views by the formal Scottish denominations. Unlike the situation in America, where "advanced" thinkers like Lyman Beecher and Albert Barnes survived judicial challenges, and where Nathaniel W. Taylor's extensively modified Calvinism became very influential in New England Congregationalism, the Scottish churches actively repulsed departures from the Westminster Confession. The Established Church deposed McLeod Campbell, Irving, and a number of other ministers who shared their views. The United Secession was the Scottish Presbyterian denomination most willing to move with the times, but it deposed Morison.[90]

The Calvinist surge continued on into the next decade as well. When in 1840 fourteen ministers of the Kirk gathered in Glasgow to discuss and promote revival, they self-consciously distanced themselves from their contemporaries in America who in the process of promoting revivals "were presuming to attempt, by [their] own devices and arrangements, to originate and guide the operations of the Holy Spirit, or entirely to supersede them." For these Scottish ministers a much better model was to be found in eighteenth-century America from Jonathan Edwards, especially his work on the religious affections. "Time itself will grow old," they said, "before the writings of Jonathan Edwards become obsolete."[91]

Not just revivalism but the general vitality in the church seemed securely Calvinistic. Evangelical Calvinism in the Church of Scotland became more prominent during the Ten Years' Conflict before 1843 among both the antipatronage party and the middle group of evangelicals willing to tolerate the old arrangements. At the Disruption, few doubted that the new Free Church was the central source of religious energy in ecclesiastical Scotland. Theological direction for the young denomination came from the hastily established New College in Edinburgh, where younger men like William Cunningham and James Bannerman joined Thomas Chalmers, David Welsh, and John Duncan as unusually forceful exponents of a general evangelical Calvinism.[92]

90. Drummond and Bulloch, *Scottish Church*, 193–219.

91. W. M. H., "Preface," in *The Revival of Religion: Addresses by Scottish Evangelical Leaders Delivered in Glasgow in 1840* (Edinburgh, 1984; orig. 1840), xvii, xix.

92. Murray, "Introduction," xvii; A. C. Cheyne, *The Transforming of the Kirk*, 7–8; and Macleod, *Scottish Theology*, 263–64.

The theological contrast to America could not have been greater. Post-Calvinist opinions on human ability, the atonement, predestination, and "new measures" had come to prevail widely in America, with the Princeton theologians and a remnant of New England Congregationalists keeping alive the objections of a minority. In Scotland, however, the Calvinistic positions were maintained in the churches with seemingly growing strength, while positions similar to those that defined the mainstream in America were under great fire inside and outside the main Presbyterian denominations. The contrast is striking. Of many ways to explain it, one at least must be that, unlike in America, religious thought in Scotland remained more completely under the control of the Scottish church and that, also unlike in America, the internal life of the Scottish church was witnessing an increasing rather than declining infusion of traditional Calvinist thought.

Scottish theology does seem to have followed the American example in the half century after 1843 because of circumstances brought about by the Disruption and the church's alliance with Victorian economic conventions. But still it sustained its independence much longer than was the case in America.

Churches maintain the independence of their theologies in different ways. Anabaptists have sought that goal by systematic separation from the world, Roman Catholics by exalted claims for their hierarchy, and Lutherans by affinity for a theory of two kingdoms. The tendency of Reformed and evangelical Protestants has been to seek theological independence through intellectual self-discipline even while working energetically at transforming the surrounding world for Christ. The histories of both America and Scotland reveal the great potential effect of such Reformed and evangelical strategies. They also show how easy it can be, because of the deep immersion in society required for such an effort, for minds to be transformed by the world they are seeking to transform.[93]

93. I am pleased to acknowledge the hospitality of Tyndale House, Cambridge (and its warden, Brian Winter), where an earlier version of this article was presented. That earlier version was published in the *Tyndale Bulletin* 40 (1989): 49–76.

4

Evangelical Institutionalization and Evangelical Sectarianism in Early Nineteenth-Century Britain and America

Ted A. Campbell

By the end of the year 1791, the first generation of evangelicals lay moldering in their graves in Britain and North America. "The Divine Dramatist," George Whitefield, had been buried in 1770 before the pulpit of the Old South Presbyterian Church of Newburyport, Massachusetts.[1] The first preacher of the revival, Howell Harris, was buried within the walls of his parish church at Trevecca in Wales in 1773. Charles Wesley died in 1788, and his mortal remains were buried in the churchyard of St. Marylebone, London. In January of 1791 William Williams of Pantycelyn, the great hymnodist of the Welsh revival, had died and was buried at Llanfair ar y Bryn. John Wesley died

---

1. Quoting the title of Harry S. Stout's recent biography, *The Divine Dramatist: George Whitefield and the Rise of Modern Evangelicalism* (Grand Rapids, 1991).

on 2 March of that year, and his body lay in the unconsecrated burial ground behind his chapel on City Road, London. Finally, Selina Shirley Hastings, the Countess of Huntingdon, who had engineered much of the early revival in Wales and England, died in June of the same year, and her remains were buried at her estate in Ashby. The year 1791 thus marked a clean sweep of the earliest advocates of evangelicalism.

With the first generation of its leadership gone, the advocates of the Evangelical Revival now faced the characteristic problems of a cultural movement that has succeeded but must attempt to pass on its genius to a new generation. It is the classic problem that Max Weber described in 1922 as "the routinization of charisma."[2] Indeed, by 1791, the various children of the Evangelical Revival had already begun to build the institutions necessary for the continued life of their movement. Some, such as "The Countess of Huntingdon's Connexion" of traveling preachers, or Wesley's North American societies, had organized themselves as independent religious denominations. Others, such as the Methodist conferences in England and Wales, existed still nominally as Anglicans, though de facto separate, having their own ordained ministries, chapels, organizational structures, and other institutions and celebrating eucharistic and preaching service at the same hours as neighboring Anglican parish churches. Within two decades these nominally Anglican societies would recognize their independence as denominations.

Other evangelical leaders had found different means of carrying on the life of the revival besides the formation of evangelical denominations. Some existed as informal and loosely networked fellowships within existing churches. Within the Church of England there was a growing and respectable party of evangelicals centered in Henry Venn's parish of Clapham and supported by numerous parish clergy who had disavowed the itinerant preaching of earlier evangelicals. Within British and North American churches with Reformed roots—Presbyterian, Congregationalist, and Baptist—there were now prominent evangelical parties who had taken up the itinerant preaching of the earlier decades of the awakening. The growing pre-

2. Max Weber, *The Sociology of Religion*, trans. E. Fischoff (orig. 1922, in German; Boston, 1963), chap. 5, pp. 60ff.

dominance of the New Light party within New England Congregationalist churches represents the transatlantic phenomenon of a pro-
awakening or pro-revival party flourishing in a variety of church traditions in the 1780s and beyond.[3]

All of these early moves toward the routinization of the evangelical
charisma—both the formation of new denominations and the existence of informal parties or networks within older denominations—
might be described as relatively predictable responses to the challenges posed by the passing of the evangelical flame to a new generation of leaders. But two momentous political events began to bear
upon the evangelical movements at the end of the eighteenth century
that threatened to tear apart the fledgling denominations, parties,
and informal networks by which the revival's leaders had carried on
its life—namely, the revolutions in North America in the 1770s and
1780s and in France in 1789. They forced evangelicalism in Britain
and America onto a rather startling and unpredictable new track. The
American Revolution, as Nathan Hatch has shown, gave a kind of
sanction to the rising tide of democratic ideals in this period.[4] The
French Revolution both fascinated and horrified its observers across
the twenty-one-mile strait that separates England and France. In both
places, evangelicalism now flourished in a wild coterie of sectarian
movements.[5] In both places, more conventional evangelicals found it
necessary to enunciate a socially and politically conservative stance
that nevertheless maintained evangelicalism's core commitment to
social and individual Christian conversion.

Although I am convinced that evangelicalism was a transatlantic
phenomenon from the eighteenth century, and remains so up until
our own time, I am also convinced that British and North American
evangelicalism began to diverge in some critical ways in the period
from 1791 to 1832. I shall argue in what follows that although more
conservative or institutional evangelicalism in this period could be
described as a truly transatlantic phenomenon, various evangelical

3. Deryck W. Lovegrove, *Established Church, Sectarian People: Itineracy and the Transformation of English Dissent, 1780–1830* (Cambridge, 1988).

4. Nathan O. Hatch, *The Democratization of American Christianity* (New Haven, Conn.,
1989), 5–9.

5. James K. Hopkins, *A Woman to Deliver Her People: Joanna Southcott and English Millenarianism in an Era of Revolution* (Austin, Tex., 1982), xi–xix.

sectarian movements that developed simultaneously in Britain and America did not generally maintain the transatlantic networks that more institutional evangelical groups maintained. Consequently, evangelicalism as a transatlantic phenomenon from this period carried much more the character of the institutional evangelicalisms of Britain and North America.

In order to pursue this claim about the character of transatlantic evangelicalism in the period between 1791 and 1832, I shall examine three particular clusters of historical material. In the first place, I consider the sectarian pole of evangelicalism by studying the pamphlets of two English sectarians of the period, namely, Richard Brothers and Joanna Southcott.[6] I shall have relatively little new information to contribute to the study of this colorful pair, except to note some nuances of their tract publications. These nuances will be relevant to a second focus, namely, the response of the more institutional pole of British evangelicalism, the so-called Clapham Sect, looking in particular at the tracts of Hannah More. In the third place, I shall inquire as to the ways in which these polarities of British evangelicalism made it across the Atlantic, and what this may reveal about the character of transatlantic revivalism, at least in this very early and transitional period.

Evangelical Polarities: The Sectarians

The French Revolution unleashed a new episode in the long history of British millennial speculation, a history that extended from the Middle Ages through the sectarians of the English Revolution (Ranters, Levellers, Diggers, Muggletonians, and the like) and thence to the Camisards and "Shaking Quakers" of the eighteenth century. Two books published in the 1790s have titles revealing the prevalence of eschatological motifs in the decade: *Popular Commotions Considered as Signs of the Approaching End of the World* and *The Present State of Europe Compared with Ancient Prophecies.*[7] In the

---

6. J. F. C. Harrison, *The Second Coming: Popular Millenarianism, 1780–1850* (New Brunswick, N.J., 1979); and Hopkins, *A Woman to Deliver Her People*.

7. The first by William Jones, the second by Joseph Priestley; both are cited in Hopkins, *A Woman to Deliver Her People*.

decade of the 1790s the poet (and artist) William Blake turned to metaphysical and millennial speculation, experienced visions and illuminations, and carried on conversations with angels and demons. His poetry captured the sense of awesome global change that British people perceived in the American and French Revolutions:

> . . . terror appeared in the Heavens above
> And in Hell beneath, & a mighty & awful change
>   threatened the Earth.
> The American War began. All its dark horrors
>   passed before my face
> Across the Atlantic to France. Then the French Revolution
>   commenc'd in thick clouds,
> And My Angels have told me that seeing such visions
>   I could not subsist on Earth.[8]

The social history of this period has been described by E. P. Thompson and a host of followers, who have shown how, in the Industrial Revolution and then especially in this revolutionary period, groups of workers began to band together to form associations that had a clear sense of proletarian social class-consciousness. Thompson himself argued that during the years immediately after the French Revolution it was not just the influence of the Continent that affected the development of English movements, but that an older chiliastic tradition in English religious life, hidden since the failure of the Cromwellian Revolution, resurfaced.[9]

In the year in which John Wesley died—and two years after the French Revolution—a Newfoundlander and erstwhile naval commander named Richard Brothers began to believe that God had given him a unique calling to announce the fulfillment of the prophecies of Daniel and the Revelation. Being convinced that military service was inconsistent with a Christian life, and having refused to collect his pension from the navy, Brothers began a barrage of letters to the king, the queen, and members of the Houses of Parliament to con-

8. Blake, cited in ibid., xiv.
9. E. P. Thompson, *The Making of the English Working Class* (New York, 1966); cf. p. 50 and chap. 2, more broadly for his suggestion about the reappearance of a submerged tradition of English millenarian speculation.

vince them to give him a hearing. Though this was not granted, Brothers began to attract considerable public attention, and in 1793 it was revealed to him that his name "Brothers" indicated that he was none other than a descendant of James, the brother of Jesus.

This peculiar belief was but part of an elaborate scheme that had captivated Brothers's imagination. The tribes of Israel, he believed, had been dispersed among the modern peoples of Europe. These would be gathered together within a few cataclysmic months, after which he himself would be acknowledged "Prince of the Hebrews." The rebuilding of Jerusalem would begin soon thereafter. Brothers's prophecies were announced in a spectacular volume published in 1794 and entitled *The World's Doom, or, A Revealed Knowledge of the Prophecies and Times.*[10] In this book, Brothers demanded that the world and its present rulers acknowledge his authority: "The Lord God commands me to say to you, George the third, king of England, that immediately upon my being revealed, in London, to the Hebrews as their prince, and to all nations as their governor, your crown must be delivered up to me, that all your power and authority may instantly cease."[11]

Within a few months of the publication of these tidings, Brothers had been committed to an asylum on charges of treason and criminal lunacy. He continued to write pamphlets while in his captivity, and although the predicted dates of his manifestation came and went, he still attracted disciples, some from the higher social class. Eventually released from asylum, Brothers died in 1824.

One might argue that Richard Brothers was at the extreme periphery of evangelicalism throughout his career, since he did not share the passion for "experiential religion," which was at the core of the eighteenth-century evangelical experience. More intimately related to English evangelicalism, though, was the career of Joanna Southcott, to whom Brothers's mantle seems to have passed early in the nineteenth century, and beside whose body Brothers was eventually

10. Richard Brothers, *A Revealed Knowledge of the Prophecies and Times: Wrote under the Direction of the Lord God, and Published under His Sacred command, it Being the First Sign of Warning for the Benefit of All Nations* (West-Springfield, 1797). This is a later printing. The *National Union Catalog* and the *British Museum Catalog* list numerous editions from 1794, some of which have the prefixed title *The World's Doom*.

11. Ibid., 109.

laid to rest in St. John's Wood cemetery. In the year in which John Wesley died, this Joanna Southcott had become a member of a Methodist society. A year later she had a vision in which it was revealed that she was the "woman clothed with the sun" spoken of in Revelation 12:1. She eventually rejected (or was expelled by) the Methodists of both Arminian and Calvinist camps. "As high as the Heavens are from the Earth," she wrote, "so high are my Writings from the thoughts, knowledge, and understandings of the Methodists."[12]

Joanna Southcott's first pamphlet appeared in January 1801 and was entitled "The Strange Effects of Faith." Over the next decade and a half she produced more than sixty-five books of prophecies, and at one point her publisher was said to have on hand 792 pounds sterling of her books.[13] Southcott's prophecies, like Brothers's, centered on the claim that a messianic age was about to dawn. Her followers expressed their faith in this creed: "We believe that there will be a New Heaven, as declared by the Spirit, and a New Earth, wherein dwelleth righteousness. We believe that Man will be created anew in Heart and Life. We believe that there is a Time to come for the millennial World, a Rest for the People of GOD; that he will come to destroy the works of the Devil, and send his Holy Spirit up—on the Sons of Men."[14]

From 1803 Southcott "sealed" her followers, giving them a token that they were to be among the elect. Toward the end of her life, in the 1810s, Southcott, who was in her sixties at the time, announced that she was to bear a son. His name would be Shiloh, and he would usher in the reign of God. Southcott was cruelly deluded; what she thought was pregnancy turned out to be cancer, and she died on Christmas Day, 1814. Her followers set a watch over her grave at St. John's Wood, believing that she would soon rise with the babe Shiloh in her arms.

Richard Brothers and Joanna Southcott were dismissed by respectable evangelical leaders of widely different persuasions. Yet they represent, in many respects, an aspect of evangelicalism that evangelicals might rather forget, and indeed many would disavow

12. Joanna Southcott, "A Warning to the Whole World" (London, 1804), 35; cf. Hopkins, *A Woman to Deliver Her People*, 55–56 and n. 66.

13. Hopkins, *A Woman to Deliver Her People*, 117.

14. A manuscript entitled "The Faith of the Believers in the Divine Mission of Joanna," cited in ibid., 112–13.

their alleged evangelicalism, especially where this term has come to connote a pattern of Protestant theological orthodoxy. There can be little question, however, that their movements emerged from the general milieu of English evangelicalism in the late eighteenth century and that they represent a polarity to which many evangelicals were attracted at this time. They were, however, an embarrassment to other evangelicals, for millenarians and other sectarians left evangelicals open to charges of rank enthusiasm by their more sophisticated opponents. The very respectable *Dictionary of National Biography*, for example, edited by the freethinker Sir Leslie Stephen, includes entries on both of them, and they are not flattering. The entry for Brothers begins, "Brothers, Richard (1757–1824), enthusiast." Similarly the entry for Southcott begins "Southcott, Joanna (1750–1814), fanatic." On the one hand, then, there would appear to be little doubt that the millenarians were perceived as a threat or at least a nuisance to the social fabric of England.

On the other hand, the fact that Brothers and Southcott attracted some well-bred followers, along with the rather more obvious fact that their works were intended for a literate public, have led some (J. F. C. Harrison, in particular) to claim that Brothers's and Southcott's followers were not really from among the poor.[15] This claim has been roundly contested by scholars such as James Hopkins, who has stressed that the great ranks of followers of Brothers and Southcott were in fact from the lower classes and that although some could read their pamphlets, many followers could not.[16] It is quite conceivable that the advocates of these millenarian movements, like so many of the earliest Methodists, were drawn from those levels of society that one might describe as "elite poor," namely, laborers who had steady occupations, owners of small shops, artisans, keepers of small farms, and the like, who had somehow acquired at least a minimal degree of literacy.

There can be little doubt, in fact, about the reading audience targeted for their various writings. The physical appearance of their tracts and pamphlets is revealing in this regard. In almost each case

15. Harrison, *The Second Coming*, 221.
16. Hopkins, *A Woman to Deliver Her People*, 76–83, where Hopkins utilizes lists of Southcottians to argue that the bulk of the movement was from the poorer ranks of society.

I have examined (Duke University holds a considerable collection of English tracts and pamphlets in the Baker Collection of Wesleyana and British Methodism), these writings are printed in small duodecimo-size pamphlets or fascicles, often with a price (e.g., "Sixpence") printed in a colophon, giving also the address of the printer. They are almost all printed on coarse brown paper, the telltale sign in this period of the use of wood pulp in paper production.

Each of these indications of material production suggests a clear intention to reduce the price of the pamphlets and tracts in order to make them more widely available. The small duodecimo size and the fact that the tracts and pamphlets went unbound reduced their price from those of larger (octavo, quarto, or folio) bound books. The fact that a price was advertised, often in pence as opposed to shillings, shows that book producers had consciously attempted to make the publications widely available. The use of wood pulp as opposed to linen or other cloth in paper production was a very new development in the 1780s and 1790s and was introduced to reduce the cost of paper production.[17] Moreover, Joanna Southcott's books (as opposed to Brothers's) apparently were of machine-produced paper, again quite a new development designed to reduce production costs even more.[18] When these considerations of book production are laid beside the relatively simple (if often mystifying) content of the works, the case appears very clear that Brothers's and Southcott's works were targeted at the literate (or semiliterate) poor. As we shall see in the case of Hannah More, the millenarians' opponents seemed to recognize this social targeting as well.

Evangelical Polarities: The Clapham Sect

We now move from the radical and democratic polarity of English evangelicalism to the conservative and elite polarity represented by

17. Dard Hunter, *Papermaking: The History and Technique of an Ancient Craft* (New York, 1947), 328–40.
18. Ibid., 341–49. I believe that I am correct in identifying the paper in Southcott's works as machine produced. At least in the works to which I have had access, the paper is woven (not laid), and at some points it shows signs of the use of rollers for smoothing the paper. The paper in Brothers's *World's Doom*, by contrast, is laid, although it is apparently made of wood pulp, as is the case with the paper in Southcott's books.

the Anglican evangelicalism of the so-called Clapham Sect. "Sect" in this case is a rather unfortunate title, since it might suggest a religiosity more like the millenarians than the group to whose attention we now turn, namely, the circle of Anglican evangelicals that gathered at Henry Venn's parish of Clapham, south of London. This circle included Venn, William Wilberforce, Zachary Macaulay, and—the subject of our particular attention here—Hannah More. The Clapham Sect represents a broader range of Anglican evangelicalism that had rejected itinerant preaching but retained the experiential stress and moral activism of the Evangelical Revival. As E. P. Thompson saw them, they represented a foreshadowing of the conservative ethos of Victorian England.[10]

In the year in which John Wesley died, Hannah More was busy at the task of establishing new schools in Congresbury, Yatton, and Axbridge. These schools, patterned after the original Sunday schools of Robert Raikes, offered a small degree of literacy for poorer parishioners—but not much; she offered, in her own terms, "such coarse works as may fit them for servants."[20]

At this point one may see the importance of the details noted above concerning the material production of popular books. A biographer describes More's own procedure for producing tracts in the 1790s:

> To the amusement of Hannah's friends, that well-bred lady made a startling collection of chapbooks; anti-governmental and anti-church tirades, histories of notorious murderers dying on the scaffold, careers of thieves, vulgar ballads, bawdy songs, and obscene jests. She studied these seriously to learn the secret of their popularity, and borrowed therefrom for her own works. Her tracts were printed on coarse brown paper, adorned with lively woodcuts, and titled to attract attention.[21]

The series of tracts that More began in this period came to be known as the Cheap Repository Tracts. Again the inexpensiveness of the tracts as well as their means of production suggest that More had tar-

---

19. Thompson, *Making of the English Working Class*, 56–57.
20. Letter to William Wilberforce, cited in *Dictionary of National Biography*, 13:864.
21. Mary Alden Hopkins, *Hannah More and Her Circle* (New York, 1947), 212.

geted precisely the same population that Brothers and Southcott had targeted, namely, the literate poor.

More's tracts, though cleverly disguised as revolutionary pamphlets, consistently advocated political stability, reverence for the state and its church, and the need to stay within one's appointed "station," or social class. The first and best known of her Cheap Repository Tracts was published anonymously and entitled "Village Politics, addressed to all the Mechanics, Journeymen, and Laborers, in Great Britain, by Will Chip, a Country Carpenter."[22] Set as a dialogue between a blacksmith and a mason, the pamphlet steadily guides a seeker of "liberty" and a "new constitution" (terms he had heard from the French) back to a realization that the stability of England is to be preferred to the revolution of France. "O the roast beef of Old England!" they sing together toward the conclusion, and at the very end the seeker is finally admonished to "study to be quiet, work with your own hands, and mind your own business."[23]

Village Politics has been described as "Burke for Beginners," recalling Edmund Burke's *Reflections on the Revolution in France.* But in this regard, Hannah More represents the interests of the Clapham Sect and Anglican evangelicalism more broadly. The Claphamites, who were involved critically in such social programs as the abolition of slavery, the establishment of schools for poor children, and the education of women, were at least partially motivated by a concern for social stability. During the 1790s Wilberforce himself wrote a book entitled *A Practical View of the Prevailing Religious System of Professed Christians, in the Higher and Middle Classes in this Country, Contrasted with Real Christianity.* He stressed the need for stricter morality, quoted Adam Smith liberally, and argued that a renewal of moral discipline would encourage persons to pursue the duties appropriate to their "station" and so would make for political stability.[24]

It should be stressed at this point that between the polarities represented by millenarians at one end and the Clapham Sect at the

---

22. Title as given in *The Works of Hannah More* (New York, 1868), 1:358.

23. Ibid., 369.

24. William Wilberforce, *A Practical View of the Prevailing Religious System of Professed Christians, in the Higher and Middle Classes in this Country, Contrasted with Real Christianity,* 18th ed. (London, 1830); see, for example, p. 248.

other, there existed a very broad and colorful spectrum of British evangelical life that included Wesleyans; Welsh Calvinistic Methodists; Primitive Methodists (from the 1820s); itinerant evangelicals within Baptist, Congregationalist, and Presbyterian churches; and an amazing complex of intricately interrelated but often formally independent religious societies, congregations, and preachers. Each one of these produced its own literature, often vying for the same readers that Brothers, Southcott, and More had targeted. What this little sketch prompts us to envision, then, is a struggle for the minds and hearts of the emerging, literate working class, a struggle in which the pamphlets of Brothers, Southcott, and More represent but a few small volumes in a cavernous library of coarse brown-paper tracts and chapbooks. I have called attention to them primarily to illustrate a range of British evangelical culture in the period from 1791 to 1832 and to offer a test of how these polarities of British evangelical culture were expressed as a transatlantic phenomenon.

The North American Context

Shifting our attention from Great Britain in the latter years of George III to the early American republic, we may see a similar range of evangelical polarities. At the conservative end of the polarity, the earlier enthusiasm of the Great Awakening had calmed down and had been institutionalized in the theological system of Samuel Hopkins, in Lyman Beecher's ideal of a "continuous revival," and in the broad triumph of the New Light party in the older Reformed churches of North America. By the earliest decades of the nineteenth century, a rather staid Episcopalian evangelical party was gathering around Bishop Charles Petit McIlvaine in the Old Northwest.[25] Moreover, in the period between 1791 and 1832 such interdenominational organizations as the American Tract Society, the American Bible Society, and the Board of Commissioners for Foreign Missionaries gave well-established American evangelical denominations the appearance of a common front.

25. Diana Hochstedt Butler, "Standing against the Whirlwind: The Evangelical Party in the Nineteenth Century Protestant Episcopal Church" (Ph.D. diss., Duke University, 1991).

At the other end of the polarity, a congeries of democratic and sectarian movements emerged in the United States in the period between 1791 and 1832. These have been studied recently in Nathan Hatch's *Democratization of American Christianity*, which argues that the Second Great Awakening in general, early American Methodism, the various "Christian" Church movements, African-American religion, and even Mormonism had in their own ways heightened the democratic ideologies of the early republic. Because Hatch deals with such distinctively American movements as the Restorationists or the Mormons, his book can give the impression that popular democratic religiosity in this period was a uniquely American phenomenon. This, I think, would be a mistaken impression, because it is in precisely this period that democratic sectarian movements sprang up in Britain as well as America. The American groups did utilize anti-European rhetoric (James O'Kelly, for example, remarked that Francis Asbury grew up in the land of kings and so could not understand American ways), and in this respect the American democratic movements could play themselves off against the *anciens régimes* of Europe. In the 1790s in both Britain and America, however, democratic evangelical movements were arising.

Although a similar polarity existed in America and Britain, a polarity with conservative institutionalized evangelicalism at one end and with more radical, democratic, and sectarian movements at the other, how much of religious culture in this period actually passed from one side of the Atlantic to the other? To what extent was evangelicalism, in the period between 1791 and 1832, truly a transatlantic phenomenon?

I realize, of course, that the Atlantic can be crossed both ways, but at this point I want to consider how the British tract and pamphlet literature considered above came to North America. In the first place, Richard Brothers's initial book, *The World's Doom*, was indeed published in the United States—in fact, by five different publishers within a few months of its publication in England.[26] Despite its spectacular success, though, none of Brothers's writings from asylum (or later in his career) was ever published in North America. Similarly, a check of the *National Union Catalog* shows that of Joanna South-

26. *National Union Catalog: Pre-1956 Imprints*, 685 vols. (London, 1968–80), 78:366–68.

cott's sixty-five or more writings, not a single work was printed in the United States before the twentieth century, and then only when a small remnant of her supporters established a colony in southern California.[27]

The story is widely different with Hannah More. Beginning as early as 1774, More's works were published by American presses year after year, up and down the Atlantic seaboard. The *National Union Catalog* lists at least 133 publications of More's works by presses in the United States between 1774 and 1832. The fact that some of her pamphlets were printed without dates would increase the overall number.[28] The various tract societies in the United States (especially the New England Tract Society, founded in 1814, which became the American Tract Society in 1823) were eager to publish More's works and sponsored uniform editions of the *Cheap Repository Tracts*. Although it is not always possible to associate particular publishing houses with particular denominations, it is clear that More's works were published by Methodists, Episcopalians, and Presbyterians as well as by the interdenominational Tract Society. All of this suggests that her works were enthusiastically received and reprinted in the early American republic.

Conclusion

Hannah More's works, then, made it across the Atlantic in a very impressive way; Richard Brothers managed to get one book published in America, but of all the pamphlets and tracts of Joanna Southcott, not a single one was published in the early American republic. All of this suggests that the Atlantic Ocean served as a kind of cultural filter through which institutionalized forms of evangelicalism passed much more readily than evangelicalism's more radical forms. Having looked here at only the top and bottom ends of the

27. Ibid., 558:256–64. There is one work by listed as having been published in San Diego in 1804, but the listing is certainly wrong; all others of the San Diego publications of her works are from the twentieth century. Presumably the printer simply carried the original date of publication of the tract without noting the new publication date.

28. Ibid., 394:201–25.

evangelical polarity, I am not able to say just how fine the grid was; it was certainly coarse enough to allow Lorenzo Dow across, and Dow was on the radical fringe of the Methodist churches of Britain and the United States. I suspect that there was no real cutoff point at which an evangelical movement could be predicted to pass or not pass the Atlantic test, only a general tendency for more institutional and wider-based evangelical movements to make it across. A broader examination of what evangelical literature made it across the Atlantic—both ways—might reveal a great deal more about the character of transatlantic evangelicalism in this period and others.

It was noted at the beginning of this essay that the various polarities in late eighteenth- and early nineteenth-century evangelicalism represented different approaches to the routinization of the evangelical charisma. But although I have focused on this passing of the first generation of evangelicals, the fact is that this same problem has repeated itself in the history of the evangelical movement. Consistently, an evangelical movement will begin with a flourish of charismatic power among relatively poor folk and will find itself fifty years later with colleges, universities, hospitals, established congregations, and denominational bureaucracies.

When William and Catherine Booth seceded from the Methodist New Connection, for instance, it seemed to them that Methodism's birthright, its claim to be a religion of the heart proclaimed to the poor, had been sold for a mess of Victorian pottage. The story could be retold in regard to Wesleyan Methodists, Free Methodists, and holiness and eventually Pentecostal churches in the United States. (Here I have touched only the Wesleyan-Arminian side of the evangelical spectrum.) One might even make a case that in evangelicalism we have a consistent "trickle-up" spirituality: what begins as a radical movement among working-class and lower-middle-class folk in one generation becomes a sophisticated cultural option in the next generation.

But if this is true, then consider its implications for evangelical leaders. It may be difficult enough for evangelical leaders to come together across the Atlantic or in an international gathering such as the Lausanne Congress on World Evangelization. It is, it may be argued, even more difficult to foster understanding between unsophisticated believers who come from radically different cultural settings. Just as the Atlantic could serve as a filter for evangelical culture in the early nineteenth century, the gap between rich and poor, sometimes expressed as the polarity between Northern and Southern hemispheres, may make understanding and cooperation between plain evangelical folk even more difficult in our own time.

Methodist Revivalism in France, Canada, and the United States

James C. Deming and Michael S. Hamilton

Around the turn of the nineteenth century, Methodism began to expand beyond the shores of Great Britain into the United States and what is now Canada.[1] In this early phase of their missionary ventures, English Wesleyans concentrated much of their work in foreign communities that were Protestant by tradition but that, in the view of Methodist preachers and other evangelicals, were spiritually dormant if not apostate and were served by churches that were largely apathetic to people's religious needs.

The historical timing of this early period of Methodist expansion is significant. At the same time that Wesleyanism began systematically to expand beyond Great Britain, it was also formally establishing its

1. Research for this essay was assisted by a Research Development grant from Penn State University, a Research Fellowship from the Department of History of the University of Notre Dame, and a Zahm Research Travel Grant from the University of Notre Dame.

independence from the Church of England. As British Methodism developed its own ecclesiastical structure, however, an increasing effort was made to strengthen church discipline and to restrain what were increasingly seen by many in the Methodist hierarchy as the dangerous excesses of revivalism. Thus Methodism developed in rather contradictory conditions. While Wesleyan leaders were expressing serious reservations at home about revivals, Methodist preachers were hard at work coaxing widespread revivals into existence in North America and in trying to transplant revivals to foreign nations like France.[2]

The energetic efforts to spread revivalistic Methodism met with a variety of fates. Methodist evangelism had its greatest success in the United States, achieving growth rates in the early years of the republic that make new religions of the twentieth century, such as the Unification Church, look lethargic and disorganized in comparison. Methodism in Upper Canada (present-day Ontario), while not the phenomenon its southern cousin was, also did quite well for itself. By 1861 it had eased past the Church of England and the Presbyterians as the largest denominational family. Methodist missionaries had perhaps their least institutional success in France, where forty years of labor failed to establish a significant ecclesiastical presence.

Why did Methodism luxuriate in some contexts and languish in others? Having produced no important institutions, the Methodist mission to France has generally failed to interest historians.[3] Methodism in Upper Canada has generated a fair amount of historical attention, but it has focused less on how Methodism spread than on Methodism's impact on politics and its loss of revival fervor in the late nineteenth century.[4] And until recently, United States historians

2. This inconsistency within British Methodism has led some to argue that Methodist missions were designed to divert revivalist fervor to foreign missions. See, for example, Bernard Semmel, *The Methodist Revolution* (New York, 1974).

3. Studies of Methodist missions in France include William Toase, *The Wesleyan Mission in France* (London, 1835); Léon Maury, *Le réveil religieux dans l'Eglise Réformée Genève et en France (1810–1850): Etude historique et dogmatique* (Paris, 1892), 387–442; Daniel Robert, *Les Eglises Réformées en France (1800–1830)* (Paris, 1961), 362–64; Alice Wemyss, *Histoire du Réveil, 1790–1849* (Paris, 1977), 53–58.

4. On Methodism and Upper Canada's political questions, see H. H. Walsh, *The Christian Church in Canada* (Toronto, 1956), 137–41, 168–84; John S. Moir, *Church and State in Canada West: Three Studies in the Relation of Denominationalism and Nationalism, 1841–1867*

have been by and large unimpressed with Methodism's growth. Methodism had no overt involvement in key political events, so political historians have seen no reason to dally with them; religious historians, preoccupied with ecumenism and theological development, have found little to say about a sectarian movement whose entire theological history could retain Sydney Ahlstrom's interest for only four pages out of a thousand.[5]

Recently, however, scholars have begun to turn their collective attention to popular forms of religion, asking why particular movements have spread in particular times and places. Given this shift, a number of recent studies have begun to piece together how Methodists became the largest denomination in nineteenth-century America.[6] The details differ, but the large picture is more or less consistent. The early republic provided a uniquely open environment that included religious freedom, widespread egalitarian sentiment, and a highly mobile, individualistic population. To this environment Methodism brought an ideally suited set of characteristics, and the movement quickly spread across the land.

But how did Methodism fare in other, less open environments in the same period? How did it adapt to less mobile societies that valued hierarchical social arrangements, societies that wanted to retain connections between church and state, societies that linked religion and peoplehood? To answer these questions, this essay turns the usual order of analysis around. After a cursory description of Methodist

---

(Toronto, 1959); and the fine book by Goldwin French, *Parsons and Politics: The Role of the Wesleyan Methodists in Upper Canada and the Maritimes from 1780–1855* (Toronto, 1962). On the decline of revivalistic enthusiasm, see William Westfall, *Two Worlds: The Protestant Culture of Nineteenth-Century Ontario* (Montreal and Kingston, 1989), 50–81; and Marguerite Van Die, *An Evangelical Mind: Nathanael Burwash and the Methodist Tradition in Canada, 1839–1918* (Montreal, 1989), esp. 7–8.

    5. Sydney E. Ahlstrom, *A Religious History of the American People* (New Haven, 1972), 326–27, 477–78.

    6. William H. Williams, *The Garden of American Methodism: The Delmarva Peninsula, 1769–1820* (Wilmington, Del., 1984); Roger Finke and Rodney Stark, "How the Upstart Sects Won America: 1776–1850," *Journal for the Scientific Study of Religion* 28 (1989): 27–44; George M. Thomas, *Revivalism and Cultural Change: Christianity, Nation Building, and the Market in the Nineteenth-Century United States* (Chicago, 1989); Nathan O. Hatch, *The Democratization of American Christianity* (New Haven, 1989); John H. Wigger, "Taking Heaven by Storm: Enthusiasm and Early American Methodism" (paper given at the spring meeting of the American Society of Church History, University of Notre Dame, March 1992).

characteristics, it asks how these fared when transplanted to dissimilar early nineteenth-century cultural-political contexts, and how those differing circumstances in turn gave Methodism varying shapes. We begin with a brief overview of Methodism in the American environment, comparing this to Methodism's more limited success in the environment of Upper Canada. We then give more extensive attention to the radically different context of France, where Methodism had a surprising influence, despite its ultimate institutional failure.

The United States

The raw numbers alone seem to indicate that Methodism and the American environment of the early republic consummated a marriage made in heaven. In 1776, only 17 percent of Americans were affiliated with any church, and the Methodists could claim only 3 percent of these. In 1850, the number of Americans affiliated with a church had doubled, but by this time over one-third of them were Methodists. In absolute numbers, Methodist membership grew from 11,000 to 2.7 million, an increase of 25,000 percent during a period in which the American population grew 800 percent. In terms of growth, no other religious group even came close.[7]

Methodism possessed a unique set of characteristics that enabled it to thrive in the American setting. It utilized a dual preaching corps consisting of itinerants and local preachers. The itinerants, as militant and single-minded as any preaching force Protestant Christianity has ever produced, were brilliantly organized into a system of districts and circuits that enabled them to expand their influence quickly over long distances. The local preachers, exhorters, and class leaders kept Methodists spiritually and temporally organized in the intervals between the visits of the itinerants. Both types of preachers were by and large ill-educated laymen and laywomen who preached wherever they could get a hearing—in houses, rude chapels, barns, woods, and fields. They disdained the privileges and trappings of elite culture and preached a simple Arminian message of sin, salvation, re-

---

7. Finke and Stark, "Upstart Sects," 29–31.

vival, and holiness in the language and style of the common people, who made up the bulk of their audiences. They encouraged an emotional, affective religion and welcomed popular forms of spiritual ecstasy. They organized local groups of Methodists into "classes" that met frequently for mutual encouragement and accountability in the pursuit of holy living.[8]

These characteristics were not of American origin. They were all present in and central to British Methodism until at least the year 1800.[9] Transplanted to America, however, they flourished even more vigorously than they had in Britain. What, then, was unique about the American environment that made the early republic such fertile ground for Methodism? The short answer is that the early republic provided more open space for religious expression than did any contemporaneous society.[10]

Most obviously, the governmental structures of the new nation, eschewing any ties to particular religious expressions, opened up political space for popular religion. The religious pluralism that immigrants brought to the colonies, especially the Middle Colonies, undermined the determined attempts of Anglicans and Puritans to perpetuate the European pattern of linking church and state into an organic unity.[11] The decentralized nature of American government helped prevent such linkage from developing. Nor were there, in the years of the early republic, connections between religion and a national sense of peoplehood. In some places and times, such as Poland after World War II, national groups have made religion a central part of their collective identity even apart from any link to their national government. Americans, embodying such wide variations in national

8. Most historical attention has been focused on Methodism's colorful itinerant preachers, but the local preachers, often laymen and laywomen, outnumbered the itinerants and were an essential part of Methodism's success. See Nancy Christie, "'In These Times of Democratic Rage and Delusion': Popular Religion and the Challenge to the Established Order, 1760–1815," in *The Canadian Protestant Experience, 1760–1990*, ed. G. A. Rawlyk (Burlington, Ontario, 1990), 23.

9. Russell E. Richey makes this point in *Early American Methodism* (Bloomington, Ind., 1991), xiv–xv.

10. David Martin, *Tongues of Fire: The Explosion of Protestantism in Latin America* (Oxford, 1990), 4.

11. Richard W. Pointer, *Protestant Pluralism and the New York Experience: A Study of Eighteenth-Century Religious Diversity* (Bloomington, Ind., 1988), ix, 68–70, 144.

origin and regional difference, as well as religion, possessed a sense of national peoplehood far too weak to define any particular religion as un-American.[12]

Less obviously, the new nation offered a great deal of open spiritual space to any sect skilled enough to occupy it. Americans were a surprisingly irreligious lot. Church adherence at the time of the revolution, even in Puritan New England, was a mere 17 percent of the population.[13] To a large extent immigrants brought their religious patterns with them from Europe, and these were often Christian in only superficial ways. Americans were just as likely to hold a cluster of popular beliefs in spirits, visions, astrology, and the like.[14] This was a highly amorphous and unsystematized sort of spirituality, however, representing not so much a challenge to Christianity as a loose cluster of supernaturalistic beliefs available for people to draw upon in the absence of a more complete and compelling religious vision.

Along with the open political and spiritual space, the early republic possessed wide-open geographic space. As Frederick Jackson Turner pointed out a century ago, Americans rushed into unsettled lands far faster than their governments thought expedient—so quickly, and in such great numbers, that their social institutions were simply unable to keep up.[15] This was as true also of religion as it was of government. The Puritan and Anglican model of church organization demanded an educated clergyman stationed in a local church, adequately supported by tax revenues—a model wholly inadequate to the challenge of westward movement. Church leaders raised the alarm about irreligion on the frontier and pleaded for money and educated men to extend their ecclesiastical structures.[16] Their efforts, however, fell short of the challenge. The American West was to belong to the religious movements the established churches regarded as the sects.

12. John M. Murrin, "A Roof without Walls: The Dilemma of American National Identity," in *Beyond Confederation: Origins of the Constitution and American National Identity*, ed. Richard Beeman, Stephen Botein, and Edward C. Carter II (Chapel Hill, N.C., 1987), 333–48.

13. Finke and Stark, "Upstart Sects," 30.

14. Jon Butler, *Awash in a Sea of Faith: Christianizing the American People* (Cambridge, Mass., 1990), 67–97.

15. Frederick Jackson Turner, "The Significance of the Frontier in American History" (1893), reprinted in *The Turner Thesis Concerning the Role of the Frontier in American History*, rev. ed., ed. G. R. Taylor (Boston, 1956), 15–17.

16. Hatch, *Democratization of American Christianity*, 17–19.

Finally, the early republic offered an astonishing amount of free social space; that is, it was a society without hardened distinctions between social classes. The American Revolution propelled limited colonial impulses toward democracy, egalitarianism, and individual liberty to the forefront of a new American ethos that elevated and enshrined these values.[17] The hierarchical class structures of Europe, which reserved social leadership and privileges to educated elites, ultimately did not survive transplantation to America. This opened opportunities for religious leadership to non-elites and cleared space for popular forms of religion that ignored the decorum, polite manners, and emphasis on intellect that had been made integral to European Christianity.[18]

Methodism, transplanted from Britain, rushed into these open spaces like air into a vacuum. Methodists never assumed that the government should help them spread their religion, and they capitalized on long-standing popular dissatisfaction with churchmen who aspired to privileged partnership with the state.

Methodists were also much better equipped to deal with the weak religious state of the American people than most of their competitors. It is noteworthy that their most successful evangelical competitors would be the Baptists, who, like the Methodists, were ardent advocates for New Birth. Anglicans, Congregationalists, and to some extent Presbyterians assumed that the norm was for individuals to be included in the religious body politic. Every person was in the fold, unless they (scandalously) declared themselves to be out. Methodist and Baptist preaching, in contrast, assumed irreligion to be the norm and all individuals to be in need of conversion. Non-Methodist and non-Baptist clerics and churchgoers took great offense at this assumption, but it comported well with the American reality.

As to America's vast geographic space, it is hard to imagine an organization better suited to it than the Methodists. The only way Congregationalist Lyman Beecher could imagine christianizing the reli-

17. Gordon S. Wood, *The Radicalism of the American Revolution* (New York, 1992), 6–7, 240–43, 271–86; Michael Zuckerman, "A Different Thermidor: The Revolution beyond the American Revolution," in *The Transformation of Early American History: Society, Authority, and Ideology*, ed. James A. Henretta, Michael Kammen, and Stanley N. Katz (New York, 1991), 190–91.

18. Hatch, *Democratization of American Christianity*, 5–9.

gious wasteland of the American West was through a massive centralized campaign of missionary recruitment and formal education that would require a great deal of time and even more money.[19] Methodists, however, recruited preachers from among their new converts, gave them a bit of on-the-job training and even less pay, and quickly pushed them out to the peripheries of American settlement.[20]

Likewise, Methodist leaders aggressively pushed outward to the American social periphery. Methodists encouraged the emotion, visions, and belief in direct supernatural intervention so prevalent in popular spirituality, which their competitors usually derided as "enthusiasm." They took seriously the rhetoric of the American Revolution, bestowing leadership upon common people and setting up egalitarian societies at the local level. They even attempted, at first, to grant relative equality to women and African-Americans. The American social environment was not, however, completely open, and it was on the matter of race that Methodism reached the outer limits of its American social possibilities. Its initial impulse to demand that its adherents emancipate their slaves and treat free blacks equally proved incompatible with the American social context.[21]

The first generation of American Methodists took a different path than did their British cousins. Under the guidance of Francis Asbury, American Methodism consciously sought to remain a common people's church that valued revivalistic enthusiasm over social prestige. In contrast, much of British Methodism, by that time under the guidance of its second-generation leaders, moved away from its popular revivalistic roots in a drive toward greater social respectability. It became more establishmentarian, more decorous, more conservative. This change naturally produced schisms attempting to retain the original Methodist vision, but the dynamic era of British revivalism had ended.[22] The second generation of American Methodist leaders

19. Lyman Beecher, *An Address to the Charitable Society for the Education of Indigent Pious Young Men for the Ministry of the Gospel* (New Haven, Conn., 1814).

20. Hatch, *Democratization of American Christianity*, 140–41.

21. Ibid., 102–13; Butler, *Awash in a Sea of Faith*, 236–41; Wigger, "Taking Heaven by Storm."

22. Hatch, *Democratization of American Christianity*, 91–93; Julia Stewart Werner, *The Primitive Methodist Connexion: Its Background and Early History* (Madison, Wis., 1984), xi–xiii, 3–20.

also pushed their church up the social ladder, but with less effect on the overall character of American religion. After 1830 the Methodist Episcopal Church distanced itself from its revivalistic past, but this did not mean the abandonment of Methodistic revivalism. Instead, the essence of the movement relocated into the holiness and Pentecostal movements that splintered out of Methodism in the mid-nineteenth and early twentieth centuries. They carried on the Methodist tradition of emotional revivalism and eventually retransmitted it to other parts of the globe.[23]

Upper Canada

In the late eighteenth and early nineteenth centuries, Upper Canada was similar to the early republic in many ways. It was a vast land, largely unsettled by Europeans and their descendants until Americans, both Loyalists and so-called Late Loyalists, began to migrate north across the border. Upper Canada proved fertile ground for the Methodism that moved in with the settlers. But unlike the United States, Upper Canada became a battleground between the American and British versions of Methodism. The story of how Canadian Methodism eventually came to resemble more closely the British variant has much to do with conditions that prevailed in the environment of this district that later became Ontario.

The Methodism originally carried into Upper Canada in the last two decades of the eighteenth century was American in every respect. It employed the same dual preaching corps. The itinerants were almost all Americans, and the circuits were organizationally situated within an American conference. Its ethos was highly democratic and egalitarian, and it attracted people from the lower rungs of the social ladder. It demanded a personal conversion and called forth emotional and ecstatic responses from the converted.[24] At first, Methodism grew at the same dizzying rate in Upper Canada as in the United States. By 1810 the Methodists counted as members approximately the same percentage of the population in both Upper

23. Martin, *Tongues of Fire*, chap. 2.
24. French, *Parsons and Politics*, 39–48; Christie, "In These Times," 30.

Canada and the United States.[25] Methodism continued to grow vigorously in Upper Canada through the middle of the nineteenth century, but after 1815 it differed significantly in one respect from the American pattern of expansion. Methodism in Upper Canada failed to supplant the churches centered in elite leadership the way it had in the United States. As the population in Upper Canada multiplied, the Anglicans and Presbyterians continued to hold the allegiance of about one-fifth of the people apiece, while the Methodist share of the market increased slightly to about one-fourth of the population by 1861.[26]

Like America in its early national years, Upper Canada offered Methodism plenty of room to grow. There was a fair amount of political space, though for different reasons than in the United States. Upper Canada's British government sought to perpetuate the link between church and state through the Established Church of England, but before 1815 the government's reach was quite short. During the Methodist invasion of Upper Canada, colonial officials remained isolated from most of the population, and British officials were preoccupied with the Napoleonic Wars. Whatever restrictions might have been latent in Upper Canada's political arrangements or percolating in the minds of the tiny Loyalist elite, they did not at first keep Methodists from going about their business.[27] Restrictions tended to be petty annoyances, like the fact that Methodist clergy were not allowed to perform legal marriages until 1831.[28] Moreover, the first settlers did not bring a unified sense of religious peoplehood with them to Upper Canada. Perhaps eight of ten Upper Canadians had come from the United States, and they seem to have brought something

25. Roughly 2.5 percent. This figure should not be confused with adherence rates (the percentage of the churchgoing population attached to particular denominations), which are quite a bit higher for the evangelical churches. The Upper Canada figure is computed from French, *Parsons and Politics*, 39, 47, which in turn comes from George F. Playter, *The History of Methodism in Canada* (Toronto, 1862), 98, 106. The percentage for the United States is computed from C. C. Goss, *Statistical History of the First Century of American Methodism* (New York, 1866), 71–72.

26. This can be seen by comparing figures from the censuses of 1842, 1851, and 1862. Upper Canada census figures are reprinted in Moir, *Church and State in Canada West*, 185.

27. John Webster Grant, *A Profusion of Spires: Religion in Nineteenth-Century Ontario* (Toronto, 1988), 47, 85; cf. Christie, "In These Times," 14.

28. Grant, *Profusion of Spires*, 87–88.

like American-style religious pluralism with them, including a broad complement of denominations.[29]

Religiously and geographically, Upper Canada before 1815 closely resembled the United States. Essentially part of the larger westward American migration, the settlement of Upper Canada outpaced the progress of basic social institutions. For every immigrant with a firm denominational commitment, there were several who brought a more diffuse spirituality that would cohere only when channeled by a compelling religious infrastructure. This the Methodists did better than any other group in early Upper Canada. While parish-oriented denominations struggled in the wilderness, the Methodists, with their circuit system and dual preaching corps drawn from the laity, quickly pushed into the open religious and geographic spaces.[30]

Upper Canada also possessed a substantial degree of free social space. The artisans, tradesmen, and farmers who originally settled Upper Canada likely had little interest in building a society in which their social betters would lord it over them. This left them highly sympathetic to evangelicalism in general, and in particular to Methodism—an egalitarian, emotional form of Christianity preached in the language of ordinary people.[31] By 1812 more than half of Upper Canadian Protestants had adopted a form of Methodism that was, in the words of George Rawlyk, "more radical, more anarchistic, more democratic and more popular than its American counterpart."[32]

After 1815, however, the environment in Upper Canada changed. As Goldwin French has observed, Upper Canadian society as a whole, and many individual Upper Canadians, carried within themselves a "latent clash of ideals." On the one hand they valued egalitarianism and a society without privilege; but on the other hand they preferred to remain loyal to the British crown rather than give their allegiance to the American experiment in republicanism.[33] The War of 1812 brought this conflict to the surface. From that point onward,

29. Ibid., 36–67.

30. Ibid., 36; French, *Parsons and Politics*, 40.

31. Christie, "In These Times," 24–25.

32. George A. Rawlyk, "The Democratization of American Christianity: A View from the North," a paper delivered at the Organization of Historians of Early America, York University, July 1992.

33. French, *Parsons and Politics*, 40.

American democracy and republicanism became powerful negative reference points as Upper Canadians shaped their society.[34] The war also marked a dramatic shift in Upper Canada's social makeup. Before the war most immigrants came from the United States, and they tended to bring American ideals. But the end of the war marked the end of immigration from the United States and the beginning of mass migration from the British Isles.[35] Naturally, the new immigrants brought their religious ideas with them, strengthening the Anglican Church, the Presbyterian Church (largely Scottish), and the Roman Catholic Church. Finally, because the end of the war coincided with the end of the Napoleonic Wars, British authorities were able to turn more attention to solidifying Upper Canada's ties to the empire. Many argued that only a strong established church could provide the social glue that would keep Canada attached to the empire.

At this historical moment the British Wesleyans launched a missionary effort into Upper Canada that had two very self-conscious purposes. The first was to wrest organizational control away from the Canadian connection. The second was to push Upper Canada's Methodism in the direction British Methodism had taken after John Wesley's death—toward more decorum, orderliness in worship, political conservatism, and deference to the state. As one British missionary put it, the Canadian preachers were "so ignorant and enthusiastic as to render their discourses ridiculous in the ears of respectable and well-informed people."[36] Naturally, the Canadians resisted outside interference, and the two groups spent the next quarter century by turns at peace and at war. Neither side won a clear-cut victory, but in the end Upper Canadian Methodism was quite different from its American counterpart.[37]

Collectively, the changes in Upper Canada's environment had tended to reduce the amount of open space in which Methodism

34. Jane Errington, *The Lion, the Eagle, and Upper Canada: A Developing Colonial Ideology* (Montreal and Kingston, 1987). The thrust of Errington's argument is that Upper Canadians were always ambivalent about the United States. They shared much with Americans, especially the New England Federalists, and they valued much about America, but virtually all Upper Canadians believed that America's democratic republicanism was a governmental disaster.

35. Christie, "In These Times," 41.

36. Thomas Catterick (1820), quoted in French, *Parsons and Politics*, 72.

37. Rawlyk, "View from the North," 2–3, 9.

could operate. Upper Canada was still a wide open geographic land-scape. But the political space closed up considerably. Before the war it had not been difficult to be both Methodist and loyal to the crown, but during and after the war Methodists increasingly were put on the defensive to prove that their democratic religion was not fundamentally linked to democratic America. As Nancy Christie and Michael Gauvreau have recently argued, to become a Methodist in Upper Canada was a politically radical act, and it was recognized as such by Upper Canada's conservatives.[38] Likewise, the religious space had closed up. Immigrants, rather than representing a pool of potential converts, came with strong attachments to churches that still clung to older European notions of the organic unity of church and state. More important, the new immigrants brought with them the belief that religious identity was central to their sense of peoplehood. By the 1861 census an astonishing 98 percent of Upper Canadians claimed a denominational preference, almost all of whom reported being Anglicans, Presbyterians, Methodists, or Catholics.[39] To a lesser extent, Upper Canada's social space also contracted. The ideal of leadership by elites gained currency in theory and practice, and all the major denominations—Methodists included—began to place an ever-higher value on social respectability.

Though the mechanics of the shift differed, Upper Canadian Methodism seems to have followed the same generational pattern seen in British and American Methodism. The first generation was marked by a thrust to the social periphery by emotionalism, egalitarianism, and rapid growth among common people. The second generation is remembered for its reversal of direction and convergence toward the more respectable center. A settled and educated clergy, rising social status of its membership, stately urban church buildings, and a new interest in political participation were the prominent features of the new Methodism.[40] By the middle of the nineteenth century Methodism had taken its place beside the Anglicans and Presbyterians in what Mark Noll calls "a confluence of opposites," where the different

38. Christie, "In These Times," 36; Michael Gauvreau, "Protestantism Transformed: Personal Piety and the Evangelical Social Vision, 1815–1867," in *The Canadian Protestant Experience, 1760–1990*, ed. George A. Rawlyk (Burlington, Ont., 1990), 49.

39. Moir, *Church and State in Canada West*, 185.

40. Westfall, *Two Worlds*, 50–81.

denominations took on rather similar characteristics; they all were fairly voluntaristic, mildly conversionistic, and always socially polite. Rather than serve as a vehicle of cultural dissent, Methodism took up an insider's role in maintaining an orderly and harmonious society.[41]

France

The Methodist Missionary Society, formally organized in 1813, increased its evangelistic efforts in France following the defeat of Napoleon. There was reason to expect they would achieve success, at least among French Reformed Protestants, similar to that in America. Though persecution followed by revolution and war meant French Protestantism had been isolated from the rest of the world for more than a century, the French Reformed religious experience contained several features that could enhance the appeal of Wesleyan ideas and practices. By the early nineteenth century most in the Reformed Church had tacitly abandoned Calvinist predestination in favor of something more akin to Methodist Arminianism.[42] In addition, as with the origins of British Wesleyanism, there was a significant Moravian influence in French Protestantism, as several small groups of these pietists had settled among Calvinist communities in southern and western France as part of the Herrnhut diaspora.[43] Finally, French Protestantism had its own tradition of illuminism, emerging out of the traumas of the Revocation of the Edict of Nantes. Abandoned by their pastors and most of their lay leaders, poor Calvinist youths experienced visions and uttered dramatic prophecies exhorting their coreligionists to remain faithful to their religion and

41. Mark A. Noll, *A History of Christianity in the United States and Canada* (Grand Rapids, 1992), 205–10.

42. Much to the consternation of French Reformed leaders, this was pointed out by the bishop of Nîmes in a pamphlet published as French Protestants celebrated the three hundredth anniversary of the Synod of 1559, which established the Reformed Church of France. In this highly polemical piece he asked why they were celebrating the Synod of 1559 when they had "abandoned its doctrines and discipline" (Henri, Eveque de Nîmes, *Lettre aux protestants du Gard, à l'occasion de leur jubilé séculaire en mémoire du synode de 1559, Par Monsigneur l'évèque de Nîmes* [Nîmes, 1859], 4–5, Archives Nationales [henceforth AN] BB [18] 1598, n⁰. 1694).

43. Small groups of Moravians settled in the Gard around the towns of Calvisson, Congénies, St.-Hippolyte-du-Fort, and Sauve, as well as near Bordeaux (Robert, *Les Eglises Réformées*, 249–50; Wemyss, *Histoire du Réveil*, 13, 45–46, 84).

resist the Babylon of Roman Catholicism.[44] The influence of these *inspirés* declined as the Reformed Church began to reestablish a presence in France after 1715, but a prophetic tradition remained a strong element of French Reformed popular religion.[45]

In the early nineteenth century, however, the French Reformed Church had lost much of its vitality. The decades of persecution followed by political, social, and religious turmoil had greatly weakened its ecclesiastical strength and spiritual vigor. At the time of Napoleon's defeat there were only 243 pastors to serve a Reformed population of 500,340, or one pastor for every 2,059 Protestants. In the Department of the Gard, the region with the greatest concentration of Calvinists, this proportion worsened to one pastor for every 2,738. Compounding this clerical shortage was the pastorate's lack of enthusiasm and vigor. Many Reformed pastors of the early nineteenth century were the product of Enlightenment rationalism and were openly skeptical of the supernatural. As a result they tended to perform their duties perfunctorily, crafting as sermons sterile dissertations on philosophy and ethics. These conditions led one nineteenth-century observer to brand this period the era of Reformed slumber.[46]

This spiritual stagnation, considered in conjunction with the tacit Arminianism, Moravian influences, and spiritualist legacy of the

44. For more on these Huguenot prophets, see Clarke Garrett, *Spirit Possession and Popular Religion: From the Camisards to the Shakers* (Baltimore, 1987), 13–34. Garrett draws a direct link between early French prophetism and revivalism in England and America.

45. A possible revival of the physical manifestations of this tradition was a prominent concern of a report presented to the minister of religion on the influence that stories of ecstatic religious experiences in American Methodism could have on French Protestants (AN F[19] 10102, "Notes pour M. le Ministre [des Cultes], Paris, 29 novembre 1859"). Methodist missionaries in France, reflecting the conservatism of English Methodism under Jabez Bunting, tried to avoid such displays. Their restraint was evident in public references to these occurrences, such as the following: "The Lord has just spread his Spirit over a meeting of Methodists in Le Vigan in a manner that made his children see some marvelous things. Following a veritable 'Pentecost' several individuals found the peace of their souls, and the work continues" ("Réveil dans le Gard," *Archives du Méthodisme* 2 [1 décembre 1854]: 94).

46. Alfred Vincent, *Histoire de la prédication protestante de la langue française au XIXe siècle, 1800–1866* (Geneva, 1870), 4. On the influence of the Enlightenment on the pastoral corps of the French Reformed Church, see John D. Woodbridge, "The Reformed Pastors of Languedoc Face the Movement of Dechristianization (1793–1794)," *Problèmes d'Histoire du Christianisme* 13 (1984): 77–89. Figures for the Reformed population are based on data provided to the government by Reformed consistories, 1814 to 1817 (AN F[19] 10477–10478). The number of pastors comes from Robert, *Les Eglises Réformées*, 118.

French Reformed experience, characterized a French Protestantism that seemed ready for, and in need of, a Methodist style of revivalism. A spiritual awakening, known as the *Réveil*, did in fact occur. Its first indications emerged in the 1820s. During the 1830s the movement gained momentum; it then burst into full strength in the 1840s and continued on into the mid-1850s. Methodist missionaries, along with other foreign organizations, played an important part in initiating and propagating this religious renewal in French Protestantism. Yet despite years of effort, the Methodists ultimately failed to establish a significant ecclesiastical presence in France. In the United States, four decades of Methodist preaching produced a rapidly expanding church of over 150,000 members, but four decades of Methodist preaching in France yielded a stagnant church of only 1,200 members by 1857.[47]

At first the creation of a distinct French church was not a priority for the Methodists. Instead their mission to France at the end of the Napoleonic Wars was framed by two impulses. The first was a deep concern to cure French impiety, demonstrated by the excesses of their revolution and wars. The second was the general enthusiasm and sense of competition that characterized much of the missionary fervor of early nineteenth-century evangelicalism. The shocks to the English psyche of the French Revolution, followed by Britain's isolation as Napoleon sealed off the Continent, had acted as a significant boost to the spread of evangelical religion in Britain. The demise of the French Empire, combined with England's success at preventing revolution at home while persevering to victory abroad, was translated into a renewed conviction among British evangelicals about the rightness of their cause and a determination to spread their message throughout the world.[48]

47. AN F[19] 10102, report, "Actes de la 6e conférence des pasteurs et ministres de la section méthodiste de l'Eglise de Christ, en France et en Suisse unis de principe aux sociétés fondées par le Rev. Jean Wesley," 10. On the *Réveil*, see Emile Léonard, *Histoire générale du Protestantisme*, vol. 3 (Paris, 1964), 188–248; André Encrevé, *Protestants français au milieu du XIXe siècle: Les réformées de 1848 a 1870* (Geneva, 1986), 87–154, 239–312, 597–811; Maury, *Le réveil religieux*; Wemyss, *Histoire du Réveil*; James L. Osen, "The Theological Revival of the French Reformed Church, 1830–1852," *Church History* 37 (March 1968): 36–49.

48. The Reverend Richard Reese, preaching the preparatory service to the creation of the Methodist Missionary Society of Halifax, claimed, "A Gospel ministry has diffused a spirit of Christian benevolence through all ranks of society, which has given birth to institutions that are an honour to our country, and a general blessing to the World" ("Religious Intelligence," *Methodist Magazine*, January 1814, 74).

From this perspective France was particularly in need of this message. Rev. Jabez Bunting declared in 1813 before the Methodist Missionary Society at George-Yard Chapel, "Did not every British heart triumph in the victories recently obtained over French tyranny; and would not every Christian heart triumph in the success of those Missions over French infidelity and wickedness?" This was especially desirable, for, as a contributor to the *Methodist Magazine* argued, "Ignorance of the book of God, with the immorality and infidelity consequent on that ignorance, was the principle cause of the French Revolution." In the years that followed, several evangelical societies and agencies, not the least of which was the Methodist Missionary Society, sought to remedy this cause of French rebelliousness.[49]

Though Methodist missionaries wanted to begin the evangelization of France by proselytizing among French Catholics, circumstances quickly convinced them that, for the time being, this was not a practical option. Restoration France provided little of the space, cultural or physical, that North America did. France was an old, established, and densely populated country. Its social and political structure, though no longer fully aristocratic, was still quite hierarchical and limited. In addition, although the Charter of 1814 proclaimed freedom of worship, cultural traditions and an alliance of throne and altar that accompanied the return of the Bourbon dynasty still restricted Protestant liberties.

The Organic Articles, promulgated by Napoleon in 1802 and maintained by Louis XVIII, had, however, established the French Reformed Church under the state. Though the French Reformed community reflected many of the same cultural and physical restrictions of the larger society, within it the Methodists found at least the legal freedom for religious action that otherwise would have been impossible. The Methodists also came to see French Protestantism as a convenient starting point from which the gospel could later spread throughout the nation. In addition, once they began work among the Reformed communities, their evangelists found a more receptive audience than they had expected. This led them to concentrate further

49. For the Reverend J. Bunting on the creation of a Methodist Missionary Society at Hull, 24 November 1813, see "Religious Intelligence," *Methodist Magazine*, March 1814, 235; see also "Review of 'Bishop Milner's Charge,' &c," ibid., 189–98.

on reviving the spiritual vitality of French Reformed congregations, even to the extent that several Methodist missionaries assumed positions in the French Reformed Church.[50]

The contribution of these Methodist evangelists to the spiritual awakening that developed in French Protestantism was widely recognized within French Reformed circles. The highly respected pastor of Nîmes, Samuel Vincent, in 1829 wrote of their ministry:

> Whether by the nature of their doctrine, their superior wisdom, or by their personal character, they have shown themselves much more adept [than other missionaries]. They carefully avoided all that could harm or wound the pastors. They were more patient and made a greater effort to justify themselves, to make themselves understood, to dissolve the prejudices that could form against them, and to profit from all favorable circumstances that their zeal afforded them.

Two decades later, one of Vincent's successors observed, "It is evident that the fortune of Methodism is not a result of its theology as such. It is a result of its devotional fervor and its prodigious activity. . . . If the struggle with Catholicism does not entirely occupy it, it will sound the *réveil* from church to church."[51]

As their work began to bear results, however, space within the Reformed community became more restricted, and cooperation between leaders of the French Reformed Church and their Methodist counterparts eroded. This was partially a result of the greater respect for religious freedom that came with the overthrow of the Bourbons in the July Revolution of 1830. Methodists wanted to take advantage of the situation to carry their message to Catholic France. They were frustrated, however, by the reluctance of many in the Reformed

50. The leader of Methodist missions in southern France, Charles Cook, initially insisted on an independent Methodist presence but soon changed his mind and twice accepted pastoral positions in Reformed congregations (Jean-Paul Cook, *La vie de Charles Cook, pasteur méthodiste et docteur en théologie, par son fils* [Paris, 1862]). Others who assumed duties in the French Reformed Church were Armand de Kerpexdron at Mer (Loir-et-Cher) and Henri de Jersey at Caveirac (Gard) (Robert, *Les Eglises Réformées*, 376, n. 1). Methodists saw the risks of proselytizing outside the Protestant community when de Jersey was arrested and imprisoned in 1821 for preaching to French Catholics (Wemyss, *Histoire du Réveil*, 126).

51. Samuel Vincent, *Vues sur le protestantisme en France* (Nîmes, 1929), 243. *Correspondance Pastorale* n⁰ 147 (Juin 1844): 4. This was a newsletter edited by Ferdinand Fontanès, pastor at Nîmes, and circulated largely among theologically liberal Reformed pastors.

Church, remembering their historical vulnerability, to risk further antagonizing the Catholic majority.[52]

The growing division between the Methodists and the Reformed Church was also an indirect result of the success of the *Réveil* within the Reformed community. By the late 1820s and early 1830s many in the Reformed Church were increasingly concerned by the lack of spiritual vitality in their community.[53] But while most recognized that a religious revival was desirable and even necessary, a division emerged within the Protestant community between the awakened and those they regarded still to be spiritually asleep. Consequently, by 1836 discussions among Reformed pastors about how to revive their congregations had shifted to debates over whether the *Réveil* was strengthening the church or weakening it by sowing discord.[54] The divisiveness that accompanied the renewal led many to regard it, and those who spread it, with suspicion and hostility.

The more church leaders hesitated to embrace the awakening, however, the more the Wesleyans were convinced they needed to separate the regenerated from the apostates in the Established Church. Consequently, by 1830 those Methodists who had assumed positions in the national church had given them up.[55] They continued to evangelize aggressively among French Protestants, particularly in the Midi under the direction of Charles Cook, but now largely as competitors rather than as colleagues with their counterparts in the Reformed Church. As one French pastor complained, divisions in the church emerged only after the arrival of "strangers who claimed to preach the Gospel with more purity than the national pastors. This is a trap held out to some simple souls. Some of these strangers have used some reprehensible means in order to achieve their goal, and

52. In 1818, Cook noted the extreme reluctance of French Protestants to engage in any activity that might provoke the Catholic population (*La vie de Charles Cook*, 51–57).

53. For example, the newly created Pastoral Conference of the Department of the Gard met three times between May 1829 and May 1830 to discuss methods by which they might improve the devotional life of their parishioners (ADG 42 J 170, "Procés-verbaux de la Conférence pastorales du Gard," 3–18, séances du 27 mai 1829, 3 mars 1830, 26 mai 1830).

54. Ibid., 129–36, séance du 9 novembre 1836. Reflecting a division already existing among the pastoral corps, debate was often quite heated and failed to reach a resolution.

55. The only exception was de Kerpezdron, who, when pressed to abandon his position, instead tendered his resignation as a Methodist missionary and integrated fully into the structure of the French Reformed Church (Wemyss, *Histoire du Réveil*, 108).

have attacked the reputation of some estimable pastors."[56] Many others echoed this sense of betrayal. They had welcomed these Methodist preachers into their pulpits hoping to revive the spiritual life of their churches, only to have them try to lure away those on whom their preaching had its desired effect.

As would be expected, the French Reformed Church tried to defend itself from this threat. The easiest and most common measure was simply to end all cooperation. As one pastor declared, "The strangers who carried separatism into our churches began by preaching in them. They abused our confidence. Do they offer us their pulpits? We will no longer allow them to mount ours." The consistory of Nîmes institutionalized this approach by forbidding, "under any circumstances," the use of its facilities to all not belonging to the Established Church. It also barred its own pastors from taking part "in any religious meetings held in Nîmes by strangers or by pastors other than those of the Consistorial Church." It then sent copies of this regulation to other consistories, encouraging them to adopt similar measures.[57]

Occasionally the Reformed Church used its position as an established church to bring governmental pressure against the Methodists.[58] For most, however, this was a rather distasteful option, as it raised uncomfortable comparisons to the Reformed community's own experience with religious persecution. In addition, it contradicted the freedom of inquiry that most French Reformed held to be an essential of Protestantism. Thus, a Reformed pastor told the authorities, "I have no love for separatism, but I respect as an act of religious liberty all the faiths that do not trouble public order."[59]

56. ADG 42 J 170, 78, séance du 13 novembre 1833.

57. ADG 42 J 47, "Régistre des délibérations du Consistoire de Nîmes," 350–51, séance du 10 avril 1835; "Réglement particulier aux pastors, articles 1,3" (ADG 42 J 170, 85, séance du 5 mars 1834).

58. See, for example, the opposition of the Consistories of Valleraugue and St.-Chaptes to the government's authorization of Methodist services in their towns (ADG 1M 607, letters, le Vigan, 20 juin 1855 and 2 juillet 1856, "Pasteur Sarrut au Sous-Préfet du Vigan"; AN F[19] 10931, letter, St. Chaptes, 6 novembre 1859, "Louis Broussous, Pasteur/Président du Consistoire de St.-Chaptes au Ministre des Cultes," and "extrait de la séance du 20 octobre 1859").

59. ADG 1M 609, letter, Nîmes, 30 mai 1853, "Pasteur Gardes au Préfet du Gard." Pasteur Broussous, in conveying to the minister of religion the opposition of the Consistory of St.-Chaptes to a Methodist chapel in its region, wrote, "I hold deeply to the freedom of religion, to the freedom of inquiry, to the freedom of conscience, but the best of things can degenerate in evil"

It was not usually necessary for the Reformed churches to seek government action. French authorities, given the cultural tradition of religious monopoly and the British nationality of the missionaries, often took action against the separatists on their own initiative. A few consistories held true to principle and protested these infringements on religious liberty. Most, however, tried to pass over the issue in silence or, if necessary, formally declared their neutrality, arguing that since it did not directly involve the rights of the Reformed Church, its leaders did not have the authority to intervene. This allowed Reformed consistories to claim their hands were clean while the government protected their interests.[60]

Government authorities and Reformed leaders were not the only ones to take exception to the activities of Methodist evangelists. On occasion members of the general Protestant population pursued their own, usually rather direct, methods to discourage religious separatism. Charles Cook told of having doors slammed shut as he went by and of being pelted with stones as he made his way from one village to the next in the Reformed bastion of the Cévennes Mountains. Another Methodist pastor had a service he was conducting in Vauvert disrupted by several men, some the husbands of women in attendance, who broke in the door to the room in which they were meeting and chased him from the building. In Ganges, the presence of a Methodist missionary elicited several charivari, and finally a minor riot, until the prefect suspended all Methodist activity in the region.[61]

(AN F[19] 10931, letter, St.-Chaptes, 6 novembre 1958, "Pasteur/Président du Consistoire de St.-Chaptes au Ministre des Cultes").

60. The Consistory of Nîmes told the minister of religion that it did not believe it should be involved, as those affected "did not have a mandate from a consistory and therefore did not put the Reformed Church in cause" (ADG 42 J 48,223, "Copie de la lettre au M. le Ministre de la Justice et des Cultes"). Action was taken against the Methodists and other religious dissidents less often during the July Monarchy (1830–1848) than either before or after. Even then, the administrative correspondence reveals the discomfort even these liberally intended officials felt regarding religious independents. The American Baptist Missionary Society was so frustrated by this regime that they claimed François Guizot, prime minister of France from 1840 to 1848 and a devout member of the Reformed Church, was the tool of Roman Catholicism (William Gammell, *History of American Baptist Missions in Asia, Africa, Europe, and North America* [Boston, 1849], chap. 9, "France").

61. AN F[19] 10927, letter, Nîmes, 11 octobre 1843, "Préfet du Gard au Ministre de la Justice"; AN BB[18] 1414 n° 7056, letter, Nîmes, 28 aout 1843, Procureur-Général du Gard aux Gardes des Sceaux; AN F[19] 10927, letter, Ganges, 20 octobre 1843, "Henri de Jersey au Ministre des Cultes."

Ecclesiastical, governmental, and popular resistance against Methodist expansion is not by itself a sufficient explanation for Methodism's disappointment in France. The Wesleyans had met and overcome similar obstacles elsewhere, nowhere more dramatically than in their home country of England. The barriers they encountered in France proved more formidable, however, because of the crowd of historical memories that reinforced them, providing little space for ecclesiastical competitors. Nineteenth-century regimes tried to rule according to principles of religious freedom, but the weight of cultural assumptions, institutions, and experience still lay in the Old Regime merger of state and church. Religious monopoly was seen as an essential corollary to this.

Historically the Reformed community had suffered under this ideal, but it had also gained certain indirect benefits. Although Catholicism's control of religion meant the social and political exclusion and repression of French Protestants, their survival had required a high degree of solidarity behind the banner of the Reformed faith. As the institutional expression of that faith, the French Reformed Church became the guardian and unifying symbol of French Protestant identity. In this way the Reformed Church was a sort of mirror image in the Reformed community of the Catholic Church in majority society.[62]

In the nineteenth century French Protestantism was no longer threatened in the same way as it had been in the past. This relieved some of the pressure for confessional unity, allowing latent tensions to come to the fore. At the same time, however, communal memory still encouraged caution, as the Reformed community had experienced before how quickly their circumstances could change with a change in regime.[63] For this reason French Protestants were wary when it came to matters that might divide them, potentially weaken-

62. James N. Hood, "Revival and Mutation of Old Rivalries in Revolutionary France," *Past and Present* 85 (November 1979): 82–115; idem, "Protestant-Catholic Relations and the Roots of the First Popular Counterrevolutionary Movement in France," *Journal of Modern History* 43 (1971): 240–83.

63. Changes such as those from Henri IV's Edict of Nantes to Louis XIV's revocation of the Edict of Nantes, to the revolution's full toleration, to the Jacobin's campaign for dechristianization, to Napoleon's establishment of the French Reformed Church, to the White Terror following the second Bourbon restoration.

ing their ability to resist a new round of assaults. Religion was a particularly delicate matter in this regard, as it lay at the core of their communal and even individual identity.[64]

This protective reflex not only limited the space available for competing churches, it also left little room for significant reform within the Reformed Church itself. Twice in the 1830s the Consistory of Nîmes rejected a reorganization of its pastoral services, although nearly everyone recognized that it would strengthen the bonds between clergy and laity, thereby enhancing the pastors' effectiveness. But it was also feared the changes could weaken the connection between congregations and the Protestant community as a whole. The same concern lay at the heart of a refusal by the Protestant elite of Nîmes to support construction of a new church in a Protestant working-class quarter, even though there was a shortage of free seating at many of the worship services and many were concerned by the declining attendance of Protestant artisans. Even alterations in the rituals of worship had to be approached with caution. A pastor warned, "Among the people the worship service is entirely confused with the religion. To change it is to challenge religion itself." Then, reflecting the influence of the past, he continued, "Our church service is worthy of our veneration. It has been tested in the desert and sanctified by tribulation." Thus, though reforms may have possessed acknowledged merits, the sense of vulnerability and history carried by many descendants of the Huguenots often meant that reforms could not be risked.[65]

When it came to the open separatism of the Methodists, the danger was that much greater and more generally felt. The major of Saint-

64. Demonstrating this cultural attachment was the exchange between a Reformed pastor and a man seeking aid from him but who could repeat neither the Lord's Prayer nor the Apostle's Creed. When told he must not be a Protestant, the man cried, "Monsieur, I would cut myself into little pieces for my religion!" Another pastor observed, "Here everyone says they are ready to die for their religions, but too few seem willing to live for it" (Cook, *La vie de Charles Cook*, 55–56; Emilien Frossard, pasteur, *Tableau pittoresque, scientifique, et moral de Nîmes et de ses environs, vingt lieues à la ronde*, 2 vols. [Nîmes, 1834–35], 89). See also James C. Deming, "The Threat of Revival to a Minority Protestant Community: The French Reformed Church in the Department of the Gard, 1830–1859," *Fides et Historia* 21, no. 3 (October 1989): 68–77.

65. The Consistory of Nîmes rotated its pastors weekly from church to church and service to service. The proposed reform would permanently assign a pastor to a specific church and service.

Jean-du-Gard warned that Protestant dissidents, "in isolating themselves in private chapels do as much harm [to the public peace] as
they do to the interests of the national Church." In the same vein a
pastor urged the government to strengthen consistorial authority
over the religious affairs of the community, noting that "while the National Church is attacked from without [by Catholicism], it is tormented from within by the combined efforts of all the dissidents. In
front marches Wesleyan Methodism. Maintained by aid from England, it sends us missionaries and opens chapels wherever it can
bring together a few adherents." Another wrote:

> The dissidents are men for whom the Charter protects their liberty, and
> with whom we would not need to concern ourselves if it were not nec-
> essary to protect our population from their sectarian spirit and their
> maxim that it is necessary to have the same beliefs to live together in
> the same Church. Resolved to remain united in a single body, desiring
> that all our Protestants form a compact mass, most pastors guard
> against their narrow ideas. They do not want to see French Protestant-
> ism fracture into small sects without strength or means of existence.[66]

In this way those engaged in the battle against sectarianism called
upon their most potent weapon—the prospect of a Protestant community too divided to defend itself.

For leaders of the Reformed Church, however, the true challenge
derived from the fact that the Wesleyans ministered to an unmet need
felt by many within the Reformed community. The stagnation of spiritual life after the revolution and the religious sterility of much of its
pastoral corps found the Established Church ill equipped to meet the
demands of a Romantic age. This left room for the Methodist missionaries, who were Arminian, egalitarian, enthusiastic, and aggressive. It was not long before an awakening began to have effects that
threatened to snap the connection between the Reformed Church
and community, providing the cultural freedom in which alternative
religious communities could develop.

This potential was evident in the plethora of voluntary religious associations that emerged as the *Réveil* grew. Some of these were na-

66. ADG 1M 607, letter, St.-Jean-du-Gard, "Léon Molines, maire, au Sous-Préfet d'Alais."

tional in scope, such as the Société Biblique Française et Etrangère, created in 1833 after a dispute over the parent organization's refusal to distribute Bibles in Catholic communities. Many more associations were local in organization and concern, established to address regional matters such as orphanages, hospitals, apprenticeships, the distribution of religious literature, or local missions. These societies were a demonstration of a new vitality in French Protestantism and had the side benefit of helping to strengthen ties between various Reformed communities in the absence of government authorization for regional and national synods. This posed some inconveniences for the consistories, however, for though pastors and elders participated in these voluntary associations, they had no official standing or representation in the French Reformed Church. Yet frequently they addressed issues directly related to the church.[67]

More troubling at the local level were the private prayer meetings and worship services that formed within Reformed congregations as a result of the awakening. With the renewal of religious vitality, a portion of the Protestant community desired additional outlets for spiritual expression or were simply dissatisfied by the services offered in the Established Church. Sometimes these private groups included the local pastor, though perhaps more as participant than leader, but frequently they were inspired and led by Methodist evangelists.

Many in the church saw these prayer meetings as a direct threat to their authority. This was particularly true when some of those involved grew so bold in their independence as to take a public stand against Established Church authorities, or to approach the govern-

---

67. Other national societies were the Société des Traites Religieux (religious tracts), the Comité pour l'Encouragement des Ecoles du Dimanche (establishment of Sunday schools), the Société pour l'Encouragement de l'Instruction Primaire parmi les Protestants de France (encouraged primary education), and the *Réveil* des Interets Generaux du Protestantisme Français (an evangelical coordinating committee). See Robert, *Les Eglises Réformée*, 418–42; Frank Puaux, *Les oeuvres du protestantisme français au XIXe siècle* (Paris, 1893). By 1860, there were more than eighteen Protestant religious and charitable associations in the Gard, such as the Société d'Evangélisation pour les Protestantes Disseminés (evangelization of isolated Protestants), Société des Dames de l'Hospice (visited Protestants in the public hospitals), several Sociétés Protestantes des Prévoyance and Secours Mutuelle (mutual aid societies for workers), Comité de la Maison des Orphelines (for a Protestant orphanage), and Société de la Maison de Santé Protestante (a Protestant hospital) (ADG 6M 770, "Sociétés religieuses et de bienfaisance").

ment directly on matters concerning the church and faith. This forced the Consistory of Nîmes to take a public position on government restrictions on the freedom of Protestant worship elsewhere in France. Because so many private individuals and groups had already written governing officials, the consistory feared they would regard these independent statements "as the expression of Protestant thought, a situation the consistories cannot accept." Another consistory felt compelled to disband its entire diaconate in order to eliminate the influence of the "Wesleyans" within it. Other consistories frequently ignored the pastoral candidate favored by a local congregation and appointed another because they believed sectarians had seized control of the candidate search.[68]

Most in these private associations professed loyalty to the Reformed Church, if not its leaders. But the risk for the Established Church was that if it did not meet the spiritual cravings of its members, a significant number would feel their need for religious fulfillment was greater than the need for confessional solidarity and would join the separatists. To prevent this from happening, many in the Reformed Church recognized that defensive measures alone were not likely to be sufficient. "Say as often as you like," a pastor told his colleagues, "that the Methodists exaggerate and distort Christian piety, that they are intolerant and that they trouble the integrity of families; if you stop there you will not impede their progress among your flock." Instead, "the means to resist Methodism," Samuel Vincent told the Reformed pastorate, "was to do much of what it does, but do it in a larger and more enlightened spirit." His son-in-law and protégé Ferdinand Fortanès reinforced this view: "In an era of awakening, like that in which we find ourselves now, it is necessary to respond to religious needs with religion, not by combatting those who exaggerate devotion. . . . If souls do not find with you the nourishment for which they feel the need, they will search for it elsewhere, and then they will slip away from you. You will remain a good pastor, but a pastor without a

68. ADG 42 J 48, 216, séance du 1 décembre 1843; ADG V 491, "Correspondance relative au renouvellement des consistoires, 1812–1904," dossier Consistoire d'Aiguesvives, 1844. Between 1837 and 1842, seven of fourteen new pastoral appointments in the Gard were bitterly disputed by competing religious factions. Six of these were resolved only when the minister of worship intervened to restore order (ADG V 353–62, "Correspondance relative a la nomination, la confirmation et la presentation de serment").

congregation or a pastor of the indifferent."[69] Essentially these leaders were arguing that the challenge of Methodism required playing the Methodists' game by altering the tie between the Reformed Church and the Reformed community from one based on cultural tradition and defensive necessity to one of attraction and free association.

Gradually, as pastor and consistories saw a significant number of the most energetic and committed members in their congregations accept evangelical ideas and participate in independent services and institutions, they began to put this strategy into action. For example, the Consistory of Nîmes added two additional worship services in 1836 as a response to the following the Methodists were gaining in the city. These services demonstrated a new concern by the church to address their people's needs and circumstances. They were scheduled for Tuesday and Sunday evenings "so that those who work during the day could attend." They were to be biblical and short, "appropriate, as much as possible to manifested needs, and by consequence efficacious for maintaining union." The message should "expose in a practical manner the truths which hold the nearest to the saving of souls by Jesus Christ." The services were not to be as "solemn as those in the temples. There will be neither pulpit nor parquet. There will be neither cantor or reader. The service will not use liturgical prayers. The pastor is not to be in a robe. . . . He will speak seated or standing before the stage." These services were quite popular, with some complaints there was not enough room to hold all who would attend, while others warned the consistory that their success "only served to reveal how much the gap you wanted to fill remains despite this measure."[70]

In fact, the Consistory of Nîmes did not limit its reforms to these two services. As time passed, aspects of the evening services gradually replaced traditional rituals of worship, particularly in singing and preaching. In addition, the popularity of Methodist Sunday schools prompted the Reformed Church of Nîmes to revive and expand its

69. Samuel Vincent, *Mélanges de religion, de morale, et de critique sacrée* (Nîmes, 1820), 167.

70. An elder spoke against them, however, arguing that there was no guarantee that the services, "considered as a defense against Methodism, would not excite a renewal of ardor instead of preventing and arresting the evil" (ADG 42 J 47, 349–51, séance du 9 september 1836; ADG 42 J 71, E 35[1], "Deux petitions, du 9 novembre 1836").

own Sunday schools as well as other educational opportunities for children and adults of both sexes. The Pastoral Conferences of the Gard organized itself to provide religious services to Protestants in regions without an established congregation. In 1856, the Consistory of Nîmes finally restructured its pastoral service by assigning each minister a particular parish, and at the same time it began building a new temple in the working-class quarter of La Placette, four years after the Methodists had established a chapel and Sunday school in the same neighborhood.[71]

In other areas, the Established Church expanded social services considerably beyond what the Wesleyans could offer. Between 1840 and 1852 the Reformed Church of Nîmes increased direct aid to the poor by 42 percent. In 1842, the Consistory of Nîmes organized and underwrote a mutual aid society for Protestant workers, a project that was repeated by consistories in at least three other towns of the Gard. In addition, the Pastoral Conferences of the Gard, beginning in 1855, organized a series of day-long religious festivals each summer. These were held in various parts of the Protestant countryside and brought together pastors and congregations from several churches for a series of open-air services. From all indications they frequently became major events in the cultural life of rural Protestant communities.[72]

The reforms and expansion of services evident in Nîmes and the Gard were indicative of a general revival taking place in French Protestantism. From the mid-1830s on, the consistories of the French Reformed Church increased their efforts to reach out to the community through charitable and devotional societies.[73] The number of religious services also increased. Worship was made less formal. Hymns were sung along with the Psalms that had been chanted since the days of the Reformation, and sermons that spoke to the heart were substituted for those that dealt exclusively with theology and philosophy. Sunday schools became commonplace, catechistic training

71. ADG 42 J 47, 187, séance de 13 septembre 1835; ADG 42 J 170, séance de 30 mai 1838; ADG 42 J 49, 166–70, séance du 7 mars 1856; *Archives du Methodisme* 4 (1 juillet 1856): 71.

72. ADG 42 J 149, "Journaux des écritures du Consistoire de Nîmes, 1840–1847"; 42 J 96, "Budgets du Consistoire de Nîmes, 1847–59": ADG 42 J 48, 108–12, séance du 10 juin 1842.

73. Between 1840 and 1852 the amount spent on charity by the Consistory of Nîmes grew by 42 percent, from 25,873Fr to 36,754Fr (ADG 42 J 149, "Journaux des écritures du Consistoire de Nîmes, 1840–1847"; 42 J 96, "Budgets du Consistoire de Nîmes, 1847–1859").

was expanded, and the examination of catechumens prior to First Communion was more tightly regulated.[74]

To a great extent these reforms worked. Whether the motivation was a genuine concern to enhance the spiritual life of the Reformed community or simply to combat separatism among their parishioners, the pastors and elders largely were able to satisfy the religious needs of the Reformed population. This helped keep Protestant sectarianism from becoming more than a limited phenomenon. In 1857, after forty years of evangelization in a Reformed population of more than 500,000 and a nation of 40 million, the Methodist Conference of France counted 141 places of worship, 25 ministers, 65 local preachers, but only 1,272 members. Even among these, a large number likely also participated in the regular worship of their local Reformed Church, as the Consistory of Nîmes claimed.[75]

The North American environment was far more conducive to Methodist growth than was the post-Napoleon atmosphere of France. Compared with the resounding statistical success of Methodism in the United States and its surprising growth in Upper Canada, the attempt to transplant Methodism to France was a complete failure. Nevertheless, Methodism had an impact upon the spiritual vitality of the French Reformed Church. Methodist missionaries played a significant role in renewing the religious vigor of the French Reformed Church.[76] In the same manner that Methodist revivalism had

74. The minister of worship commented on this new vitality in French Protestantism in an 1857 letter to prefects. "For several years one has noticed in Protestantism, both in the churches recognized by the state and in the dissident sects, some tendencies toward propaganda and an ardor for proselytizing that the Protestants themselves qualify by the name of *Réveil* (ADG 1 M 609, letter, Paris, 25 avril 1857, "Minstre des Cultures aux Préfets").

75. The Consistory of Nîmes wrote the minister of religion, "Those who frequent these meetings [at the Methodist chapel] for the most part also attend the services of the national church, and nearly all communicate there on religious festivals" (ADG 42 J 60, "Consistoire de Nîmes—Rapport sur l'Eglise réformée de Nîmes, Gard. Envoyé sur sa demande à Monsieur le Ministre de l'instruction et des cultes en 1852," 31). The fact that most of the Methodist worship services were scheduled for days and times that did not conflict with the services of the local Reformed Church would seem to support this. See the petitions for government authorization to hold private religious services in ADG 1M 607.

76. It is not fair to go as far as Alice Wemyss in claiming the *Réveil* was essentially a foreign import to France. As this chapter shows, the preconditions for the awakening were present, and it may well have occurred without foreign assistance. It is worth noting that French Catholicism experienced a similar awakening during the same period (Wemyss, *Histoire du Réveil*, 7–9). On nineteenth-century Catholicism, see Gérard Cholvy and Yves-Marie Hilaire, *Histoire*

awakened isolated communities in Upper Canada and the United States, it helped pull French Protestantism from its isolation and religious torpor. Much of this was accomplished indirectly by threatening the religious integrity of the Reformed community and by forcing the Reformed Church to assume many of the practices and themes of Methodism and thereby renew itself or sink deeper into stagnation.

The Methodism transported abroad from Britain carried radical social implications that far transcended strictly religious renewal. It eschewed the established social conventions of all three areas, reaching into the lower social orders with a vision of egalitarian relationships among people and unmediated individual relationship with God. Ruling elites quickly came to see Methodism's radical nature, for it undercut the foundations supporting clerical authority and links between church and state.[77] Methodism elevated the authority of the individual conscience, and in so doing it stripped meaning away from established national and ecclesiastical social groupings. The community of the converted became the primary social reference group, set up in opposition to a corrupt society and an apostate church.[78] Ultimately, the French environment could not accommodate a force that threatened to tear the social fabric apart, and Methodism as a movement failed. After the War of 1812, the Upper Canadian environment circumscribed Methodism somewhat, but the movement still helped feed a powerful impulse toward social reform. In the United States, Methodism was left free to develop in an alternating pattern of conservative respectability and radical renewal that continued into the twentieth century.

---

religieuse de la France contemporaine, 1800/1880 (Paris, 1985); Thomas Kselman, *Miracles and Prophecies in Nineteenth Century France* (New Brunswick, N.J., 1984).

77. Christie, "In These Times," 14–18, 35; Gauvreau, "Protestantism Transformed," 49.
78. Westfall, *Two Worlds*, 42–45.

The United States and Britain: Modern History

A Christian Cosmopolitan

F. B. Meyer in Britain and America

Ian Randall

Frederick Brotherton Meyer (1847–1929) was a leading Nonconformist minister, holiness teacher, and social reformer who reached
the peak of his national and international career during the period
1890–1914, an era that represented the heyday of Free Church influence in Britain.[1] The uniqueness of Meyer's position in England was
that as well as being on the evangelistic and socially oriented wing of
evangelicalism, he also identified, from the mid-1880s, with the increasingly important pietistic and holiness stream that had its focus in
the annual Keswick Convention.[2] Meyer had a bridging and transdenominational role. Internationally, Meyer was known primarily as an
advocate of Keswick teaching, and by the turn of the century he was
Keswick's chief international spokesperson. As a result of his friend-

1. J. Munson, *The Nonconformists: In Search of a Lost Culture* (London, 1991), 2.
2. See D. W. Bebbington, *Evangelicalism in Modern Britain: A History from the 1730s to the 1980s* (London, 1989), chap. 5, for Keswick.

ship with D. L. Moody, an association that began in 1873, Meyer became widely known in North America as a holiness speaker. Moody's commitment to evangelism had made a deep and lasting impression on Meyer as a young Baptist minister. In turn, through invitations from Moody to address his Northfield conferences, Meyer introduced Keswick doctrine, with its emphasis on holiness and the filling of the Holy Spirit, to conservative North American evangelicalism.

Meyer's American ministry in the 1890s and beyond coincided with a time of change within the American evangelical community. Three new developments, each related in some way to the others, were significant.[3] First, there was a readiness to accept new teaching on the steps to holiness and particularly on the Holy Spirit. When, however, the twentieth-century Pentecostal movement began to give prominence to the gifts of the Spirit, many evangelicals, including Meyer, feared the threat of division. Although Meyer contributed to a heightened expectation of spiritual power, he remained ambivalent about Pentecostalism. A second feature of the period was the growth of the Social Gospel, a phenomenon that became identified with liberal, rather than evangelical, Christianity. In Britain Meyer was an advocate of the Social Gospel, but in America he seemed to play down social concerns. The final development, which was to affect much of North American evangelicalism, was the advance of fundamentalism. Although Meyer was close to the center of the considerably smaller British fundamentalist movement, he studiously attempted to avoid fundamentalist schisms. Meyer's goal, it should be stressed, was reconciliation, not fragmentation. His dream was of a vigorous and united international evangelical community.

Early Influences—Britain and America

William Brock, minister of Bloomsbury Baptist Church in central London and a leader among English Baptists in the later nineteenth century, was an important formative influence on Meyer.[4] One Sun-

3. For these developments, see George M. Marsden, *Fundamentalism and American Culture: The Shaping of Twentieth-Century Evangelicalism, 1870–1925* (New York, 1980), esp. 82–101.

4. F. B. Meyer, *The Bells of Is; or, Voices of Human Need and Sorrow* (London, 1894), 15.

day at Bloomsbury, Brock laid his hand on Meyer's shoulder and prophesied that he would be a minister.[5] Brock encouraged London Baptists to take a higher profile in city life,[6] and Meyer, coming as he did from an unusually wealthy background for a Baptist minister of his time, would have readily responded to Brock's approach to ministry. Brock also supported social endeavor through Bloomsbury's mission in the poor area of St. Giles,[7] an emphasis that Meyer was to develop. Following training in 1866–69 for the Baptist ministry at Regent's Park College, London,[8] under the respected principal Joseph Angus, Meyer spent two years in Liverpool as assistant/associate to another eminent Baptist minister, C. M. Birrell. From Birrell, Meyer imbibed the expository method of preaching, which was to sustain his later wide-ranging ministry.[9] Each of the major churches that Meyer served was to be a preaching center, and from the 1890s his London churches were to serve as springboards for his international teaching activities. Meyer was a product of mainstream Victorian Particular Baptist life in urban England.

A more profound influence on Meyer was to come from the United States. In 1873, when Meyer was in his second pastorate, at Priory Street Baptist Church, York, he encountered the American evangelist D. L. Moody. Together with Sankey, his co-evangelist/singer, Moody arrived virtually unheralded in York in June 1873.[10] After a largely uneventful first week of meetings, the Americans moved to Priory Street, and Meyer observed at first hand Moody's evangelistic tech-

5. W. Y. Fullerton, *F. B. Meyer: A Biography* (London, 1929), 13.

6. C. M. Birrell, *The Life of William Brock* (London, 1878), 169; I. Sellers, *Nineteenth-Century Nonconformity* (London, 1977), 14.

7. G. W. M'Cree, *William Brock* (London, 1876), 90; Faith Bowers, "Religion amongst the Proprieties of Life: George M'Cree and the Bloomsbury Domestic Mission," *Baptist Quarterly* 33, no. 1 (1989): 29–37.

8. Regent's Park, which was then in London, was regarded as the most prestigious of the Baptist colleges (J. E. B. Munson, "The Education of Baptist Ministers," *Baptist Quarterly* 26, no. 7 [1976]: 323). The only academic thesis previously produced on Meyer, a Th.D. by R. E. Nielsen, "An Appraisal of F. B. Meyer as a Preacher" (New Orleans, 1955), 97, states that Meyer did not have the advantage of seminary training but made up for this lack through diligent private study. In fact, Meyer gained a creditable London University B.A.

9. F. B. Meyer, *Jottings and Hints for Lay Preachers* (London, 1903), 74; idem, *Expository Preaching Plans and Methods* (London, 1910), 14; *Baptist Times*, 7 April 1927, 239.

10. J. C. Pollock, *Moody without Sankey* (London, 1963), 97–98.

niques and his expansive style.[11] Priory Street marked the beginning
of Moody's hugely successful 1873–75 British campaign. For someone from Meyer's English public school and conservative Baptist
background, informality in religion was likely to be distasteful, yet
Meyer was fascinated by Moody, seeing in him "a great and noble
soul."[12] Moody taught Meyer that he should not slavishly follow the
conventional patterns of ministry set down by others.[13] He should express his own personality.[14] It was a discovery that helped to shape
Meyer's subsequent role in international evangelicalism. The link
with Moody was crucial.

Following the Moody experience, Meyer saw significant expansion in his church but began to feel restless. His unease culminated
in a move, in 1874, to the wealthy Victoria Road Baptist Church in Leicester, in the English Midlands.[15] At an early stage Meyer attempted
to introduce a Moody-style appeal for decisions into a Sunday
evening service. The result was disastrous. Despite the staidness of
the setting eighty people responded and came forward, but a deacon
ran into the group shouting: "We cannot have this sort of thing; this is
not a Gospel shop."[16] His reaction was typical of the church leadership, and in 1878 Meyer decided to give up the unequal struggle.
Urged on by supporters, he began a new congregation, with a membership of seventy-seven people, meeting initially in buildings of the
Leicester Museum.[17] Meyer's vision was to implement the evangelistic priorities he had learned from Moody. The church, in Meyer's
view, should be primarily concerned to reach those outside its normal orbit, especially the working classes.[18] Melbourne Hall was built
to Meyer's specifications in a deliberately nonecclesiastical style.
During the 1880s it housed Meyer's Leicester congregations of 1500

11. J. F. Findlay, *Dwight L. Moody: American Evangelist, 1837–1899* (Chicago, 1969),
187, 208.

12. R. R. Darsley, *A Short History of Baptists in York, 1646–1987* (York, 1987), 17.

13. A. Chester Mann, *F. B. Meyer: Preacher, Teacher, Man of God* (London, 1929), 116.

14. Fullerton, *Meyer*, 32.

15. M. J. Street, *F. B. Meyer: His Life and Work* (London, 1902), 45; Mann, *Meyer*, 42. Meyer
described Victoria Road as a church in the "front rank" of the Baptist denomination (*The Christian*, 5 February 1925, 6).

16. J. H. Shakespeare in the *Baptist Times*, 4 January 1907, supp. 4.

17. Street, *Meyer*, 45–47.

18. Meyer, *Bells of Is*, 22.

people[19] and also provided a model that influenced British Nonconformist thinking about local church mission.[20] A whole range of organizations was developed, under the umbrella of the church, for evangelism, social welfare, and spiritual teaching.[21] British and American
influences, incorporating old and new emphases, were being fused.

International Evangelical

In 1891 Meyer made his first trip to North America, invited by
Moody to speak at the annual conference that Moody arranged and
hosted at Northfield, Massachusetts. Meyer described Northfield as
committed to scriptural truths and evangelical doctrine.[22] Moody's
platform was a broad one, and Meyer identified with the emphasis on
Christian unity.[23] Between 1891 and his death, Meyer crossed the her-
ring-pond, as he termed the Atlantic, nearly twenty times.[24] Moody's
personality was the initial attraction.[25] The bond between the two men
was strong.[26] Although North America held special appeal for Meyer,
he also expanded his ministry into Europe, and to a lesser degree to
Asia, South Africa, and Australia.[27] It is likely that he personally addressed more of the worldwide evangelical community of his day than
did any other British minister. Travel fired Meyer's imagination. Places,
as well as personalities, allured him. If he were dying, he said, he could
be brought to Northfield and given a new lease on life.[28] Through the
activity of leaders such as Moody, operating from strategic centers like
Northfield, Meyer envisaged the creation of a global evangelical network. He was, as he saw it, a key facilitator in this enterprise.

19. Ibid., 89.
20. Fullerton, in *Life of Faith*, 7 February 1912, 141, and in *Meyer*, 54–55, says that Melbourne Hall provided the inspiration for the Methodist central halls.
21. Meyer, *Bells of Is*, 23–24.
22. *The Christian*, 10 March 1897, 117. Meyer regarded Northfield as similar to the London
Mildmay Park conferences , at which he was a regular speaker.
23. W. R. Moody, *The Life of Dwight L. Moody* (London, 1900), 426.
24. *The Christian*, 5 March 1925, 20.
25. Meyer loved Moody's "mother-wit" and wanted his table talk recorded (ibid., 24 August
1899, 15).
26. Ibid., 5 March 1925, 20.
27. Fullerton, *Meyer*, 196–210.
28. *The Christian*, 28 August 1902, 18.

Meyer's British ministry was known for its evangelistic thrust, both locally, in the churches he led, and on a national scale, for example through the Simultaneous Mission organized by the Free Churches in 1901. Meyer was a central figure in what was regarded as the most intensive and concentrated evangelism ever seen in England.[29] When preaching in North America, Meyer's task was different. Evangelism was vital, but in America it was being done by others. Meyer therefore addressed the Christian population. He did give an evangelistic appeal at Northfield in 1891, and several people rose in response,[30] but by 1894 he was condemning the use of evangelists to try to bring internal revival to churches. The evangelist, he argued, was for people outside.[31] Three years later Meyer warned his American audience about the vogue for "getting up a revival," which was, he considered, a concept destined to end in disaster.[32] The message that Meyer brought to North America in the 1890s was directed to the revival of the church, but not by human organization. His call was to holiness spirituality, practical Christian living, reception of the power of the Spirit, and faithfulness to the Bible. More effective evangelism in America would, he believed, be a consequence of a revived American church.[33] Meyer had a strategic plan for American evangelicalism.

Although Meyer attempted to be specific in his American emphases, he did not restrict himself to a narrow constituency. In 1910 he was in Washington as president of the World's Sunday School Association and played a part in achieving the adjournment of the House of Representatives while he reviewed a parade of several thousand Bible Class men.[34] On that occasion, and again in the following year, he met President Taft. The year 1911 saw the Anglo-American Treaty of Arbitration, and as a consequence Meyer had contact with Asquith, the British prime minister, and with Taft, to whom he presented an il-

29. E. K. H. Jordan, *Free Church Unity: A History of the Free Church Council Movement, 1896–1941* (London, 1955), 72.

30. *The Christian*, 27 August 1891, 10.

31. Ibid., 6 September 1894, 12.

32. *The Life of Faith*, 10 March 1897, 117.

33. Ibid., 118.

34. *The Christian*, 16 June 1910, 31; Munson, *Nonconformists*, 201. Munson wrongly dates this incident as 1908.

luminated address from the English Free Churches and the British peace societies.[35] Amid much interest in Anglo-American cooperation, Meyer had asserted in 1905 that visits like his own did "a great deal towards cementing the union of the great Anglo-Saxon peoples."[36] Through such links across the Atlantic, Meyer's ultimate goal was the creation of a robust international evangelical community. Referring to the fact that he had introduced British Congregationalist G. Campbell Morgan to Moody, as a result of which Morgan moved to Northfield, Meyer commented that Britain's loss had been the immense gain of transatlantic Christendom.[37]

Holiness Influences

Meyer believed that evangelicalism would be invigorated through embracing holiness teaching. From its beginnings in the 1870s, the British holiness movement steadily grew until by the end of the nineteenth century it was exercising a worldwide influence on evangelicalism. The emphasis on the "rest of faith" or on "victory" was welcomed by weary or defeated evangelicals.[38] In 1874 and 1875 Meyer attended significant holiness conventions that were held at Oxford and Brighton, and he was especially impressed by addresses given by Hannah Pearsall Smith.[39] The Pearsall Smiths were Americans, described by Meyer as highly respected members of the Society of Friends. Quaker spirituality was one ingredient in the new movement that appealed to Meyer.[40] A second element was the Romantic ethos. It is no accident that the annual Keswick Convention, which became the hub of the British holiness movement, was located in Wordsworth's country. "The setting," as David Bebbington puts it, "was es-

35. *The Times*, 20 March 1911, 6; 24 March 1911, 6; 19 June 1911, 29.

36. *The Christian*, 18 May 1905, 10. See Munson, *Nonconformists*, chap. 7, for Nonconformists and the Anglo-Saxon world. According to Munson, men like C. H. Spurgeon, R. F. Horton, or Meyer were as famous in America as in England.

37. *The Christian*, 19 March 1925, 5.

38. Ibid., 8 January 1925, 5. See also J. Kent, *Holding the Fort: Studies in Victorian Revivalism* (London, 1978), 345; and D. W. Frank, *Less than Conquerors: How Evangelicals Entered the Twentieth Century* (Grand Rapids, 1986), 141.

39. *The Christian*, 2 August 1917, 8; 1 January 1925, 6.

40. For the influence on Meyer of his maternal grandmother, Ann Sturt, who was a Quaker, see Fullerton, *Meyer*, 11; Street, *Meyer*, 10–12; Mann, *Meyer*, 22.

sential to the experience."[41] Meyer was a thoroughgoing Romantic. For him, Wordsworth and all his followers were students in the school of Jesus Christ.[42] Meyer himself came into a decisive experience of the power of the Holy Spirit on a Keswick hillside in 1887, after an earlier experience of consecration in 1884.[43] From the late 1880s Meyer became a major leader in the Keswick enterprise. He was distinctive for his practical teaching, for his position as Nonconformity's most outstanding representative on a predominantly Anglican Keswick platform,[44] and for his prodigious travels, through which he probably did more than anyone else to spread the Keswick message worldwide.[45] Meyer's first visit to Northfield, in 1891, was with this as his objective.

Moody invited Meyer to Northfield because of Keswick. According to Meyer, Moody had met a man while he was in England who was "one of the driest preachers possible," but who had been transformed at Keswick.[46] Moody was impressed. This was what America needed. Moody was favorably inclined toward Keswick's teaching on the fullness of the Spirit, since he had undergone a deep experience, not unlike a "second conversion,"[47] two years before the York mission. He gave a private account of this to Meyer, on whom it made a deep impression.[48] A tendency toward sentimentality can also be seen as something predisposing Moody to Keswick's Romanticism. In no sense did Meyer think he was the first to take holiness teaching to North America. He was himself indebted to the Pearsall Smiths and noted the contribution of the Boardmans, another American couple in the holiness camp. But Meyer was convinced that only in Keswick teaching had the different strands of holiness been "woven into a sys-

---

41. Bebbington, *Evangelicalism in Modern Britain*, 168.

42. F. B. Meyer, *Elijah and the Secret of His Power* (London, 1888), 168.

43. Fullerton, *Meyer*, 56–58, 65–67. Meyer spoke on many occasions about these experiences, which appear in numerous issues of *Life of Faith* and *Keswick Week*, from the 1890s to the 1920s.

44. W. H. Griffith Thomas, in C. F. Harford, ed., *The Keswick Convention* (London, 1907), 233.

45. W. B. Sloan, *These Sixty Years: The Story of the Keswick Convention* (London, 1935), 33; S. Barabas, *So Great Salvation* (London, 1952), 186.

46. *Life of Faith*, 10 March 1897, 117.

47. Findlay, *Moody*, 132.

48. *Life of Faith*, 18 April 1917, 393.

tematized form."[49] He was aware that Northfield and its associated conferences—Niagara and Ocean Grove—treated the theme of the "inner life," or subjective experience, cautiously. There was fear of the doctrine of sinlessness, or entire sanctification, and a perceived need to counter such perfectionist ideas.[50] Indeed Meyer had been told before going to the United States to avoid the word "holiness" because of its perfectionist connotations.[51] Undeterred by gloomy prognostications, however, Meyer set about delivering the message about holiness in a packaging that would prove to be acceptable to conservative American evangelicals.

Keswick Apostle

As a Keswick ambassador, Meyer was a diplomat. Coming from an activist and socially committed Free Church background, he had quickly endeared himself, from 1887, to pietistic Anglican audiences at Keswick. He now addressed the task, in 1891, of reassuring American Presbyterians and Baptists—two important groups at Northfield—that holiness could be respectable. In England, he announced, many have been "much worried with people who say they don't sin."[52] In fact sinless perfection was an insignificant doctrine in Britain, but Meyer wanted to woo Northfield to his side. He asked: What are we to do with sin? The answer was to reckon yourself "dead to the whole thing." Here was the heart of Meyer's approach. It was about faith, not feeling. The promises of God about deliverance from sin were simply to be "claimed." There were some protests at Meyer's teaching, but George Marsden's conclusion that the extent of the opposition has been overstated is justified.[53] Meyer was actually judged a huge success. Presbyterian minister T. L. Cuyler reported in the *New York Evangelist* on the spiritually hungry crowds, who would

49. *The Christian*, 12 March 1925, 5.
50. Ibid., 10 September 1891, 11.
51. *Life of Faith*, 10 March 1897, 117; and Harford, *Keswick Convention*, 160.
52. *The Christian*, 27 August 1891, 10.
53. E. R. Sandeen, in *The Roots of Fundamentalism: British and American Millenarianism, 1800–1930* (Chicago, 1970), 176, mentions the protests at Northfield about Meyer's teaching. Marsden, in *Fundamentalism*, 249 n. 36, argues that the extent of the controversy regarding Meyer has been overstated by hazy recollection.

not be satisfied with less than three addresses each day from Meyer, the "lion of Northfield."[54] Meyer believed that he had found what his friend R. C. Morgan described as virgin soil for teaching the inner life,[55] although Moody in fact had already prepared the ground without using Keswick terminology.[56] Cuyler, commenting on Meyer's role as a leading man in the Keswick school in England, perceptively remarked: "But while he is a man of poetic temperament, and a profound mystic . . . he is a thoroughly practical teacher; and instead of devout dreaming . . . he exhorts his hearers to work hard for the rescue of perishing souls."[57] At Keswick Meyer brought a practical emphasis to an existing holiness movement, while at Northfield he was—as far as he could see—the first to offer the successive steps to holiness: consecration, cleansing, and the filling of the Spirit, as systematized by Keswick.[58] Northfield gave Meyer the opportunity to act as a transatlantic Keswick pioneer.

Return visits to Northfield were guaranteed. It became a feature of several of Meyer's summers in the 1890s to go direct from Keswick to Northfield, and then to a similar convention at Blankenburg in Germany. Meyer's dream may well have been of Northfield as an American Keswick, although Moody would never have identified exclusively with one strand of teaching. Meyer remarked in 1892 that, like Keswick, Northfield's beauty was "a worthy setting for the conference, and in close harmony with the devotional character of the meetings."[59] The year 1892 saw Meyer working particularly closely with the American Baptist leader A. J. Gordon, as together they guided people into "consecration and the filling of the Spirit."[60] Meyer was delighted to hear "many testimonies" to the effect that his 1891 teaching had "revolutionized many lives." His 1892 strategy was to

54. *The Christian*, 3 September 1891, 13.
55. Ibid., 20 August 1891, 9.
56. Marsden, *Fundamentalism*, 78–79.
57. *The Christian*, 3 September 1891, 13.
58. Ibid., 12 March 1925, 5; 25 August 1892, 13.
59. Ibid., 25 August 1892, 13. Meyer's only complaint, when he reminisced about Northfield, was the "overcrowded and dusty" American (railway) cars, where seats had to be shared and there was no "cushioned back on which to rest back, head or neck." Meyer compared this with England's "comfortable railway carriages" (F. B. Meyer, *Reveries and Realities; or, Life and Work in London* [London, 1896], 17).
60. *The Christian*, 1 September 1892, 11.

give his audience more of the same. "I gave the message with which I had been entrusted from the Keswick Convention," he declared.[61] He emphasized that he was not teaching that the old sinful nature was eradicated (as in Wesleyan thinking) but that it was "kept as torpid as serpents and toads are kept in winter."[62] Meyer welcomed the interest being taken in truths that had been associated with "errors and extravagances."[63] Oblique references like these were presumably to the radical holiness elements in American Methodism.[64] By 1894 a band of teachers at Northfield shared Meyer's position, including A. C. Dixon, J. Wilbur Chapman, George Needham, Gordon, and A. T. Pierson, and together they discussed tactics for advance.[65] There was still, in Meyer's view, a great lack in America of what he termed—with overtones of spiritual imperialism—"the inner life as taught in England."[66] Meyer was surveying the evangelical ground still to be taken.

At the 1896 Northfield convention, Moody began to make plans to promote Meyer in the New York area.[67] The suggestion that in the late 1890s efforts were made, with Moody's approval, to dissociate Northfield from Keswick does not seem to be consistent with Moody's sustained support for Meyer.[68] In 1896 Moody announced to Meyer that Northfield was waiting to be led (by implication, through Meyer) into the promised land.[69] Following Meyer's 1897 visit Moody reported that it was now "much easier to preach."[70] Keswick teaching had evangelistic side-effects. During that tour Meyer wrote to his British audience, from Boston, to say that any prejudice against "the teachings promulgated at Keswick" had disappeared, with the principal points

61. Ibid., 25 August 1892, 13.
62. Ibid., 8 September 1892, 14.
63. Ibid., 25 August 1892, 13.
64. For background, see V. Synan, *The Holiness-Pentecostal Movement in the United States* (Grand Rapids, 1971), chap. 2. In 1921, during his later American ministry, Meyer spoke to one thousand students for a week at the summer school of the Methodist Episcopal Church (*The Christian*, 25 August 1921, 10).
65. Meyer, *Reveries and Realities*, 22. The strategy was to emphasize "deeper truths," as well as to reaffirm "the old doctrines of the Cross."
66. *The Christian*, 30 August 1894, 9.
67. Ibid., 3 September 1896, 18.
68. Findlay, *Moody*, 412n.
69. *The Christian*, 3 September 1896, 18.
70. Fullerton, *Meyer*, 39.

now being, as far as he could judge, accepted.[71] In 1899 the spiritual tide at Northfield was still rising, according to Meyer.[72] Despite Moody's death that year, Meyer continued the link with Northfield.

Inevitably Meyer's relationship with the United States changed after this point, but the establishment of a holiness ethos went beyond any one individual. Meyer recognized the importance of A. B. Simpson, the Christian and Missionary Alliance leader, and had many discussions with him. In 1905 Simpson criticized Meyer for an address in which Meyer had suggested that "the regenerated man by gradually and steadily yielding his being to God would become so filled with the Spirit of God that Christ would at last be formed in him just as the embryo in the egg gradually absorbs the viscous matter of the egg and at the end of a certain period becomes a living bird."[73] This, countered Simpson, was not possible without the "crisis" of a "distinct supernatural addition to our life," a baptism of the Holy Ghost. In fact Meyer did teach such a baptism, although he accepted the fact that in at least one aspect of his teaching on holiness, he was at variance with Simpson. Meyer believed that the self-life was not "extirpated" but was kept in "absolute subjection," and he considered that Simpson went further than this in the direction of entire sanctification.[74] Meyer contended, however, that the experience was much the same and found American Christians amenable to his experiential approach to spirituality. North America provided Meyer with some of his most satisfying achievements as a Keswick apostle.

"Undenominational" Baptist

Keswick was explicitly undenominational. Its motto was "All one in Christ Jesus." Nevertheless, denominationalism could not be ignored. Meyer, as a Nonconformist/Baptist leader, was crucial at Keswick as a demonstration that the holiness message was for all, not

71. *Life of Faith*, 3 March 1897, 104.
72. *The Christian*, 24 August 1899, 15.
73. A. B. Simpson, editorial, in the *Christian and Missionary Alliance Weekly*, 27 May 1905, 321. I am grateful to Charles Nienkirchen, the author of *A. B. Simpson and the Pentecostal Movement: A Study in Continuity, Crisis and Change* (Peabody, Mass., 1992) for pointing me to this passage.
74. *The Christian*, 19 March 1925, 6.

just for Anglicans. Meyer's encounter with Moody had radically altered his denominational perspective. He entered into a "wider, larger life," turning away from what he saw as "mere denominationalism."[75] The love of God, he came to believe, "knows no favored sect."[76] Meyer was strongly committed to the Baptist doctrine of believer's baptism, but the "rite of Immersion," for him, had to be totally independent of questions of "church order and discipline."[77] His thinking on baptism and denominationalism was highly individualistic, which probably aided his acceptability in North America. It was suggested that Meyer had immersed more members of other denominations, including Anglican clergy, than any other English Baptist minister.[78] Meyer became president of the Baptist Union in 1906 and in addition had an important place on the international Baptist stage, but he was a Baptist whose vision was primarily transdenominational.

In 1891, when Meyer began his American ministry, he was minister of Regent's Park Chapel, a London Baptist Church with a uniquely upper-middle-class congregation. His influence in the English Baptist Union in the previous few years had been growing. Perhaps most significantly, he had introduced Keswick's emphases into the denomination through the formation, in 1887, of a Prayer Union for Baptist ministers.[79] By 1890 an enthusiastic supporter of Meyer could announce that the Prayer Union was bringing under its influence "the entire ministry of our denomination."[80] It does not seem that at Northfield Meyer directed particular attention to Baptists, although he was undoubtedly impressed by the freedom given by Moody to A. J. Gordon to baptize five people in a lake during the 1894 Northfield conference. Thousands watched the event.[81] This would have been unthinkable at Keswick. Meyer was once accused of breaking an unwritten rule at Keswick by distributing Baptist tracts and urging rebaptism.[82] At Northfield one of those baptized was a Methodist minister who,

75. Meyer, *Bells of Is*, 17.
76. F. B. Meyer, *The Call and Challenge of the Unseen* (London, [1928]), 61.
77. F. B. Meyer, *Seven Reasons for Believers' Baptism* (London, 1882), 3.
78. Street, *Meyer*, 85.
79. *The Freeman*, 20 May 1887, 336; 30 September 1887, 629; 2 December 1887, 801.
80. *Life of Faith*, 9 May 1890, 306.
81. *The Christian*, 30 August 1894, 9.
82. J. C. Pollock, *The Keswick Story* (London, 1964), 104.

Moody informed Meyer, would probably continue in his present ministry. Meyer approved of the "greater liberty" he found in America.[83] Less rigid ecclesiastical attitudes gave greater scope for new directions, especially in terms of the understanding of holiness Meyer wished to introduce.

Interdenominational Holiness

Meyer's American ministry followed Moody's nondenominational approach, but he was also able to take to North America his British experience, which showed that with judicious handling, holiness teaching could be spread within mainline denominations. During his 1897 American tour Meyer spoke to ministers in Boston, New York, and Philadelphia and to general audiences of around three thousand in the Tremont Temple, Boston, and in the Carnegie Rooms, New York.[84] He took the opportunity to expose "exaggerated and unsound views" of holiness.[85] Presbyterian ministers seem to have been predominant, and Meyer knew the importance to the Presbyterian tradition of sound doctrine, having been brought up on what he called the "juicy doctrines of grace," which were characteristic of Calvinism.[86] He may well have seen himself as especially equipped to convince leaders of doctrinally oriented American denominations of the truth of the Keswick system. In Britain Meyer was regarded as uniquely able to communicate with ordinary people and lead them into spiritual power.[87] It gave him, therefore, additional satisfaction to influence American evangelical policy-makers. Moody helped by publicizing Meyer's books in advance of the meetings.[88] Meyer's usual

83. *The Christian*, 30 August 1894, 9.

84. *Life of Faith*, 10 March 1897, 117–18. Meetings in Boston were arranged by Dr. Lorimer; in Philadelphia Meyer spoke in Wilbur Chapman's Bethany Church.

85. *The Christian*, 11 March 1897, 10.

86. F. B. Meyer, preface to *The Directory of the Devout Life* (London, 1904). Meyer is referred to as a Presbyterian by R. M. Anderson in *Vision of the Disinherited: The Making of American Pentecostalism* (Oxford, 1979), 44.

87. F. S. Webster, in *Life of Faith*, 25 July 1917, 813.

88. Ibid., 10 March 1897, 117; Fullerton, *Meyer*, 41. It is clear that Moody went to considerable lengths to introduce Meyer to ministers. In 1894 he wrote to Meyer to say that he was building his new Northfield auditorium seating 2,500 and that he wanted Meyer to lecture in it for thirty days. Moody promised to get ministers there "by the hundreds" (Fullerton, *Meyer*, 39, quoting a letter from Moody dated 31 March 1894).

approach was to speak for about an hour to ministers, showing "our position on controverted points."[89] He then invited questions, dealing typically with about twenty.[90] In Boston, where he was questioned by four hundred ministers, Meyer reported that all knelt together at the end of his meeting.[91] He reveled in an audience of five hundred ministers in New York, describing it as a great body of divinity.[92] Cuyler was involved in sponsoring meetings, in his New York Presbyterian church, and again Meyer was questioned to ensure that his teaching was theologically and biblically sound.[93] For Meyer, the high point was when "venerable servants of Christ" stopped questioning and "melted under the power of God."[94] Meyer believed that the most important contribution he could make to American denominational life would be to ensure that spiritual experience became paramount.

Meyer's visits to America in 1899, 1900, and 1901 saw him exploiting growing opportunities among denominational leaders. There was a large delegation of Presbyterian pastors at Northfield in 1899, as well as Methodists, Baptists, and Congregationalists.[95] In addition, Meyer addressed the New York Presbytery and was delighted to find the hold that Keswick teaching was taking in the United States.[96] W. R. Moody supervised Northfield following his father's death in 1899. Meyer commented that in 1900, under W. R. Moody, the convention was one of the best and that there was "evidently a great movement among the ministers of the Evangelical Churches in the States."[97] These ministers included clergy from, in Meyer's words, distinguished pulpits. It was clearly more conservative and Reformed denominational life, rather than existing holiness elements, that Meyer touched. Indeed Meyer indicated that the only opposition he received in America was, perhaps conveniently, from perfectionists of

89. *Life of Faith*, 24 February 1897, 90.

90. Ibid., 3 March 1897, 104. Meyer described the questioning as "intelligent, reverent, and appreciative."

91. Ibid., 10 March 1897, 117.

92. Ibid.

93. Fullerton, *Meyer*, 43–44.

94. *Life of Faith*, 10 March 1897, 118.

95. *The Christian*, 24 August 1899, 22.

96. Ibid., 31 August 1899, 16.

97. Ibid., 23 August 1900, 11; 30 August 1900, 20.

the "old school."[98] Through supportive ministers, Meyer had the opportunity to conduct a preaching tour in the southern states in 1901. Meyer, the interdenominationalist, was thrilled that invitations came from local ministerial associations.[99] In his 1901 tour, which included Richmond, Atlanta, and Cincinnati, Meyer was accompanied by Moody's lieutenant, R. A. Torrey.[100] Meyer was able to report that many ministers were planning to visit Keswick.[101] The holiness movement was, as Meyer had hoped, bridging across national and ecclesiastical divides.

Social Activist

Meyer's commitment to holiness did not mean, as it tended to do with other Keswick leaders, that he withdrew from the world. He believed churches should "save souls" and "right social wrongs."[102] During his Leicester ministry Meyer met, over a period of years, between 4,500 and 5,000 former prisoners, with the aim of helping in their rehabilitation.[103] He set up in business as "F. B. Meyer, Firewood Merchant" to give former convicts employment.[104] Temperance issues also occupied Meyer's attention. His temperance campaigns were marked both by agitation and by positive efforts to reclaim alcoholics.[105] In 1921 Meyer expressed pleasure that American churches had been influential in the fight for Prohibition. The Christianity of "this wonderful country," he concluded, "is neither dead nor sleeping."[106] For him, effective social action was a fruit of spiritual life.

From 1892 to 1907, while minister of the undenominational Christ Church, set in the middle of some of South London's poorest areas, Meyer launched significant sociopolitical initiatives. His aim was

98. Harford, *Keswick Convention*, 160.

99. *Life of Faith*, 6 March 1901, 127. Meyer was probably also pleased to pioneer the South at a time when most British ministers avoided it (Munson, *The Nonconformists*, 194).

100. *Life of Faith*, 3 April 1901, 200.

101. Ibid., 17 April 1901, 241.

102. *The Times*, 22 June 1907, 12.

103. Meyer, *Bells of Is*, 89–90.

104. Ibid., 102.

105. For background, see D. W. Bebbington, *The Nonconformist Conscience: Chapel and Politics, 1870–1914* (London, 1982), 46–51.

106. *The Christian*, 25 August 1921, 10.

that Christ Church should be a center in which all classes of people would be able to meet together to worship, and in America Meyer used his success in attracting congregations of 2,500 drawn from all levels of society as an object lesson to prove that separate mission halls were not needed.[107] A huge "institutional church" network of organizations or societies was formed, and Christ Church was reckoned to be "probably the biggest thing of its kind in London."[108] At the hub of the outreach was Meyer's Sunday afternoon Brotherhood, which grew to eight hundred men.[109] This working-class congregation expressed Meyer's belief in a new social and spiritual reality, a brotherhood.[110] Meyer also achieved the closure of between seven and eight hundred local brothels during 1805 1007.[111] This period saw Meyer becoming increasingly involved in party politics. Like many Nonconformists, he campaigned for the election of a Liberal government in 1906. He vigorously opposed Tory policy to support church schools from public money, calling it "absurd and retrograde."[112] Meyer's political activity alienated some of his Keswick supporters, but he was able to show British evangelicals that spirituality could undergird social activism.

In America, Meyer appears to have formed the view that the churches tended to overemphasize social questions. For many years, he asserted in 1897, the American pulpit had been given to sensational instead of expository preaching, and a certain proportion of preachers had given their people "the muddy waters of political and social debate."[113] One instance that appalled Meyer was that of a minister who had preached eight sermons on suicide. How, Meyer wondered, could a herald of eternal life be so pressed for subjects?[114] In 1905 Meyer was still lamenting the fact that the pulpit

107. Ibid., 16 May 1907, 11; 1 June 1905, 12.

108. Interview with H. G. Turner, Meyer's private secretary, on 19 July 1899 (Booth Collection, London School of Economics Archives, B271, 79).

109. Street, *Meyer*, 92; Fullerton, *Meyer*, 108; Turner, Booth Collection, B271, 85.

110. Meyer insisted on the term "brothers," not "brethren." The latter term he described as a "cant expression" used by clergymen when only women were present (*British Weekly*, 19 October 1905, 37).

111. *Free Church Year Book* (London, 1908), 179.

112. *Christian World*, 12 June 1902, 3.

113. *Life of Faith*, 10 March 1897, 117.

114. *The Christian*, 6 September 1894, 12.

"across the water" was reflecting the current life of the time, rather than dealing in systematic exposition of the Bible, which was, he pronounced smugly, "the characteristic of the English pulpit," and he was also wary of the way the institutional church was being emphasized in America, issuing a caution that the religious elements could be overwhelmed.[115] In Britain he was insisting, in 1904, that he had no sympathy with Christians who spoke only of heaven "while the wrongs of earth are unredressed."[116] In 1906 Meyer was anticipating righting of wrongs that made a few rich and many poor. Along with this Meyer looked for the redemption not only of individuals but also of the state,[117] and he affirmed, in 1908, that the "humanitarian side" of the gospel was coming to the fore.[118] Meyer's gospel was a social one. It seems that when in America, however, he rarely diverged from the position adopted by Moody, which was that the transformation of individuals would eventually produce social change.[119]

One social issue that Meyer addressed more directly through his American visits was race. In 1901 Meyer visited the cotton plantations. He was pleased, he reported, to be able to hold services for blacks. Meyer referred tactfully to the fact that they did not attend meetings with whites, but he became increasingly aware of the feelings of black people about the ban they suffered. He talked to black ministers, who he said were often highly educated.[120] Meyer had seen racial demarcation in British India, which made him reluctant to pronounce on America's "sore problem." His hope was the fundamentally spiritual one that God's power would raise the status of African-Americans.[121] The enthusiastic responses of black southerners to his messages fascinated Meyer, but on one occasion he asked one of the "Aunties" to moderate her interjections, as they were unduly exciting his congregation. She stopped crying out, observed Meyer, and con-

115. Ibid., 1 June 1905, 12. As an example of the decay of religious life. Meyer was horrified to find that in one American town the ministers had come to an arrangement with baseball organizers by which tickets for Sunday evening baseball games were issued only to those who came to Sunday morning services (*The Christian*, 30 June 1910, 29).

116. *British Weekly*, 17 March 1904, 611.

117. *Baptist Times*, 27 April 1906, 308.

118. *Free Church Year Book*, 33.

119. Marsden, *Fundamentalism*, 37.

120. *The Christian*, 11 April 1901, 16; *Life of Faith*, 10 April 1901, 220.

121. *The Christian*, 11 April 1901, 16.

tented herself with rocking to and fro.[122] Probably the American racial situation strengthened Meyer in his subsequent stance on the issue. By 1906 he was sufficiently stirred up by events in South Africa to say that the term "niggers" was damnable.[123] In 1908 Meyer spent a winter in South Africa, subsequently writing a book in which he condemned repressive racial policies, praised the "Christianized and educated" native peoples, and suggested a forum to give Africans a voice, though with whites retaining a veto.[124] During his visit Meyer was delighted to meet Gandhi and promised him support in his passive resistance campaign.[125] Back in Britain, in 1911 Meyer managed to stop a world boxing prizefight between a black and a white, on the grounds of its brutality but also, significantly, its potential to create racial tension.[126] Meyer admitted during this well-publicized crusade that he considered the races were "differently constituted,"[127] but his underlying belief was that religion had the power to bring the world to a new racial kinship.[128]

Holy Spirit Preacher

During the 1890s Meyer's Keswick and Northfield ministry placed increasing stress on the Holy Spirit. Meyer confessed to his Northfield hearers in 1891 that at one time he could not endure too much preaching about the Holy Spirit.[129] He then went on to address the subject in such a way as to make it acceptable at Northfield.[130] First he made a persuasive appeal to millenarians, suggesting that God was preparing for the second advent, and that at the end of the dis-

---

122. Ibid., 4 April 1901, 15; 11 April 1901, 16. Meyer admitted that some southerners found him "rather stolid."

123. *British Weekly*, 3 May 1906, 80.

124. F. B. Meyer, *A Winter in South Africa* (London, 1908), 152, 179, 201.

125. *British Weekly*, 16 July 1908, 358.

126. Meyer's battle was chronicled in *The Times* (see issues of 18 September 1911, 5; 20 September 1911, 4; 21 September 1911, 5; 22 September 1911, 6; 29 September 1911, 7). For an account of this episode, see S. Mews, "Puritanicalism, Sport, and Race: A Symbolic Crusade of 1911," in *Studies in Church History* 8 (1972).

127. *The Times*, 22 September 1911, 6.

128. F. B. Meyer, *Religion and Race-Regeneration* (London, 1912), 60–62.

129. *The Christian*, 3 September 1891, 10.

130. The points that follow are recorded in *The Christian*, 3 September 1891, 11.

pensation people might be "filled with the Holy Ghost" as happened in that "first blessed age." It was a "Latter Rain" vision. Second, he brought in the historical context by referring to John Wesley's experience. Third, Meyer was at pains to show that his teaching was Bible-based and Christ-centered. Just as electricity passes along the wire, he explained, so the Holy Ghost passes through the Word. Seeking the Holy Spirit apart from Scripture spelled trouble. The Holy Spirit also came from Christ, who received the Spirit for the whole church and in whom, Meyer argued, was each person's "share of Pentecost." Meyer's appeal to people not to take the train home from Northfield until they had claimed the gift seems to have been heeded, since in 1892 Meyer reported that everyone at Northfield in 1891 had received a "most gracious in-filling of the Holy Ghost."[131]

In 1893 Keswick was beginning to become nervous about differences of exposition in messages on the Spirit.[132] A conference of Keswick leaders, Meyer recalled, decided to restrict the word "baptism" to the Spirit's outpouring at Pentecost and to use the words "filled" or "anointed" to describe the experiences of individual believers.[133] It is not clear when this position was officially defined, but it was probably around the turn of the century. Keswick wanted to emphasize its moderation, by contrast with the more sensational views about Spirit baptism that were being formulated.[134] Meyer clearly did not feel bound by Keswick's ruling, since from the 1890s to the 1920s he used "baptism" with reference to contemporary experiences of the empowering of the Spirit. In 1897, for example, Meyer related how ministers in Boston received "an overwhelming baptism of the Holy Spirit,"[135] and at Keswick in 1922 he was still unashamedly preaching baptism in the Spirit.[136] Meyer appears to have been more inclined in America than he was in Britain to call for public response to his teaching on the Spirit. He probably enjoyed being free from au-

131. Ibid., 1 September 1892, 11.
132. Ibid., 10 August 1893, 9.
133. Ibid., 19 February 1925, 15.
134. See D. W. Dayton, *Theological Roots of Pentecostalism* (Grand Rapids, 1987), 87–108. Meyer defended the baptism-filling distinction in 1900 (F. B. Meyer, *John the Baptist* [London, 1900], 85).
135. *Life of Faith*, 10 March 1897, 117.
136. *Keswick Week*, 1922, 114.

diences bound by British reserve. At meetings in Richmond in 1901, Meyer reported that nearly everyone remained at an after-meeting to wait for an anointing of the Spirit[137] and that a whole assembly stood up "to claim the fulfillment of the promise of Pentecost."[138] Meyer was evidently in full flight, speaking three times a day to audiences of between three and four thousand in Chattanooga and Louisville.[139] His teaching was a factor in pointing the way toward new conceptions of the Spirit's power.

Preaching on the baptism of the Spirit helped prepare the way for twentieth-century Pentecostalism. A second element, also associated with Meyer, that contributed to Pentecostalism was the Welsh revival of 1904–5.[140] Meyer had contact in 1903 with some young Welsh ministers whom he persuaded to come to a convention at Llandrindod Wells in 1903 at which he was a speaker.[141] He saw this convention as a "seed-plot" of the revival,[142] although he denied allegations that he claimed to be the revival's originator.[143] It was through observing Evan Roberts, the enigmatic hero of the revival, that Meyer experienced a world in total contrast to "stereotyped religious forms."[144] In 1905, Meyer took to America the message about the power he had seen released in Wales. In Los Angeles he spoke for eight days, twice a day, to audiences of over three thousand. One of those present—on 8 April 1905—was Frank Bartleman, who was to be a central figure in the Pentecostal explosion in Azusa Street in 1906. Bartleman was stirred as Meyer "described the great revival going on in Wales."[145] Meyer went on to Portland, where he found that people who were tired of "cranks," "fads," and "perfectionists"

137. *The Christian*, 4 April 1901, 15.
138. *Life of Faith*, 10 April 1901, 220.
139. *The Christian*, 18 April 1901, 11.
140. For the Welsh revival, see R. B. Jones, *Rent Heavens: The Revival of 1904* (London, 1931); and E. Evans, *The Welsh Revival of 1904* (Bridgend, 1979).
141. Jones, *Rent Heavens*, 27–28: B. P. Jones, *The King's Champions* (Cwmbran, 1968), 48; B. P. Jones, *The Spiritual History of Keswick in Wales, 1903–1983* (Cwmbran, 1989), 7, 8.
142. *The Christian*, 26 March 1925, 5.
143. *Daily News*, 2 January 1905, 3.
144. *The Christian*, 12 January 1905, 11. See also Anderson, *Vision of the Disinherited*, 44.
145. F. Bartleman, *How Pentecost Came to Los Angeles* (Los Angeles, 1925), 11. Also Anderson, *Vision of the Disinherited*, 64–66. For Meyer's report on his Los Angeles meetings, see *The Christian*, 4 May 1905, 23.

accepted his teaching.[146] Again he spoke about the Welsh revival.[147] After ten weeks and 14,600 miles of traveling, Meyer concluded that there was, in America, "a tidal wave of Revival" about to roll over the land.[148] For some at least, Wales, with Meyer's tales of "Spirit-baptized ministers," visions, and "days of Pentecostal overflowing,"[149] was the precursor of a new, worldwide Pentecost.

A crucial question with which Meyer had to grapple when Pentecostalism arrived was whether gifts of the Spirit, such as tongues, were still to be expected in the church. In the late 1880s he was ambivalent, suggesting that the special gifts of the apostolic age were for a limited period and purpose,[150] but also hinting that they could have continued if the church had been more faithful.[151] When he was in Estonia in 1902, Meyer heard at first hand from Baron Uexküll, a Baptist leader, about experiences of speaking in tongues and deliverance from evil spirits that were taking place in local congregations. Meyer was impressed by the testimonies given.[152] In 1905 he associated the Welsh revival with Paul's teaching on the supernatural gifts of the Spirit in 1 Corinthians 12.[153] After 1906, however, the reaction from Meyer's circle to the growth of Pentecostalism became increasingly negative. Horror stories abounded, and there was great fear of division.[154] By 1912 Meyer was prepared to commend the fiercely anti-Pentecostal stance taken by a fellow Baptist, W. Graham Scroggie.[155] Toward the end of his life Meyer's position moderated, and he was careful not to condemn all use of tongues, but he remained doubtful about the Pentecostal movement.[156] Meyer always thought of himself

146. *The Christian*, 18 May 1905, 10.

147. Ibid., 19 March 1925, 6.

148. Ibid., 1 June 1905, 12.

149. Ibid., 26 March 1925, 5.

150. Meyer, *Elijah*, 183.

151. F. B. Meyer, *Christian Living* (London, 1888), 102.

152. *The Christian*, 27 February 1902, 19; 6 March 1902, 18.

153. Ibid., 12 January 1905, 11.

154. In 1907 and 1908 Jessie Penn-Lewis, with whom Meyer at times worked closely, wrote articles against Pentecostalism in *Life of Faith* and in *The Christian*. M. N. Garrard, in *Mrs. Penn-Lewis: A Memoir* (London, 1931), 228, indicates that Meyer supported this line.

155. Letter from Meyer to Scroggie dated 24 August 1912, a copy of which is held in the Donald Gee Centre, Mattersey Hall, Mattersey, North Dorchester, United Kingdom.

156. Meyer's mature position on pentecostalism is found in Meyer, *Call and Challenge of the Unseen*, 63–64.

as part of mainstream evangelicalism. When faced with a choice between the Keswick/Northfield axis and Azusa Street, his decision was never in doubt.

Fundamentalist?

With his background as a unifier, Meyer was hardly likely to be a supporter of the kind of hard-line fundamentalism that emerged in America and, to a much lesser extent, in Britain.[157] From the 1880s Meyer was mixing a great deal in premillennial circles, which provided a seedbed for fundamentalism, but it was not until 1917 that he openly aligned himself with the premillennial movement.[158] Indeed, in 1904, Meyer toyed with the idea that the second advent had taken place in A.D. 70.[159] Moody was a premillennialist, and this view was part of the accepted teaching at Northfield.[160] Cuyler, reporting on the 1891 Northfield conference, said that while premillennialism was not his position, he enjoyed "the rapture" (the pun seems unintended) with which people sang about it.[161] Meyer's friend Gordon advanced the thesis that Baptists were committed to premillennialism by their history and approach to Scripture.[162] For a long time, however, Meyer remained cautious. Neither did he comment to any great extent, when in the United States, on the issues behind fundamentalism. In 1899 he did proffer the view that America had pursued higher criticism and had seen the "waste and horrid Sahara" that resulted.[163] Meyer took a rather different line in Britain, arguing in 1904 that the

157. For a treatment of British fundamentalism, see D. W. Bebbington, "Baptists and Fundamentalism in Inter-War Britain," in *Protestant Evangelicalism: Britain, Ireland, Germany, and America c. 1750–1950: Essays in Honour of W. R. Ward*, ed. K. Robbins (Oxford, 1990).

158. Fullerton, *Meyer*, chap. 16. For premillennialism and fundamentalism, see Marsden, *Fundamentalism*, 5; Sandeen, *Roots*, 207.

159. *British Weekly*, 29 December 1904, 333: *Christian World*, 22 November 1917, 10; 29 November 1917, 7.

160. Marsden, *Fundamentalism*, 38. Meyer recalled meeting C. I. Scofield at Northfield. The latter was famous for the Scofield Reference Bible, which did much to popularize dispensational premillennialism (*The Christian*, 5 March 1925, 20). Sandeen suggests that millenarians did not speak at Northfield during 1887–1893 (*Roots*, 175), but the premillennial coming was regarded as part of Northfield's creed in 1891 (*The Christian*, 10 September 1891, 11).

161. *The Christian*, 3 September 1891, 13.

162. E. B. Gordon, *A. J. Gordon* (London, 1896), 356.

163. *The Christian*, 31 August 1899, 16.

conflict over criticism was about the "outer husk" of the truth.[164] His concern was to maintain spiritual unity between evangelicals who differed in their degree of acceptance of critical theories.

Meyer's attitudes changed perceptibly after 1917, the year when, with the backing of leading Keswick figures, he launched the Advent Testimony movement in Britain.[165] He was coming to believe that the present age was heading for dissolution[166] and that the true church was but a remnant, distinguished from the unfaithful church by its adherence to prophetic truth and to Scripture.[167] This definition has clear fundamentalist overtones. But Meyer was still a reconciler. He had to work hard to keep together the historicist and futurist wings of British premillennialism.[168] Meyer's Advent Testimony movement upheld biblical inerrancy and thus was close to being a fundamentalist group,[169] but Meyer himself was not a fundamentalist. He deplored debates not carried out in Christian love,[170] was open to scientific inquiry and accepted evolution,[171] and refused to become involved in battles for the Bible.[172] Meyer was ideally placed to lead a conservative uprising in Britain, but, like Moody, he had no love for theological controversy.[173] Also, Meyer was on friendly terms with all the major Free Church leaders in Britain and many of their Anglican counterparts and was not prepared to alienate himself from them. Meyer's stance was an important reason why British evangelicalism did not see a major fundamentalist split.[174] On his visits to America in the 1920s Meyer

164. F. B. Meyer, *In the Beginning God!* (London, 1904), 197.

165. Accounts are in the *Monthly Bulletin of the Advent Preparation Prayer Union* (hereafter, *MBAPPU*), June 1919, 1; *Advent Witness*, December 1923, 135–36; *Advent Witness*, January 1925, 1. The premillennial manifesto that appeared in the British Christian Press caused considerable controversy. See *Christian World*, 8 November 1917, 7; 15 November 1917, 7; 13 December 1917, 11.

166. *MBAPPU*, September 1919, 26.

167. *AW*, June 1926, 95.

168. *MBAPPU*, December 1919, 51; *AW*, February 1921, 161; *Life of Faith*, 23 December 1925, 1564. For background on the variations within premillennialism, see R. G. Clouse, ed., *The Meaning of the Millennium: Four Views* (Downers Grove, Ill., 1977).

169. *Advent Witness*, May 1923, 59.

170. Meyer, *Directory of the Devout Life*, 188.

171. *The Freeman*, 9 January 1891, 19; *Baptist Times*, 24 December 1909, 935.

172. *Regions Beyond* 47 (1926): 58.

173. Marsden, *Fundamentalism*, 33.

174. See D. W. Bebbington, "The Advent Hope in British Evangelicalism since 1800," *Scottish Journal of Religious Studies* 9, no. 2 (1988): 108–9.

was not impressed by the fundamentalist offensive. "Religious people," he said in 1926, were "sick of the conflict" between fundamentalists and modernists because of the spirit in which it had been conducted.[175] Sandeen is incorrect when he suggests Meyer was one of those who intensified fundamentalist militancy.[176] In 1927, Meyer's affinity was clearly with those outside the hostilities who longed for the "deeper aspects of spiritual truth."[177] Both in Britain and America, spirituality, rather than strict doctrinal purity, was Meyer's priority.

Despite his coolness toward aspects of American fundamentalism, Meyer had contacts within North American evangelicalism that enabled him to continue his ministry there in the 1920s. He was particularly pleased with a visit to Canada in 1925, which he described, with characteristic enthusiasm, as the greatest thing of his life.[178] He crossed the Atlantic again in 1926 and 1927. At this stage his teaching included talks on the second coming,[179] although Meyer tended to emphasize premillennialism less in North America than he did in Britain. He knew that across the Atlantic the subject had received a great deal of exposure, and he would also have been wary of the dominance of futurism in America. The possibility, in the American context, of unity between futurists and historicists was not strong.[180] Meyer was glad that a movement similar to British Advent Testimony was being formed in Philadelphia in 1926, but he was more excited at the opportunity he had there to expound the truths of "spiritual fellowship with God" and of Pentecost.[181] In 1927 Meyer spoke in all but two Canadian provinces and in six states. He could still draw audiences of 2,500 people. On this occasion Meyer remarked: "I fear whether the influence of so-called Modern thought may not, as in Britain, be seriously affecting the united influence of the Christian Church."[182] Meyer's instincts were still inclusivist. His was not the spirit of fundamentalism.

175. *The Christian*, 16 September 1926, 12.
176. Sandeen, *Roots*, 233–35.
177. *Baptist Times*, 3 November 1927, 733.
178. Ibid., 28 May 1925, 385. Meyer met the Canadian prime minister and Earl Haig.
179. *The Christian*, 19 August 1926, 11.
180. Sandeen, *Roots*, 208–25.
181. *The Christian*, 9 September 1926, 14.
182. Ibid., 4 August 1927, 10; 22 September 1927, 10.

Conclusion

Meyer's ministry represents an amalgam of American and British influences, which he blended in such a way as to bring together an emphasis on practical evangelism and an equal stress on holiness spirituality. Through his strategic approach, his interdenominationalism, and his links across the evangelical spectrum, Meyer operated, to a large extent, as the British equivalent of Moody. He differed from Moody in being a local church leader with an expository ministry, in his position within his own denomination and British Free Churches generally, and in his willingness to become involved in political affairs. When in America, however, Meyer generally devoted himself to acting as an apologist for the Keswick variety of holiness teaching, which he saw as the key to the renewal of evangelical vitality throughout the world. With support from Moody, and with Northfield as his platform, Meyer had widespread credibility, and he successfully differentiated his teaching from radical Wesleyan holiness in order to make his message acceptable within conservative American denominations.[183] Meyer also distanced himself from Pentecostalism and fundamentalism. His aim was to produce an evangelicalism of the center. Meyer's timing was important. He came to America in the 1890s, when a body of teachers around Moody was ready to accept and spread Keswick doctrines. On occasions Meyer was tempted to make America his base.[184] It was a country that fascinated him. Other Keswick teachers followed Meyer to America, but none came so often or made such an impact.[185] In Britain and America Meyer was, from the 1890s to the 1920s, a uniquely influential evangelical statesman.

183. Northfield, said Meyer in 1897, was very influential in America and had been "so largely reinforced from Keswick" (*Life of Faith*, 3 March 1897, 104).

184. *The Christian*, 1 September 1892, 11; *BW* 1 June 1905, 195. Moody suggested that Meyer could do more in America in a month than he could in London in a year (Fullerton, Calif., *Meyer*, 38).

185. At the time of his death, about five million copies of Meyer's books were in circulation, approximately half of these in North America (J. H. Rushbrooke, in *Dictionary of National Biography* [London, 1937], 583; *The Christian*, 18 April 1929, 5).

Evangelicalism in Modern Britain and America

A Comparison

David W. Bebbington

For the last two and a half centuries there has been a strong evangelical presence in both Britain and America. Those Christians who have emphasized the need to "evangelize"—to pass on the gospel message—have formed a large proportion, often a majority, of the members of the various Protestant denominations.[1] But has evangelicalism been the same phenomenon on the two sides of the Atlantic? Sometimes it has been assumed that the national versions of Britain and the United States are identical. Both, after all, share the same label. Evangelicalism, furthermore, is often supposed not to have changed much over time. With its fierce loyalty to the Bible, evangel-

---

1. An earlier version of this chapter was first delivered at the Annual Public Lecture of the Bible Training Institute, Glasgow, in 1986. I am very grateful for comments on its text to Richard Carwardine, Mark Noll, and Ian Rennie—none of whom, however, is responsible for the views that have emerged.

ical religion is thought to have been incapable of substantial change. As will appear, however, evangelicalism has in fact altered its nature enormously over time. Evangelicals of the mid-eighteenth century differed greatly in attitude from those of the mid-nineteenth century, let alone from those of the mid-twentieth century. Once its variation over time is perceived, the likelihood of its variation over space can also be appreciated.

Sometimes, in fact, it is suggested that the American form is entirely distinctive. According to Nathan Hatch, the evangelicalism of the United States possesses unique American characteristics. The movement, it is argued, expresses the views of commoners, who have unbounded confidence in their ability to grasp total truth. It is at its core "democratic." "Where but in America," asks Hatch, "could a converted seaman . . . make bold to undertake the same kind of rational study of biblical prophecy that had taxed the mind of . . . Isaac Newton?"[2] The expected answer is nowhere, but the accurate answer is that similar studies were published aplenty by converted butcher's assistants, grocer's assistants, and other humble folk in nineteenth- and twentieth-century Britain. It is assumed that evangelicalism was in this respect distinctive to the United States, when in reality it was not. This supposition is grounded in a central theme of American historiography, namely, the contention that Protestant evangelicalism was one of the forces that indigenized a disparate immigrant population. Because a common evangelicalism did help foster Americanness, it can be imagined that evangelicalism itself has been intrinsically American. But that is open to doubt. The issue is therefore worth exploring.[3] How different have been the evangelicalisms? The similarities and then the contrasts will be reviewed in turn.

2. Nathan O. Hatch, "Evangelicalism as a Democratic Movement," in *Evangelicalism and Modern America*, ed. George Marsden (Grand Rapids, 1984), 78–79. Hatch is referring to Hal Lindsey, the author of *The Late Great Planet Earth* (Grand Rapids, 1970). For expansion, see Hatch, *The Democratization of American Christianity* (New Haven, 1989).
3. The question has been addressed before, notably in W. S. Hudson, "How American Is Religion in America?" in *Essays in Divinity*, ed. J. C. Brauer (Chicago, 1967); Richard Carwardine, *Transatlantic Revivalism: Popular Evangelicalism in Britain and America, 1790–1865* (Westport, Conn., 1978); and George M. Marsden, "Fundamentalism as an American Phenomenon: A Comparison with English Evangelicalism," *Church History* 46 (June 1977): 25–32; which is partly reflected in Marsden, *Fundamentalism and American Culture: The Shaping of Twentieth Century Evangelicalism* (New York, 1980), chap. 25.

Transatlantic Similarities

The similarities must begin with the nature of evangelicalism itself. The defining characteristics were the same in Britain and the United States. The phenomenon was *biblicist*. Evangelicals never failed to stress the importance, and especially the authority, of the Bible for the Christian life. American evangelicals shared the "intense veneration and love for the Bible" that was displayed by Brownlow North, a nineteenth-century Scottish evangelist.[4] In terms of doctrine, this form of Christianity was *crucicentric*. Evangelicals selected the cross as the fulcrum of their theological system. By contrast with other Protestants who emphasized the incarnation or the example of Jesus, they concentrated on his death as a sacrifice for sin. Those who neglected the atonement were suspected of slipping their evangelical moorings. The great American Congregational minister Henry Ward Beecher was criticized by an English Wesleyan reviewer for giving too little prominence in his teaching to redemption in the blood of Christ.[5] Next, the movement was *conversionist*. There was an insistence that conversion was essential to being a Christian. Robert Bickersteth, the bishop of Ripon from 1857 to 1884, spoke for evangelicals on both sides of the Atlantic in teaching that "a conscious turning from sin to God was the crisis of the religious life."[6] Finally, evangelicals were *activist*. Because of the commands found in the Bible, because of the work of Christ on the cross, and because of the indispensability of conversion, they felt a powerful obligation to translate their beliefs into missionary activity at home and abroad. The great object of the minister, according to an evangelical clerical handbook of the late nineteenth century, was "saving souls."[7] Other tasks of an educational or philanthropic kind might often be entailed, as similar American works of many periods would have agreed, but

4. Kenneth Moody-Stuart, *Brownlow North: The Story of His Life and Work* (Kilmarnock, Scotland, 1904), 180.

5. William Strawson, "Methodist Theology, 1850–1950," in *A History of the Methodist Church in Great Britain*, vol. 3, ed. Rupert Davies, A. R. George, and Gordon Rupp (London, 1983), 188.

6. M. C. Bickersteth, *A Sketch of the Life and Episcopate of the Right Reverend Robert Bickersteth, D.D.* (London, 1887), 48.

7. Herbert James, *The Country Clergyman and His Work* (London, 1890), 25.

evangelism was the overriding priority. The gospel had to be spread. Each of these four features marked the movement throughout the whole period of its existence in both countries.[8] The basic religious impulse was the same in Britain and the United States.

The movement originated almost simultaneously in the two countries. American evangelicalism is normally dated from the outbreak of revival under Jonathan Edwards at Northampton, Massachusetts, in 1734–35. In the latter year in Wales, Howell Harris and Daniel Rowland were converted and began their preaching ministries. George Whitefield and John Wesley took the same path in England in 1735–37 and 1738 respectively. The account by Edwards of the Northampton revival helped precipitate similar outbreaks at Cambuslang in 1742, so launching a fresh concern for evangelism in Scotland. Until his death in 1770 Whitefield, by his repeated personal presence in each, bound together the whole movement in America, Wales, England, and Scotland.[9] The branches of the movement remained interlinked over the centuries. Preachers regularly traversed the ocean, specially from North America to Britain. Some of the chief developments among subsequent generations of British evangelicals were the fruit of visits by Americans, among them Lorenzo Dow, James Caughey, Dwight L. Moody, and Billy Graham. John Wimber, the contemporary prophet of evangelism through "signs and wonders," maintained the tradition in the mid-1980s. Others traveled in the opposite direction. Some went as emigrants from Britain. John Witherspoon, the only minister of religion to sign the American Declaration of Independence, had gone out from Scotland to become president of the largely Presbyterian College at Princeton.[10] Others such as F. B. Meyer were only visitors.[11]

Personal friendships cemented the international solidarity of the movement. Literature had the same effect. The common language ensured that books and journals circulated freely across the Atlantic.

8. The four characteristics are more fully analyzed in David W. Bebbington, *Evangelicalism in Modern Britain: A History from the 1730s to the 1980s* (London, 1989; Grand Rapids, 1992), chap. 1.

9. H. S. Stout, *The Divine Dramatist: George Whitefield and the Rise of Modern Evangelicalism* (Grand Rapids, 1991).

10. V. L. Collins, *President Witherspoon: A Biography* (Princeton, N.J., 1925).

11. W. Y. Fullerton, *F. B. Meyer: A Biography* (London, n.d.), 36–45, 198ff.

Most religious works of any importance were published simultaneously in Britain and the United States. Worship likewise tended to foster unity. Sankey's hymns were a determinative influence on popular evangelicalism worldwide for many decades after their appearance in the 1870s. Even in matters of detail, such as the introduction of hygienic individual cups at Communion, there was imitation. (This idea began in the United States in 1894 and was taken up with enthusiasm in England, initially at Thorne Congregational Church, near Doncaster, in 1898.)[12] From the origins of evangelicalism onward, therefore, there was constant flow of people, literature, and practices backward and forward across the ocean. The stronger influence in the eighteenth and nineteenth centuries was no doubt Britain, but, as in other fields, the predominant partner changed in the twentieth century. The flow was nevertheless reciprocal at all stages. There was in fact a religious "special relationship" throughout the era.

The Cultural Setting

The cultural context was another common factor for British and American evangelicalism. The same broad intellectual currents swept both countries molding the ways of thinking, and especially the fundamental assumptions, of evangelicals along with the rest of the population. The Enlightenment was the first cultural mood to affect them. It was essentially the typical tendency of eighteenth-century thought to exalt rational inquiry. Far from being alien to the evangelical mentality (as is often supposed), the Enlightenment marked the movement from its beginnings. Acceptance of the "enlightened" style of thinking was a trait that separated the evangelicals from their Puritan forbears. Jonathan Edwards, the greatest American theologian of the eighteenth century, while dissatisfied with the limitations of Locke's sensationalist psychology, nevertheless entered fully into the framework of thought created by Locke and his contemporaries. Edwards's defense of Calvinism in *The Freedom of the Will* (1754), for example, draws heavily on the teaching of Locke's *Essay*.[13] Likewise John Wesley, with all his influence over early evan-

---

12. *Christian World*, 22 November 1894, 871; 9 August 1900, 12; 16 August 1900, 9.

13. Edwards, *The Works of Jonathan Edwards*, vol. 1: *Freedom of the Will*, ed. Paul Ramsey (New Haven, 1957), 47–65.

gelicals, is properly seen as an Enlightenment thinker. Wesley, too, owed a great debt to Locke.[14] Evangelical leaders were among the standard-bearers of the new learning.

Consequently a range of "enlightened" attitudes was professed by American and British evangelicals. Their stance entailed a rejection of scholastic method with its careful a priori distinctions. In America, Edwards condemned all views built upon "what our reason would lead us to suppose without, or before experience."[15] Similarly among the Baptists of England, the elaborate systematic divinity of John Gill, a high Calvinist, began in the late eighteenth century to give way to the simpler evangelical theology of Andrew Fuller, which was cast in an Enlightenment mold.[16] Robert Hall, sharing Fuller's perspective, roundly dismissed Gill's scholastic thought as "a continent of mud."[17] The spirit of inquiry was the new avenue to truth. William Carey, another Baptist of kindred mind to Fuller, called his book that launched the modern British missionary movement *An Enquiry into the Obligation of Christians to use Means for the Conversion of the Heathen* (1792). The choice of the word "enquiry" was no accident. The same word was selected for the title of their major works by two of the greatest figures of the English-speaking Enlightenment. David Hume wrote an *Enquiry concerning Human Understanding* (1748), and Adam Smith *An Inquiry into the Nature and Cause of the Wealth of Nations* (1776). The essence of the intellectual method of all three men was investigation. Theology overlapped with science, for both disciplines adopted empirical techniques. Thus in Scotland the most powerful sermons delivered by the leader of the early nineteenth-century evangelicals, Thomas Chalmers, were his Astronomical Discourses, on the wonders of the heavens. Chalmers's set of premises, the "common sense philosophy" that sprang from the Scottish Enlightenment, also underlay the thinking of American evangelicals.

14. R. E. Brantley, *Locke, Wesley, and the Method of English Romanticism* (Gainesville, FL, 1984). Cf. Frederick Dreyer, "Faith and Experience in the Thought of John Wesley," *American Historical Review* 88 (February 1983): 12–30.

15. Quoted in Perry Miller, *Jonathan Edwards* (Boston, 1949), 45.

16. W. R. Ward, "The Baptists and the Transformation of the Church, 1780–1830," *Baptist Quarterly* 23 (1973): 167–73.

17. Olinthus Gregory, ed., *The Works of Robert Hall*, vol. 6 (London, 1841), 125; cited in Raymond Brown, *The English Baptists of the Eighteenth Century* (London, 1986), 93.

For over a century from its introduction into America by Wither-spoon in 1768, common sense provided the philosophical framework for all their attitudes.

Its corollary in the field of practice was pragmatism. It is often held that pragmatism was a distinctive feature of American life, an adaptation to the conditions of the New World.[18] In fact, however, Enlightenment evangelicals in Britain were equally prepared to experiment. Wesley's field preaching was but one instance of many innovations of technique. Early evangelical churchmen were far less insistent on the punctilio of church order than has been supposed,[19] and many Baptists went so far down the road of pragmatism as to abandon their traditional demand for believer's baptism as a condition of Communion for the sake of fraternizing with other evangelicals.[20] The pragmatic temper of the Enlightenment and evangelical zeal went hand in hand in both the United States and Britain.

The next great cultural wave to sweep across the Western world was Romanticism. The term is used here not in the narrow sense of the literary generation that was fading by the 1820s but in the much broader sense of the whole mood that was inaugurated by that generation and lasted throughout the nineteenth century and beyond. This was the movement of taste that stressed, against the mechanism and classicism of the Enlightenment, the place of feeling and intuition in human perception, the importance of nature and history for human experience. Goethe embodied the Romantic spirit in Germany, where the initial impact of the movement was strongest, while Wordsworth, Coleridge, Keats, Shelley, and Byron represented its various expressions in English verse. In the United States it enjoyed a vogue only with the rise of transcendentalism in the circle around Emerson in the 1830s. Its late American success, it has been suggested, helps account for the enduring strength of Enlightenment styles of thought among the evangelicals of the United States. In England and most of Europe, on this view, Romanticism

18. Robert T. Handy, for instance, writes of "certain major tendencies of American religion, such as . . . pragmatism" (*A History of the Churches in the United States and Canada* [Oxford, 1976], 227).

19. W. D. Balda, "Spheres of Influence: Simeon's Trust and Its Implications for Evangelical Patronage" (Ph.D. diss., Cambridge University, 1981), 41ff.

20. Ward, "Baptists and the Transformation of the Church," 176ff.

was undermining Enlightenment categories from the 1780s onward. The common sense philosophy, it is argued, persisted among American evangelicals after it had withered in Britain.[21] It is a mistake, however, to drive such a wedge between the two countries. Romanticism gained little favor with the educated public in Britain until the second decade of the nineteenth century. It was not until the 1820s that it impinged significantly on evangelicalism through Edward Irving and his friends.[22] The delay between the reception of Romantic thought by British evangelicals and its infiltration among American evangelicals in the following decade is very small. The new cultural mood appeared in the two national movements at broadly the same time.

The effects of Romanticism were also virtually identical. The style of the evangelical movement was affected before the content of its belief. Preaching became more florid. Edward Irving, when pioneering the new manner in the 1820s, deliberately cultivated what was called "the Miltonic or Old-English Puritan style" of declamation.[23] He was widely followed in English pulpits by the middle of the century. Similarly in urbane American congregations, particularly on the East Coast, preaching became more elaborate, rhetorical, and charged with metaphor. Dr. William Adams of New York, a Presbyterian minister of the middle years of the century, was celebrated for his mastery of imaginative pulpit idiom. "Sometimes when his soul was on fire," it was recalled, "and his voice trembled with emotion, he rose into the region of lofty impassioned eloquence."[24] In both countries the incidentals of worship were also altered as the century wore on. Romantic taste eventually dictated that flowers, once denounced as symptoms of heathen worship,[25] should beautify the sanctuary. Gradually, however, the content of evangelical teaching broadened. The process was rightly diagnosed as the result of influences emanating from the German heartland of Romantic thought

21. Marsden, *Fundamentalism and American Culture*, 226–27.
22. Bebbington, *Evangelicalism in Modern Britain*, chap. 3.
23. Thomas Carlyle, *Reminiscences* (1887), ed. C. E. Norton (London, 1972), 195.
24. T. L. Cuyler, *Recollections of a Long Life: An Autobiography* (London, 1902), 203.
25. In 1880 it was still being claimed by a Protestant churchman that floral decorations in church served a "Pagan purpose" (James Bateman, *The Church Association: Its Policy and Prospects Considered in a Letter to the Chairman*, 2d ed. [London, 1880], 86).

and denounced by the sterner evangelicals as "neologism." Its tendency was to blur the sharp edges of dogmatic belief. The new blend of aesthetic sensibility and humanitarianism swayed some toward Unitarianism. This development took place chiefly in New England, but there were comparable instances in Britain. George Dawson of Birmingham, for example, deserted his early Baptist associations to become a preacher of elevating influences and municipal duty. "I love religion and flowers," he is said to have remarked, "but I hate botany and theology."[26] Among the orthodox the same forces were at work, softening the contours of doctrinal statements. The trend was especially marked among the Congregationalists, the friends and followers of Henry Ward Beecher in the United States and of R. W. Dale in Britain. Although there was an impact on specific doctrines, the chief change was a general inclination to put ethics before dogma. The effect of Romanticism was to push evangelicalism in the direction of more liberal thinking.

Romanticism was succeeded in the twentieth century by another all-pervading cultural fashion—modernism. This cultural mood, which must be distinguished from theological modernism, began in many Western cities around and just after the turn of the century. Its first onset in Germany was called expressionism, and its hallmark was a willingness among creative artists to express how they felt rather than how they believed they ought to feel. Under the sway of Nietzsche, Freud, and their contemporaries, new literary and philosophical forms gave vent to the unconscious.[27] Modernism first affected evangelicalism through the Oxford Group movement of Frank Buchman, later rechristened Moral Re-Armament. It emphasized total openness in group confession of secret thoughts, immediate divine guidance in the everyday affairs of life, and an exuberant delight in Christianity as the remedy for the ills of the modern world.[28] Similar motifs were seen in the movement of charismatic renewal that from about 1960 began to transform the idiom of evangelicalism and

26. Dawson quoted by M. G. Pearse, "Some Modern Theories Tried by an Old Experiment," *Wesleyan Methodist Magazine*, 6th ser., 8 (1884): 8.

27. Malcom Bradbury and James McFarlane, eds., *Modernism, 1890–1930* (Harmondsworth, Middlessex, 1976).

28. David W. Bebbington, "The Oxford Group Movement between the Wars," in *Voluntary Religion*, Studies in Church History, 23, ed. W. J. Sheils and D. Wood (Oxford, 1986).

a broader Christian constituency. It added a fresh dimension of free expression in worship. Both movements flowered earlier in the United States but rapidly took root in Britain. Modernism, like the Enlightenment and Romanticism, became a vehicle for the gospel on both sides of the Atlantic. The cultural setting that did so much to form evangelical religion as it changed over time was common to the two countries.

Popular Theological Views

The story is the same for theology. Important shifts of popular theological thinking united the English-speaking evangelical world rather than dividing it on national lines. This is true of the emergence of premillennialism, the belief that the second coming of Christ will precede the millennium and is therefore imminent. Modern premillennial teaching originated in the circle of Edward Irving in Britain during the 1820s, spread gradually during the nineteenth century, and advanced more rapidly in the twentieth century. A major reason for its increasing acceptance was the publication in 1909 of the Scofield Reference Bible, replete with marginal notes expounding a coherent premillennialist scheme.[29] Another reason was the issuing in 1917 of the Balfour Declaration, followed shortly by the capture of Jerusalem by British forces. Hopes for the return of the Jews to Palestine were kindled; that event, it was believed, would herald the return of Christ. In Britain the Advent Testimony and Preparation Movement was immediately founded under F. B. Meyer,[30] and similar bodies sprang up in the United States. Premillennialism became the normal eschatology of conservative evangelicals in the interwar period.

Belief in biblical inerrancy, not a precisely formulated view in early evangelicalism, grew up in harness with premillennialism. According to most premillennialists, Old Testament prophecy addressed to Israel and Judah would be fulfilled in the millennium of their lineal descendants, the Jews. The message of the prophets must not be applied spiritually to the church, but literally to the Jews. Literal interpretation became a battle cry. It was associated with a stricter

---

29. E. R. Sandeen, *The Roots of Fundamentalism: British and American Millenarianism, 1800–1930* (Chicago, 1970), 221–24.
30. Fullerton, *Meyer*, chap. 16.

doctrine of inspiration than had hitherto been accepted by evangelicals. The new argument took a deductive form. Because God speaks in the Bible and because God cannot lie, the Bible must be inerrant.[31] Such an argument was not used in the eighteenth century, even by evangelicals, but it became popular during the nineteenth century in Britain and America. It was entrenched as the conservative evangelical orthodoxy of the twentieth century.

Holiness teaching likewise took a similar course in the two countries. In the eighteenth century, the distinctive doctrine of holiness belonged to the Methodists. Following John Wesley himself, they taught that the believer can be entirely sanctified in this life. In the United States during the mid-nineteenth century, the idea was taken up by non-Methodists and recast in a new shape. No longer was holiness the end of a long and arduous quest; now it was the immediate gift of faith. The doctrine became the basis of a range of American holiness churches that sprang up in the late nineteenth century.[32] It was transmitted to Britain by Robert Pearsall Smith and his wife, Hannah, in the early 1870s. There it became widespread throughout the existing evangelical churches in the form of Keswick teaching. "Victory through faith" was the watchword.[33] It became the general view of conservative evangelicals in the first half of the twentieth century that a higher spiritual life can be attained by faith alone.

Fundamentalism was in large measure the outcome of these currents of popular theology. In America, as is well known, it gave rise in the 1920s to a series of controversies that split evangelicalism. Fundamentalists denounced their more liberal opponents as modernists. The fundamentalist controversies have sometimes been seen as absent from British religious life.[34] That was not the case. In 1922 the Church Missionary Society, the organization that more than any other bound together evangelicals in the Church of England, was racked by argument over whether or not it was committed to biblical infallibility. Since the issue was not settled to the satisfaction of the conservatives, a section of them seceded to found the Bible Church-

31. W. J. Abraham, *The Divine Inspiration of Holy Scripture* (Oxford, 1981), chap. 1.
32. M. E. Dieter, *The Holiness Revival of the Nineteenth Century* (Metuchen, N.J., 1980).
33. J. C. Pollock, *The Keswick Story: The Authorized History of the Keswick Convention* (London, 1964).
34. For example, J. T. Wilkinson, *Arthur Samuel Peake: A Biography* (London, 1971), 195.

men's Missionary Society.[35] Already in 1913 there had been a dispute in Wesleyan Methodism over the appointment of George Jackson to a theological college chair. When Jackson's appointment was confirmed despite his allegedly unsound views on the Bible, the disgruntled conservatives formed the Wesley Bible Union, which in the 1920s avowed its fundamentalism.[36] Again the election of T. R. Glover to the chair of the Baptist Union in 1924 aroused strenuous opposition from those who supposed him too liberal in theology.[37] The same vitriolic temper that was displayed in America stained fundamentalism in Britain. Glover's family, for instance, destroyed the critical letters he had received because they were so abusive.[38] Fundamentalism not only existed in Britain but evidently adopted a tone comparable to that of its American counterpart. It was another of the theological products of evangelicalism shared by Britain and America.

Structures and Social Policies

The denominational pattern was a further common feature. Most denominations had cousins across the ocean for the good reason that the main American bodies had been exported from Britain in the first place. There was enormous variation in the relative strength of the denominations in different parts of America, and the same was true of Britain. The Presbyterian dominance in Scotland was reproduced during the colonial period in the Delaware Valley, and the competitive variety of early nineteenth-century Wales was similar to the kaleidoscope of the American frontier. Again, the spirit of interdenominational cooperation in bodies like the Bible societies was a strong force in both countries during the nineteenth century. The "evangelical united front" of such organizations in the United States was in fact copied from Britain. While these bodies sustained links between de-

35. Gordon Hewitt, *The Problems of Success: A History of the Church Missionary Society, 1910–1942*, vol. 1 (London, 1971), 461–73.

36. David W. Bebbington, "The Persecution of George Jackson: A British Fundamentalist Controversy," in *Persecution and Toleration*, Studies in Church History, 21, ed. W. J. Sheils (Oxford, 1984).

37. D. W. Bebbington, "Baptists and Fundamentalism in Inter-War Britain," in *Protestant Evangelicalism: Britain, Ireland, Germany, and America, c. 1750–c. 1950: Essays in Honour of W. R. Ward*, Studies in Church History Subsidia, 7, ed. Keith Robbins (Oxford, 1990).

38. Information from the late Mrs. A. R. Wade, daughter of T. R. Glover.

nominations into the twentieth century, they were complemented among conservative evangelicals by a new range of institutions that are better described as nondenominational than as interdenominational. In the United States nondenominational institutions, of which the Bible schools were chief, bound together the fundamentalist movement. Likewise in Britain there were Scripture Unions, Crusaders, and faith missions like the China Inland Mission that formed the common ground of conservative evangelicalism. Furthermore, both countries produced sects. The United States is justly celebrated for the range of its indigenous sects. There were innumerable Pentecostal bodies as well as remarkable, though tiny, structures like the National Baptist Evangelical Life and Soul Saving Assembly of the United States of America, Kansas City, Missouri, founded in 1920.[39] But Britain, proportionate to its size, generated a similar range of sects. Apart from three substantial Pentecostal bodies, there were half a dozen separate sects in the holiness category alone in the early twentieth century.[40] Sectarianism was certainly no American monopoly. It seems that the subdivisions of the evangelical world were similar in the two countries.

Attitudes to social action among evangelicals were also quite similar. Although opinion changed greatly over time, the trajectory of change was broadly the same in Britain and the United States. In the early nineteenth century individual charitable efforts were supplemented by a range of voluntary societies performing philanthropic activities. Moral crusades, mass movements of opposition to particular social evils, increased in number during the nineteenth century. Like antislavery, the model campaign on both sides of the Atlantic (though not in the southern United States), such crusades often entailed political pressure. The major cases taken up were similar in Britain and the United States, and included Sabbath observance, anti-Catholicism, and temperance. From the 1880s to the 1920s the Social Gospel appealed to many. This movement was an intensification of the moral crusading temper, a desire to reconstruct the whole of so-

39. F. S. Mead, *Handbook of Denominations in the United States*, 2d ed. (New York, 1961), 46.

40. W. J. Hollenweger, *The Pentecostals* (London, 1972); Jack Ford, *In the Steps of John Wesley: The Church of the Nazarene in Britain* (Kansas City, Mo., 1968).

ciety on a Christian basis. It is clear that, far from being an alternative religious prescription to the simple gospel, the message of the American movement was rooted in evangelicalism. That was also the case in Britain. One of the leading social radicals of Scotland, A. Scott Matheson, a United Presbyterian minister at Dumbarton, was typical in rejecting any downgrading of the gospel for the individual. "Social reform," he declared in 1894, "ought never to draw the church aside from her proper work of saving men."[41]

In the succeeding period, however, from the 1920s up to the 1960s, there was a reaction among conservative evangelicals. Social action was denounced in Britain and the United States alike as a diversion from the true gospel.[42] That phase in turn was superseded by a growing inclination among evangelicals to pay attention to the material needs of humanity. The Lausanne Congress on World Evangelization in 1974, at which evangelical leaders confessed that they had neglected social action, was a landmark in this worldwide trend. The pattern over time of evangelical attitudes to organized humanitarianism was common to Britain, the United States, and (like many of the other developments noticed here) the rest of the English-speaking world. Overall, it is clear that in many fundamental respects evangelicals in Britain and America proceeded on parallel lines.

Transatlantic Contrasts

Nevertheless it can by no means be concluded that the two evangelical communities were virtually identical in their experience. The contrasts between them deserve equal exploration. Significant differences existed, some of them in the areas that have been discussed so far. Notwithstanding the substantial similarities in the area of popular theology, for instance, there were differences in each of the theological fields already covered. Premillennialism, in the first place, may take one of two forms, the historicist or the futurist, according to the interpretation of the Book of Revelation adopted. Historicists hold that Revelation supplies a predictive view of the Christian cen-

41. A. Scott Matheson, *The Church and Social Problems* (Edinburgh, 1894), v.
42. Marsden, *Fundamentalism and American Culture*, chap. 10; E. L. Langston, *How God Is Working to a Plan* (London, 1933), 20, 32.

turies in chronological order, a panorama of history. Individual prophecies can be correlated with recorded events. Futurists claim, on the contrary, that all the predictions of Revelation await fulfillment in the future. The dispensationalism of J. N. Darby, an early Brethren leader, is a version of futurism.[43] In the United States as well as Britain, historicism was the dominant type of premillennialism in the middle years of the nineteenth century, but later on the paths of the two countries diverged. A series of books published in the 1870s and 1880s by Henry Grattan Guinness, the founder of the Regions Beyond Missionary Union, entrenched the popularity of the historicist interpretation of Revelation in Britain. Guinness's *Approaching End of the Age* (1878) was especially influential. Brethren, however, were zealous students of prophecy, and most of them advocated Darby's dispensationalism. In British prophetic circles there was therefore a major ideological division. After 1917 the Advent Preparation Movement had to agree to differ on the question of interpreting Revelation.[44] In the United States, by contrast, dispensationalism gained the edge by the beginning of the twentieth century.[45] Historicism became the apparently idiosyncratic hobbyhorse of the Seventh-Day Adventists, and the mainstream of conservative evangelical opinion flowed in dispensationalist channels. American premillennialists were therefore united, whereas their British equivalents were divided. Americans could be far more insistent on the details of their vista of the cosmos than the British.

The contrast in attitudes to Scripture was comparable. Inerrancy was widely asserted in both countries at a popular level. In Britain, however, there was a dearth of scholarly defenses of inerrancy in the late nineteenth and early twentieth centuries. Only W. H. Griffith Thomas of Wycliffe Hall, Oxford, attempted an academic case, and he did so with great caution. Otherwise evangelical scholars stopped short of asserting the absence of errors in the Bible.[46] In the United

43. T. P. Weber, *Living in the Shadow of the Second Coming: American Premillennialism, 1875–1925* (New York, 1979), 10.

44. D. W. Bebbington, "The Advent Hope in British Evangelicalism since 1800," *Scottish Journal of Religious Studies* 9 (1988).

45. Weber, *Shadow of the Second Coming*, 11.

46. D. F. Wright, "Soundings in the Doctrine of Scripture in British Evangelicalism in the First Half of the Twentieth Century," *Tyndale Bulletin* 31 (1980).

States, in contrast, inerrancy was massively expounded by the Reformed theologian B. B. Warfield of Princeton.[47] The doctrine was consequently held with much greater confidence in the United States than in Britain.

In the field of holiness teaching there was another contrast that had the same effect. Although the Keswick message did affect the United States, its origin and strength were in Britain. There its style of spirituality virtually swept the field among evangelicals, marginalizing both traditional views and the more extreme form of doctrine that continued to flourish in the holiness churches. In the American West there were some remarkable beliefs about sanctification. In the 1890s the Fire-Baptized Holiness Association of southeastern Kansas, for instance, held that beyond the second blessing the believer should progress through the baptisms of fire, dynamite, lyddite, and oxydite.[48] Keswick teaching took root in Britain precisely because it was far more gentle, appealing to the leisured who could frequent the superior resort in July, the Calvinists who wanted nothing savoring of Methodist error, and the Anglicans who loved decency and order in religion. Speakers on Keswick platforms insisted that there is no guarantee of the permanence of the "higher spiritual life." It has to be maintained through faith, moment by moment.[49] There was therefore less assurance that a sanctified state would persist and more self-scrutiny for signs of devotional declension in Britain. The British version of holiness was altogether more restrained.

Although fundamentalism, as we have seen, existed in Britain, it was not strong. The Primitive Methodist biblical scholar A. S. Peake, in commenting on the British situation in 1923, remarked that "we are not submerged, as I fear America seems likely to be[,] by the tide of obscurantism."[50] The committed supporters of fundamentalism in the 1920s were few and lacked able leadership. By 1955, when *The Times* carried a correspondence on fundamentalism occasioned by the visit of Billy Graham, John Stott, a rising leader of Anglican evangelicals, contributed a denial that conservative evangelicals were

47. Sandeen, *Roots of Fundamentalism*, chap. 5.
48. R. W. Anderson, *Vision of the Disinherited: The Making of American Pentecostalism* (New York, 1979), 35.
49. Pollock, *Keswick Story*, chap. 9.
50. Peake to J. E. McFadyen, January 1923, in Wilkinson, *Peake*, 92.

necessarily fundamentalists.[51] In the United States fundamentalism gave rise to a number of separatist organizations that denounced the "liberalism" of their parent bodies. They created a united front in the American Council of Christian Churches in 1941. These "come-outers" remained hostile to the existing denominations and bitterly opposed to the emerging ecumenical movement.[52] In Britain there was a body professing similar separatist convictions, the Fellowship of Independent Evangelical Churches, which showed traces of *odium theologicum* for mainstream denominations and ecumenical developments. Yet even when, in 1966, its principles were publicly espoused by the eminent minister of Westminster Chapel, Dr. D. Martyn Lloyd-Jones,[53] it was much weaker than its American counterparts and lacked their aggressive edge. It is thus possible to conclude that the shared popular theological movements were significantly more moderate in Britain.

The Mosaic of Denominations

The denominational pattern, despite the similarities already noticed, showed divergence in other respects. The balance of denominations was crucially different. Among the evangelicals of Britain, those in the Anglican tradition were numerous and influential. From the early eighteenth century there were evangelicals in the Church of England (Wesley himself was her devoted son), and in the nineteenth and twentieth centuries they formed a high proportion of the evangelical community. Although there were exceptional evangelicals of stature in the American Episcopal Church—men like Bishop McIlvaine of Ohio (1833–73)[54]—they were relatively few. The American Episcopal Church was normally more like the Scottish Episcopal Church than the Church of England—small in numbers, high in

51. John R. W. Stott to editor, 25 August 1955, in *Fundamentalism: A Religious Problem: Letters to the Editor of The Times and a Leading Article* (London, 1955), 15–16.
52. J. A. Carpenter, "From Fundamentalism to the New Evangelical Coalition," in *Evangelicalism and Modern America*, ed. George Marsden (Grand Rapids, 1984), 12–13.
53. John Peters, *Martyn Lloyd-Jones: Preacher* (Exeter, 1986), 83–94. Cf. D. G. Fountain, *E. J. Poole-Connor (1872–1962): Contender for the Faith* (Worthing, England, 1966), 121–28.
54. William Carus, ed., *Memorials of the Right Reverend Charles Pettit McIlvaine, D. D., D. C. L.* (London, 1882). On Anglican evangelicalism in America, cf. A. C. Zabriskie, ed., *Anglican Evangelicalism*, Church Historical Society Publication no. 13 (Philadelphia, 1943).

churchmanship, and catering for members of the social elite and their dependents. Consequently leadership of the evangelical community in the United States was assumed by others—commonly by Presbyterians or Congregationalists in the realm of theology, by Methodists or Baptists in the realm of evangelism. The example of vigorous Methodist techniques for harvesting souls was particularly potent in the early nineteenth century. Whereas unremitting outreach carried the greatest prestige in the United States, the order and the decorum of the Church of England were relatively more important in Britain. Revivalism among the Methodists of Britain was deliberately restrained, largely for the sake of ensuring the respect of the Anglicans. The Anglican belief that real conversions may be gradual gained ground in Britain, and far fewer than in America were prepared to insist on sudden conversions. As in the wider society, so within the evangelical community, the strength of the Church of England was a force for moderation.

The existence of other parties within the Church of England was another significant feature of the denominational mosaic. Evangelicals in the Church of England could not avoid responding to the presence of High Churchmen within the fold. A measure of rivalry grew up, particularly in the wake of the Oxford Movement of the 1830s. A great deal of evangelical energy was directed into repressing ritualism in the later nineteenth century, chiefly through the Church Association. Until about 1960 there were persistent attempts through the National Church League and similar bodies to prevent a revision of the Book of Common Prayer favorable to the Anglo-Catholics.[55] There can be no doubt that ecclesiastical party warfare was a diversion from Christian mission. Rubbing shoulders with High Churchmen also had a very different effect. High Churchmanship exercised a fascination over many evangelicals. Because they coexisted within the same communion, it was easy for evangelical clergy to transfer by almost indistinguishable stages to the other camp. The adoption of reading the daily service, as directed by the Book of Common Prayer, was often one of the points in a pilgrimage away from identification with the evangelical party. Especially in the later nineteenth century,

55. Randle Manwaring, *From Controversy to Co-existence: Evangelicals in the Church of England, 1914 to 1980* (Cambridge, 1985), 31–36.

there was a constant hemorrhage of young talent. The appeal of High Churchmanship, particularly on its liturgical side, touched ministers outside the Church of England. From the 1880s, for instance, there was a Scoto-Catholic movement north of the border.[56] Likewise Broad Churchmen pulled evangelicals in their direction. Because they formed part of the same church, Broad Church thinkers were more readily appreciated by Anglican evangelicals. Because of the prestige of the Church of England, writers who can be classified as Broad Church also caught the attention of those beyond its bounds. F. D. Maurice in particular was a powerful influence among Congregationalists.[57] By contrast, in the United States the relative weakness of the Episcopalians restricted their impact on others. In Britain the diverse churchmanship of the Church of England affected evangelicals both by sapping their strength and by widening their horizons.

Although both countries generated sects, their balance relative to each other and to the larger Christian denominations was different. The so-called Plymouth Brethren were far more numerous in Britain. There were thought to be between 75,000 and 100,000 in the British Isles in 1968.[58] There were only just over 25,000 in the whole of the United States in 1936.[59] Brethren therefore played a much greater role in the evangelical community of Britain, helping to mold the tone of conservative evangelicalism in the twentieth century. Their sense of deference to social superiors, including the aristocracy and gentry, several of whom joined their ranks, reinforced the traditionalist values of the wider evangelical community. Their weakness in the United States meant that dispensationalism was perceived less as a party badge and so was free to spread more widely. In general, however, the sects attracted much larger numbers of adherents in the United States. The holiness-Pentecostal sector in particular was immense. As early as 1907 there were twenty-five holiness sects;[60] eighty years later the largest of the innumerable Pentecostal bodies,

56. James Whyte, "The Setting of Worship," in *Studies in the History of Worship in Scotland*, ed. D. B. Forrester and D. M. Murray (Edinburgh, 1984), 147ff.

57. R. T. Jones, *Congregationalism in England, 1662–1962* (London, 1962), 253.

58. F. R. Coad, *A History of the Brethren Movement: Its Origins, Worldwide Development, and Its Significance for the Present Day* (Exeter, England, 1968), 185.

59. Mead, *Handbook*, 59.

60. Anderson, *Vision of the Disinherited*, 37.

the Assemblies of God, boasted well over two million members.[61] The typical vigor of sectarian religion was far more a feature of the United States than of Britain.

An aspect of denominational life that deserves special mention is the role of the clergy. The difference between the two countries in this field was primarily a consequence of the social standing of the established churches of Britain. The clergy of the Churches of England and Scotland enjoyed widespread popular respect in the eighteenth and nineteenth centuries, for they had entered a profession closely connected with the landed gentry. Ministers of other churches endeavored, with some success, to bask in their reflected glory. The respect decayed during the twentieth century, but, especially within their own congregations, their prestige was by no means extinguished. There was a certain respect for the cloth. In the United States the dividing line between clergy and laity was commonly less marked. Frequently a preacher had a trade, a practice still not unknown today. The fact that prosperous twentieth-century churches enjoyed the services of specialist ministers—for youth or for music—further blurred the line marking off the clergy from their flocks. The laity took the lead in many ventures, especially from the 1857–58 revival onward. Greater participation in church management by American businessmen imparted a lay tone to much of American religion that has never been discarded. That in turn meant that churches reflected the characteristics of the ordinary American, especially the successful American. This factor contributed to the cumulative effect of the different denominational balance in the two countries. It tended to make British evangelicalism less assertive than its American counterpart.

Education

The analysis can be widened to take in aspects of church life that yielded no similarities in the international comparison. Education is a field where the differences were overwhelmingly preponderant. In England, literacy made little progress beyond its mid-eighteenth-century level of 60 percent for males and 40 percent for females for

61. C. M. Jacquet, Jr., ed., *Yearbook of American and Canadian Churches, 1988* (Nashville, 1988), 246.

over half a century.[62] The typical dissenting pastor of this period was dismissed, with only a certain degree of exaggeration, as "an illiterate peasant or mechanic."[63] Some learning, however, was expected of the ministry in the later nineteenth century. Baptist ministers, whose academic standards were probably lower than those of other denominations at the beginning of the century, made rapid strides later on. By 1870, about half still lacked a theological education; by 1900, only 18 percent.[64] Training was more often at a low standard in the United States, especially away from the more sophisticated East Coast. As late as the 1970s, 18 percent of pastors serving with the Southern Baptist Convention had received no education beyond high school.[65] In the United States there was greater scope for anti-intellectualism. There was a general view, it was said in 1853, "that an intellectual clergyman is deficient in piety."[66] Consequently, for instance, the rejection of evolution was much stronger in the United States in the interwar period.[67] In England as well as in Wales and Scotland, both of which were famed for educational aspirations, learning was generally esteemed even by those who lacked it in the churches. In American congregations, although many counterexamples could be found in any generation, respect for scholarship was less widespread among those whose educational opportunities had been limited.

The content of education represented almost as important a difference between the countries as its level. The persistence of the classics in Britain is the key. Whereas even Harvard University, at the apex of the American educational system, abandoned its requirement of Latin and Greek in 1886,[68] Cambridge and Oxford continued

62. R. S. Schofield, "Dimensions of Illiteracy, 1850–1950," *Explorations in Economic History* 10 (Summer 1973): 446.

63. Samuel Horsley, "Second General Visitation Charge to the Clergy of the Diocese of Rochester, 1800," in *The Charges of Samuel Horsley* (London, 1830), 103.

64. J. E. B. Munson, "The Education of Baptist Ministers, 1870–1900," *Baptist Quarterly* 26–27 (July 1976): 321.

65. R. A. Baker, *The Southern Baptist Convention and Its People, 1607–1972* (Nashville, 1974), 448.

66. B. B. Edwards, "Influence of Eminent Piety on the Intellectual Powers," in *Writings*, vol. 2 (Boston, 1853), 497–98, quoted in Richard Hofstadter, *Anti-Intellectualism in American Life* (London, 1964), 87.

67. Marsden, *Fundamentalism and American Culture*, 169–70.

68. Hugh Hawkins, *Between Harvard and America: The Educational Leadership of Charles W. Eliot* (New York, 1972), 173–77.

to make Greek compulsory until 1919 and 1920.[69] The classics retained their place in the curriculum of grammar schools in England
and Wales until their phasing out in the 1960s and 1970s, and margin-
ally longer in Scotland. Training in Greek, the language of the New
Testament, was therefore much more common in Britain. It was natural for biblical scholars to emerge from the ranks of evangelical denominations. There was also a greater awareness of issues surrounding biblical criticism.[70] Even among conservative evangelicals in the
twentieth century there was more sympathy for academic standards
in biblical interpretation. There was less scope in Britain for colorful
but idiosyncratic exegesis of the Bible.

Partly as a result, British churches continued to send candidates
for the ministry to the universities. No aspect of training for the ministry of the Church of Scotland was provided outside the universities
at any point in the period. In England, Nonconformist colleges actually moved to Oxford and Cambridge in the sixty years after the abolition of the university tests that had excluded them prior to 1871.[71]
There candidates for the ministry mingled with contemporaries of all
theological opinions and none. The evangelicals among them, though
often remaining firm in their own convictions, were normally delivered from a narrowness of outlook. The tendency in the United
States was in the opposite direction, to send men for training away
from the universities, away even from denominational theological
colleges. The separate Bible schools that were created from the late
nineteenth century onward became bastions of conservative attitudes to the Bible.[72] Although certain missionary training establishments showed comparable leanings and for a while around 1950 an
avowedly fundamentalist college existed as a counterweight to the
Scottish Baptist College, there were only half a dozen equivalents in
Britain, of which the best known were the Bible Training Institute in

69. T. E. B. Howarth, *Cambridge between the Wars* (London, 1978), 87.
70. Mark A. Noll, *Between Faith and Criticism: Evangelicals, Scholarship, and the Bible in America*, 2d ed. (Grand Rapids, 1992), chap. 4.
71. E. A. Payne, "The Development of Nonconformist Theological Education in the Nine-teenth Century, with special reference to Regent's Park College," in E. A. Payne, ed., *Studies in History and Religion* (London, 1942), 252.
72. See V. L. Brereton, *Training God's Army: The American Bible School, 1880–1940* (Bloomington, Ind., 1990).

Glasgow and, from 1943, the London Bible College.[73] Neither became a rallying point for opposition to the existing denominations on the American model. There was therefore a bifurcation among institutions for theological education in the United States that hardly affected Britain. It helped ensure that there persisted a great polarization in American Protestant life between fundamentalists and modernists.

Social Patterns

Features of the wider society impinged directly on evangelicalism in both countries. Social class was more sharply defined in Britain. There the traditional norm was deference to the landed interest. Subscription lists to evangelical societies, especially in the established churches, were headed by the names of aristocrats and gentry in the nineteenth century and well into the twentieth.[74] In the United States, by contrast, there was a repudiation of deference in the name of democracy. The very notion of being termed a servant was anathema in some parts.[75] The lay right to appoint clergymen as a form of patronage was tolerated for long years by evangelicals in the Church of Scotland and throughout the period by those in the Church of England. A certain obsequiousness was maintained toward the social elite as it assimilated leading businessmen in the early twentieth century. British evangelicalism, in being wedded to social conformity, was also wedded to class distinctions. Sometimes the resulting attitudes may have obscured a sense of evangelistic responsibility toward the working classes. Certainly the tone of evangelicalism was affected. The most valued figures were not men like Billy Sunday, the raucous American preacher of the years round the First World War, but Brownlow North, "The Gentleman Evangelist."[76] There were of course exceptions. Wealthy evangelical philanthropists in America,

73. H. H. Rowdon, *London Bible College: The First Twenty-Five Years* (Worthing, England, 1968). The other institutions so far lack histories.

74. F. K. Brown, *Fathers of the Victorians: The Age of Wilberforce* (Cambridge, 1961), 353–60.

75. Frances Trollope, *Domestic Manners of the Americans* (1832; 5th ed., edited by Richard Mullen,Oxford, 1984), 44.

76. William G. McLoughlin, *Billy Sunday Was His Real Name* (Chicago, 1955); Moody-Stuart, *Brownlow North*.

especially the merchant princes of the East Coast, expected and received their share of deference. Early Primitive Methodists in England, for their part, were prepared to defy convention—to the extent, for example, of permitting female preaching for the sake of the gospel.[77] But East Coast philanthropists were notorious for aping English fashions, and the Primitives were strongly influenced by the rugged personality of the eccentric American revivalist Lorenzo Dow.[78] In general, social distinctions were much more a feature of the movement in Britain. An aura of respectability enveloped most evangelicals there.

The ethnic factor also played a part in differentiating the movements. From long before the Great Awakening in the thirteen colonies, there was a variety of nationalities alongside those of British descent. Germans and Dutch were strongly represented. Immigration reinforced the diversity over the centuries. Usually the religion of the newcomers was insulated by language for the first generation or two, so that there was little interaction with the trends of the host culture. But in due course mutual influence was unavoidable. Thus a branch of Lutheranism, the Missouri Synod, came to express fundamentalist positions. And American evangelicalism came to be more receptive to developments in Continental Protestantism than was its British counterpart. There was greater access to German and Dutch literature through individuals and churches of German and Dutch origin. Walter Rauschenbusch, the leading American spokesman of the Social Gospel, could draw on contacts in Germany as well as ideas from Germany in the evolution of his convictions. Ethnic diversity ensured that American evangelicals were touched by a wider range of influences. If at some stages their beliefs were diluted as a result, at others the experience proved enriching.

This was particularly true of the black presence in American evangelicalism. Blacks did not at first worship in separate congregations, but with the heightening of racial tension in the early nineteenth century, they created their own congregations, usually intensely evangel-

77. D. M. Valenze, *Prophetic Sons and Daughters: Female Preaching and Popular Religion in Industrial England* (Princeton, N.J., 1985).
78. J. S. Werner, *The Primitive Methodist Connexion: Its Background and History* (Madison, Wis., 1984), 45ff.

ical.[79] The process led to the launching of the African Methodist Episcopal Church in 1816. Like immigrant Protestants in the early years, they lived out their religious existence in isolation from the white Anglo-Saxon churches. But their influence could not be contained in the twentieth century. Their music in particular helped reinvigorate the worship of other evangelicals. Only from the 1950s did Britain possess a comparable tradition of black evangelical Christianity. The Pentecostal bodies brought by West Indian immigrants remained almost entirely apart from the existing churches until the mid-1980s.[80] It was therefore in the United States that black Christianity made its mark on its neighbors. American evangelicalism was undoubtedly more diverse on account of the ethnic factor. Perhaps the result was to inhibit evangelical solidarity, but ethnic variety was also a source of vigor.

A further significant divergence between the two movements began in the 1920s with the appearance of radio. In Britain it was entrusted to a public body, the British Broadcasting Corporation, which adopted a policy of excluding contentious religious themes from the airwaves. Evangelizing evangelicals were defined as contentious. Despite protests, access to broadcasting continued to be denied them when television began in the 1930s and became a way of life in the 1950s.[81] Independent television pursued similar policies from its commencement in 1955. The contrast with the United States could hardly have been sharper. There, local radio and television stations proliferated. By 1946 there were some 1,000 radio stations alone; by 1963, the number had increased to 5,000; and by 1986, to 10,000.[82] Religious content was almost universally welcomed—as long as it was paid for. An evangelical organization, the National Religious Broadcasters, by 1984 bound together 922 radio stations, 65 television stations, 535 radio producers, and 280 television/film producers.[83] Evangelistic messages were numerous and presented according to the

79. See A. J. Raboteau, *Slave Religion: The "Invisible Institution" in the Antebellum South* (New York, 1978).

80. M. J. C. Calley, *God's People: West Indian Pentecostal Sects in England* (London, 1965).

81. See K. M. Wolfe, *The Churches and the British Broadcasting Corporation, 1922–1956: The Politics of Broadcast Religion* (London, 1984).

82. *The Times,* 23 April 1986, 16.

83. R. N. Ostling, "Evangelical Publishing and Broadcasting," in *Evangelicalism and Modern America,* ed. George Marsden (Grand Rapids, 1984), 49.

latest taste of a popular audience. Television preachers became household names—even before some attained notoriety in public scandals. At least up to that time, the evangelical media empire, lacking any equivalent in Britain, greatly influenced the impact of the gospel in the United States.

Economy, Secularity and Geography

Behind the communications network, and behind many other features of twentieth-century American evangelicalism, was the power of the dollar. The economic disparity between the United States and Britain dictated differences in the religious sphere. In the eighteenth and nineteenth centuries, there had been a disparity, but it was in favor of Britain. Enjoying the rewards of being the first country in the world to industrialize, Britain was by far the richer. One obvious consequence was the much greater extent of publication in Britain. Americans learned what Britons taught. After the First World War, however, the United States experienced the greater prosperity. The flow of literature and ideas, at least at the popular level, was therefore reversed. Economic attitudes, furthermore, were as important as economic realities. Enterprise was part of British life in the eighteenth and early nineteenth centuries. Respect was paid to the entrepreneur. Congregationalists in particular celebrated the rising industrial civilization as an expression of the same unfettered spirit they represented in religion. Gradually, however, there was a decline of esteem for business success. Matthew Arnold set a new course with his mockery of the narrowness of the same Congregationalists, together with the other Nonconformists, for their devotion to material advantage and confinement of culture to tea parties.[84] Zeal for money-making was less socially acceptable, at least in public. In the United States there was no comparable process. Business ambition retained its fascination for the young. As a boy, President Jimmy Carter began buying and selling peanuts at a profit. At the age of nine, he was able to acquire a quantity of cotton at a bargain price. With the proceeds

84. Matthew Arnold, *Culture and Anarchy*, ed. J. Dover Wilson (Cambridge, 1960; orig. 1869). Cf. M. J. Wiener, *English Culture and the Decline of the Industrial Spirit* (Cambridge, 1981).

of its sale, he purchased five houses. As a teenager, he enjoyed a private income from their monthly rents.[85] Such confidence and thrust were not rare among evangelicals. These qualities were naturally carried over from the business world into the religious sphere. The result was the "brashness" that British eyes saw, for example, in American religious advertising on television; but that spirit of enterprise, with its expectation of concrete achievements, often led to much more effective evangelism.

Another feature differentiating the two societies was the degree of secularization. Churchgoing relative to population was quite high in eighteenth-century America, and probably higher than in contemporary Britain. Some of the leeway may have been made up during the nineteenth century, so that religiosity was not markedly different in the two countries by 1900. In the twentieth century, however, there developed a striking contrast. Churchgoing collapsed in England to less than 10 percent of the adult population in the 1980s, but in the United States the proportion was as high as 42 or 43 percent. There was a corresponding decline in the social salience of religion in Britain. Weddings had traditionally been performed in church, but by 1980 fully half the marriage ceremonies were conducted in register offices.[86] Religion became a weaker force in Britain. Evangelicals, furthermore, formed a much higher proportion of the population in the United States.[87] The greater support in the United States for religion in general, and for evangelicalism in particular, flowed from the various other factors that have been discussed. Success, however, breeds success. The buoyant temper of the American movement was encouraged by its strength in society.

Geography, it is clear, has also done much to mold the contrasting forms of religious practice in the two countries. Although there were instances of remote and self-contained Christian communities within Britain, the island's narrow confines meant, even at an early date, that its evangelical movement tended to form a fairly integrated whole. In particular, denominational leaders readily created networks that

85. Jimmy Carter, *Why Not the Best?* (New York, 1976), 22.
86. *Social Trends No. 12: 1982 Edition*, ed. Deo Ramprakash (London, 1981), 193.
87. George Marsden, "The Evangelical Denomination," in *Evangelicalism and Modern America*, ed. Marsden (Grand Rapids, 1984), x.

bound them together in solidarity. By contrast, the vast distances within the United States dictated that new ideas spread only slowly in remoter areas during the era before the mass media revolution. Parts of the Appalachian Mountains were not touched by religious change—or by almost any other form of change—for series of decades at a time. Even long into the twentieth century, there persisted local religious cultures. Consequently, there was great scope for misunderstandings. Denominational splits based on local allegiances ensued. In many cases the lines of division followed the boundaries between the great sections of the United States. The East Coast, the Midwest, the Far West, and the South had entirely different characters—especially the South. Below the Mason-Dixon line was a region almost entirely untouched by immigration from continental Europe but deeply marked first by slavery and then by the legacy of the Civil War in white supremacy and dominance of the Democratic party. There evangelical religion held a hegemony unrivaled in the Western Hemisphere.[88] In Britain, the nearest equivalents—the remoter Scottish Highlands and Welsh-speaking Wales—never adopted evangelical values as community norms to the same degree. The South was able to generate distinctive expressions of evangelicalism, of which the chief was the Southern Baptist Convention—populist, extraordinarily centralized for a denomination theoretically upholding local church independency, and the largest Protestant body in the world. Its character was partly shaped by the other significant aspect of geography, the vast rural tracts of the United States.

Despite urbanization, the United States retained a higher proportion of rural population than Britain. In many areas, particularly where smallholding was customary, the tradition of frontier religion lived on long after settlement had been pushed further west. Because people were called together for a preaching service only rarely on the frontier, it was thought essential to set out the gospel with great force. The intensity of evangelistic appeal often striking among Americans was a product in the first place of the backwoods. Localism, sectionalism, and the frontier combined to sustain the pristine vitality of American evangelicalism.

88. K. K. Bailey, *Southern White Protestantism in the Twentieth Century* (New York, 1964), ix.

Conclusion

How similar, then, were the evangelicals of the two countries? An overall evaluation must suggest that the British and American varieties were far more alike than is often supposed in literature that concentrates on one alone, making only tangential reference to the other. Evangelical religion in itself was originally planted simultaneously in Britain and America. The shaping waves of cultural influence, theological developments, denominational patterns, and the changing types of social action were all broadly parallel. Those authors who have examined the tight bonds between the two movements are undoubtedly right to conclude that American religion was primarily a westward outgrowth from its European roots, and not something new. Nevertheless, the differences were real. There were contrasts resulting from the strength of theological tendencies and the balance of denominations, together with those deriving from the impact of education, other social factors, and geography. Each of these, with the partial exception of the first, was a consequence of inhabiting a new world. The weakness of the Episcopalians, the earlier abandonment of Greek, the casting aside of deference, and sheer distance all sprang from the conditions of the Western Hemisphere. Such circumstances transformed many contingent features of popular religion. In essentials, however, there was common ground. Preachers who crossed the ocean discovered an immediate rapport with their hearers. The presentation of the message, like the accent, might be strange, but its substance, like the language that was used, was familiar. In fundamentals, evangelicalism remained a single entity on the two sides of the Atlantic.

The differences between the movements in Britain and the United States were not constant over time. At their origin, when the American colonies were merely far-flung dependencies of Great Britain, their religious life was unlikely to be highly distinctive. So it proved. The evangelicalism of the eighteenth century showed the weakest contrasts. Differences in the nineteenth century were greater as the American western frontier advanced, but still the circumstances of the two countries were relatively similar. No more education was required to be a Bible Christian exhorter in Cornwall than to be a backwoods evangelist in Kentucky. Entrepreneurship had not yet fallen under a cloud in Britain. It was in the twentieth century that the contrasts became greatest. In a very few respects, it is true, previous differences were eroded. Immigration, for instance, brought a black presence into British popular religion. But in most ways differentiation increased. Fundamentalism became the dominant force in American evangelicalism, whereas in Britain it was contained; Britain produced no evangelical media circus; and wealth became rare in the British churches. The movements gradually diverged. At no stage was there any significant check to the natural process by which two stems from a common stock grew in different directions.

Perhaps what is most remarkable is that virtually all the contrasts reinforce each other. All the differences that came to light in the twentieth century tended to make the American version more intense, more confident, and less inhibited. That is not to say that evangelical religion in the United States became more attractive or more Christian. But it is to point out that it became more vigorous and growth-oriented. It is commonplace among historians to contrast British with American foreign policy from the Second World War onward. Britain habitually pursued a course that was more moderate, restrained, and prudent. The United States adopted a more idealistic, clear-cut, crusading style.[89] The difference between the British and the American varieties of evangelicalism was parallel. Popular religion, like foreign policy, was shaped by the total range of factors that created the British and American experience. The two countries distilled similar versions of evangelicalism, but the American brand was certainly the headier brew.

---

89. For example, "The general American attitude was that there was a need to move . . . into the new era of efficient world organization. . . . Britain was, perhaps, more pragmatic and more concerned with the realities of power" (Ritchie Ovendale, *The English-Speaking Alliance: Britain, the United States, the Dominions, and the Cold War, 1945–1951* [London, 1985], 6–7).

Australian
Vistas

Evangelical Anglicans Compared

Australia and Britain

Brian Dickey

The impact of evangelicalism upon Australian Anglicanism has been profoundly significant—in the founding years, in urban and rural settings, in constitutional affairs, and more.[1] That evangelical tradition was imported from the world of the late eighteenth- century Evangelical Revival in England. The flow of influence continued with great power from both England and Ireland through the nineteenth century and well into the twentieth. But the Australian evangelical tradition within Anglicanism has also responded to local circum-

1. This essay and a similar piece by Stuart Piggin have been developed from a shared intellectual base stretching back some years. I am grateful for his comments and stimulation in the preparation of this chapter. We are jointly engaged on a series of projects in the history of evangelicalism in Australia. Piggin is the senior author of "Australian Evangelicalism, 1788–1988" (working title of a forthcoming monograph), while Dickey is general editor of the forthcoming "Australian Dictionary of Evangelical Biography." Much of the empirical data underlying this chapter is drawn from these larger projects.

stances and opportunities, especially in the twentieth century, in ways that increasingly have reflected its independence from its formative inheritance from the United Kingdom. In missionary strategy, bush church work, church growth, theological scholarship, and more, Australian evangelical Anglicans are, in the late twentieth century, finding their own way, responding to the challenges of their own choosing. The British heritage has shrunk to modest proportions.

Setting the Scene

The Church of England in Australia was part of the Church of England in the eighteenth century. From 1801 to 1869 it belonged to the United Church of England and Ireland; then it was part of the Church of England until the creation of the Church of England in Australia (1962), now the Anglican Church of Australia (1972).

The most notable characteristic of the Church of England, and of the United Church of England and Ireland, was that it was "by law established"; that is, it was a state-controlled agency whose senior officials were appointed by the crown and whose central documents possessed legal validation from Parliament. The Church of England in Australia was never explicitly established in this way. Nevertheless, "Anglican"[2] ministry began in the colony of New South Wales from 1788 onward with the deployment of government-appointed and salaried chaplains as part of the colony's administration, serving the convict and the military establishments. They were immediately answerable to their colonial superiors, and only in a distant and ineffectual way to the bishop who licensed them.[3] With the appointment of these chaplains, Anglicanism was the official Christian faith of the colony, but possessing no separate independence. The chaplaincy system lasted till transportation ceased (New South Wales, 1840; Van Diemen's Land, 1853).

2. I shall use this term somewhat anachronistically in this article as the common adjectival referent to the Church of England, the United Church of England and Ireland, the Church of England in Australia, and the Anglican Church of Australia, as the context demands. The term evolved in the nineteenth century to meet this grammatical problem.

3. This was, in the case of the military chaplains, the archbishop of Canterbury, and also, by extension, the convict chaplains. Episcopal supervision was delegated to the slightly closer bishop of Calcutta from 1823. There is no evidence that these "ordinaries," or episcopal superiors, ever exercised any pastoral care over the chaplains in NSW.

For a short period from 1823 to 1836, when a more elaborate state-sponsored but slightly more self-governing Anglican structure was developed, the Church of England in Australia possessed a form and style recognizably similar to its established English progenitor. But in 1836 the colonial government distanced itself from the Anglican Church by legislating for shared subsidies to such churches as chose to apply and could meet certain minimum criteria as to congregational identity and so on. From this point onward the Church of England in Australia became but one denomination among many competing for government funds and favor. Furthermore, when state aid to religion completely ceased in the various colonies between 1851 ('South Australia') and 1895 ('Western Australia'), the Anglican Church became completely free of direct state control or supervision, except for enabling acts in some colonies permitting it to exist as a corporation and of course laws that applied equally to other organizations.

This also prompts the reflection that the evangelical Anglican strategy, enunciated by the Clapham Sect leadership in England, that to hold to the established character of the Church of England would promote the interests of the evangelical party, was even less likely to possess validity in Australia. Don Lewis makes a major point of this strategic debate, asserting that in England by 1860 the *pan*-evangelical model had emerged as dominant among evangelicals, especially as an institutional model for evangelism, over against the earlier preference of "church evangelicals."[4] Both models rejected the third, which we might label "sect evangelicalism," where the whole worshiping assembly deliberately espoused evangelicalism. He shows that senior English evangelicals such as J. C. Ryle continued to promote the virtues of church evangelicalism and establishment in the later nineteenth century, when Roman Catholics, nonconformists, and ritualists preferred the liberal political view that disestablishment was best for the future of the Church of England. There were also twentieth-century examples of the use of state power in England to shore up the evangelical position in the Church of England, notably the rejection by the House of Commons of prayer book revision in the late 1920s.

4. Donald M. Lewis, *Lighten Their Darkness: The Evangelical Mission to Working-Class London, 1828–1860* (New York, 1986).

If, as it may be argued, open and equal competition was so much more highly regarded in Australia, it is to be expected that the pro-state church evangelical strategy would be even less popular. It was easily labeled subordination, state interference, or worse, by its critics, especially from outside the evangelical tradition. The reliance by evangelicals on arguments about the established character of the Church of England in Australia, when they sought legal declarations in 1947 that the use of the 1928 prayer book was illegal, was the most striking Australian example of this tendency.[5] Whether there are still traces of this reliance on the virtues of state power to shore up evangelical influence in the Australian case is now unlikely. There remain hints. Donald Robinson, who retired in 1993 as archbishop of Sydney, made much of the legal bases of his power as archbishop in disputes with some of his clergy. It is hard to know if another archbishop would act in the same way. Robinson also gladly used the opportunity provided by public ceremonial occasions to offer a Christian component, for example, offering prayers for the nation on Australia Day. (He took turns annually with the Roman Catholic cardinal-archbishop of Sydney.) Again the question is whether nonevangelicals would still accept such a close link with the state on such occasions. Another example relates to the method used in early 1992 to stop the bishop of Canberra and Goulburn from ordaining women to the priesthood in advance of the next General Synod meeting. It was to obtain an injunction from the NSW Court of Appeal.[6] Since evangelicals were obviously part of the opposition to the ordination of women, though by no means the only ones, their participation in the use of this civil power of the law was consistent with previous actions. Consistent or not, they must grapple with the predictable and well-rehearsed odium their tactics have evoked. Even more difficult is the position of the many evangelical Anglicans who support the or-

5. Ruth Teale, "The 'Red Book' Case," *Journal of Religion History* 12 (1982): 74–89.

6. Another attempt was made in Perth to block the ordination of ten women as priests by Archbishop Carnley. Again it was based on seeking a civil court injunction. However, the plaintiffs were not necessarily to be labeled evangelicals; like the Goulburn case, they reflect a coalition that only in part overlaps evangelicalism. As of April 1992 the matter was back in court, attracting wide media attention. In this legal process there is no doubt that a group of Sydney evangelical Anglicans was taking the lead. Their behavior has generated much debate and a great deal of criticism.

dination of women as priests; they are less likely, however, to resort to the use of state power to impose their views on the Anglican Church of Australia.

Another obvious social contrast between *settled* societies in England and Ireland and *settling* colonial societies must be considered in this discussion. Churches, along with all else in the colonies, had to be created as institutions from the beginning. There were no endowments, no inheritances of buildings, no established scholarly traditions, no supplies of leaders on hand. All these and more had to be imported or created locally. It was a tremendous and exhausting task, even if it was easily assumed that the British models and methods should be replicated, without much thought for the differences between the two cases. In particular, the settling communities had largely to import clerical staff from England (and Ireland) until the early twentieth century. Thus, the evolving character and availability of this stream of metropolitan clergy remained crucial to the character of the Church of England in Australia.

One more factor that is significant in this analysis is timing. This first affected the terms of the opportunities for evangelicals within the Church of England framework in England to influence the choice of chaplains to New South Wales; it was an era of elites, of patronage, of personal influence. Timing also mattered in the impact of ongoing developments within the Church of England and the Church of Ireland in the nineteenth century such as the rise to influence of Tractarianism, or the collapse of opportunity for employment in the Church of Ireland after disestablishment in 1869. In this sense, there will sometimes be direct linkages explicable in United Kingdom terms, rather than a process of concurrent and independent development in Australia.

It should also be remembered that evangelicalism among Australian Anglicans has never evolved solely from or been informed completely by immediate contemporary English Anglican primary sources. Established traditions of faith in published form deriving from the previous three hundred years' history of Protestantism in the United Kingdom have always been available in Australia; furthermore, the process of open competition in the colonies has encouraged borrowing from other denominations, as have the imperatives of settling in a new land. Importation of ideas and methods has also occurred more recently from the United States direct to Australian evangelicalism. Consequently the argument about Australian evangelical Anglicanism is certainly not one about a simple one-to-one relationship with its metropolitan progenitors.

Having made these introductory statements about the frame of reference, I now address the comparisons and contrasts observable between the United Kingdom and the Australian expressions of evangelicalism within Anglicanism. The aim of this essay is to draw out the distinctives of the Australian Anglican case of evangelicalism. I am not trying to compare the metropolitan case with some colonial offshoots simply as part of the story of the expansion of the metropolitan dimension of evangelicalism, let alone Anglicanism. Rather, what is noteworthy is the Australian expression of evangelicalism, in its Anglican guise: What are the informing traditions? What are the special local developments that set it apart from its creating matrix? How has it interacted with its local environment in ways that are different from those in the United Kingdom? The British cases illuminate the Australian one, which is the central concern. It is necessary now to sketch a narrative sequence of the developing evangelical Anglican tradition in Australia that explores some of these introductory points with historical detail.

The Early Chaplaincy

English Anglican evangelicals provided the Christian base for the foundation of the colony of New South Wales in 1788. John Newton, William Cowper, William Wilberforce, and Henry Venn all joined in a vision of evangelizing the South Pacific, the Aborigines, and the prospective colonial white population of convicts to be transported to New South Wales. They saw the project in the largest and most comprehensive terms as an exercise in world evangelization, a distinctive evangelical concern in the late eighteenth century. William Wilberforce, in particular, exercised decisive influence with his friend Prime Minister William Pitt to ensure the creation of a religious institution for the colony (i.e., the chaplaincy) and in ensuring the appointment of an evangelical Anglican clergyman, Richard Johnson, to the post.[7]

---

7. For fuller details of this tale, see Piggin, "Australian Evangelicalism," chap. 1.

The cultural and racial base of the white community of New South Wales presented significant difficulties to the exponents of evangelical Christianity in the colony. Most of the settlers were convicted criminals, drawn from the working classes of the United Kingdom. About a third were Irish, most of whom were Roman Catholics. Given the eighteenth-century methodology of the Church of England, with its focus on settled parochial ministry based on deference and trust, these were enormous handicaps. In England the Church of England was weakest in its efforts to minister to the working classes; in Ireland the Church of Ireland was the faith of the Establishment, the foreign ruling colonizers. Displaced urban workers who had become convicts, let alone Irish transportees, were unlikely to respond to Church of England ministry, however dedicated and biblical.[8] The present scholarly opinion is that the first generation of Christian effort at evangelism and pastoral care, evangelical Anglican in character as it was, was a failure, especially in the ministry to the convicts, former convicts, their families, and the Aborigines.[9] There remains some doubt about how this judgment has been framed. With respect to the white community it is probably true that the Australian mission was no less effective (if no more) than its English and Irish counterparts.[10] And it is certain the evangelical clergy in New South Wales tried hard. The tradition of hostility among historians in Australia toward evangelical Christianity may have underrated both the effort and the outcome of this ministry.[11]

8. Richard Johnson, first colonial chaplain in NSW, published a thoroughly evangelical tract laced with biblical selections (*An Address to the Inhabitants of the Colonies Established in New South Wales and Norfolk Island* [London, 1794]). It emphasized the necessity to repent from present sinfulness and underlined the inevitable judgment to come. He addressed his convict flock in the pamphlet with great fervor. Could they—would they?—read it?

9. The main study of this link between Christianity and convicts is A. Grocott, *Convicts, Clergymen, and Churches: Attitudes of Convicts and Ex-convicts towards the Churches and Clergy in New South Wales from 1788 to 1851* (Sydney, 1980). The related question of the relationships between early evangelicals and the Aborigines is studied in John Harris, *One Blood. Two Hundred Years of Aboriginal Encounter with Christianity: A Story of Hope* (Sydney, 1990).

10. Alan Gilbert, *Religion and Society in Industrial England: Church, Chapel, and Social Change, 1740–1914* (London, 1976), makes the case of the inadequacy of eighteenth-century English Christian ministry to the working classes, especially in the towns.

11. By contrast, Robert Knopwood, the Anglican chaplain in Van Diemen's Land, was a Tory who seemed to enjoy the chase and the table as much as his pastoral duties, and who was

Could the early evangelical leadership, the clergy Richard Johnson and Samuel Marsden in particular, have made things worse simply because they were evangelicals? Australian scholarship argues that Marsden probably did.[12] Whereas in England the process of establishing settled parochial ministries was largely in place except, as Gilbert reminds us, in the north, and clergy came and went, producing something of a wide spectrum of ministries, the predominance of evangelicals among the chaplaincy in New South Wales meant that evangelical Christianity was being tested on behalf of Christianity at large in New South Wales. To reject Marsden's Christianity was to reject Christianity generally. There were few if any other versions to choose from in the colony, and only a small minority consciously brought a viable alternative with them.

What Marsden preached above all was the awesome and inevitable judgment of God upon a sinful world. He offered grace always, but grace surrounded by dreadful warnings of eternal punishment. It was a terrible and demanding setting for the gospel, and one that people then and since have found psychologically unwise. Furthermore, Marsden sought and gained personal security in farming, and public recognition and authority as a leading magistrate. Both his financial and his public achievements were consistent with eighteenth-century Anglican social modes; both were also imposed on him by the requirements of the colonial environment—he had to eat, feed his children, and, more significantly, finance his missionary endeavors to the Maoris of New Zealand, a dangerous 1,200-mile sea voyage away. As for his work as a magistrate, he was ordered to serve by his colonial superior, the governor. These characteristics of Marsden's situation combined to gain for him the reputation as the "flogging parson" and to identify evangelical Anglicanism with money-grubbing, authoritarian, threatening, ruling-class oppression. It should not be forgotten, however, that in New Zealand he is commemorated as the Apostle to New Zealand.

---

far less urgent, biblical, crucicentric, or conversionistic. While his recent biographer has tried to rescue his reputation, the received image of Bobby with dog and hunting horse probably remains accurate. See, for example, the cover illustration in Geoffrey Stephens, *Robert Knopwood: A Biography* (Hobart, 1990).

  12. A. T. Yarwood, *Samuel Marsden: The Great Survivor* (Melbourne, 1977).

How much was personal in this less than triumphant outcome?
How much depended, for example, on the high profile of the senior
chaplain, or on the deliberate criminal libels of Marsden published at
the behest of Governor Macquarie?[13] How much, by contrast, arose
from the demanding and divisive impact of gospel preaching? Would
a different Christian tradition have produced a less contested and
more successful relationship with the largely convict community? At
the very least, the examples of William Cowper, of his son, William
Macquarie Cowper, and of Thomas Hassall, all colonial chaplains between 1810 and 1860, suggest that when free of some of Marsden's
personal burdens and obsessions, Australian evangelical Anglicans
could revert to the best features of the British evangelical Anglican
type. They were utterly dedicated pastors, offering a comprehensive
range of ministries including worship, preaching, education, exhor-
tation, welfare, evangelism, and advocacy. These men developed a
ministry based on the notion of a specific parish location, as they had
been taught by their English mentors of the Clapham tradition. They
modified it to cope with the vast distances of the Australian landscape, so that Hassall became known as the galloping parson. When
they did that, with great dedication, and despite the vast distances of
a settling Australian community, they succeeded. In these men, then,
we can observe the successful transference of a Christian tradition—
namely, the role of the energetic pastor-teacher of a local congregation—that became crucial in the long-term survival and development
of evangelical Christianity in Australia.[14]

Evangelical Anglicans Become a Party (c. 1820–1860)

By the 1820s other Anglican traditions were exercising clerical
leadership in Australia. Archdeacons Scott and Broughton were High
Churchmen appointed at the behest of influential patrons (in Broughton's case, the Duke of Wellington as prime minister). In this, we are

13. Ibid., 194–200, establishes this startling sequences of events.
14. Another example was Charles Beaumont Howard, the first colonial chaplain to the colony of South Australia. Formed in the Trinity College Dublin model and then in the diocese of
Chester under the evangelical bishop J. B. Sumner, he too gave himself totally to Christianity
defined in evangelical terms. It cost him his life after six and a half years of unceasing effort
(Brian Dickey, *Holy Trinity Adelaide: The History of a City Church, 1836–1988* [Adelaide,
1988], chap. 2).

reminded again of the importance of English government patronage to the colonial situation. Australian Anglicanism was long vulnerable to such interventions, delivering new, perhaps unwanted, fashions shaped in the homeland and embodied in the persons of powerful new leaders for the colonial church. Thus critically, William Broughton (bishop 1835–53) resisted evangelical influence and imported to Australia the English division, so fashionable in the first half of the nineteenth century among churchmen, that disdained and suspected evangelicals and depicted them as weak on episcopacy, overemphasizing personal commitment and activity, making too much of evangelism, and threatening the settled parochial ministry with itinerancy (e.g., in Ireland). Above all, because High Churchmen were Laudian-Arminian in theological outlook, they were suspicious of the evangelical emphasis on Calvinist doctrines of salvation and election deriving from the Protestant Reformation.

By the 1840s, then, Australian evangelical Anglicans were experiencing a contested situation, as were their English colleagues. By virtue of Broughton's behavior they were turned into "party"—and they were no longer the party in power. But it would appear, meanwhile, that, as in Ireland and England, evangelical Anglicanism was widely acceptable among the respectable middle classes of New South Wales. Low Church Protestantism became for many the norm. We do not know if this was (1) merely conventional religiosity, (2) an expression of rampant laicism suspicious of a High Church bishop, (3) the product of a faith chosen to distinguish them from the Irish, the former criminals, and the working classes, or (4) the product of energetic clerical evangelical ministry; all could be true. Or none. Or something else. Whatever the causes, an evangelical tradition was well rooted in Sydney by 1850.[15]

The major new development in the life of the Church of England in the nineteenth century was Tractarianism, which started in Oxford in the 1830s and developed into ritualism by the 1860s and Anglo-Ca-

---

15. In a suggestive note, Richard Ely strengthens the case for this Erastian, respectable, Low Church Protestantism as a significant component of Anglicanism in the nineteenth century in Australia. He criticized David Hilliard, "Anglicanism," *Australian Cultural History* 7 (1988): 64–82, for implying that Anglicanism in Australia was largely about cathedrals and architecture and style (Richard Ely, "'Anglican' Religious Culture and 'Anglo-Australian' Religious Culture: A Comment on David Hilliard's Paper," *Australian Cultural History* 7 [1988]: 83–85).

tholicism by the late nineteenth century. The emphasis within these movements was upon tradition as superior to the Bible, on priest as superior to the people, on bishops and their authority, on ancient forms and practices such as confession and religious orders, on public processions, vestments, and elaborate ceremonies. By the early twentieth century, the movements seemed to have rejected everything evangelicals stood for. The Reformation was at risk, and with it salvation by faith alone. By later in the century *sola scriptura* was also seen to be at risk as the ritualists started to make common cause with theological liberals, or at least so some evangelicals believed. Consequently, English evangelical Anglicanism was on the defensive from the 1840s, and this same process can be followed in the colonies. From the 1850s the quality of evangelical clerics coming to Australia declined or simply dried up. Australian Anglicanism became more diverse as the range of Anglican clergy arriving expanded. The center of gravity of the Church of England was shifting away from evangelicalism, both in England and in the colonies.

More important still to this trend away from evangelicalism was the first wave of bishoprics: Australia in 1835, New Zealand and Tasmania, both in 1842 (when "Australia" was reduced merely to Sydney!), and in 1846, Adelaide, Newcastle, and Melbourne, all created by the British government, with financial help from generous English donors. The establishment of this "normal" Anglican structure, which was based on the diocese with a bishop who could confirm, ordain, and discipline, emphasized the High Church view of Anglicanism, in which the existence of diocesan bishops was of the essence, one of its necessary characteristics. This was probably a view to which earlier colonial evangelicals had not given much attention; for them the pastor and congregation was the defining entity, sustained by the Bible and then the prayer book.

In Adelaide, for example, Bishop Short had a thirty-five-year battle with evangelicals both lay and clerical. What had been a predominantly evangelical Anglican style established by the first wave of clergy in 1836–46[16] was overlaid by broad, high, and eventually (in

16. Dickey, *Holy Trinity Adelaide*, chaps. 2 and 3. See especially the manifestos published by Howard in 1838, in which he speaks of setting forth "'Jesus Christ and Him crucified' as the only foundation for a sinner's hopes" (37) and Farrell in 1848 in almost exactly the same words (54).

the twentieth century) ritualist styles that weakened the evangelical emphasis on Bible, evangelism, action, and the cross, replacing them with greater attention to tradition, settled form, reserve, and incarnational theology, increasingly within a more liberal doctrinal framework.

In Newcastle, to give another example, Bishop Tyrrell arrived full of suspicion of the early evangelical clergy and set out in similar vein to remake the diocesan tradition along High Church lines, following the advice of his mentor Broughton.[17] Melbourne, however, under Charles Perry,[18] had an evangelical leader who set about his immense tasks with conviction. But his successors, Moorhouse and Goe, put no effort into maintaining such an evangelical tradition. As a result, that diocese proved more vulnerable than Sydney to the shifts in Anglicanism occurring in England. To this day, Melbourne Anglican evangelicalism is a party, often at odds with the official leadership, but powerful in lay strength and some clergy, sometimes granted some proportionate political influence within the diocese, but equally often condemned by Anglican critics for circumventing Anglican structures by frequent use of lay interdenominational agencies with evangelical charters. The election of David Penman as archbishop of Melbourne in 1984 makes the point: it was an electoral coup after a long, drawn-out deadlock among the more expectant nonevangelical pretenders. Nor did Penman ever enjoy the undivided support of his diocese.[19]

17. G. P. Shaw, *Patriarch and Patriot: William Grant Broughton, 1788–1853* (Melbourne, 1978), 209, 220.

18. A. de Q. Robin, *Charles Perry, Bishop of Melbourne: The Challenge of a Colonial Episcopate, 1847–76* (Perth, 1967).

19. Alan Nichols, *David Penman: Bridge Builder, Peace Maker, Fighter for Social Justice* (Sydney, 1991). The contrasts between Sydney and Melbourne have attracted a variety of scholarly writings; indeed it is something of a cottage industry where opinion sometimes prevails over evidence. Nevertheless, see Stuart Piggin, briefly summarizing his Perry Memorial Lecture "Pietism, Pluralism, and Provincialism: The Divergent Paths of Melbourne and Sydney Evangelicalism, 1848–1988" in *Southern Cross* (February 1991): 12–13: "Melbourne's evangelicalism has been gentler, but then the laity are always less quarrelsome than the clergy." More generally, see Jill Roe, "A Tale of Religion in Two Cities," *Meanjin* 40 (1980): 48–56; David Hilliard, "God in the Suburbs: The Religious Culture of Australian Cities in the 1950s," *Australian Historical Studies* 24 (1991): 399–419, for further references.

Evangelicals Lose the Bush (c. 1860–c. 1920) . . .

Some bush dioceses—for example, Goulburn, North Queensland, Riverina, Bathurst, and Bendigo—began evangelical in leadership but were overtaken by other styles of Anglicanism later in the century or (e.g., Bendigo) early in the next. All of the newer dioceses in the distant parts—Willochra, Carpentaria, North-West Australia, and St. Arnaud—began with similar High Church or Anglo-Catholic traditions dominant. The important doctoral study recently completed by Ruth Frappell offers some powerful explanations for this shift in the dioceses of rural Australia.

The importance of the shift already noted in the balance of English church parties in mid-century away from evangelicalism toward High Church and Anglo-Catholic styles was plainly central to this process by which evangelicalism lost the bush. It meant that the men offering for the bush dioceses of Australia were less likely to be evangelical, more likely to be High Church or Anglo-Catholic. Even more important, during the period when English bishops selected men for Australian bishoprics (i.e., before the twentieth-century practice of election by synod became established in the Australian bush), they were likely to select men they favored theologically as well as personally. The same outcome applied with even more important results for the character of the Australian bush dioceses. All of this was exacerbated by the failure of city-based clergy to reproduce themselves socially. Few Australian clerical dynasties emerged, and even fewer were willing to proceed to the poor, toilsome bush dioceses. Evangelicals were the prime examples. Few went from the urban dioceses for rural service, thus reinforcing the weakness of evangelicals in rural Australia. It must be said in their defense that their decision was strategic, not personal; they went where the people were in large numbers, to preach the gospel to them and to minister to congregations.

Nevertheless, the outcome in the bush meant that the bishops in those dioceses had to make do with what was on offer, mainly from England, which was sometimes, as Frappell shows, pretty poor stuff. Furthermore, when the bishops got round to addressing the problem of supplying clergy from locally trained men, they created their own training colleges, all weak, limited, and likely to reinforce the style and preferences of the bishop.

Again, the theological and liturgical preferences of the late nineteenth-century bishops and the more active "modern" clergy in the bush dioceses were, with few exceptions, High Church or even Anglo-Catholic in the fullest sense. These clergy judged that such emphases were most likely to promote pastoral success and a distinctive Anglican identity in the countryside of Australia. It led to some startling applications of "proper" Gothic architecture and late nineteenth-century ecclesiastical furniture to unexpected locations in the hot and dusty Australian countryside.[20]

At the same time, from the 1870s to the 1920s, the bishops observed what they believed to be the oppressive and threatening behavior of the metropolitan dioceses of Sydney and Melbourne. In wishing to be separate and independent of them, they reinforced their sense of difference from the entrenched evangelicalism of those two dioceses, for evangelicalism and centralism were united in the minds of these country leaders as twin evils.[21] The development of Anglican constitutional forms toward a province of dioceses in New South Wales in the 1870s involved conflict, especially over endowments and the fear of being outvoted in matters of doctrinal importance. In resisting Sydney, the New South Wales country dioceses were also resisting evangelicalism. As Frappell shows, Sydney had become identified in the eyes of the dioceses with overpowering metropolitan centralism (and probably still is). The steps Sydney took to maintain the weakness of the legal structure of the Church of England in Australia in the debates of the 1920s, preferring to rely on the legal links (the "nexus") each diocese possessed with the English church, had the effect of reinforcing that sense of exalted diocesan authority, that dispersed federalism of the Australian part of the Church of England that made it so different from this English progenitor, and from its Canadian cousin. The adoption of the constitution of the Church of England in Australia in 1962 was a significant cession of diocesan power, especially by Sydney evangelicals. In 1992 proposals have surfaced to return a large degree of power to individual dioceses. This 1992 initia-

20. Other, more moderate, Anglicans also adopted the same cultural mode, favoring the same Gothic style, though perhaps with less self-conscious "religious" justifications than the Anglo-Catholics.

21. Stephen Judd and Kenneth Cable, *Sydney Anglicans* (Sydney, 1987), 89–91.

tive reinforces the point that the institutionalized strength of evangelicalism within the Anglican Church continues to generate organizational tensions and outcomes quite different from those experienced in other parts of the Anglican communion.[22]

Turning from that constitutional and organizational issue to the problem of clergy supply reinforces the argument. The most sustained effort to provide clergy for the poorer and more remote Australian dioceses, which Frappell rightly labels not merely country dioceses but missionary dioceses, was through the medium of the "bush brotherhood." This was a notion developed in Australia, in which groups of clergy agreed to a form of regular life, including poverty, chastity, and obedience to a superior for a period, usually five years. Some hundreds of English (though few Australian) clergy were recruited to such brotherhoods for service in many Australian dioceses. They served groups of vast parishes with energetic commitment. They worked best when their leader was a man of outstanding personal character, larger than life for the great outback. But the rank-and-file clergy came and went in five-year stints, or less if they were utterly inadequate to the demands of the bush. Only rarely, as Frappell shows, did this method survive beyond the 1920s as a more settled and domestic ministry became appropriate.[23] Nonetheless, for fifty years or more these brotherhoods exercised a significant and anti-evangelical influence on many Australian dioceses.

. . . And Move to Regain It (c. 1920 Onward)

It is essential to pursue Frappell's argument one further and important step. In the second decade of the twentieth century, evangelicals, mainly in Sydney, at long last began to address this loss of the countryside. They hit upon a creative alternative. They established the Bush Church Aid Society, at first in connection with the Colonial and Continental Church Society of Great Britain, which was an English evangelical missionary society that had already had some influence

22. These remarks are based upon conversations with a variety of participants and upon a reading of a portion of the frequent press commentary, some of it ill informed.
23. Ruth M. Frappell, "The Anglican Ministry to the Unsettled Rural Districts of Australia, c. 1890 to 1940" (Ph.D. diss., University of Sydney, 1991), 36, 50, 64, 158, 169, 220–22, 353–61.

in church-planting in early Western Australia. This was the application of a classic English evangelical method, namely, the centralized missionary society with a clear agenda and doctrinal basis acting on behalf of the church at large and in cooperation with the local bishop by negotiation. BCA, as it quickly became known, deployed clergy, often married, as well as deaconesses and nursing sisters. They went, like the bush brothers before them, to remote frontier towns and districts. They exercised a practical, hands-on ministry of health care and Christian encouragement. They attracted much support from city-based but susceptible evangelicals who were responding to the appeal to support these proponents of the "Australian Legend" in evangelical garb, emphasizing self-sustaining competence in the bush. They gained a fair degree of approval in the bush from lonely men and women (especially in the crisis of childbirth). Some rigid bishops were rather cautious about these potential Trojan horses. Others welcomed them in recognition of their dedication and in desperation at the difficulty of finding anyone else. Unlike the bush brotherhoods, now gone, this evangelical counterattack remains an active and positive contribution to the maintenance of the evangelical tradition in the Anglican Church of Australia.[24]

Sydney since c. 1860

As suggested above, the underlying evangelical strength in Sydney was not obliterated by Bishop Broughton, even as the bush was being lost. His successor, Frederic Barker (1854–81), was a fine sprig of Chester-Liverpool evangelicalism. He gained wide support and embedded evangelical style, theology, and preferences into Sydney's Anglican Christianity, so much so that in the competitive environment of denominationalism, Anglicanism with an evangelical voice became and has remained the dominant Christian style in Sydney at least since 1860. Church evangelicalism and a touch of sect evangelicalism were growing apace in this diocese.

24. Most notably in the dioceses of Willochra (in northern South Australia) and of North-West Australia, where an evangelical, Tony Nicholls, formerly head of the CMS training college, has recently been elected bishop, the second in succession of this tradition, thus confirming a turnaround in that diocese's principal tradition.

The immediate question that must then be addressed is why this was so. Did the 35 percent, mainly Irish Roman Catholic proportion of Sydney's population reinforce the wide acceptance of evangelicalism, both within and outside the Anglican denomination? The analogy with Liverpool, and indeed with the diocese of Liverpool under J. C. Ryle, is an obvious and suggestive one. Here it is similarity of circumstances, not difference, that emerges from our comparison, although it should be pointed out that Sydney never endured sectarian rioting, politicking, party structuring, or campaigning in the Kensit style, as did Liverpool, nor famine, disease, and unemployment, nor poverty fed from Ireland and battened on by the British Conservative Party.[25] The Sydney case was more moderate in all respects than this; above all, it developed within an environment of optimistic economic growth and relatively narrow bands of social separation and competition. Yet the large Irish Roman Catholic challenge remained. That challenge reinforced the Protestant evangelical account of Christianity among Sydney Anglicans. In the hands of the combative T. C. Hammond in the 1930s and 1940s, this combativeness became a significant and widely publicized characteristic of Sydney Anglicanism.[26] That it did not also become so in Melbourne might be explained by the later and less convict-dominated character of the Irish presence, or perhaps by the triumphalism of Roman Catholic Archbishop Mannix, or simply the more irenic personality of Melbourne's evangelical Anglicans, for in the McCartneys, father and son, they were not without vigorous Irishmen, even if not as abrasive as Hammond.

But more important than this anti-Catholicism to the apologists for evangelical Anglicanism of Sydney would be dedicated parish work and truthful gospel preaching in season and out, the established and proven characteristics of British evangelicalism. They were right: It worked in Sydney.[27]

Few English dioceses became so thoroughly evangelical as Sydney, or for that matter as ritualist as some country dioceses of Austra-

---

25. Frank Neal, *Sectarian Violence: The Liverpool Experience, 1819–1914* (Manchester, 1988).

26. Warren Nelson, "T. C. Hammond and the Irish Church" (forthcoming).

27. Without exception the biographical entries of Sydney Anglican evangelicals, especially clergy, in Dickey, "Australian Dictionary of Evangelical Biography," illustrate these characteristics.

lia. In England the role of lay control over the appointment of many clergy, even when modified by mid-nineteenth-century legislation against self-appointment and the sale of reversions, permitted the development of trusts controlling many parochial appointments. Thus could an evangelical tradition be maintained over many generations, and be given an opportunity to show its strength and best competence in an active parish ministry. Few such opportunities existed in Australia. Almost all clerical appointments were effectively controlled by the bishop. Such centralized power was defended in principle by High Churchmen as an essential characteristic of Anglicanism (even if they were acting politically, as bishops of all hues act). The strategic survival of Holy Trinity, Adelaide, as an evangelical parish in a High Church–liberal diocese is a splendid case in point, Appointment to the incumbency is controlled by trustees who are not answerable to the bishop. They possess and expect to maintain an evangelical outlook, which has been expressed quite consciously in the appointment of an unbroken line of evangelical clergy since the colony began in 1836.[28]

Free Trade in Religion

Australian evangelical Anglicanism experienced earlier than the English case the pressure of open denominationalism. From Governor Bourke's Acts of 1836 there was competition for government grants, later (from roughly 1860) simply open competition without even that benefit of subsidy. In South Australia evangelical Anglican laypeople in the 1840s found good fellowship with many non-Anglican Protestants in the eager endeavors of settling, where a shared common Protestantism mattered more to them than distinctive Anglicanism. The arrival of Bishop Short in 1847 and some sharp controversies soon ensured that official South Australian Anglican action would proceed independent of other denominations.[29] The pan-evangelical mode of action Lewis noted developing in the 1850s in

28. The story of the survival of this parish into late twentieth-century evangelical effectiveness is the principal theme of Dickey, *Holy Trinity Adelaide*.

29. Brian Dickey, "Marginalising Evangelicals: Thomas Binney in South Australia, 1858–59," *Journal of the United Reformed Church History Society* 4 (1991): 540–65.

London and elsewhere in England was now unlikely. Less self-conscious arguments occurred elsewhere. What this meant was an emphasis on denominational differences rather than shared traditions. "Anglicanism" was becoming for some more important than "evangelicalism." In such a developing context of strengthened separateness, it was no longer possible to take the Church of England for granted and to work in active cooperation with others of a like mind, as Lewis showed occurred in London. It should be noticed that in that case active Anglican participation required the active tolerance of Bishop Tait. Nor should it be forgotten that in both England and Australia there were some evangelical Anglicans among the clergy in particular who spoke of themselves as church evangelicals, who therefore resisted notions of such cooperation as undermining some of the essentials of Anglicanism.[30] Likewise the other Protestant denominations developed their own independent vision of influence and structures. Methodism in South Australia, for example, was the most successful, rising to claim the allegiance of 25 percent of the population between 1875 and 1933, which effectively made it the largest single denomination in that state. For that denomination there was no question of pan-evangelicalism at all.

As already hinted, by 1900 many Anglican evangelicals addressed the problem of unsympathetic diocesan leadership and the difficulties of competitive denominationalism by moving into interdenominational organizations with an evangelical charter. Pan-evangelicalism in this way got a second wind from approximately 1890 in Australia, but based on a conscious decision to move in this direction *as an alternative* to such action supported by diocesan leadership. The first such efforts were the faith missions, notably the strong Australian support given to Hudson Taylor's China Inland Mission.[31] Not many Anglicans would go down that track at first. But from the 1930s some interdenominational agencies became respectable for Anglicans, most notably the Inter-Varsity Fellowship (campus evangelism), Children's Special Service Mission (children's evangelism),

---

30. In the 1858–69 debate in Adelaide on his issue, Bishop Short received crucial support from evangelical clergy unwilling to weaken Anglican distinctiveness (Dickey, "Marginalising Evangelicals").

31. M. L. Loane, *The Story of the China Inland Mission in Australia and New Zealand, 1890–1964* (Sydney, 1965).

and the Scripture Union (Bible reading). These agencies possessed strategic significance that readily commended them to evangelical Anglicans.

Anglicans entered these activities most vigorously when, as in Sydney, diocesan approval was publicly provided, notably by Archbishop Howard Mowll (1933–58).[32] The convention, or Keswick, movement was imported from England in the late nineteenth century, promoted in Sydney largely by a group of Brethren and a small coterie of Anglican clergy focused on Nathaniel Jones, principal of the local theological college from 1897 to 1911.[33] By the time J. C. Ryle had Anglicanized Keswick, it became increasingly acceptable for evangelical Anglicans to participate at Katoomba conventions (Sydney's venue). From the 1930s to the 1970s this convention was controlled by Anglicans with strong links to the diocesan leadership. More recently it has been taken over by Phillip Jensen and others who have a less intimate link with the diocesan leadership but are nevertheless strongly evangelical. In Melbourne the Upwey–Belgrave Heights equivalent was more interdenominational, less dominated by Anglican evangelicals.

Both developments were thoroughly English in style, reflecting needs common to both societies, where the Established Church structures were perceived by evangelicals to be inadequate, unresponsive to new emphases such as holiness teaching. Both English and Australian evangelical Anglicans moved away from an emphases on Keswick holiness from about 1960, influenced by the Billy Graham campaigns in Australia, which acted as something of a circuit breaker in this shift away from Keswick-style holiness emphases. The present group of Sydney Anglicans exercising control over the Katoomba convention deliberately seeks to deny any opportunity for wrong teachings on holiness (which might be Arminian-Methodist, Pentecostal, or simply overemotional) to gain currency. There remains, of course, the question of what tradition of piety is being de-

32. David Parker, "Fundamentalism and Conservative Protestantism—Australia, 1920–1980" (Ph.D. diss., University of Queensland, 1982), esp. part 3. Parker has published several articles based on this substantial dissertation.

33. Bill Lawton, *The Better Time to Be: Utopian Attitudes to Society among Sydney Anglicans, 1885–1914* (Sydney, 1990).

veloped to replace that earlier one. Some have been heard to exclaim "Sandemanianism!" with scorn.[34]

Missionary Effort

Evangelical Anglicans led by Marsden were also consciously conversionist. They soon established an Anglican missionary agency, a Corresponding Committee (1819), and then an Auxiliary, of the Church Missionary Society (1825). Marsden in fact dominated the thinking and action of CMS London for twenty years with his call to evangelize the Maoris of New Zealand. There has been a long scholarly debate as to whether he meant civilize first, then gospelize, and if so whether he was wrong. What matters is that Marsden taught Australian evangelical Anglicans by precept and example of the importance of missionary evangelism, crossing the Tasman Sea fourteen times to promote and supervise the endeavor.

That practical commitment to overseas evangelism waned mid-century in the face of the desperate effort to plant churches to keep pace with the spread of white settlement in Australia. But it was readily fanned into action again in the 1890s, prompted by a delegation from CMS UK.[35] By 1926 CMS Australia was independent, taking full responsibility for support of Anglican CMS missionary work in East Africa, and continuing to grow as a concurrent, sister organization alongside CMS UK.

The Canadian Anglican decision to mount missionary work through the diocese and the bishop rather than through voluntary association was resisted in Anglican evangelical circles in Australia. They preferred the associational model, sustained by the countenance and leadership of powerful evangelicals (preferably bishops), the most notable examples being Archbishops Mowll and Loane. Nor was the English split of the 1920s leading to the creation of the Bible Churchmen's Missionary Society experienced in Australia. It has

34. See the brilliant essay by Martyn Lloyd-Jones, "Sandemanianism," in *The Puritans: Their Origins and Successors. Addresses Delivered at the Puritan and Westminster Conferences, 1959–1978* (Edinburgh, 1987), 170–90.

35. Keith Cole, *A History of the Church Missionary Society of Australia* (Melbourne, 1971), 58–63.

been suggested that Mowll worked to avoid it (though there have been plenty of competing evangelical missionary organizations in Australia attracting Anglican evangelical support). So CMS Australia has become a major expression of Anglican evangelical identity in Australia. In Sydney it is in effect the overseas missionary arm of the diocese and enjoys close, privileged relations with diocesan leadership. In Adelaide from its founding years (1910–17) onward it has served as a focus for evangelical identity within a diocese otherwise generally unsympathetic to evangelicalism outside one or two parishes.[36] It might be asked if English evangelical Anglicanism has been as proportionately or absolutely committed to missionary action.

The mission field of Aborigines has been a challenge to all denominations; evangelical Anglicans were first to try, though those early efforts were unsuccessful. Marsden gave up, utterly discouraged. Most nineteenth-century Anglican congregations, clergy, and bishops agreed. A few tried and tried, and almost without exception they were evangelicals. Notable examples are Daniel Matthews and his wife, and the Gribbles, father and son. Some bishops proved responsive to negative community pressure. The worst example was the collapse of nerve of the bishop of Perth in the face of concerted community attacks on John Gribble after Gribble challenged the violent racism of landowners and others in the colony.[37] As a result much evangelical effort at evangelizing Aborigines became nondenominational until about 1900. CMS took up Aboriginal ministry in Northern Territory from 1908, though only after Gilbert White, bishop of Carpentaria, had given his strongly worded approval.[38] There were other denominations engaged in Aboriginal missionary work—for example, Lutherans in Central Australia—but among Anglicans it was evangelicals who took up the challenge.[39] The late twentieth-century outburst of Aboriginal Christianity has built on the work of Anglican

36. Brian Dickey, "The Origins of the Church Missionary Society in South Australia, 1910–1917," *Journal of the Historical Society of South Australia* 17 (1989): 62–77.

37. Harris, *One Blood*, 411–31.

38. Keith Cole, *From Mission to Church: The CMS Mission to the Aborigines of Arnhem Land, 1908–1985* (Bendigo, 1985).

39. It should also be noted that the Australian Board of Mission, the major nonevangelical Anglican missionary agency, began a vigorous and dedicated work in Papua New Guinea about the same time.

evangelicals in CMS as well as on much else, and CMS retains good ministering relations with Aboriginal Christians in Northern Territory and elsewhere.

The Church of Ireland

This church has been actively engaged in evangelism among Roman Catholics in its own country, for at least two hundred years. That engagement with the conversion of the Roman Catholics of Ireland has been an influential model for Anglican evangelicals in Australia. This has often been conveyed by the clergy migrants from Ireland, who were especially numerous after the disestablishment of the Irish church in 1869. Given the difficulty of training or recruiting clergy, those who offered tended to be accepted by Australian bishops. Perry of Melbourne was particularly happy to appoint Irish clergy. Some significant examples were the H. B. McCartneys (the father was a long-time dean of Melbourne, the son a speaker at Australian Keswick-style conventions and founder of a missionary society targeting socially enclosed Indian women), John MacCullagh, long-time dean of Bendigo, and later T. C. Hammond in Sydney. What did they bring? A convinced evangelical stance in doctrine, a suspicion of ritualism and "Romanism," combined with activism, dedication, missionary fervor, and willingness to work with or without diocesan approval as self-starters.

Slightly different was the case of Howard Guinness. He, as so many Irish evangelicals, possessed an upper-class link that gained him wide acceptance with a certain layer of Sydney Anglican evangelicalism. This social strata was known for superior wealth, support for the crown, hostility to organized labor, and a preference for respectability that often appeared to be simple snobbery. Whatever the link, the impact of the Church of Ireland on Australian Anglican evangelicalism over more than a hundred years cannot be underestimated. It is a major factor in making the Australian case different from the English model.

Politicking

Another much-publicized characteristic of Anglican evangelicalism, especially in its Sydney guise, has been its politicization. Organized clusters of clergy were operating in Sydney from the 1880s, and they were especially active in the elections for the archbishop in 1910 and 1933.[40] Indeed, as a conscious response to the outcome of the 1910 election, a reorganized Anglican Church League (ACL) took deliberate and positive steps over a generation to gain control of the key agencies of the diocese, and above all to influence the election of the archbishop. In Bebbington's terms, this political behavior of the ACL would be an example of activism. They succeeded in 1933 and exercised significant and deliberate power within the affairs of the diocese for a generation, especially through the issue of how to vote tickets for the standing committee of synod and its office bearers. In short, they politicized the decision-making processes of the diocese of Sydney. This was a result of a conscious decision to ensure that control of the diocese remained in evangelical hands. They were using the usual methods of political activism within a party environment created by the size of the membership of Sydney's synod (over five hundred lay voters and nearly two hundred clergy). This political action attracted widespread criticism (criticism fed by a naive Burkean view of politics, party, and power held in some church circles that asserts that party arrangements are somehow improper). Sydney Anglican evangelicals justified their protectiveness as a concern for the gospel and its truths. Their critics point to the love of power, politicking, and the self-perpetuating momentum of a party machine, together with the absence of similar tight ticketing among other groups. The evangelicals have been acutely sensitive to historical process and opportunity, and to the negative behavior of High Churchmen in other times and places when these have had similar power.

I cannot think of similar Irish or English examples, although others might, and not forgetting the much shorter history of diocesan synods in England. There have been suggestions, including that of Archbishop Robinson, that the influence of the ACL has waned significantly over the last decade. "What began as a comprehensive, middle-of-the-road evangelical group, backing the position of J. C. Wright has become a much narrower group indeed, with little or no diocesan leadership."[41] If Robinson is right, then a more mature and self-confi-

40. Judd and Cable, *Sydney Anglicans*, chap. 14.
41. Donald Robinson to Brian Dickey, 28 April 1992.

dent era has arrived for evangelical Anglicans, in Sydney as in other dioceses in Australia. That group was decisively defeated in the election of Robinson's successor in March 1993, but it would be wrong to think that Archbishop Harry Goodhew is anything other than a conservative evangelical, even if widely acceptable among the parties of the Diocese of Sydney.

Conclusion

Has Australian evangelical Anglicanism been more open to influences from the United States than has its English counterpart, since the 1950s? Examples that spring to mind include Billy Graham,[42] *Christianity Today*, some Reformed colleges feeding back into Anglicanism via Sydney, bookshops selling discounted American volumes, though often books written by Englishmen working in the United States or just American printings of British books. Credentialism and the cost of higher-degree education in Britain has spread the sources of intellectual influence. Australian Anglican evangelicalism has changed substantially in the last thirty years as this new wave of ideas and practices has reached Australia across the Pacific, not the Atlantic. The former dominance of English models has been doubly broken—by nationalism and by Americanism.

A continuing flow of English scholars and gurus, however, continues to the antipodes: John R. W. Stott and Dick France are two well-known examples. They and others visit Australia and are listened to politely, though probably more on Australian terms and less frequently than a generation ago. Concurrently Australia has produced some evangelical Anglican leaders of world influence, such as Marcus Loane and Leon Morris for the period 1960–90; it remains to be seen if there are more to come.

Thus a relatively independent mode of existence has evolved in Australia among Anglican evangelicals, as compared with their counterparts in England, let alone Ireland. There is a self-conscious life of its own about Australian evangelical Anglicanism. There is a develop-

---

42. Stuart Piggin has argued that Billy Graham reinforced changes already in motion in the area of piety, and especially toward a more Reformed emphasis. See especially his "Billy Graham in Australia, 1959—Was It Revival?" *Lucas* 6 (1989): 2–23.

ing, long-term, and worldwide influence being exercised by Australian evangelical Anglicanism. This independence makes the link with the United Kingdom almost irrelevant. This capacity for independent action is not as apparent among other, more nostalgic, less dynamic elements of Anglicanism in Australia. That is to say, by the 1990s we are now examining in Australian evangelical Anglicanism self-contained, self-directing phenomena whose linkages are tenuous and various, whose driving forces are largely endogamous, whose endeavors are largely independent.

⑨

Rough Blocks

The Transoceanic Triangle in Planting Pentecostalism among Italian Immigrants to Australia, 1907–1979

Mark Hutchinson

Why include a discussion of Italian Pentecostalism in a book about English-speaking, transatlantic evangelicalism? Any cross-cultural study has its basis in the simple observation about the way that people know things; one cannot know the inside of something without at least recognizing its edges. This chapter, then, deals with the edges of evangelicalism in the English-speaking world, by looking at what lies beyond those edges and the way that inside and outside relate to one another. If, for instance, evangelicalism is essentially evangelistic and missionary-minded, surely the impulse did not simply end with the centers of power in the English-speaking world![1] What happens

1. See Richard V. Pierard, "Pax Americana and the Evangelical Missionary Advance," in *Earthen Vessels: American Evangelicals and Foreign Missions, 1880–1980*, ed. J. Carpenter and W. R. Shenk (Grand Rapids, 1990), 160.

to religion when it crosses cultural and linguistic barriers, when entering other milieus, other climes?

In the spread of Italian Pentecostalism from the United States after 1906, we have an example of the transmutation of evangelicalism from a northern European and American phenomenon with particular denominational and class distinctions, into a populist southern European form that had a dynamic relationship, through migrant communities, with many parts of the world. In particular, this chapter focuses on the triangular relationship that was established after World War II between a host culture (in the United States), the development of a national church on classical lines (in Italy), and a third-stage colonial settlement in another country with a Protestant background (Australia).

Pre-Azusa Street

One of the first things a cross-cultural comparison demonstrates is that things are not always what they seem. Ask Italo-American converts to Protestantism about the Reformation, for instance, and they will tell you proudly that they had it first. Ever since the twelfth century, the Waldensians had been dissenting religious voices in that most Catholic of countries. When the followers of Wesley came as missionaries to Italy from England in 1859, with the aim of renewing that country bound up in the "superstitions of popedom," they found the Waldensians already there. English missionaries were backed up by American Episcopalian Methodists from 1872. These two forms of Methodism joined each other in 1946 and then merged with the Waldensian church in a common synod from 1979 to form the Chiesa Evangelica Valdese (Waldensian Evangelical Church).

The Valdesi were not the only Protestant group working in Italy. As internationalism, liberalism, and secularization advanced, the ability of the religio-political clique that ruled Italy to impose Catholicism by force necessarily waned (the last violent gasps of legally sanctioned repression of Italian Protestants came under the Fascist regime through to the end of the Second World War). The Valdesi had won some political and civil liberties with the liberal revolutions of 1848, and the rise of British and American power made opponents think twice about suppressing works begun by foreign nationals. When Italian troops marched into Rome in 1870 after the battle of Porta Pia, six colporteurs of the British and Foreign Bible Society were hot on their heels. All Italian nationals, they included two Valdesi, two Methodists, and two "free church."[2] Baptist influence had begun in Italy in 1863, when the England-based Baptist Missionary Society sent the missionaries Wall and Clarke; by 1911 there were 32 churches with 814 members. Their transatlantic cousins, the Southern Baptist Convention, began work in Italy in 1870 and by 1907 had equaled the English total—in fact, from 1921, the Americans took over the work, and by the 1920s had some 50 churches with 2,200 members. Like most American works, the Baptists aimed to establish a national church that could work independently among its own people, so obviating the problems of culture and language, a goal it reached in 1956. In 1886 the first Salvation Army work began in Rome, and though it was forced to close, it quickly reopened in the liberal stronghold of Piedmont. And so it went: Through the nineteenth and twentieth centuries the Italian religious scene received almost all the expansionist Christian movements of the time.[3]

In part, of course, this was because the whole world was opening up and becoming more subject to cultural interpenetration through advances in transportation, industry, and communications. What made Italy particularly open to the variety of these influences, if not their penetration in depth, was the nature of its economy and society. A poverty-stricken South, and a rich, industrializing and liberal North, presented the centuries-old Catholic hierarchy with a challenge to their power under the new conditions. On the one hand, this made any political hold tenuous and resentment at the corruption of the religio-political state considerable; on the other, it created a seedbed from which, later in the twentieth century, the Catholic

2. M. Cignoni, "Colportori evangelici a Porta Pia nel 1870," *Bollettino della Società Studi Valdesi*, no. 168 (June 1991): 7.

3. "In all European and American Protestantism in the last hundred or hundred and fifty years, there have been no churches (perhaps it would be more exact to say 'ecclesiastical denominational areas'), interdenominational organizations and ecumenical movements, currents of thought and religious studies, that have not also gained a foothold, to greater or lesser extent, in Italy" (G. Spini, "Introduzione: Un mestieraccio: Me ne vale la pena," in *Movimenti evangelici in Italia dall'unità ad oggi: Studi e ricerche*, ed. F. Chiarini and L. Giorgi [Turin, 1990]).

Church itself would become first divided from the state and then "Protestantized."

The grinding poverty of the South also created a channel by which Italy would be evangelized, namely, by the return of people converted in that evangelical pressure cooker, the United States of America. Waldensian, Methodist, and Baptist evangelism in the South had created a consciousness of the possibility of a different form of religiosity toward the end of the nineteenth century (it was notable that the Southern Baptist outreaches were almost all in the Mezzogiorno and Sicily).[4] When the uprooting process that took millions of Italians to the United States broke up, to some extent, the absolute social conditions of support for the Catholic Church, quite a few Italians either converted to Protestantism or changed the form of their Catholicism.[5] By 1919 the Italian Presbyterian minister Enrico Sartorio could say that "sixty percent of Italian immigrants are completely free of the control of the Catholic Church after a few years of residence in America."[6] Catholic sources estimated that, of the 6 million Italian-born immigrants and their descendants living in the United States before 1939, one-third were still active Catholics, one-half were nonattenders, and the remaining one-sixth had converted to some form of Protestantism. This chapter examines one form of Protestantism, namely, evangelical Pentecostalism.

Early Italo-American Pentecostalism

It is important to note a number of things about the beginning of Italian Pentecostalism in the United States. First, it was rooted in the evangelistic outreach of the mainline denominations. It has been estimated that in 1919 there were approximately 400 Italian Protestant churches with a total membership of around 25,000. The most impor-

4. See S. Cucchiari, "Between Shame and Sanctification: Patriarchy and Its Transformation in Sicilian Pentecostalism," *American Ethnologist* 17 (November 1990): 687.

5. For studies of the effects of the postwar breakup of monopolistic Catholicism on Italian life, see David Kertzer, *Comrades and Christians: Religious and Political Struggle in Communist Italy* (New York, 1980); Salvatore Cucchiari, "Sicilian Pentecostalism: An Interpretive Study in Cultural Discontinuity" (Ph.D. diss., University of Michigan, 1985).

6. Enrico Sartorio, *The Social and Religious Life of Italians in America,* with a foreword by Francesco Cordasco (Clifton, N.J., 1974; orig. 1919), 104.

tant of these was the Presbyterian Church, with seventy-six churches and missions; large Italian congregations in New York, Philadelphia, Chicago, and Pittsburgh; and a widely circulated Italian-language publication, *Era Nuova.* Such groups were characterized by their mobility, resulting in congregations with extremely high turnover. One author likened the work to that of a sculptor "who is compelled to do the rough work of cutting a block and then when he is on the point of carving out the delicate lines of the figure has his work taken out of his hands and another rough block put in its place."[7] Considering the minimal training of Italian church workers, the extreme respect for the Bible that emerged as a reaction to the Catholic limitations on the uses of Scripture, the poverty and illiteracy common among the immigrant population, and the antagonism between the Catholic majority and this "apostate" minority, it is not surprising that there should be an attraction among Italians for a creed that preached power, biblicism, and authority. As Sartorio has observed, Italian Protestant ministry has historically tended to produce either failures or apostles.[8]

Pentecostalism, then, was just the sort of creed to appeal to emigrant Italians, and around the turn of the century it seemed to be breaking out in little "spot fires" all over the world. Azusa Street in 1906, however, was special. It was here that a neo-Pentecostal revival first touched thousands of people, and these fanned out all over the United States to touch others. One group so touched was that which formed the first Italian Pentecostal church in the world: the Assemblea di Dio on West Grand Avenue, Chicago. Its history would be typical of, and indeed linked to, much that followed. Its great figures were all converts in mainline denominations: Pietro Ottolini, Luigi Francescon, and Giacomo Lombardi were all Italian Presbyterians of a biblicist and literalist stamp. While still Presbyterian, Francescon, convinced by Scripture of the necessity of baptism, in 1903 led twenty members and an elder of the church down to Lake Michigan, where they were baptized by immersion. Performing the honors was another Italian Presbyterian, Giuseppe Berretta, who had converted under Free Methodist evangelism, and indeed in the 1890s had gone

7. Ibid., 112.
8. Ibid., 114 and 119.

through an early Pentecostal experience that he had rejected out of fear of error. It was because of this fundamentalist understanding of the Scriptures that the group had already begun drifting from the Presbyterian mainstream and established themselves as an autonomous Bible study group in the Ottolini household. This core of twenty or so people, most of whom had already been in contact with either Methodist or Presbyterian evangelists, received the message of the Pentecost then being preached in the North Avenue congregation of William Durham, himself just returned from Azusa Street. From there, Ottolini brought it back, so that, on "15 September 1907, 'a day of sacred memory,' in the church on Grand Avenue, there was manifested the divine blessing and many were baptized in the Holy Spirit, with initial signs of glossolalia (speaking in tongues)."[9] It was the beginning of a worldwide ethnic movement.

None of the three leaders stayed at the church for more than a year. "Ottolini felt that he couldn't stay in Chicago, but that he needed to begin an evangelistic and missionary work among Italians in other places." Through 1908, Ottolini and Francescon worked in New York, Buffalo, and St. Louis, in particular, and Giacomo Lombardi went back to Italy. All of these works began as renewal rather than purely evangelistic works, though they became evangelistic in time as the mainline denominations rejected their distinctive Pentecostal teachings on the Holy Spirit. Ottolini's work in New York began in the Presbyterian church at Holley, and Lombardi, on landing in Rome without any directions except his habit of receiving extraordinarily clear divine guidance, sought out the Waldensians and "free church," only to be "decisively ejected by the pastor of a church who was tired of seeing him make contacts with members of his congregation."[10]

A "faithful servant of God, without any theological instruction or preparation, except only that given him by the fire of the Holy Spirit and by a passion for the lost,"[11] Lombardi still had a powerful effect. The lawyer Mauro Paretti, who became an early convert to the new message, was "attracted by Lombardi's message, full of warmth and

9. F. Toppi, "Profili di pionieri del movimento evangelico pentecostale italiano: Giacomo Lombardi," in *Cristiani Oggi* (celebration issues of eighty years of Italian Pentecostalism, 1908–1988), 16–31 December 1988, year 7, no. 24 (all translations by author).

10. Ibid., 3.

11. *Annuario Evangelico, 1983–84*, 91.

authority, and was above all amazed that this simple man, who generally spoke an incorrect Italian with a heavy Abbruzzese accent, could, when he pronounced the message of the gospel, express himself in a correct and even oratorical form."[12] Having established a number of small groups in Rome, Calabria, and Abruzzi, Lombardi laid the ground for those who returned after him. These small groups became churches as other emigrants returned home, each having an effect on the evangelization of their particular region.[13] Francescon and Ottolini were also to go back to Italy but perhaps did their greatest work in the Italian diaspora in South America, developing large congregations following strict dress and behavior rules.[14] Where the written word could not go, and indeed where the high seriousness and emphasis on the written word of the Valdesi had not made much ground, the spirit still flowed. In 1915 in the United States just after his conversion, Giovanni Spinella, father of a future Italian Pentecostal immigrant to Australia, had a vision that God loved Sicily too. Returning to Catania, Spinella—like Lombardi, totally without theological education or even skill in preaching—was used in personal evangelism to lay the basis for a future congregation. This pattern was reproduced many times.

Italo-American Evangelical Theology

What sort of evangelical theology did the founders of the Italian Pentecostal work develop? The theological bases for the division from Italian Presbyterianism were twofold: a fundamentalist understanding of the Bible that was shot through with Restorationist tendencies, and an emphasis on the experience of a moment of apostolic revelation.[15] This reversion to the Bible as absolute standard demon-

---

12. Toppi, "Profili di pionieri," 3.

13. Pietro Ottolini, *La storia dell'opera italiana* (1945); L. Francescon, *Fedele testimonianza* (1945).

14. W. Hollenweger, *The Pentecostals* (Peabody, Mass., 1988), 85ff., 253.

15. Note that Cucchiari sees these two poles as typical of southern Italian Pentecostalism and reinforcing of the family structures that typify traditional life: "Word domination," typified by the male-dominated ministries of preaching, teaching, and pastoring, "is held in check by the centrality of Spirit experience," in which women are free to move as the recipients of gifts. In this sense it reflects the traditional patriarchy, while at the same time opening up a space in

strates Everett Wilson's point that Pentecostalism thrives as a form of "religious assertiveness following social upheaval."[16] Catholicism, the traditional religion, had been undercut at its social roots by the move to the United States, and Presbyterianism was something that, in a sense, was grafted on. Italians, from an earthy, patriarchal, and agricultural culture (Francescon, Ottolini, and Lombardi were all born in small agricultural towns), were attracted to a gospel that, like that noted by Wilson among the Central American Pentecostal missionaries, was "rugged, authoritative and persuasive."[17] As Donald Dayton has pointed out, Restorationist tendencies in Pentecostalism also made it easier for converts from traditional churches not to miss the solidity of a historical base. They could leap two thousand years of history via the doctrine of the Latter Rain, appropriating apostolic authority directly (rather than by succession) through promises based on the unchangingness of God.[18]

The Italian Pentecostal churches had been established by returnees from the United States and were partially supported by offerings collected in the United States. Now it looked as if an organic union might be effected—the bridge across the Atlantic was rapidly firming up. The national Italian group, calling itself the Christian Churches of North America (CCNA), in the interwar period looked as if it was poised to become the primary Pentecostal body in Italy.

Two things interposed to stop this from happening. First, with its solution of the Roman Question, the Fascist government erected a framework of punitive legislation that smashed local Pentecostal assemblies and drove them underground.[19] What little central organization had been put in place by 1929 was swept away.[20]

---

which women can operate freely and negotiate new relationships within the church (Cucchiari, "Between Shame and Sanctification," 702–3).

16. E. Wilson, "Identity, Community, and Status: The Legacy of Central American Pentecostal Pioneers," in *Earthen Vessels: American Evangelicals and Foreign Missions, 1880–1980*, ed. J. Carpenter and W. R. Shenk (Grand Rapids, 1990), 141.

17. Ibid., 135.

18. D. Dayton, *Theological Roots of Pentecostalism* (Metuchen, N.J., 1987), 25–27.

19. See M. Hutchinson, "Non siami considerate come uomini ma come bestie: Buffarini Guidi and the Mind of Persecution." *Lucas: An Evangelical History Review* 13 (June 1992).

20. See Giorgio Peyrot, *La circolare Buffarini-Guidi e i pentecostali*, Associazione Italiana per la Liberta di Coscienza (Rome, 1955); and Hutchinson, "Non siami considerate."

The second interruption was based on the ambivalence the CCNA had towards organization generally, something particularly evident in the CCNA works in the U.S. and Italy. The basis of union was basically negative or circumstantial, embracing a language and cultural group that would necessarily decline as migration slowed down, and a doctrinal statement that defined itself *against* a mystical minority (the Petrelli-ites) rather than *for* a group of common beliefs. As Edith Blumhofer has indicated, Holy Spirit evangelicalism tended this way even in American congregations; under the power of the conviction that the congregations were restoring the New Testament pattern of the church, the old denominational lines tended to break down, and new patterns began to form.[21] On the smaller scale of the congregation, the Pentecostal experience of "*culto*-ecstacy" broke down "the structural boundaries of experience."[22] Countering this tendency toward union, however, were the extreme congregationalism of such autonomous groups, the converts' fear of hierarchy and bureaucracy, and the continuing suspicion that the tendency toward centralization would undermine the restoration of the church of the Book of Acts. The older generation even banned the use of notes by preachers in the pulpit. Notes meant preparation, obduracy of heart in the face of the working Spirit, a vaunting of the intellect over the revealed knowledge of God. On a more serious level, a suspiciousness about programs for evangelization and pastoral training created dissatisfaction among their youth and a sort of shotgun monetary support for congregations that produced "new groups and churches scattered wherever."[23]

Significantly, when the independent Italian Pentecostal congregations met in Rome for the 1947 Convegno Nazionale to form a single overarching organization, they chose the more centralized, internationally recognized, and powerful Assemblies of God (AOG) to act as the sponsoring body. With the previous disorganization of the work, a negative attitude from Italian government circles, and Italy aflood with American soldiers and money after the war, it was a natural choice. Nevertheless, it was one that caused considerable distress

21. E. Blumhofer, *The Assemblies of God*, 2 vols. (Springfield, Mo., 1989), vol. 1, chap. 1.
22. Cucchiari, "Between Shame and Sanctification," 691.
23. *Annuario Evangelico, 1983–84*, 92.

among CCNA circles, which had expended considerable resources in evangelizing their home country.[24] The switch to the AOG, however, gave the Italian churches an international link for which, given the stultifying conditions of Italian religious life and the absolute dominance of the Catholic Church, most evangelical churches sought.[25] The CCNA did not offer this, being rather a union of Italians, albeit based in another land.

Migration to Australia and the Religious Reception There

The history of Italian immigration to Australia is, in a sense, the reverse side of the American coin. The United States was the great goal and, until the 1920s, the first choice of Italians. As the immigration policy of that nation tightened up through the 1920s, Italians sought alternatives, among them Australia. When Australia finally started relaxing its draconian "White Australia" legislation after 1945, Italians sought it out as if there, in the southern oceans, there was a new America that had opened its doors. Some idea of the impact on Australian society can be gained from the rapidity and size of expansion of the Italian community after the war. From 91,550 in 1947, the community's size jumped to over 400,000 in 1961, and to over 940,000 in 1986. By the end of the 1980s, the Italian community made up between 4 and 6 percent of the total Australian population, and the Italian-born approximately 1.8 percent.

As religions move across cultures, they inevitably, for one reason or another, encounter difficulties of adaptation of the greatest magnitude. Such adaptation is possible, of course, only when church authorities realize that there is a cultural shift in process. For the Australian churches, their acculturation was to the status quo prior to the war. The Anglican Church was largely set within its dependable body of Britons, the Catholic Church within its Irish-based community,

24. The Italian churches in the sway of Francescon persisted in considering the AOG a church that had fallen away from its original calling because it had submitted to organizational methods, while considering its own plantings closer to the ideals of the Reformers, given their recent emergence from Roman Catholicism.

25. F. Chiarini, "Gli studi sulle singole denominazioni evangeliche," in *Movementi evangelici in Italia dall'unità ad oggi: Studi e ricerche*, ed. F. Chiarin and L. Giorgi (Turin, 1990), 5.

while others straddled the two (the Presbyterians, for instance, had strong ties in Scots, English, and Northern Ireland communities). In consequence, they shared a willing ignorance of the magnitude of the change their society was facing through the 1950s.[26] In effect two whole generations of immigrants were consigned by Australian Protestantism to arranging their own affairs in matters of religious belief: those who had come to Australia as adults, already acculturated but in a state of temporary uprootedness, and those who had come as children and would be mainly acculturated in the mixed environment of Italian home and Australian school. While the mainline Protestant churches did much by the way of works of charity and assistance among migrant communities, they never did come to understand migrants as possible converts, as part of a new church for new conditions. By any measure, and in hindsight, it must be considered a great opportunity missed by these denominations.

The reception of migrants by the Catholic Church was slightly different.[27] Of the two and a half million people that the postwar immigrations brought to Australia, about half were from Catholic backgrounds. From its position in 1933, when it formed 17.5 percent of the population, the Catholics by 1971 had risen to some 27 percent, challenging the ascendancy of the Anglicans, who had based much of their claims to being the national church on their retaining over 30 percent of the population. The postwar influx was a shock, then, in both Protestant and Catholic quarters. To the Protestants, it seemed as if the sea had lapped in over King Canute's knees,[28] while the Catholics suddenly found the ethnic roots that they had long counted on to unite the church were being eaten out from underneath their very feet.[29]

26. D. Penman, "Comment: Religions in Australia—Can They Cope with Multiculturalism?" *Journal of Intercultural Studies*, 8, no. 1 (1987). Typical of Italian humor, the pronunciation of "Anglican" by migrants has been played on to produce jokes. One person known to the author feigns to stumble over the word, making it come out as *manco gli cane* ("not even the dogs").

27. F. Lewins, *The Myth of the Universal Church*, quoted in ibid., 58.

28. Canute is the British king who, according to legend, showed his fawning supporters that their flatteries were vain by sitting at the edge of the sea and commanding the tide to stop coming in. Postwar immigration to Australia's British based churches appeared similarly unstoppable and upsetting of the common religious platitudes of the day.

29. P. O'Farrell, *The Catholic Church and Community in Australia: A History* (Melbourne, 1977), 404.

Yet as badly as the Catholic Church performed in not being "decisive or comforting when the postwar immigrants needed it most," it did better than almost all other denominations.[30] Equivalent figures to the Italo-American experience of conversion to Protestantism would have established an Italian Protestant population in Australia of some 150,000, an incredible figure that suggests the failure of Australian Protestantism to react to the migrant presence. The truly significant missionary work was done by Italian Roman Catholic priests who came to Australia specifically for that purpose, though it was not until 1959 that the first parish was handed over specifically to Italian groups, followed by the second in 1968. Meanwhile, the Salesian, Capuchin, and Scalabrinian orders had long been staffed by Italians working among Italians, having started well before Vatican II began to bring about such changes more widely from the mid-1960s. Such orders of priests reimposed the condition dominant in Italo-American Catholicism whereby the priest became the intermediary between the Italian folk religion and "Little Italy"-type society on the one hand, and the hierarchical Australian Catholic Church on the other.[31] In this, the Catholic Church was taking advantage of its international status by bringing in staff from overseas. This should not be confused with internal openness—it did so in order to get around the entrenched cultural hegemony that was driving people from its pews.

Americans to Australia

The position filled by Scalabrinians for the Catholic Church was for Pentecostalism filled by American missionaries. Among the trickle of American investment that was rapidly widening into a flood through the 1950s was the work of the Carnation Milk Company. One of its senior executives, Andrew Nelli, was an Italo-American Pentecostal whose business took him through many cities on repeated trips to Australia. He was also a member of a wide variety of voluntary organizations, combining commerce and the work of the cross in the best traditions of evangelical mercantilism. As assistant direc-

---

30. S. Judd and K. Cable, *Sydney Anglicans* (Sydney, 1991).
31. This problem merits further study.

tor of the Board of Evangel College, he was in a position to influence decision-making about Australia as a mission field, and as the chairman of the Foreign Missions Board of North Hollywood Assembly, he had access to funds and the means of encouraging missions. During his trips abroad he made three contacts that were to be vital for the future of the Italian AOG work in Australia. He became aware of the condition of Italian migrants to Australia, which he reported back to the AOG-USA's international headquarters in Springfield, Missouri; he encouraged the work of the budding AOG in Italy; and he became friends with two influential Australian Pentecostals: Philip Duncan of Petersham Assembly and Charles Greenwood of Richmond Temple.

Nelli's contacts were not limited to Australia, however. As already suggested, there was already an American presence in Italy through funding and literature arrangements. There was also a physical presence in the figure of a missionary field secretary, based in Rome. Anthony Piraino filled that position for a substantial part of the period between 1945 and 1960. Like the pioneers of the Italian work before him, Piraino felt the burden of missions very strongly, at least partly because "my family migrated to America when I was but a boy of six and God in his mercy permitted me to hear the Gospel and be saved in America." His gratitude had led him to Italy as missions secretary under the Italian District of the Assemblies of God in the United States, where he took part in the fight to win religious liberty for the Pentecostal churches by leading representations to government, established Sunday schools, and "literally flooded Italy with Gospel literature."[32] He was prepared to stand on his record in requesting permission to lead a mission to Australia: "I feel I can be the means of salvation to many of these good people who have been forced to leave their native land to go to a foreign land—Australia—to find work."[33] Furthermore, "I see a tremendous need in Australia—all those Italians and NOT ONE PENTECOSTAL CHURCH! A pioneer field—a real missionary field. . . . God in his mercy saved me—a poor immigrant boy and now, I feel a tremendous burden to go to Australia to try to

32. Piraino to Carmichael, 27 May 1958, Archives of the Division of Foreign Missions Research Center, Springfield, Mo. (henceforth ADFMRC).
33. Piraino to Carmichael, 15 July 1958, ADFMRC.

do to those poor immigrants what God in His great love did for me."[34]
The problems he faced, however, were manifold.

The first and greatest of these was the fact that Australia, to the
AOG-USA, was not a mission field. There was already an established
Australian AOG, and so American efforts were stymied on policy
grounds. While the Italian AOG could have done something out of
their brief to deal with Italian people everywhere, they were poor and
small in numbers. Enthusiastic support was all that Piraino could expect from Rome; money would have to be raised in the United States.

While a way was eventually to be found around this organizational
impasse, the net effect was to restrict the vision for the Australian
work. It would always remain an "Italian" work, and thus peripheral
to the global thrust of AOG missionary work, and so would be under-
funded and underorganized. This, however, was not Piraino's fault.
The vision he sketched for work in Australia was original and bold,
as was suitable for a work that needed to span an entire continent
and operate with little outside help.[35]

But Piraino clearly had not gauged the feeling back in Springfield
at all well when he said things like "I feel that I am mobilizing for an
all-out attack in Australia." If the thought that they might feel responsible for the funding of this commando raid did not scare the Foreign
Missions Department off, then consideration of the repercussions
this would have on relationships with the Australian AOG did. Piraino
asked for an army; all he got was a small reconnaissance mission.[36]

Contrary to his earlier impression that there was "no Fundamental
or Full Gospel" work among Italians in Australia, small groups had
preempted Piraino's arrival by some months in all the eastern seaboard capitals. Despite his enthusiasm and the breadth of his original
plans, it must have seemed a daunting task to Piraino. Italians were
scattered throughout the country, in pockets quite unlike the communities he had been used to in the United States.[37] How was he to reach
them? There was no ethnic radio and little ethnic press, and his chief
pipeline into the country, the Australian AOG, was as small and scat-

34. Piraino to Carmichael, 27 May 1958, ADFMRC.
35. Piraino to Carmichael, 15 July 1958, ADFMRC.
36. A. Nelli to Noel Perkin, n.d. [1959?], p. 2, ADFMRC.
37. Piraino to S. Totaro, 6 October 1959, ADFMRC.

tered as that in Italy. The task was so much larger than he expected, even though the actual number of Italians was not. There was a note of desperation in his voice in writing his report for Springfield, perhaps in the realization that even his minimum demands of the previous year were not going to be met: "I do not know what else to do but pray and believe God to work a miracle as far as you good brethren [at Springfield] are concerned."[38] His miracle did not happen. The team he had dreamed about did not materialize, and the great "now or never" push into Australia's Italian population did not eventuate. The baton was passed over to rugged individualists such as Giuseppe Giusti.

Giusti was an Italian-born American missionary who had been evangelizing in Catania, Sicily, for some years. It was there that he heard of the large numbers of Italians who had emigrated to Australia.[39] Returning from the Italo-American diaspora to work in Italy suggests the cut of the man—he felt called of God to take the gospel to his own people wherever they might be found. He was also a driven personality. Although he was toward the end of his working life, hardly had he found out about this new field than, on returning to the United States, he broached the matter with the Italian District of the AOG-USA. He said that he had conceived a plan to carry the work he had already been involved in for some time to the shores of Australia, and he announced that he would be pursuing this as a missionary calling. He began to take to the missionary circuit—Anthony Foti remembers him coming to Shelton, Connecticut, and preaching a missionary message about Australia, about the great towns there, and about the multitudes of Italians lying "in Egypt" waiting to be set free by the gospel of Christ.

Giusti was supported by a general enthusiasm for missions in American Pentecostalism through the 1950s. Through the war, American AOG Missionary Secretary Noel Perkin had restructured the AOG missionary endeavor around a global vision for growth. Through the 1950s, support structures such as Speed the Light

38. Anthony Piraino, "Report of Findings in Australia Relative to the Evangelization of One Million Italians—September 1959," 3, ADFMRC.

39. Interview with Giovanni Spinella (M. Hutchinson, June 1991), Archives of the Center for the Study of Australian Christianity (henceforth ACSAC).

(which by 1986 had raised some $53 million for mission equipment and building) multiplied, missionaries were increasingly well trained, and from 1957 a new strategy, known as Global Conquest, was introduced.[40]

Having raised money on the missionary circuit, Giusti sailed for Australia, arriving in early 1959. His first action was to travel between the major cities to size up the situation. There were already groups operating in Melbourne and Adelaide when he arrived there. And he soon ran into an enraged Piraino, who denounced him for his religious imperialism. While Piraino was fighting hard to make Australia a national priority through an attachment to Springfield's global goals, Giusti's personality-centered evangelism, informed by a view that extended no wider than the Italian District back in the United States, kept pushing it into the periphery. Piraino begged Springfield and the Italian District to "inform Brother Giusti as quickly as possible for your decisions."[41] In fact, this kind of coordinated planning, whereby the national body took over responsibility for missionary work from the district, was not to happen until 1965.

A gruff, forthright man, with traditional views on dress and male-female relations, Giusti imported to the Australian work the use of the veil, separate seating for men and women in the congregation, and a ruling passion for the dignity of the pastorate. These elements were clearly tied into the Italian idea of respect. An imposing figure in his blocky, dark, pin-striped suits, some remember him as "looking like a mafioso," and one could see in his idea of subjection to the pastor a paternalism similar to that found in some southern Italian families.

Anthony Foti, another American-influenced Italian Pentecostal, was of a different stamp. A second-generation Italo-American and a Bible school graduate, he had a pastoral rather than an apostolic approach; he was prepared to bend where perhaps a more rigid man might have been broken. They were characteristics that brought out the worst in the controlling part of Giusti's nature.

This side of Giusti particularly affected Foti and his wife when they came to take over the work. Giusti let people know he was not entirely happy about the new couple, in a sense importing the same

40. Blumhofer, *Assemblies of God*, 2:143–47.
41. Piraino, "Report of Findings," 1.

struggle that had been fought out between the AOG and CCNA, and within the CCNA itself, twenty years before. The Fotis were too American—Jean, in particular, had a modern hairstyle (though she hid it under a veil) and spoke hardly any Italian. Anthony was too loose on the enforcement of "tradition." Even after Giusti left, to return to America in June 1962, he continued to attempt to control the way the church ran, though this came to nothing with his death in a car crash in 1965.

Interplay between Italy and the United States

Though the American AOG organized fairly effectively through the 1950s, the Italo-American work was, it should be remembered, directed out of a small and underfinanced Italian District. Few possible replacements for the Fotis were available—even among those of Italian descent in the United States. The few who might consider going on missions either did not speak their parents' language or spoke it (in the case of dialect) too well to fill pastoral positions. In his very first report back to the United States, Foti summed up the situation as he had found it in Australia and made a call, above all, for workers. Any Italian workers that might consider coming out had need of English as well. Again, Foti called the attention of the Italian District (USA) to the problems of sending out unsuitable missionaries: "I call your attention to the inadvisability of [sending] workers from Italy without command of the English language. Bi-lingual is a must for here. In order to perform marriages, each minister must be registered with the state and this calls for the understanding of the English language to qualify and satisfy legal requirements."[42]

The United States, therefore, would have to be the source of missionary personnel, as it was for Italy itself in earlier years. In immigrant work, moreover, the standard AOG "Global Conquest" position did not apply; there were no "native" people, as that term was ordinarily understood, to train for the ministry and take over. The Australian work, meanwhile, while open to contacts, was also comparatively small and scattered. The only congregation with which the

42. Report, 9 March 1962, 2, ACSAC.

Italian work had much contact was the Petersham Assembly under Philip Duncan, and that only with the pastor. The Australians were not so interested in the Italian work as to invest large amounts of their own scarce resources, and the Italian AOG was too small. It was not, for instance, until December 1964, nearly three years after their arrival, that the Australia Commonwealth Executive Presbytery formally voted to welcome the Fotis to work in Australia.[43] When the second Italo-American missionary came out in 1966, the Assemblies of North America expressed its concern openly: "We have frankly wondered just to what extent Brother Foti had been able to reach out for fellowship among the ministers of the churches of the Assemblies of God in Australia."[44] This problem of the relationship with the Australian AOG was to raise its head again and again over the next four decades. As Giusti had found, it began as a problem of jurisdiction. It continued for the fledgling Italo-American congregations as a problem of identity. In a society that identified itself as British and was only in the early stages of internationalization, this also had legal ramifications, as Foti warned his former fellows back in the States:

> Concerning our organization as an offshoot of the IAG [Italian Assemblies of God], this would involve the recognition of you (as a foreign corporation) in Australia. Our lawyer informs that this would be rather difficult unless someone like the Australian Assemblies vouched for you (rather doubtful). It would be rather a simple matter (that is legally) to organize as a separate movement such as the Italian Assemblies of God of Australia. Before we further pursue this matter we would like to know your wishes since the above action may incur displeasure from Springfield.[45]

In the short term, this problem of whose flag the Italian Assemblies would march under was resolved with their constitution as an autonomous committee within the Australia AOG. This, apparently, was the understanding that the Australian Assemblies (particularly Duncan) had from quite early, but it did not help to simplify things that Rome and Sydney were talking at cross-purposes to the Italian Dis-

43. Irish to McGlasson, 17 December 1974, ADFMRC.
44. R. T. McGlasson to I. J. Hewitt, 18 March 1966, ADFMRC.
45. Report, 9 March 1962, 2, ACSAC.

trict in the United States. Foti called for all such agreements to be brought out into the open:

> I suggest that an investigation and subsequent *questioning* of any commitments or concordat be made concerning the organization of the Italian work in Australia as discussed by Mr. Duncan and the officials of the Assemblies of God in Italy. Giusti informs me that in a very recent conversation with Duncan, it was made known that the Italians of Italy had agreed that the work in Australia be directly under the supervision of the Australian A of G, no Branch relation. . . . the matter should be thoroughly aired.[46]

Foti's concern related to the very real threat that, in any agreement between Italy and Australia, the vital American support line would be squeezed or even cut. In the short term, such questions obtained amicable provisional solutions. In the long term, however, the autonomous nature of congregations in general and the Italian operation in particular, together with the forces pulling these operations away toward an independent identity with ties to the United States and Italy, kept the issue on the agenda. Not the least of these was the fact that the Australian AOG was increasingly aware of its own identity. In 1966, A. T. Davidson became the first full-time chairman of the Australian AOG, while the 1967 national convention began taking steps toward the foundation of a permanent national headquarters.[47] The consequence of more efficient oversight and the increasing conceptualization of the church as a denomination meant that it sought to regularize its relations with other groups. The Italian works, in response to a similar tightening up in administration in Springfield, also groped for a more definite form of organization. But the ongoing bitter conflict between the pro- and anti-traditionalists weakened the movement.

While the traditionalists maintained a splendid isolation, stressing a theology of the elect, the Assemblies of God committee maintained its strength through the openness of the USA-Italy-Australia triangle. A regular visitor from the United States was C. E. Greenaway,

---

46. Ibid., 1. Al Perna was the foreign missions secretary of the Italian District of the AOG.
47. D. Smith and G. Smith, *A River Is Flowing: A History of the Assemblies of God in Australia* (Adelaide, 1987).

Springfield's Far Eastern missionary secretary. He entertained people with his bottomless fund of personally experienced missionary stories, his great good humor and wisdom, and his persistent willingness to take things as he found them. Nor was he alone. The list of visiting American ministers and missionaries is testimony of the increasing interconnection of Australian and American religious life across this period. Even on the ship out, the Fotis had met and accompanied a group of American missionaries who were sailing for service in Papua New Guinea. These links were reinforced in 1964 with the visit of Bert Schaad from Papua New Guinea, who ministered to the congregation by the use of color film, and two American sisters (returning to the United States from a mission station in India) "who shared some of their interesting experiences with us and enlightened us further concerning the need of India. It was a delightful time of fellowship."[48]

In the same year, when Foti was away touring with the American C. C. Grant, the Americans Jim and Dorothy Adams came down from their position in Gosford, New Guinea, to minister with their highly professional, "beloved gospel duets and the sharp two-edged Word of God," while in later years Foti attended a ministers' seminar at which "Bro Gene Martin of the States was the main evening speaker and proved to be a blessing and inspiration to all."[49] In 1965, Oral Roberts led a team to Australia to hold a ministers' seminar, which proved refreshing; for Foti, the main attraction of the seminar was the testimony of a spirit-filled Methodist minister. The next year, the church saw a great harvest from another of their contacts through the T. L. Osborne organization, Brother R. Remick,[50] whose mission to the Sydney congregation was a formative breakthrough for the church. Like many other churches, it had started with the conversion and fairly rapid baptism in the Spirit of wives and mothers, followed by husbands and families. In bridging the transition period between a seedling church that was really an extension of the national work to a strong local autonomous congregation with its own defined leader-

48. "Greetings to our American prayer partners and friends," 11 June 1964, ACSAC.

49. "Greetings to our American prayer partners and friends," n.d. [ca. 1964], ACSAC.

50. Interview with A. Foti, 30 April 1987, ACSAC; Christian Friends and prayer partners in America, September 1966, ACSAC.

ship, the assistance of visiting preachers was essential. Remick was followed by many others, including (among the Americans) the free-lance Latter Rain evangelist Terlizzi, the Osborne representative and Indian missionary Bill Thompson (1967), and in 1968–69 the Four-square Gospel ministers A. S. Worley, H. Ferrel, and Hal Herman.

By the end of the 1960s, more American missionary help was also becoming possible. The first of these was Joe Vitello and family. Vitello was an evangelist and Bible teacher who had pastored for a number of years in Jamestown, New York. Like Foti, Vitello was a graduate of Eastern Bible Institute; some assumed he would have much the same sort of pastoral thrust. Like Giusti, however, he had spent time touring in Italy, preaching and planting churches with support from the United States. Arriving toward the beginning of the year, he toured Queensland in order to ascertain the scale of the task. It was huge. His first missionary letter home (which he called, amusingly, a "Vitello-gram") gave some idea of this to supporters who gauged states by the size of Texas:

> It is our responsibility to evangelize the Italian community of Queensland. Queensland, Australia's second largest state, covers 667,000 square miles, or 22 percent of the continent, and it has a population of almost 2 million. Its greatest distance from north to south is 1300 miles, and from east to west 900 miles. It is 2 times the size of Texas, U.S.A., and is large enough to contain the British Isles, France, Belgium, Germany, Italy and Greece together.[51]

The description of the task, however, hid at its core the seed of a problem. Vitello saw a huge land and, drawing on his experience as a traveling evangelist, desired to travel it as an apostle. Times, however, had changed from when Giusti first arrived, if indeed that sort of ministry was ever appropriate for Australian conditions. Giusti himself had found Brisbane and Melbourne hard ground. The limitation was, again, "laborers, fluent in the Italian language."[52] Under those conditions, pastors were needed who would gather and nurture what enthusiastic laymen had often begun. In the mid-1970s, and

51. Vitello-gram, Spring 1970, ADFMRC.
52. Ibid.

possibly earlier, Foti demonstrated his conviction about the nature of the Australian work by encouraging Italian layworkers in Brisbane to develop centers from which they could spread. In this he recognized a streak of stubborn individualism among his charges that would re-emerge repeatedly even on his own home turf.[53]

Vitello, however, was used to large organizations and an extended and literate fellowship rather more like the Australian assemblies. In Brisbane, he also had to deal with determined personalities and the tight (to some suffocating) atmosphere of a small church made up of large families. In time, he began to spend more of his time between preaching in the larger Australian churches and traveling as secretary of the national Italian work.

Italo-American Relationships in Australia

Since 1943, it had been AOG policy to appoint field secretaries for all major areas, to provide appropriate training for missionaries, and subsequently to ensure the harmonious running of "mission fields" by the establishment of appropriate structures.[54] In 1970, Springfield finally began bringing the funding of the Australian missionaries under an accounting system separate from the European work, a technical detail to which they had to resort to avoid insulting the Australians.[55] With the advent of Vitello, Greenaway also began to see the need for a steering committee, with Foti as senior missionary chairman.[56] In April 1970, the new committee was established on a set of guidelines that declared the need for closer cooperation and stated that all members were considered equal and responsible in their own sphere but that all would cooperate "to coordinate the total program with definitive objectives that can at any time be justified and explained to any part of our constituency at home or in Australia." He underlined

53. Foti to Campisi, 11 October 1974, ACSAC.

54. Blumhofer, *Assemblies of God*, 2:143.

55. J. Kilpatrick to M. Best, 25 May 1970, ADFMRC.

56. Greenaway had clearly signaled this to Vitello previous to his arrival, as the latter commented to Foti that "Roma doesn't have the profile, he's too far out in the front" (Foti interview). Vitello's minutes of the field committee meetings are the sign of a neat mind used to working with formally constituted bodies, unlike the rough-and-tumble approach of most Italo-Australian missionaries.

the key point: "One prime requisite . . . will be the complete and total harmony with the Australian Assemblies of God."[57] If there were repercussions, he wanted the American and the Australian work alike to be insulated (wisely, as it turned out, when disagreements with the CCNA arose).[58]

The local group clearly agreed. Soon after Foti's return, the field missionary committee decided that "the Executive committee of the Commonwealth Assemblies of God in Australia, be approached with the suggestion that each American Assemblies of God missionary be permitted to represent the Italian work in his respective state at the state executive level, in order to promote a harmonious working relationship between the Italian work and the Australian Assemblies of God."[59] It was a shrewd move—it gave the group representation virtually without obligation, as well as instant standing in Australian Pentecostal circles. It avoided the disappointments of the experiment with ethnic branches in the United States, effectively making the Italian works "integrated into the overall structure of the National Church."[60] They informed the independent Adelaide work that they were "moving toward a closer association with the Australian Assemblies of God, and in the light of present existing ties between him [the minister] and the Assemblies of God in Italy, it will recommend that he favorably consider doing likewise." In March 1971 Greenaway (who was again passing through Sydney) moved to reassure the Australians that the Italian work was "moving in the right direction."[61]

Despite the fact that this increasing organization forced local congregations, especially that in Adelaide, to make choices that often resulted in church splits, after a decade there was enough evidence to support Greenaway's optimism. As Foti was to say in the mid-1970s, "Some problems are like prickly pears; but Italians peel the skin and thorns off and then eat the succulent fruit!"[62] The main churches in Sydney and Melbourne were growing (each with more than fifty full members in 1970); the former preaching points in Newcastle, Oak-

57. Guidelines, 13 May 1970, ADFMRC.
58. Field committee minutes, 13 April 1970, ACSAC.
59. Field committee minutes, 26 June 1970, ACSAC.
60. Perna to Hogan, 8 May 1971, ADFMRC.
61. Field committee minutes, 19 January 1971 and 17 March 1971, ACSAC.
62. Foti to Greenaway, 29 May 1974, ACSAC.

leigh, and Brisbane were becoming established (with around twenty full members apiece); and new opportunities were still opening up. From seventy members in 1971, the number of Italian AOG worshipers in Sydney grew to eighty-five the next year, while growth rates in Melbourne were even greater. If the congregations could avoid disaster and find adequate leadership resources, the future was promising, if not bright. Certainly, compared with any other Australian migrant community depending upon conversion rather than cultural adherence, the Italian AOG was doing reasonably well. It was with some good reason that it was reported in December 1971 that "the Assemblies of God is the only evangelical fellowship with an effective outreach to Italian emigrants in Australia."[63]

Conclusion

Between 1907, when Pentecost burst upon the Italian community in Chicago, and 1979, when Italian Pentecostal work had reached its full maturity in Australia, a series of fascinating cultural dynamics developed that shaped (and often impeded) evangelistic work among Italians in the triangle formed by the United States, Italy, and Australia. Founded in the United States, it spread to Italy, which in turn fed back through the incredible porosity of international barriers for migrant communities. In this sense, and as Edith Blumhofer has indicated, Italian Pentecostalism has been an archetypically evangelical movement.[64] It was, from the start, an intercontinental force, and it has continued as such to the present. Theological trends cultivated in North America and Europe, and in the petri dish of South America, reinforced one another on some points (such as the rugged, apostolic nature of leadership) and produced opposing parties on other points ("literalist" against "mystical," "open to the world" against "closed to the world," "centralizing" against "radically congregationalist"). These parties became conflated with generational effects, as the Italian population in the United States aged and migration dried up, pro-

---

63. *Evangel*, December 1971.
64. E. Blumhofer, "Transatlantic Currents in North Atlantic Pentecostalism," in *Evangelicalism: Comparative Studies of Popular Protestantism in North America, the British Isles, and Beyond*, ed. M. A. Noll, D. W. Bebbington, and G. Rawlyk (New York, 1994).

ducing a further split with the younger generation and a loss to the more organized and centrally energized bodies like the Assemblies of God. In turn, as American migration closed up and Australian migration opened up, the theological differences between these parties were brought into a new field, which the more Italian sources treated as a colony, an appearance that the more internationalist American AOG tried to avoid. There too, tendencies both toward extreme holiness and separation from the world and toward corporate centralization were to be found. With a smaller and more scattered Italian population, however, and with preestablished Pentecostal structures in place, these tendencies did not reach full institutional form. Rather, they were catapulted early into the strains of generation change that hit the American churches just after the Second World War, with their consequent shifts in emphasis on holiness and increased openness to the broader Australian culture. What had started as a Italian evangelical colony was supported by American personnel and cultural insight through a more gentle transition to an intelligent openness to the changing culture around it.

Evangelicalism in Modern Canada

10

Of Canadian Presbyterians and Guardian Angels

Barry Mack

The twentieth century has been a very difficult one for Protestants throughout the Western world, but it has been particularly rough on Canadian Presbyterians. Given that there are now in the 1990s fewer Presbyterians in Canada than Muslims, it is perhaps difficult to recall that in 1875, it was the largest Protestant denomination in the Dominion and played a key leadership role in shaping modern Canada. Although never more than 16 percent of the population,[1] Canadian Presbyterians exerted a cultural influence out of all proportion to the census figures.[2]

Part of that cultural impact may well be due to the fact that Presbyterianism in Canada has been closely tied to Scottish ethnicity. The

1. *Census of Canada* (Ottawa, 1941), 290, 292.
2. Two of Canada's longest-serving prime ministers, Sir John A. Macdonald and W. L. Mackenzie King, grew up as Presbyterians. Canadian novelists from Lucy Maud Montgomery (of *Anne of Green Gables* fame) and the best-sellers of Ralph Connor to Hugh Maclennan, Robertson Davies, and Margaret Laurence have spent an inordinate amount of attention on the wintry Presbyterian past that apparently still haunts the Canadian psyche.

Scottishness of the Canadian Presbyterian Church is a recurring theme in John Moir's official history of the denomination, *Enduring Witness*. According to Moir, British suspicions that the American Revolution was all a Presbyterian plot made it expedient for Presbyterian Loyalists to stress their British credentials and to downplay any connection with "democratical tendencies" of the new republic to the south. The War of 1812 and the slavery issue reinforced this orientation in the nineteenth century. When the various strands of Presbyterianism in Canada united shortly after Confederation in 1875, the new church was marked, according to Moir, by a national consciousness—"Scottish Canadianism"—that limited its appeal for other ethnic groups.[3] Even today, moderatorial lace, Robbie Burns suppers, haggis, and the "Kirking of the Tartan" are not unknown to Canadian Presbyterians.

Denominational bonds were thus reinforced by ethnic loyalties, which may have provided Presbyterians with a particularly potent sense of cohesion and identity. This, by itself, however, is hardly sufficient to explain the cultural impact of Canadian Presbyterianism on Canadian society, which was considerable. The ethnic chauvinism of a minority group is at least as likely to repel others as to impress them. More important is the fact that the Presbyterian Church managed to provide spiritual and intellectual leadership to the nation during the years in which Canada entered the modern world. In a time of transition and uncertainty, the Presbyterian Church answered questions that many Canadians were asking.

Clarence MacKinnon, principal of the Presbyterian Theological College in Halifax (Pine Hill), ventured the opinion in 1924 that the Presbyterian Church in Canada had adapted to the theological turmoil at the end of the nineteenth century "with perhaps less irritation than any other part of Christendom." It had softened the harsh outlines of Westminster Confession Calvinism with a measure of evangelical piety, a new historical understanding of the Bible and the creeds, and an appreciation of the social responsibilities of the church in a pioneer society. MacKinnon attributed the smoothness of this shift to a special "spiritual tact . . . a peculiar practical instinct, [which] like a guardian angel, sifted for her what was eternal in the

---

3. John Moir, *Enduring Witness*, 2d ed. (Toronto, 1987), 215. Cf. 35, 43, 126ff., 144.

old and what was of advantage in the new, and enabled her to make the inevitable adjustments."[4]

At least some of MacKinnon's satisfaction with his church was warranted. Unlike their sister church in the northern United States, Canadian Presbyterians avoided much of the disruptive theological polarization of the New School and Old School camps that, by the 1890s, had resulted in that church officially adopting a stand on biblical inerrancy and driving distinguished and devout scholars such as Charles Briggs, Henry Preserved Smith, and Arthur Cushman McGiffert out of the Presbyterian ministry.[5]

Unlike both the American and Scottish churches, Canadian Presbyterians did not remain silent and counsel passivity in the face of the social and economic horrors of the Industrial Revolution. In nineteenth-century Scotland, Presbyterians were seriously inhibited in their response to industrialization by a hyperindividualistic Calvinism that combined easily with laissez-faire economics. Nor were they helped by Thomas Chalmers's quixotic notions about charity in an industrial society. In the resulting alienation of the working class, leadership for social reform passed to the trade unions, Kier Hardie, and the Labour Party.[6] In the United States, Presbyterians were probably more resistant to the Social Gospel than any other mainline denomination. Certainly they lagged far behind Unitarians and Episcopalians in demonstrating any sympathy for the labor movement or con-

4. John Thomas McNeill, *The Presbyterian Church in Canada, 1875–1925* (Toronto, 1925), ix.

5. Lefferts A. Loetscher, *The Broadening Church: A Study of Theological Issues in the Presbyterian Church since 1869* (Philadelphia, 1954), 94ff.; George M. Marsden, *The Evangelical Mind and the New School Presbyterian Experience: A Case Study of Thought and Theology in Nineteenth-Century America* (New Haven, 1970).

6. T. C. Smout, *A Century of the Scottish People: 1830–1950* (London, 1987). Smout is able to tell the story of working-class radicalism and the rise of socialist idealism in nineteenth-century Scotland without any reference to the Presbyterian churches. Cf. Donald C. Smith, *Passive Obedience and Prophetic Protest: Social Criticism in the Scottish Church, 1830–1945* (New York, 1988), 313: "In the 1880's and 90's a remarkable change in the Church's attitude to the organized labour movement had begun to take place. Set free from the now discredited economic dogma of the 'iron law' of wages, it was no longer axiomatic that all churchmen would side with the masters and capitalists in denouncing the workers when they sought to raise wages through strikes. Henceforth, among progressive clergy and lay leaders, labour was always to have a few, sometimes many champions within the Church." The impression Smith's book leaves, however, is that the Scottish church followed rather than led in these developments.

cern for social justice. According to Henry May, "Their periodicals, for the most part, held fast to traditional social theories. Though the General Assembly fairly often discussed city evils, radicalism and strikes as menaces to society, it showed little effort to formulate suggestions for improvement."[7] Social Christianity would gain a hearing in the church's national councils only after the turn of the twentieth century, under the flamboyant leadership of Charles Stelzle.

Of course, Canada industrialized later than either Scotland or the United States, but when the process began in the 1880s, the Presbyterian Church led the agitation for social justice and pointed the way to liberal reform. The origins of the Social Gospel movement in Canada are usually traced to Queen's University during the years in which George Monro Grant was its principal and Primaritus Professor of Divinity.[8] If radical Methodists like Salem Bland found their inspiration at Queen's, so too did more moderate Presbyterians. It is hardly too much to say that the origins of the welfare state that developed under the aegis of Prime Minister W. L. Mackenzie King in the twentieth century are to be found in the Presbyterian Church, in which he was raised, and at Queen's University, to which he felt a lifelong attachment.[9]

Guardian angels may well have had something to do with this result, but as Clarence MacKinnon has elsewhere acknowledged, it also had a great deal to do with specific personalities and leadership. No one was more important to the outcome than Principal Grant of Queen's College, Kingston. Grant was a powerful debater, a masterful church politician, and a dominating presence on the floor of the General Assembly. In John Moir's words, he was "the acknowledged giant among giants of Canadian Presbyterianism."[10] While he certainly received help from many quarters, it was Grant who directed attention to theological developments in Scotland and who prevented the Ca-

7. Henry F. May, *Protestant Churches and Industrial America* (New York, 1949), 192.

8. Richard Allen, *The Social Passion: Religion and Social Reform in Canada, 1914–28* (Toronto, 1971), 6, 10; Ramsay Cook, *The Regenerators: Social Criticism in Late Victorian English Canada* (Toronto, 1985); Doug Owram, *The Government Generation: Canadian Intellectuals and the State, 1900–1945* (Toronto, 1986).

9. George Henderson, "Mackenzie King and Queen's University, 1893–1950," *Historic Kingston* 39 (1991): 62–79.

10. Moir, *Enduring Witness*, 143.

nadian Presbyterians from following the Princeton lead into a conservative defense of Calvinist orthodoxy. His role in steering the Canadian church into an accommodating evangelicalism during the 1880s and 1890s is roughly comparable to that of a Henry Boynton Smith in the American church a generation before him[11] or Robert Speer a generation after him.[12] And it was Grant who made Queen's College in particular and the Presbyterian Church in general the nursery of liberal political reform in Canada.

The outcome could certainly have been very different. The forty-ninth parallel has always been porous to theology, and in the nineteenth century, a significant number of Canadian Presbyterians learned Calvin under the Hodges, father and son, at Princeton. In general, it was the Canadian-educated Free Church and the Secessionist elements in the church that looked to Princeton for theological direction. Included in this category are men such as Daniel Harvey MacVicar, principal of Presbyterian College, Montreal,[13] and William Caven and William McLaren at Knox College, Toronto.[14] Not surprisingly, the "Auld Kirk" element and those who had been educated in Scotland were better informed about, and relatively more open to, developments there. Besides Grant at Queen's, they included Allan Pollok, Daniel Miner Gordon, James and Robert Falconer, and Clarence MacKinnon at the Pine Hill Divinity College, Halifax,[15] as well as the Rev. D. J. Macdonnell.[16]

11. Marsden, *Evangelical Mind*, 157–82, esp. chap. 8, "The Mediating Theology of Henry B. Smith." Smith, like Grant, was firmly rooted in Scottish common sense philosophy but much influenced by the Romanticism and historical consciousness of reverent German scholars such as Tholuck, Hengstenberg, and Neander.

12. Loetscher, *Broadening Church*, 105; Bradley J. Longfield, *The Presbyterian Controversy: Fundamentalists, Modernists, and Moderates* (New York, 1991), 185ff.

13. H. Keith Markell, *History of the Presbyterian College, Montreal, 1865–1986* (Montreal, 1987), 17–21.

14. Cf. Moir, *Enduring Witness*, 176.

15. Wilhelmina Gordon, *Daniel M. Gordon: His Life* (Toronto, 1941); James G. Greenlee, *Sir Robert Falconer: A Biography* (Toronto, 1988); Clarence Mackinnon, *Reminiscences* (Toronto, 1938).

16. J. F. McCurdy, *The Life and Work of D. J. Macdonnell* (Toronto, 1897). John Mark King, principal of Manitoba College in Winnipeg, does not fall into either category. While he did not come from an Auld Kirk background, certainly by the 1890s he was sympathetic to theological developments in Scotland. See Gordon Harland, "John Mark King: First Principal of Manitoba College," in *Prairie Spirit: Perspectives on the Heritage of the United Church of Canada in the West*, ed. Dennis L. Butcher et al. (Winnipeg, 1985).

Grant was appointed to Queen's College two years after the various strands of Presbyterianism united in 1875 to form the largest Protestant denomination in the country. Within months of that union the question of the theological orientation of the new denomination was posed in a particularly sharp way. Macdonnell, minister of St. Andrew's in Toronto, preached a sermon that included some injudicious speculation on the subject of eternal punishment of the reprobate. He ventured to doubt that the Westminster Confession represented the final word on the subject and pointed to various passages in the Bible that could be construed as allowing the possibility of purgatorial parole.

Strict Calvinists were outraged, and Macdonnell soon found himself called to account for his views at the General Assembly in 1876 and again in 1877. The underlying issue was liberty in interpreting the Westminster Confession—the same one over which John MacLeod Campbell had been deposed forty-five years earlier in Scotland. Was the Westminster Confession to be accepted as the final authority in establishing doctrinal orthodoxy in the newly formed Presbyterian Church of Canada, or was it a "subordinate standard" subject to the superior authority of Scripture? Those in the Canadian church who looked toward Princeton were as determined as their counterparts in the United States to bind their church tightly to the Westminster Confession. Grant played a leading role in the fight against what he called the "keen, relentless, inquisitorial attitude" of conservative Calvinists like William Caven and William McLaren—which he considered a "break of faith" of the Union agreement. He wrote to his predecessor at Queen's, William Snodgrass,

Everybody knew that we were and are in favour of a revision of the Confession, but that realizing its present impracticality we were satisfied to leave matters as they were with the understanding that we have a general assent to the scheme of doctrine in it, and would work loyally for the church side by side with the straightest of them. Would one of us have ever dreamed of Union had we dreamed that the first result would be to stretch us one by one on such a bed of Procrustes as they have been torturing Macdonnell on?[17]

17. George M. Grant to William Snodgrass, 4 May 1876, Grant Papers, Queen's University Archives, Kingston.

While recognizing the practical necessity of creedal confessions if the church was to avoid intellectual anarchy, Grant warned the General Assembly about the dangers of human words being fashioned into idols. "The two points seemingly contrary that we must hold are (1) that the confession is our interpretation of scripture and must, in its main scope be adhered to (2) that it is only a subordinate standard and must never theoretically or practically be elevated into a supreme position."[18] For Grant, theological statements and systems like the Westminster Confession had a necessary but limited use.

The result of the trial was very different from that of the famous Swing case in the United States a few years earlier. Even after he had been acquitted of heresy by a sympathetic Chicago Presbytery, David Swing left the church when faced with the prospect of another trial before the General Assembly. This gratifying lesson was not lost on the conservative party, and Old School Presbyterians soon consolidated their control of the McCormack Seminary.[19] Macdonnell, the very popular minister of one of the largest congregations in Toronto, in contrast, was quite ready for a fight at the assembly. Although he eventually promised to adhere publicly to the teaching of the confession on the subject of the endless duration of future punishment, "notwithstanding doubts or difficulties which perplex my mind,"[20] the unity of the orthodox party had been badly strained during the debate and, as Grant accurately predicted to Agnes Maule Machar, the effect of the trial was to "legitimize doubts, difficulties and perplexities to any extent as far as other ministers and other doctrines are concerned."[21]

The Macdonnell case dampened zeal among Canadian Presbyterians for heresy hunting, and there were no subsequent attempts to enforce creedal conformity to the Westminster Confession. The Auld Kirk element in the new church, from which Macdonnell came and which stood solidly by him during the trial, represented only 25 per-

18. Grant diary for 1876, notes for his speech to the General Assembly on the Macdonnell heresy trail, Grant Papers, vol. 8, Public Archives of Canada (henceforth PAC). Cf. William Caven, *A Vindication of Doctrinal Standards: With Special Reference to the Standards of the Presbyterian Church* (Toronto, 1875).

19. Loetscher, *Broadening Church*, 15.

20. *The Acts and Proceedings of the Third General Assembly of the Presbyterian Church in Canada, Halifax 1877* (Toronto, 1877), 135.

21. W. L. Grant and F. C. Hamilton, *Principal Grant* (Toronto, 1904), 164.

cent of the membership in the national church—but it had effectively resisted the attempt by the much larger group of former Free Church and Canadian Presbyterian Church ministers to insist on strict creedal conformity to the confession. The net effect of the trial was to weaken the church's adherence to scholastic Calvinism and to open it to an accommodating evangelicalism.

In 1880, at the Pan-Presbyterian conference in Philadelphia, Grant and Macdonnell urged a revision of the creed, but their suggestion met with little favor in a city that was close to the center of Princeton influence.[22] It was sufficient, however, to make Grant an ally of those in the American church who were in favor of nudging the church into a similar theological stance and who had run afoul of Princeton influence.[23] Although McLaren and MacVicar continued to look to Princeton for their theological use, Grant was just as sure that Charles Hodge was pointing the church into a cul-de-sac. He saw Hodge's attempt to defend orthodoxy in the nineteenth century by donning the whole panoply of seventeenth-century theological armor as fundamentally misguided. Like his friend Charles Macdonald, professor of mathematics at Dalhousie University, Grant was amazed at how a man of Hodge's obvious intellectual abilities "could live so entirely on words—words—words—no reality in nature or life corresponding."[24] By insisting on the last jot and tittle of the Calvinist system, Hodge's Princeton, instead of being a breakwater against heresy, risked becoming a grand provocation to atheism.

Grant had himself been educated in Scotland during the 1850s, a decade in which Calvinism in Scotland was breaking up. His mentor was the Reverend Norman Macleod, cousin of MacLeod Campbell, whose great work *The Nature of the Atonement* was published in 1856. Grant's awareness of the theological situation in Scotland made

22. D. Macrae to W. L. Grant, 14 May 1903, Grant Papers, vol. 7, PAC. Cf. John B. Dales and R. M. Patterson, eds., *Presbyterian Alliance: Report of Proceedings of the Second Council of the Presbyterian Alliance, convened at Philadelphia, Sept. 1880* (Philadelphia, 1880).

23. George Muller to George M. Grant, 6 March 1889, Grant Papers, PAC. Muller, whose father had been one of the original professors of the Princeton Seminary, looked to Grant for support in drafting a new evangelical creed for the church. Their mutual friends included Prof. J. F. McCurdy of the Department of Near Eastern Studies, University of Toronto, and Dr. Reinsford of New York.

24. Charles Macdonald to Grant [1878? first pages of letter are missing], Correspondence, 406, Grant Papers, PAC.

it difficult for him to regard Hodge's efforts at Princeton as anything more than sophisticated obscurantism. Grant believed that Protestant theology needed to be reformulated if it was not to be discarded as unintelligible verbiage in the modern world. This did not make him a liberal modernist, however. He is better described as a Romantic evangelical who retained both a strong Calvinist awareness of original sin and a belief in God's electing purpose in history even as he broke away from the Calvinism of double predestination and limited atonement that Robbie Burns had satirized so effectively in poems like "Holy Willie."

Grant was a Romantic in the sense that he had read Coleridge and especially Carlyle with appreciation, believed that reason was tied to intuition, and was thoroughly imbued with the historical sense that characterized the nineteenth century. He was an evangelical in the sense that he looked theologically to Paul and to Luther, was open to revivalism, and could function fairly effectively in that role himself— whether preaching to the revivalistic Presbyterian Macdonaldites on Prince Edward Island or during a 1875 revival in Pictou County, Nova Scotia.[25] He was also a great admirer of D. L. Moody. During his years in Kingston he became increasingly skeptical of professional revivalists and the advertising techniques and psychological manipulation that came to characterize North American revivalism, but he never ceased to regard Moody as a wonderful exception. He was also genuinely sympathetic to the work of the Salvation Army, and when General William Booth visited Kingston, he stayed at Summerhill, the principal's residence.[26] Grant told his students that conversion was the aim of every minister's sermon every Sunday. Christians needed to be revived "or awakened from slumber into which all are prone to fall, and in every congregation there ought to be conversions all the time."[27]

While Grant was in favor of revising the Westminster Confession, he was certainly not in favor of recklessly casting it aside. His main

25. J. Fraser Campbell to W. L. Grant, 25 June 1902, Grant Papers, vol. 7, PAC; *Presbyterian Witness*, 24 April 1875; G. Lawson Gordon, *River John: Its Pastors and People* (New Glasgow, 1911), 88–93. For an account of one man's conversion under Grant's ministry, see John Ingram to G. M. Grant, 7 March 1883. Ingram was a bandboy with the Seventy-eighth Highland Regiment who eventually felt called to the ministry and served as a missionary in Jamaica.

26. Grant and Hamilton, *Principal Grant*, 493.

27. Grant Papers, PAC, "Subjects Treated in 1890–91 Vol. II," 53.

point was that it had to be understood historically as a powerful testimony to the faith of the Puritans rather than as an improvement on the New Testament. Grant warned:

> Extreme views about the excellence of the Westminster Confession lead to the opposite extreme of depreciation of it. The latter is the worse extreme of the two. It not only argues an unhistorical spirit, as the other view does, but indicates self-sufficiency which is generally the sign of superficiality. The Westminster divines were a noble body of men, but the modern point of view is quite different than theirs, and we can only accept their work as the high water mark of the religion of that age. We have developed since, but to discard such a document would be to break the continuity of religious life. Therefore we keep it, without pressing it in detail, until circumstances enable us to draw up such a confession as will faithfully reflect the higher life of our own day. The time for that is not yet, for this is an age of criticism rather than construction and criticism has not yet done its work. We must therefore be patient, unless we choose to break the Church into fragments instead of uniting it, and I am inclined to think that hasty utterances and one-sided language do harm.[28]

Grant was a skillful church politician who saw his task in terms of keeping the Presbyterian family together until a new theological consensus emerged. His manner was conciliatory and even-handed. At his inaugural address at Queen's in 1877, he alluded to theological tensions in the new church and stressed that the fault lay not just on one side. There were two classes of people who obstructed the policy of constructive dialogue in the church that he wished to pursue:

> The one class believes nothing but what is old; the other believes nothing but what is new. It is difficult to decide which are the greater enemies to truth, though a characteristic of both is that they always speak

28. G. M. Grant to W. L. Grant, Winnipeg, 21 July 1893, Grant Papers, PAC, vol. 32. Cf. "Notes for Divinity Lectures, Session 1899–1900," 3: "When we awaken to the perception of this fact of the necessary limitation of dogma, we are apt to go to the extreme of belittling dogma altogether. That for the generality of persons is a greater mistake than the mistake of identifying our dogmas with pure truth" (Grant Papers, vol. 15). See also Diary 1901–1902, W. L. Grant Papers, vol. 27, PAC; see also dialogue on the subject, pp. 30ff. Another indication of this attitude is that a chair of "Church History and the History of Dogma" was established at Queen's in 1900 (D. C. Masters, *Protestant Church Colleges in Canada* [Toronto, 1966], 148).

as if they had sole monopoly of truth. When a man boasts in the newspapers and at public meetings that he is orthodox, suspect him. When he assures you he is an advanced thinker, avoid him. As a rule both are pretentious humbugs and will come to naught.[29]

Grant's own theology was evangelical and christocentric, and he frequently stressed that if people began theological discussions by talking about Jesus, they would see many of the issues on which they disagreed as peripheral rather than as essential. No one better exemplified the board church motto "In necessariis unitas, in dubiis libertas, in omnibus caritas."

Increasingly, it was Grant's voice, rather than that of Caven's or MacVicar's, that young ministers heeded at General Assembly.[30] The struggle in the Canadian church between Princeton Calvinism and the accommodating evangelicalism that prevailed in Scotland took many forms. When the issue of a new Presbyterian hymnal came up in the 1890s, for example, Grant counseled consultation with the Scottish rather than the American church and defeated the conservative faction opposed to any selections being made from the Psalms. He boasted to his wife that "Caven, MacVicar, McLaren all united against selections being made from the psalms and we beat them by 156 to 89. The young men are coming in like a flood. Language from Caven and MacVicar that would have swept the Assembly like a whirlwind a few years ago is now listened to respectfully by their own students and then calmly disregarded."[31] Significantly, it was one of Grant's students, Alfred Gandier, who was appointed principal of Knox College when William McLaren retired in 1908.

The debate about the status of the Westminster Confession in the church was related to the controversy over the higher criticism of the

---

29. *The Globe*, 8 December 1877, 2.

30. G. M. Grant to J. L. Grant, letter headed "Peterboro—Tues. morning": "Friday, I moved for a committee to consider what matters could with advantage be taken from the jurisdiction of the Assembly and entrusted to Synods. At once, all the combined fatherhood of Montreal, Knox, and Winnipeg Colleges, including McVicar, Warden, Proudfoot, McLaren, Laing, King and Caven, who though in the Chair shook his head ominously and thundered at me, but I—as mover—had the right of reply and to their amazement carried the House by a vote of 126 to 59. This is a good omen of what can be done. There are a good many Queen's men at the Assembly and they are going to dine together this evening and of course they have invited me" (Grant Papers, PAC, vol. 31).

31. Ibid., letter headed "Friday St. John."

Bible. The difference between Grant and his conservative opponents was that he regarded the confession as a historical document in a way that they did not. The same could be said of their respective views of the Bible. Grant was open to what he termed the "reverent criticism" of the Bible from the time he assumed the principalship of Queen's.[32] Shortly after his inauguration he pointed his students to the "new school" in Scotland:

> of whom several Free Church Professors, such as Lindsay, Davidson and ex-Prof. Robertson Smith are the best known representatives. Its position may be characterized as a resolute and scholarly attempt to combine old dogmatic faith with new criticism. Accepting the results of criticism in the most extreme form if necessary, they see nothing to shake their faith in the inspiration of Scripture and the supernatural character of the record. They consider that the new criticism brings out much more clearly and fully than the old view of the Bible did the historical character of the record and gives us new and beautiful evidence of the continuous intercourse of Jehovah with his people.[33]

It was to the Scottish school and writers like Marcus Dods, A. B. Bruce, and George Adam Smith that Grant continued to look for intellectual guidance until his death in 1902. His personal judgment of the "the celebrated heretic" W. Robertson Smith was that he was "very pleasant, very clever, very decided in all his opinions."[34] In 1882, he consulted with Professor Bruce about the possibility of filling the Old Testament Chair at Queen's with someone who, while essentially holding Smith's views, was wiser and more patient with those of average intelligence—one not given to "rash or impetuous judgments."[35] In the event, however, Grant decided that it was politically inexpedient to retire John Mowat—the brother of the premier

32. John S. Moir, *A History of Biblical Studies in Canada: A Sense of Proportion* (Chicago, 1982). Moir points to the key role of J. F. McCurdy at the Department of Near Eastern Studies, University of Toronto, and to the appointment of the prolific John E. McFadyen to the Old Testament Chair at Knox in 1898 in introducing biblical criticism to Canada. But twenty years before McFadyen arrived in Toronto, Grant was pointing his students to developments in Scotland.

33. Divinity Lectures 1878–79, 54, Grant Papers, PAC, vol. 14.

34. George M. Grant to J. L. Grant, 12 October 1882, Grant Papers, PAC, vol. 34.

35. A. B. Bruce to Grant, 13 September 1882, Grant Papers, PAC.

of Ontario—from the job, whatever his views on Jonah and the whale. In 1899, after many years of part-time involvement at Queen's, the British-born and educated William George Jordan was appointed as Mowat's successor. He combined sound scholarship with strong pastoral sense and a prolific pen. Author of *Prophetic Ideas and Ideals* (1902) and *Biblical Criticism and Modern Thought* (1909), among many other works, long before his own retirement in 1929, Jordan became one of the great men of Queen's.

If Grant's best contacts were with British scholars like his classmate at Glasgow, Robert Flint, professor of theology at Edinburgh, and Andrew Martin Fairbairn, principal of Mansfield college, Oxford, he was also aware of developments in Germany and the United States. He felt a particular affinity for the Romantic historian Heinrich Ewald. Much of Grant's early lecture notes are a condensation of the German historian's *History of Israel*, which had been translated into English in 1874. Although Grant had moved away from such distinctively Calvinist doctrines as double predestination and limited atonement, Ewald's emphasis on Israel's election within the process of history and his openness to the possibility of miracle impressed him. Ewald's influence is evident in the only book Grant published on a theological topic, *The Religions of the World* (1894). The book is a fairly sympathetic treatment of other world religions from the point of view of an accommodating evangelical who believed "that Jesus is the way, the truth and the life, and that His religion is the absolute religion."[36] Other faiths in the world served as a preparation to the fuller revelation of God afforded by the life, death, and resurrection of Jesus.

A recent study has suggested that this moderately liberal position became normative for American Presbyterians in the 1930s under the influence of Robert Speer.[37] Although Grant did not control the vast missionary empire that Speer did, he was always an active and influential member of the Mission Board of the Canadian church and exerted a comparable influence. The difference is that views on mission

36. George M. Grant, *The Religions of the World in Relation to Christianity* (Edinburgh, 1894), viii.
37. Grant Wacker, "A Plural World: The Protestant Awakening to World Religions," in *Between the Times: The Travail of the Protestant Establishment in America, 1900–1960,* ed. William R. Hutchison (Cambridge, Mass.2, 1989), 263–64.

that became acceptable in the American church only in the 1930s were widely held in Canada many decades earlier. The position that Grant outlined in *The Religions of the World* was one he had held when he first came to Queen's, and in fact one that he had acquired in Scotland in the 1850s under the influence of Norman Macleod and Max Muller.[38] John R. Mott, founder of the World's Student Christian Federation and chairman of the International Missionary Council, was still recommending his book, as the best short introduction to the subject, in the 1940s.[39]

Students at Queen's were also encouraged to read American theologians such as Horace Bushnell and Charles Briggs.[40] In the midst of the controversy that eventually forced Briggs out of the American church, he delivered one of the Sunday afternoon addresses at the 1892 Theological Alumni Conference at Queen's.[41] Grant's openness to biblical as opposed to scholastic theology is also reflected in the fact that he published in the *Andover Review* and the *American Journal of Theology*.[42]

The Briggs trial was reaching its climax when Grant spoke on behalf of Canadian Presbyterians at the World Congress of Religions, held in Chicago in 1893. During his address "Presbyterian Reunion" he stressed the importance of the church remaining "broad enough to include varieties of thought not inconsistent with its life." He ended it with a rather pointed warning:

> The ablest expounder of the New Testament that I heard when a student in Scotland was Morrison, the founder of the Evangelical Union.

38. Lecture on mission, Diary for 1878, January 1, Grant Papers, PAC, vol. 9. Cf. George M. Grant, *Our Five Foreign Missions* (Toronto, [1886?]); Donald McLeod, *Memoir of Norman Macleod, D.D.* (Toronto, 1876), 356, 364, 481.

39. J. R. Watts, "George Monro Grant," in *Some Great Men of Queen's*, ed. R. C. Wallace (Toronto, 1941), 12; Grant and Hamilton, *Principal Grant*, 488.

40. Lectures for 1881–82, 171, 198; and Exams and Lectures for Session 1892–93, 198, Grant Papers, PAC, vol. 14.

41. Charles Briggs, "The Bible and Other Books," in *Sunday Afternoon Addresses* (Kingston, 1892), 3–11.

42. George M. Grant, "The British Association at Montreal," *Andover Review* 2 (October 1884): 381–93; and "The Outlook of the Twentieth Century in Theology," *American Journal of Theology* 6 (January 1902): 1–16. Grant also published book reviews on the subject of comparative religion; see *American Journal of Theology* 1 (January 1897): 163–65; 1 (October 1897): 1002–7; 2 (July 1898): 651–54; 2 (October 1898): 849–51.

Him the United Presbyterian church cast out. The holiest man I ever knew was John McLeod Campbell, whose work on the "Atonement" is the most valuable contribution to the great subject that the Nineteenth Century has produced. Him the Church of Scotland cast out. The most brilliant scholar I ever met, the man who could have done the church greater service than any other writer in the field of historical criticism, where service is most needed, was Robertson Smith. Him the Free Church of Scotland cast out from his chair.

Acknowledging that "the ashes of controversy [were] still hot," he nevertheless urged the American Presbyterian Church to confess its sin and repent of its handling of the Briggs case.[43] It was a particularly nasty example of scapegoating in his view, which would be remembered with shame and embarrassment.[44]

Such unsolicited advice from an outsider was probably resented in Chicago—which was by then an Old School bastion. But after the Presbyterian General Assembly officially adopted the Princeton position on biblical inerrancy, the scattered moderate elements within the church continued to look to Grant for support. The editor of the *New York Evangelist,* one of the few Presbyterian periodicals not dominated by the influence of Princeton, published "A Bystander's View of the Church," in which Grant predictably denounced inerrancy as a "baseless dogma. It is a poor modern invention, or, rather, a repetition of the old rabbinic views of Holy Scripture, against which Paul protested so emphatically when he declared that the letter killeth, but the spirit giveth life."[45]

Unlike the Presbyterian Church in the northern United States, the Canadian church showed itself to be remarkably open to the higher criticism of the Bible in the late nineteenth century. In this regard it followed the lead of both the Established and Free Church colleges in Scotland. In 1893, Professor John Campbell of Presbyterian College, Montreal, was charged with heresy for a sermon he had preached at a Queen's Alumni Conference that questioned the bibli-

---

43. "Presbyterian Reunion and Reformation Principles," in J. W. Hanson, *The World's Congress of Religions* (Chicago, 1894), 1044, reprinted in the *Queen's Quarterly* 1 (January 1894): 173ff.

44. *Queen's Quarterly* 1 (July 1893): 76.

45. "A Bystander's View of the Church, " *The Evangelist,* 10 August 1899, 8.

cal depiction of God in some passages of the Old Testament.[46] The charges, however, were dropped by the presbytery in favor of a statement about scriptural inspiration, and he retained his teaching position. Perhaps the incident cost him the principalship of Presbyterian College a few years later, but more likely it was his poor judgment rather than his openness to the higher criticism of the Bible that made people doubt his suitability for the job.[47]

Canadian Methodists were more resistant to biblical criticism than were Presbyterians. When George Workman was dismissed from his post at Victoria College for comments on the subject of messianic prophesy, Grant defended him and "reverent" biblical criticism in the columns of *The Week*.[48] Grant saw the substitution of a biblical theology for Calvinist scholasticism as presenting an opportunity for a theological rapprochement with Methodists—a first step toward the formation of a national church, which remained one of his fondest hopes. If Presbyterians dropped double predestination and limited atonement from their creed, Methodists abandoned talk about perfectionism and exaggerated notions of human initiative in the economy of salvation, and both churches rediscovered their common biblical inheritance, then a theological deal could be struck. As he explained (citing Charles Briggs) to readers of the *Methodist Monthly* in 1884, differences between Presbyterianism and Methodism were in intellectual emphasis, not in spiritual truth. He proposed the possibility of organic union.[49] That such a union eventually took place is another reflection of the fact that the Canadian Presbyterian Church took a different path theologically in the last decades of the nineteenth century than its American sister.

Another related respect in which the Canadian Presbyterians took a different path than either the American or the Scottish church was

46. J. Campbell, "The Perfect Book of the Perfect Father," *Sunday Afternoon Addresses* (Kingston, 1893), 10–21.

47. Markell, *History of the Presbyterian College*, 21–28.

48. *The Week*, 5 February 1892, 149; 26 February 1892, 198 (signed "Presbyter").

49. George M. Grant, "Organic Union of the Churches: How Far Should It Go?" *Canadian Methodist Magazine* 20 (September 1884): 252. On a personal level, Grant was a good friend of Samuel Nelles, principal of Victoria College until his death in 1887. It is perhaps more than coincidence that in 1889, when Grant was moderator of the General Assembly, a delegation of Methodists presented a resolution to the gathered Presbyterians earnestly praying for closer union (*Acts and Proceedings of the Fifteenth General Assembly* [Toronto, 1889], 31).

in its advocacy of liberal reform in social and economic matters. Again Grant's role was pivotal. As a national policy of protectionism, immigration, and the construction of the railway to the Pacific took hold and Canada began to industrialize in the 1880s, the issues of industrial capitalism, working-class slums, agrarian discontent, and labor strife all came to the fore.[50] The Royal Commission on the Relations of Labour and Capital reported to Parliament in 1889. In 1891, a memorial to the annual meetings of the Anglican, Methodist, and Presbyterian churches by a joint committee of the Knights of Labour, the Single Tax Association, the Trades and Labour Council, the Woman's Enfranchisement Association, the Eight Hours League, and the Nationalist Association called for the churches to affirm their solidarity with the poor against the oppression by the rich. The Anglicans and Methodists rejected the petition.[51] The General Assembly of the Presbyterian Church indicated a willingness to take the matter under study and asked Grant, who had been elected moderator in 1889, to convene the committee.

Never far behind the times, Grant had appointed Adam Shortt to lecture on economic and political science at Queen's in 1888, the same year in which he had reviewed Henry George's *Progress and Poverty* for the *Presbyterian Review*, then coedited by Briggs.[52] Despite serious misgivings about George's analysis of the problems of industrial society in North America and his "single-tax" remedy, Grant identified it as an important book because it called attention "with a trumpet voice to the social evils of our times."[53] Grant had long been concerned about social justice in the relationship between employers and employees. His student commonplace books from the 1850s are filled with Carlyle's sayings about the inadequacy of the "cash-nexus" between human beings, and Grant shared with his literary mentor a radical streak that sympathized with the sansculottes

50. Greg Kealey, *Canada Investigates Industrialism* (Toronto, 1973); idem, *Toronto Workers Respond to Industrial Capitalism* (Toronto, 1980); Greg Kealey and Bryan Palmer, *Dreaming of What Might Be: The Knights of Labour in Ontario, 1880–1900* (New York, 1982).

51. Cook, *Regenerators*, 116.

52. George M. Grant, "Progress and Poverty," *Presbyterian Review* 9 (April 1888): 177–98. The periodical was still coedited at that point by Charles Briggs.

53. Ibid., 197.

rather than the complacent aristocracy in revolutionary France. It was Carlyle who taught Grant to thunder prophetically against the sins of the industrial world.

For most of the nineteenth century, the Scottish church listened not to Thomas Carlyle but to the man Karl Marx once sneeringly dubbed "arch-parson Chalmers."[54] However eloquent Thomas Chalmers was in the pulpit on evangelical themes, his notions of how to deal with the social conditions spawned by the Industrial Revolution were sadly anachronistic. He opposed the Poor Law legislation of 1834, for example, in favor of a scheme of charity modeled on the seventeenth-century rural parish.[55] His strict Calvinism, which owed much to the deterministic vision of Jonathan Edwards, fitted easily together with laissez-faire capitalism. And his enormous prestige helped propagate the economic dogma known as the iron law of wages. Prosperous middle-class congregations were assured that wages could not be permanently raised "artificially" either by labor agitation or by government regulation, above the "natural" level dictated by the market price of labor. The gross inequities of the economic system were thus invested with the authority of divine sanction. It was, no doubt, a comforting thought to some, but by the 1880s such an approach had effectively alienated many members of the working class from the Scottish churches. They looked elsewhere for intellectual and spiritual leadership.[56]

Whereas in Scotland, the churches maintained almost complete silence or worse in relation to the problems of industrial society—at least until after the issue had been taken up by society at large—the response in Canada was quite different. On social questions, Presbyterian clergy in Canada looked more to Thomas Carlyle than to Thomas Chalmers. They insisted less on the so-called iron law of wages than on the Book of Amos. Part of this change of attitude is explained

54. Donald C. Smith, *Passive Obedience and Prophetic Protest: Social Criticism in the Scottish Church, 1830–1945* (New York, 1988).

55. Stewart J. Brown, *Thomas Chalmers and the Godly Commonwealth in Scotland* (Oxford, 1982); and Boyd Hilton, *The Age of Atonement: The Influence of Evangelicalism on Social and Economic Thought, 1795–1865* (Oxford, 1988). In my judgment, Hilton gets the better of the argument. The ideal of the "godly commonwealth" in nineteenth-century Scotland owes far more to Thomas Carlyle than it does to Chalmers.

56. Callum G. Brown, *The Social History of Religion in Scotland since 1730* (London, 1987), 169–207.

by the general theological shift in Canada away from strict Calvinism. Grant's biblical theology had little time for scholastic definitions of divine sovereignty that logically eliminated any role for human freedom and thus encouraged passive acceptance of the morally intolerable. Moreover, historical criticism of the Bible highlighted the role of the prophets in Israel as social critics (rather than as fortune-tellers) and suggested obvious parallels to current circumstances. Part of the change was personal. Grant was taught by Carlyle to shout defiance at the alleged necessity of social arrangements in the world, and he taught his students to do the same. He insisted on human freedom and responsibility in constructing a just social order. During his years as a parish minister in Halifax during the 1860s and 1870s, the obligation of capital to labor was a frequent theme in his sermons: workers needed to be treated as people rather than simply as factors of production.

It was the widespread influence of Henry George's book, however, and the populist reaction that it triggered in the United States and Canada, that provided the opportunity for Grant to speak to the issue on behalf of the Presbyterian Church and from his public platform at Queen's. In 1892 he delivered an address entitled "The Wage Question" to the Fifth Pan-Presbyterian Council meeting in Toronto.[57] Although loudly opposed by at least one American minister in the audience, Grant's case for progressive reform defined what was soon to become orthodoxy on the subject of political economy for Canadian Presbyterians. While dismissing socialist talk about the abolition of private property as quixotic, given the fact of "original sin," Grant recognized that there was considerable truth in the socialist indictment of industrial society. He affirmed the importance of the churches' taking an active interest in issues of social justice and preaching about the "moralization of capital."[58] He recognized a role for government regulation, and he defended trade unions on the basis of the need for the working class to be treated with respect.

57. George M. Grant, "The Wage Question," in *Alliance of the Reformed Churches Holding the Presbyterian System: Proceedings of the Fifth General Council, Toronto, 1892* (Toronto, 1892), 351–62; also published as "Principal Grant's Address on the Wage Question," *Weekly Witness*, 5 October 1892; and "The Problem of Wages," *Journal of the Knights of Labour*, 20 October 1891.

58. Ibid., 355.

His own preferred solution to the obvious inequities produced by unfettered capitalism was the cooperative movement in some industries and profit sharing in the rest. Anticipating King's *Industry and Humanity* by twenty-five years, he insisted that both labor and capital had a right to both wages and a share of the profits and that society as a whole also had rights. This would eventually provide the rationale for extensive government intervention in the economy.[59] It is quite possible that King, then a student at the University of Toronto, was among those sitting in the audience as Grant delivered his address. In any event, he soon wrote Grant to ask for advice about graduate work in economics and political science. Grant encouraged King in his educational ambitions and urged him to "hold fast your confidence in God as your friend and in His purpose for you."[60]

Drawing on rhetoric that he had learned from Carlyle, Grant challenged the hyperindividualism to which many nineteenth-century Calvinists were prone and alerted the Presbyterian Church to its social responsibilities. On this as on many other topics, he slipped into the role of prophet. In the columns of the *Queen's Quarterly*, which he edited, he worried publicly about the dangers of social polarization and plutocratic power.

> The one-eyed man can see sinister influences at work. In former times, he felt that the press could be depended on as the sure bulwark of liberty. Now, he is prone to ask, who is the millionaire behind the press? Then, he believed in the ministers of religion, pointing out with pride that a state establishment was not needed to ensure devoted service of God. Now, he views the Church with suspicion, and perhaps calls clergymen the "watch-dogs of the propertied classes." He made sacrifices for education, and honoured college presidents and professors. But even the universities—institutions whose freedom medieval bishops and popes respected—are now tainted. He consequently feels that the very wells from which he must drink are being poisoned, and he is be-

59. Ibid., 358.
60. Grant to King, 14 January 1897, W. L. M. King Papers, vol. 1, PAC. King's letters have not survived, but it is clear that he wrote more than once. Cf. Grant diary for 1896, Feb. Thursday 13, "W. L. M. King, Hull House Cor. Polk and Halstead, Chicago," Grant Papers, vol. 9, PAC. Among the addresses listed at the back of the diary (with the notation, "Glad you left Hull House") is W. L. M. King, 5728 Madison Ave., Chicago.

ginning to suspect that a vast conspiracy is on foot to pauperize and enslave him.[61]

He warned the clergy attending the Queen's Alumni Conference in 1894, "Armies of the unemployed, with starving wives and children in their rear, muster even on this new continent on which barns and elevators are full to bursting and banks cannot find investments for their money."[62] Carlyle lay in the background as Protestant clergy slipped into the role of Old Testament prophets to denounce the social consequences of the unregulated pursuit of unrighteous mammon.[63]

Having alerted church and nation to the problems and having argued for the broad outlines of a response, Grant was quite content to leave the details of state involvement in the economy to a younger generation of specialists. For the relative merits of specific proposals on tariffs, taxation, and other forms of regulation, he referred students and ministers to Shortt. Shortt often received requests for his opinion in economic matters from concerned church members, and he sometimes lectured on economic subjects at synod and presbytery meetings, as well as at the annual alumni conferences at Queen's.[64] In 1907, one correspondent who had heard him give a lecture at Knox College on the subject "Lawson and His Critics" invited him to the church at Nairn "for an intelligent hearing."[65] Another correspondent complained that "we have some very aggressive men on single tax here in the pulpit and Presbytery. I feel they are wrong but have not yet got my mind sufficiently enlightened to just answer them as is requisite. Where can I best read to see clearly the fallacy of single-tax advocates?"[66] Sometimes he received requests from ministers on the

61. *Queen's Quarterly* 5 (October 1897): 167.

62. George M. Grant, "The Lesson of the Book of Jonah," *Sunday Afternoon Addresses* (Kingston, 1894), 47.

63. Michael Gauvreau, *The Evangelical Century: College and Creed in English Canada from the Great Revival to the Great Depression* (Montreal and Kingston, 1991). Gauvreau emphasizes the extent to which Protestant clergy in Canada began to see themselves as modern-day successors of the Old Testament prophets. This, he argues was far more central to the rise of the Social Gospel in Canada than the alleged influence of Hegelian idealism or the rise of sociology.

64. Macdonnell to Shortt, 17 December 1906; and Shortt diary, 25 January 1908, Adam Shortt Papers, QUA.

65. Rannie to Shortt, 16 April 1907, Shortt Papers.

66. Milligan to Shortt, 13 January 1907, Shortt Papers.

scrounge for sermon material. The Reverend D. M. Solant, whom Shortt had helped get a call to the church in Smith's Falls, asked for reading suggestions. "I have people to whom I can give anything as long as it is sensible."[67] Many of the ministers had studied political economy with Shortt as part of their theological training.

In 1910, the General Assembly of the Presbyterian Church of Canada approved a Reading Course in Social Science, which had been recommended by its Board of Moral and Social Reform.[68] True to the Reformed tradition of respect for education and scholarship, it was designed for readers who shunned both "the enthusiasm of zealous ignorance" and "the paralysis of partial knowledge" for "the way of patient investigation and scientific knowledge." The reading list included texts on political science, sociology, economics, labor and industrial relations, socialism, trusts, the city, municipal ownership, poverty, temperance, gambling, the "social evil," criminology, philanthropy, children, political purity, immigrants, and public health. It also advertised the fact that Queen's University, at that point still a Presbyterian institution, offered an extramural course on economics, political science, and sociology. The reading list was prepared by the three acknowledged experts in social science within the Presbyterian Church, all of whom had a connection with Queen's: King, Shortt, and O. D. Skelton.

Intellectual clarification of the social and economic issues facing an urbanizing and industrializing Canada was linked to moral and spiritual leadership. It was clearly understood around Queen's that the state and the churches would need to cooperate if the problems of industrial society were to be successfully addressed. Knowledge of the technical details of government activity was important, but such knowledge would be sterile without the moral and political support of a "social passion" for reform generated by the churches. Both sorts of leadership were equally important. Skelton, in a chapter that he contributed to a primer on social service, designed for the edification of Presbyterian youth groups, stated that besides the traditional evangelical approach of "saving society through saving the individual," there

67. Solant to Shortt, 13 January 1907, Shortt Papers.
68. *Acts and Proceedings of the General Assembly of the Presbyterian Church of Canada* (Toronto, 1910), 293–98.

were several ways in which churches could join with the state in solving "the problem of the city."[69] It could "find ample scope in initiating educational or recreational measures to be taken up by school and state when grown beyond the Church's resources, and . . . carry on permanently those activities in which personal sympathy is most requisite." The other possibility was more directly political. Besides generally "developing in its members social conscience and enthusiasm," the church as a body might advocate the adoption by the state of particular policies—although, like Grant, Skelton was anxious not to confuse faith and politics and was "chary about committing the Church to hard and fast endorsation or condemnation of policies (prohibition, municipal public houses, single tax, municipal ownership) on which there is wide difference of opinion among honest men."[70]

Scholarly interest in the problems of social reform soon gave way at Queen's to a desire to actively shape government policy. After some successful work as a labor relations conciliator, Shortt accepted an appointment in Ottawa in 1908 as the civil service commissioner.[71] For a variety of reasons, he was not entirely successful. But in 1923, his replacement in the Sir John A. Macdonald Chair of Political Economy at Queen's, O. D. Skelton, also made the trip to Ottawa. As deputy minister for external affairs, he created and ran the civil service for the prime minister, then King. The acknowledged experts in the Presbyterian Church on social questions in 1910 had by 1923 become the acknowledged experts in Canada. They were experts who controlled the levels of power in Ottawa.[72]

In 1924, Clarence MacKinnon thus had some reason for being satisfied with how the Presbyterian Church had handled the challenges of the preceding half century. While it had produced little that could be classified as original theological scholarship, it was unreasonable to expect either great erudition or theological creativity in a pioneer

69. O. D. Skelton, "The Problem of the City," in *Social Service*, ed. W. R. McIntosh (Toronto, 1911).

70. Ibid., 42.

71. S. E. D. Shortt, *The Search for an Ideal: Six Canadian Intellectuals and Their Convictions in an Age of Transition, 1890–1930* (Toronto, 1976), 95–116.

72. J. S. Granatstein, *The Ottawa Men: The Civil Service Mandarins, 1935–1957* (Toronto, 1982); Doug Owram, *The Government Generation: Canadian Intellectuals and the State, 1900–1945* (Toronto, 1986).

society that was still engaged in the task of clearing the land. Canadian Presbyterians were perforce dependent in this respect, as in many others, on the older and more established parts of the Anglo-American world of which they were an extension.[73] They had, however, chosen wisely between the alternatives represented by Princeton and Scotland. The isolation of the backwoods tended to foster religious and cultural conservatism. It was natural, therefore, that many ministers born and educated in Canada should have looked for guidance to the bastion of Calvinist conservatism at Princeton. But this influence had not ultimately been decisive.

Instead, Canadian Presbyterians had edged away from Westminster Confession Calvinism and cautiously appropriated the fruits of Scottish biblical scholarship. They had turned away from seventeenth-century scholasticism and embraced a nineteenth-century biblical theology. In doing so, they had chosen a different path than had their American cousins and avoided the late nineteenth-century theological polarization in that church. Much of the difference must be attributed to George Monro Grant's skills as a mediator and church politician. From MacKinnon's perspective, a guardian angel had prevented Canadian Presbyterians from taking Charles Hodge too seriously in matters of theology—or Thomas Chalmers on the subject of social reform. They had, in fact, navigated the troubled years between 1875 and the First World War with particular grace, providing Canadian society with intellectual and spiritual leadership that can be summed up as moderate and socially concerned evangelicalism.

The church union debacle of 1925, however, and the secularized climate of the 1920s were clear indications that all was not well. The Presbyterian ship was about to strike the rocks of the modernist-fundamentalist controversy that Grant worked the tiller so hard to avoid. MacKinnon must at times have looked around ruefully and wondered what had happened to the guardian angel. Perhaps Grant, looking down on the proceedings from a more exalted perspective, asked the same question.

---

73. Cf. George M. Grant, "The Religious Condition of Canada," *Christianity Practically Applied: The Discussions of the International Christian Conference, held in Chicago, October 8–14, 1893*, 2 vols. (New York, 1894), 68–75.

11

The Holiness Movement and Canadian Maritime Baptists

George A. Rawlyk

In 1871, Baptists in New Brunswick, Nova Scotia, and Prince Edward Island, consisting of a New Light–Calvinist majority and a Free Christian minority, reached the zenith of their influence and power in the Canadian Maritimes.[1] According to the 1871 Canadian census, out of a total New Brunswick population of 285,594, of whom 33.6 percent were Roman Catholics, 15.0 percent were Calvinist Baptist, and 9.8 percent Free Christian Baptists. In Nova Scotia, out of a population of 387,800, 26.3 percent of whom were Roman Catholic, 14.0 percent were Calvinist Baptists and an estimated 4.9 percent Free Christian Baptists. On tiny Prince Edward Island in 1881 only 5.7 percent of the population of 94,021 were Baptists, all of whom were of the Calvinist variety.[2] It should be stressed that Maritime Baptists, in

---

1. This chapter was originally written for the "Wesleyan Holiness Project" located at Asbury Seminary, Wilmore, Kentucky. I am grateful to the directors of this project for permission to use a revised version of the essay for this book.
2. See my discussion of some of these demographic trends in my *Ravished by the Spirit: Religious Revivals, Baptists, and Henry Alline* (Montreal and Kingston, 1984), 170–72.

1871, were the largest group of Protestants in New Brunswick and Nova Scotia combined—and the second largest if Prince Edward Island is also taken into account.

Calvinists and Free Christian Baptists in the Maritimes, despite their theological differences, shared a common New Light–evangelical heritage, one profoundly shaped by two remarkable late eighteenth-century charismatic preachers, neither of whom was a Baptist and neither of whom was Maritime-born. The most influential was Henry Alline (1748–84), a "Free-Will" Congregationalist who, almost single-handedly, coaxed into existence Maritime Canada's First Great Awakening during the American Revolution.[3] The other was the extraordinarily gifted Methodist itinerant Freeborn Garrettson (1752–1827), who, though he spent only twenty-six months in the region in 1785, 1786, and early 1787, nevertheless played a key role in strengthening not only the New Light–evangelical thrust of Allinism but also its concern with transforming lives on earth. Garrettson was quite explicit about his espousal of sanctification and holiness, and this concern with what he once referred to as "rising higher and higher in the divine image"[4] gradually became an integral part of the Allinite-Garrettson evangelical legacy within the Maritime Baptist tradition. This legacy, it should be stressed, would be a far more significant force within the early nineteenth-century Maritime Baptist tradition—especially among the Free Christians—than the Methodist and would also help to explain why the Baptists were so much more successful in the post-Garrettson period than were the Methodists.[5]

In the 1870s, just when the two groups of Maritime Baptists, particularly those in New Brunswick and Nova Scotia, seemed to have become the largest Protestant body, they experienced a bitter schism. Then a decade later, there was yet another acrimonious schism. Each of these two secession movements involved far more Maritime Baptists than did the fundamentalist split of the 1930s,[6] and

3. See my *Wrapped Up in God* (Burlington, Ont., 1988), 1–54.
4. Quoted in Nathan Bangs, *The Life of the Rev. Freeborn Garrettson* (New York, 1830), 154.
5. I have dealt with this issue at much greater length in my *Wrapped Up in God*, 65–75.
6. See my "Fundamentalism, Modernism, and the Maritime Baptists in the 1920s and 1930s," *Acadiensis* 13 (Fall 1987): 3–33.

each originated within the Free Christian Baptist Conference of New Brunswick. It was within this conference that the Allinite influence, throughout the period from 1840 to 1880, was, without question, most significant and long lasting.[7]

The first schism, in 1874, was orchestrated by a New Brunswick Free Christian Baptist preacher, George Whitefield Orser, who was certain that his fellow Baptists had abandoned the pristine purity of Henry Alline's New Light evangelicalism. Reacting violently against what he considered to be the growing respectability and "churchiness" of the Free Christian Baptists, Orser struck a surprisingly responsive chord in the Free Christian Baptist heartland in the Woodstock region on both sides of the St. John River. Orser's primitivism was superbly captured in the 1874 declaration to his former associates that:

> In the beginning of the denomination they took the Word of the Lord as their only rule in all things. But as the denomination has advanced, certain things have grown up, and are endorsed by the Conference, that he does not find any warrant for in the Bible. Sabbath Schools and Missions are among these things. He thinks that we are following other denominations, rather than the revealed truth. He does not say that there is no good in these things, but he finds no warrant for them in the words of Christ.[8]

By the time of his death in 1885, the Orserites, also known as the Primitive Baptists, were worshiping in approximately forty churches "in the Upper St. John valley of New Brunswick and Maine, several in western Nova Scotia, one on Deer Island and one in Lowell, Massachusetts."[9] What may help to explain the Orserite movement? There are a number of possible answers to this deceptively complex question. The extraordinary leadership abilities of Orser should never be underestimated, nor should the power of his appeal to Allinite primitivism at a time when acute church-sect and urban-rural tensions

---

7. D. G. Bell, "The Allinite Tradition and the New Brunswick Free Christian Baptists, 1830–1875," in *An Abiding Conviction: Maritime Baptists and Their World*, ed. R. S. Wilson (Saint John, 1988), 56–65. Bell's article is the best available study of the topic.

8. New Brunswick Free Christian Baptist, *Minutes* (1874), 35.

9. Bell, "Allinite Tradition," 70.

were beginning to undermine the foundations of the Free Christian Baptist movement, especially in New Brunswick.

The Orserite controversy set the stage for the departure in 1888 of the Reformed or Holiness Baptists from the ranks of the Free Christian Baptists. In the period after 1874, the Free Christians found themselves suffering from the aftershocks of the Orserite secession. The leaders of the conference, especially an influential editor of the *Religious Intelligencer*, Joseph McLeod, believed that only denominational respectability would keep in check the embarrassing manifestation of Allinite anarchy. In underscoring their respectability, they merely "succeeded in detaching themselves from their unserviceable past at the cost of jettisoning the very thing which made them distinctive and justified continued separate existence."[10] According to David Bell, "Respectability in the eyes of the world had been achieved, but only through the entire negation, suppression and abandonment of the tradition of Henry Alline."[11]

Like the Orserites, the Reformed Baptists in the 1880s were disturbed, among other things, because of what they regarded as the spiritual declension of the Free Christian Baptists. To deal with this problem, the Reformed Baptists turned not to Allinite primitivism but rather to American "holiness"—something they considered to be an integral part of the Free Christian Baptist tradition. When the holiness solution was summarily rejected in 1888 by the Free Christian Baptist Conference, nine ordained Free Christian Baptist ministers and three licentiates quit the conference to establish the Reformed Baptist Church. It has been estimated that by the end of 1888 there were 433 Reformed Baptist church members, all of them in New Brunswick.[12] Two years later there were 736, and in 1966, when the Reformed Baptists officially became part of the Wesleyan Methodist Church of America, there were 2,160 Canadian members and 431 American, all in Maine.[13]

10. Ibid., 71.
11. Ibid.
12. *History of the Organization of the Reformed Baptist Denomination* (Saint John, 1890), 47.
13. *Minutes of the Alliance of the Reformed Baptist Church of Canada* (1966), "Statistical Report."

In the 1870s and 1880s in the three Maritime Provinces, it has been estimated that for every one church member there were five adherents.[14] Though this appears to be a conservative estimate, it may be argued that in 1888 more than 2,160 Free Christian Baptists became Reformed Baptists. The Reformed Baptists have received amazingly little serious historical attention. Maritime Wesleyans probably would like to forget their Baptist roots, and Maritime Baptists, preoccupied with the Calvinist, or "Regular" Baptist tradition, have pushed groups like the Reformed Baptists to the Siberian scholarly periphery.[15]

In his massive 520-page *History of the Baptists of the Maritime Provinces*, published in 1902 in Halifax, Nova Scotia, Edward Manning Saunders devotes merely one short paragraph to the Reformed Baptists. According to Saunders:

In 1888 the [Free Christian Baptist] Conference suffered the loss of nine ordained ministers and three licentiates—the result of an unhappy schism, caused by the doctrine of "instantaneous entire sanctification." For a time there was a severe struggle caused by the influence of those who had become separated from the denomination. But much more quickly than many feared, the churches recovered from the shock and loss, and the work went on more encouragingly than for five or six years before the separation. (433)

In 1946, George E. Levy published *The Baptists of the Maritime Provinces, 1753–1946*. Levy's book is still the best overview on the topic largely because it is the only modern general survey available. Where Saunders had one paragraph dealing with the Reformed Baptists, Levy was satisfied with one problematic sentence. "A heated controversy over the doctrine of Holiness," Levy observed, "was soon precipitated and eventually led to the formation of the 'Primitive' and 'Reformed' Baptists bodies."[16] The Orserites are then transformed into holiness advocates, the 1870s are merged into the 1880s,

14. See W. H. Brooks, "The Changing Character of Maritime Wesleyan Methodism, 1855–1883" (M.A. thesis, Mount Allison University, 1965), 73.

15. See David Bell, "All Things New: The Transformation of Maritime Baptists Historiography," *Nova Scotia Historical Review* 4, no. 2 (1984): 69–81.

16. George E. Levy, *The Baptists of the Maritime Provinces, 1753–1946* (Saint John, 1946), 263.

and Levy can rush on to his main concern in the same paragraph—
preparing for the decision made in 1905 and 1906 by the Calvinist and
Free Christian Baptists to create "one denomination under the direction of the United Baptist Convention of the Maritime Provinces."[17]

In the only general history of Canadian Baptists, Harry A. Renfree's
Heritage and Horizon: The Baptist Story in Canada, a very brief
view of the Reformed Baptists similar to Levy's is presented. Because
of what Renfree refers to as the "second blessing . . . entire sanctification" problem of the 1880s, "two factions did leave the Free Baptists,
one taking the name Reformed Baptists, the other Primitive Baptists."
According to Renfree, "The latter, who adopted a very simple form of
church government and resisted an educated and salaried ministry,
continue as a very small company; the Reformed eventually joined
forces with the Wesleyan Methodists who held congenial views on
the holiness issue."[18] Renfree's inaccurate reading of the 1870s and
1880s unfortunately sets the scholarly tone for his entire volume.

The Origins of the Maritime Reformed Baptists

The Reformed Baptists of the Maritime Provinces were the only
Canadian Baptists in the nineteenth or twentieth centuries who, because of their belief in the crucial importance of "entire sanctification" and "holiness," established their own new denomination. In
their church polity and their theology, the Reformed Baptists at the
beginning merely added a special emphasis on holiness to their Free
Christian Baptist polity and theology. They were, in a very real sense,
"Holiness Baptists"—Baptists who also believed in entire sanctification. Until the Second World War, the Canadian Free Christian Baptist tradition probably outweighed in importance the American holiness tradition. Consequently, it is not surprising that in the interwar
years, serious consideration was given at least at the leadership level
to some kind of union with the United Baptist Convention. The period after 1945, however, witnessed the almost inexorable drift of the
Reformed Baptists to the Wesleyans, as a result of the coming to ma-

17. Ibid., 264.
18. Harry A. Renfree, *Heritage and Horizon: The Baptist Story in Canada* (Mississauga,
1988), 207.

turity of a new group of Reformed Baptist leaders who were profoundly influenced by things American and who also were eager to cut all ties with what they considered to be an increasingly irrelevant nineteenth-century Baptist past.[19] The Woodstock region of New Brunswick in the 1880s was the epicenter of the Reformed Baptist movement in the Maritimes. Throughout the nineteenth century the religious culture of the area had been significantly affected by the powerful impulses of radical sectarian and evangelical Christianity originating in neighboring Maine. The Woodstock region, moreover, was, as has already been pointed out, the heartland of the Free Christian Baptists, where the Allinite-Garrettsonian legacy continued to be especially salient and influential. The upper St. John River area was also, it should be emphasized, the corner of the Maritime Provinces, where the holiness gospel, as preached by Phoebe Palmer in the late 1850s, had had its greatest immediate impact.

Phoebe Palmer's remarkable ministry in the Maritime Provinces in general, and western New Brunswick in particular, has received surprisingly little attention from religious scholars—either in the past or the present. Yet, according to Palmer herself, she probably had a greater immediate impact on New Brunswick than on any other North American or British area. Taking full advantage of what has recently been referred to as the "vibrantly alive . . . Holiness" tradition still existing in what is now Canada, Phoebe Palmer breathed new life into the movement and gave it a new Yankee shape and substance.[20]

After her remarkable evangelistic successes in 1857 in what is now Ontario, in the summer of 1858 Phoebe Palmer and her husband, Walter, decided to visit New Brunswick on their way to Great Britain. At a camp meeting held near Woodstock, "the flame that broke out . . . spread to the surrounding country." The "gracious work . . . of holiness" was especially noticeable at Woodstock. Hundreds flocked to hear the Palmers preach not only in Woodstock but also in the commercial center of St. John and later in Halifax, the capital of Nova Scotia, and Charlottetown, the capital of Prince Edward Island. Many

19. These conclusions are based on a careful reading of *The King's Highway* for these years as well as the annual *Minutes* of the Maritime Reformed Baptists.

20. See Peter Bush, "James Caughey, Phoebe and Walter Palmer, and the Methodist Revival Experience in Canada West, 1850–1858" (M.A. thesis, Queen's University, 1985), 145.

were converted to evangelical Christianity, and almost as many experienced, for the first time, "the baptism of the Holy Spirit."[21]

According to the Palmers, in their western New Brunswick revival, "Never have we witnessed a more extraordinary demonstration of the fact that our God loves to take the weak things of this world to confound the mighty."[22] From her vantage point at St. John in November 1858, Mrs. Palmer observed that "it is astonishing how the people come out from all the surrounding country, going and returning from ten to twelve miles daily, and others coming, and remaining day after day, from a distance of fifty miles and over."[23]

On a number of occasions Phoebe Palmer noted that at her revival services Methodists were probably outnumbered by Baptists, and at least once she pointed out that in New Brunswick "on Sabbath morning our friends of the Baptist Church would omit their own services in order to be present at the Wesleyan Church."[24] Realizing that such a Baptist policy was disconcerting to Methodists, she officially discouraged it.[25] But of course she could never prevent hundreds of Baptists from flocking to hear her on Sunday morning or evening or during the week.

There is no existing evidence to support the contention that the Palmers reshaped the religious contours of Maritime Methodism in the period after 1858.[26] Obviously, for a time, a number of Methodists, especially rural Methodists, were positively affected by the holiness gospel. But most Maritime Methodists at this time continued to be obsessed with British respectability and order and were increasingly embarrassed when they read about any "new baptism of fire."[27] In February 1873 it was noted in the *Provincial Wesleyan* that the Methodist "heavenly planting" was showing "signs of decadence and withering."[28] The class meeting was a dead institution; even the new "sci-

21. Phoebe Palmer, *Promise of the Father* (Boston, 1859), 279.
22. Ibid., 194.
23. Ibid., 295.
24. Ibid., 300–301.
25. Ibid., 300.
26. In his "Changing Character of Maritime Wesleyan Methodism," Brooks implicitly and explicitly argues that Palmer had no real impact on Maritime Methodism. Brooks, however, seriously downplays the immediate impact of the Palmer revivals.
27. *Provincial Wesleyan*, 24 February 1864.
28. Ibid., 26 February 1873.

entific societies" sweeping the Maritimes, it was bitterly contended, "were less formal and more natural than the present state of the Class-Meetings."[29]

For most Maritime Methodists, Phoebe Palmer's gospel seeds had briefly flourished as tiny plants, and then most had withered away and died as what has been called the heroic age of Maritime Methodism came to an end.[30] All of the Palmer plants, however, had not died, which many Maritime Baptists, particularly in the 1880s, began to realize. In the 1860s and 1870s a handful of American Wesleyan holiness preachers, notably Joshua Gill, G. D. Watson, H. D. Pepper, J. Parker, and H. N. Brown, visited New Brunswick, attempting to revitalize the tiny "bands of holiness people" still remaining in the western and central parts of the province. They were not particularly successful. Licentiate Aaron Hartt, however, a young New Brunswick Free Christian Baptist preacher, saw more results. In the fall of 1882 he began the process that ended six years later in the creation of the Reformed Baptist Alliance.

Hartt was the son of Samuel Hartt, one of the founders of the New Brunswick Free Christian Baptists. In 1882, after experiencing "entire sanctification" at a Methodist camp meeting in New England, Aaron Hartt was licensed to preach by the Free Christian Baptist Conference meeting in Victoria, New Brunswick, in the summer of 1882. Soon afterward, Hartt was invited by G. W. MacDonald, the pastor of the Albert Street Free Christian Baptist Church, Woodstock, to conduct revival services in the community. Within a short period of time, MacDonald and many members of his congregation "experienced the second blessing."[31] The so-called Hartt holiness stir radiated in all directions, and by the end of the year "the revival spread to Jacksonville and Hartlang where many entered the holiness experience,"[32] among whom were two influential Free Christian Baptist pastors, Bamford Colpitts and G. T. Hartley. During the following year, the holiness stir continued to affect the Free Christian Baptists along the St. John River Valley. Among those experiencing entire

29. Brooks, "Changing Character of Maritime Wesleyan Methodism," 120.

30. Ibid., 118.

31. L. K. Mullen, "The Organization of Reformed Baptists" (Unpublished paper, October 1978), 5, Wesleyan Archives, Bethany Bible College, Sussex, N.B.

32. Ibid.

sanctification were the Free Christian Baptist pastors William King-
ham, G. B. Trafton, J. H. Coy, and G. N. Ballantine. The New Brunswick border could not contain the movement as "Houlton, Maine,
and all of Arrostook County came under the teaching of perfect love
as preached by Hartt."[33]

Perhaps the most evocative description of the holiness experience
of 1882 and 1883 and its implications was penned by MacDonald,
who was certainly at the inner core of the revitalization movement.
Writing in March 1894, MacDonald observed, often using the language of Phoebe Palmer:

> Twelve years ago, the 19th day of this present month, after praying and
> wrestling with God in the hope of making my heart clean by my own
> struggles, but in vain, my soul gathered strength to lay everything on
> the altar, and claimed the blessing of perfect love by faith in the cleans-
> ing blood. My struggling eased, and my soul rested on the bosom of
> Jesus as a poor weary child, wearied of its loving mother. Such rest,
> only to be experienced, never fully told. Rest from all the inward war-
> fare caused by remaining evil in my heart, and withal a sense of clean-
> ness, purity and such a deep satisfied assurance of having reached the
> place where the soul could dwell with God, and that God had perfected
> His love in me. There was no doubt about it; the Comforter had come.
> How easy now to pray, to praise; what a constancy of faith; how deep
> the peace; how bright the hope. Since that memorable night I have
> never doubted my soul's entire sanctification.

MacDonald then went on to describe some of the costs of his holiness
but also some of the benefits:

> I look back over the past twelve years and they have been full of la-
> bours; struggles severe and long have been passed; burdens heavy
> have been borne; the world has been cruel in its opposition; the devil
> and his emissaries have made their heaviest assaults upon my soul, my
> reputation and my work. Friends whose love I valued have turned
> away; loved ones have sickened and died, and men have said his light
> is going out in darkness. . . . But I wish to say in this, my first written
> testimony, that never once during those years has faith been permitted
> to fail or hope to grow dim; never once has discouragement triumphed;

33. Ibid.

and today as I write, my love takes in a larger scope, my peace of mind deeper and broader than ever before. The Comforter who came to my heart twelve years ago came to stay. He abides with me still. The blood of Jesus Christ cleanseth me from all sin.[34]

Unlike MacDonald, William Kinghorn, of Nashwaaksis, was at first somewhat timid and cautious about testifying to his "second blessing." Yet he was absolutely certain of it. "It was a deeper and altogether different experience from my conversion. . . . It was something that went down to the very depths of my being, and put an end to old carnality, Hallelujah to Jesus!"[35] G. G. Gray, a layperson from Woodstock, echoed in a somewhat muted voice the statements of MacDonald and Kinghorn. According to Gray, "In the autumn of 1882, under the teaching of Reverends Aaron Hartt and G. W. MacDonald and others . . . [I] was sanctified wholly by faith in the atonement made by our Saviour for this very purpose according to Ephesians 5:26–27, also in our Lord's prayer in John 17:17."[36]

1883–1885, Years of Conflict

Not all Free Christian Baptists were pleased with the "Hartt stir," many regarding his American-influenced holiness message as "Methodistic, unscriptural, promoting absolute perfection and . . . a divider of churches."[37] At the Free Christian Baptist Conference in October 1883, held at Tracy's Mills, the holiness issue, for the first time, became *the* major issue confronting the conference. Bombarded by conflicting arguments, the conference decided that the "chapter on 'Sanctification' in 'Butler's Theology'" . . . be read aloud in open conference, that all might clearly understand what Butler taught on this subject." Later the conference "reaffirmed its acceptance of the views on Sanctification, set forth in Butler's Theology, consider[ing] it advisable also to counsel the ministers, in presenting this doctrine, to use the utmost care to avoid a real or seeming denial of any part or phase of the truth bearing on it." It was also explicitly resolved that

34. *King's Highway*, 15 March 1894.
35. Ibid., 5 February 1913.
36. Ibid., 15 January 1913.
37. Quoted in Mullen, "Organization of Reformed Baptists," 6.

all Free Christian Baptist preachers "need to make plain the necessity and importance of growth in the Divine life; that such life, beginning with regeneration, is one of the stages and development, and
that growth does not cease till the Christian ceases to live." To
weaken even more the position of instantaneous sanctification, it
was further resolved:

> That each step in the Christian life involves surrender to God; and each
> surrender is attended by the blessing of God; that the blessing, in its be-
> stowment, is instantaneous, and that each believer may have the ful-
> ness of spiritual blessing.
>   That in order for the proper edification of Christians there must be
> the reception of Gospel truth in its entirety. Since such doctrine is es-
> sential to the completeness of the whole system of Christian doctrines,
> the belief and practice of all are essential to completeness of Christian
> character.[38]

It is clear that conference leaders in October 1883 were still trying to
walk the sanctification knife-edge that they felt Butler provided them.

Since 1865, J. J. Butler's *Natural and Revealed Theology*, published in New England in 1861, had provided the standard and authoritative doctrinal statement for Maritime Free Christian Baptists. Butler, a native of Maine and a graduate of Bowdoin College and Andover
Theological Seminary, was an ordained minister of the Free Baptist
Church of the United States. In 1865, the New Brunswick Free Christian Baptist Conference had recommended that "all our young brethren who enter the ministry to procure Butler's theology and strive to
become thoroughly acquainted with the doctrines therein treated,
which is the best exposition of the leading sentiments held by our denomination of which we have knowledge."[39] So much, however, depended on how one interpreted Butler, whose chapter "Sanctification," it has been correctly pointed out, carefully "attempts to present
both sides of the question."[40]

    38. William Kinghorn, *The Doctrine of Sanctification As Taught by Free Christian Stan-
dards of Faith* (Fredericton, 1886), 6–7.
    39. Ibid., 4.
    40. E. G. Britten, "A History of the Reformed Baptist Alliance of Canada" (B.Div. thesis, Ac-
adia University, 1964), 39.

The 1883 conference decision did nothing to resolve the holiness issue, which continued throughout the winter and spring and summer months of 1884 to divide Free Christian Baptists into warring theological camps, especially in the Woodstock region. A strongly worded petition against MacDonald was circulated by his opponents, charging him and other members of his church with being "propagators of heresy."[41] The antiholiness petition was forwarded to the General Conference, which met in October 1884 in Fredericton.

According to the beleaguered MacDonald, at the conference "the feeling on the question of holiness was intense." He went on: "The opposition, having enlisted some of the leading ministers and laymen of the conference, contended that the doctrine was absurd and evil in its tendencies and must be suppressed. In the Elder's Conference especially the discussion was hot and excited. The preaching of perfect love was declared by many of the ministers to be decidedly unscriptural."[42]

After a bitter, acrimonious debate, which took place behind closed doors, the Elder's Conference finally issued the following statement, which reflected a majority view but certainly not, in any way, a consensus:

> Your committee, having considered the teachings of the brethren who claim to be entirely sanctified, find their teachings in several particulars [are] not in agreement with the teachings of this denomination.
> (a) That they do not admit growth between justification and sanctification, whereas in justification partially we are sanctified, for in justification we devote, surrender ourselves to God, which is a central element of sanctification.
> (b) That they do not admit that sanctification is progressive, gradual, beginning in regeneration, justification, and completed in glorification, but is a special work upon the heart subsequent to justification.
> (c) That they claim that purity is not of growth but a special act of cleansing, whereas in conviction we are made "new creatures in Christ" and by regeneration we are changed in spirit, purpose, desire and in putting on of Christ we grow into the divine nature,

41. Quoted in ibid., 7.
42. *King's Highway*, 31 March 1894.

which is growth in holiness, and growth in holiness is a growth in purity.[43]

It was decided by the elders—the ordained ministers—to present a somewhat more conciliatory statement to the General Conference in an attempt to placate an aroused holiness minority. The declaration was cogent and to the point. "We believe that sanctification is a work of growth, gradual and progressive, that it begins in justification and is completed in glorification. That there are special blessings in the enlargement of knowledge, in greater consecration and devotedness. That it is the duty of Christian believers 'to perfect holiness in the fear of God.'" When the declaration was read to the evening meeting, it was denounced by the holiness advocates, who vociferously argued that it needed to be modified; moreover, they contended, the three recommendations of the Elder's Conference should be reconsidered. When the vote was called on MacDonald's "reconsideration" motion, it passed by a vote of 39 to 15.[44]

After hours of even more acrimonious debate, and after the preaching licenses of two holiness licentiates, Aaron Hartt and W. B. Wiggins, were canceled, it was unanimously agreed to publish the following two resolutions rather than the elders' official statement, which had begun with the words "We believe that sanctification. . . ."

Resolved That the doctrine of sanctification, as taught by some of our brethren of late, is not according to the views held and taught by this denomination.
Resolved That the holy Bible is the recognized standard of faith and practice of the denomination and that all other books are used by us only as aids or as explanatory of the scriptures.[45]

It is difficult to understand how holiness supporters could have voted for these two resolutions, for they were adopted at the same evening session that witnessed the removal from potential Free Christian Baptist ministry of their champion Aaron Hartt. The first

43. Clipping from undated *Religious Intelligencer*, 1884, quoted in Britten, "History of the Reformed Baptist Alliance," 12.
44. Ibid., 13
45. *Religious Intelligencer*, 17 October 1884.

resolution denounced "the doctrine of sanctification" as being opposed to Free Christian Baptist principles, and the second effectively
removed Butler's troublesome chapter on sanctification from the
Free Christian Baptist tradition. MacDonald and his friends had been
badly outmaneuvered by their most astute antiholiness enemies.
These men and women realized that the holiness advocates threatened their positions of power and influence in the denomination. If
entire sanctification became the litmus test for denomination leadership, they realized that their opponents would easily push them aside
in any power struggle. And this they were determined to prevent, almost at any cost. They harbored a growing animus for the American-
ized upstarts who threatened their hegemony in the denomination.
This was not, however, the only reason for their implacable opposition. They feared that an overemphasis on the importance of the second blessing significantly distorted the essence of the Free Christian
Baptist faith and practice. They also saw a growing anti-establish-
ment impulse in the holiness movement as well as an anti-education
bias and what was perceived as a virulent anti–Roman Catholicism.
It is painfully evident that some young Free Christian holiness
preachers blended a powerful anti–Roman Catholicism into their
message of entire sanctification. This blend would help to explain
some of the early growth of the Reformed Baptists in parts of New
Brunswick and neighboring Nova Scotia.[46]

In 1885 the Free Christian Baptists met in Sussex, when once again
the sanctification issue took center stage. Seeking to pour oil on troubled denominational waters, it was decided to emphasize once again
the Tracy's Mill compromise of October 1883. A very conciliatory
statement was therefore issued by the ordained ministers present:

> The Elder's Conference, having reaffirmed its acceptance of the views
> on Sanctification set forth in Butler's Theology, considers it advisable
> also to counsel the ministers, in presenting this doctrine, to use the ut-
> most care to avoid a real or seeming denial of any part or phase of the
> truth bearing on it.

46. L. J. King, *House of Death and Gate of Hell* (Toledo, Ohio, 1932); and L. F. Martinique,
The Scarlet Mother on the Tiber: Trials and Travels of Evangelist L. J. King (Queensbury,
York Co., N.B., 1908). Professor David Bell of the University of New Brunswick has made me
aware of these two vitriolic books.

They need to make the necessity and importance of growth in the Divine life; that such life, beginning with regeneration, is one of stages and development, and that growth does not cease till the Christian ceases to live.[47]

It was also pointed out that "the conference wishes to say that the disagreements on this subject are less serious than they have seemed to be, having largely grown out of misunderstanding and the use of phraseology new to our people."[48] Stressing the fact that "perfect uniformity in all things is scarcely possible," it was nevertheless hoped that everything possible would be done by all Free Christian Baptists to "seek the closest possible union with each other in thought, feeling and manner of work."[49]

Conciliatory words were one thing, whether concerning the "use of phraseology new to our people" or the quest for "the closest possible union with one another." While the leadership played down the divisiveness of the sanctification issue, a growing number of Free Christian Baptists were publicly repudiating their leadership, contending:

1. That Entire Sanctification is a separate and distinct work from justification.
2. That one may grow in Justification, also in Entire Sanctification, but one cannot grow from Justification into Entire Sanctification.
3. That Entire Sanctification is an Instantaneous work.
4. That the roots of sin are taken away by Entire Sanctification.
5. That Entire Sanctification does not give perfection of judgment.
6. That one may fall from Entire Sanctification.[50]

Despite growing tensions between the two sides, the holiness minority in late 1885 did not want to quit the conference, and the majority did not want to drive them out. It seems as though that even in early 1886, the minority felt certain that it was an integral part of evangelical Christianity's cutting edge and that it was foreordained that they should be victorious. Their opponents were just as certain of the

47. Free Christian Baptist Conference (henceforth FCBC), *Minutes* (1885), 19.
48. Ibid.
49. Kinghorn, *Doctrine of Sanctification*, 8.
50. FCBC, *Minutes* (1885), 22.

absolute rightness of their own cause and were determined to bring their coreligionists back to basic Free Christian Baptist principles.

October 1886: Saint John and "The Deliverance"

By the late summer of 1886, however, the two sides had drifted even further apart as compromise eluded even the most conciliatory leaders. What Freud once referred to as the "narcissism of small differences" pushed the two warring factions into what seemed to be irreconcilable positions.[51] These positions were significantly consolidated at the October 1886 conference, held in Saint John. On October 12, the executive of the New Brunswick Conference presented a Deliverance and Recommendations to the Free Christian Baptist Conference.[52] In the preamble to the Deliverance, the executive underscored the fact that "for several years past, an unpleasant spirit of discord and division over doctrinal views, has disturbed our harmony, so that many of the burden-bearers, and most devoted of our ministers and laymen, feel anxiously concerning the peace of our beloved Zion." Condemning the bitter divisiveness introduced by the advocates of the "new and strange teaching . . . in 'entire instantaneous Sanctification,'" the conference executive had reluctantly come to the conclusion that if these people did not abandon their "anti-Free Christian Baptist" views, they were to leave the conference. "If the brethren adopting those views [of entire sanctification] regard them as of such supreme importance," it was argued "and feel that they must promulgate them, we think that, to be honest and consistent, they should do so at their own expense, and in their own name, not using the machinery of the denomination to its injury, or for the overthrow of doctrines, for the promulgation of which the denomination doctrinally exists." The Deliverance attacked frontally three contentions of those "who believe in entire instantaneous Sanctification," namely, "(1) That Entire Sanctification is a separate and distinct work from Justification . . . (2) That one may grow in Justification and also in Entire Sanctification but one cannot grow from

51. See D. Akenson, *Small Differences* (Montreal and Kingston, 1988), 149.
52. The Deliverance is reprinted in Kinghorn, *Doctrine of Sanctification*, 18–23.

Justification to Entire Sanctification . . . (3) That Entire Sanctification is an instantaneous work."

The Deliverance concluded with the following seven resolutions.

1. *Resolved,* That the Ministers of this Conference who have changed their views and teachings on the doctrine of Sanctification from those held and taught by the denomination, and all who believe in "entire instantaneous Sanctification," as it has been taught amongst us by some of late, be affectionately requested to prayerfully reconsider the whole question, with a view of returning to the belief of the denomination, and the restoration of doctrinal harmony.

2. *Resolved,* That this Conference cannot ordain any man holding the views on Sanctification condemned in this paper.

3. *Resolved,* That this Conference cannot license to preach any man holding these views.

4. *Resolved,* That this Conference recommend the District Meetings of the denomination not to grant licenses to any persons holding these views.

5. *Resolved,* That the Conference requests the Churches of the denomination not to license to preach any man holding such views.

6. *Resolved,* That the Conference recommend all the Churches not to elect any person holding these views to any office in their respective Churches, or to appoint any of them Trustees of Church Property.

7. *Resolved,* That the Recording Secretary notify the District Meetings and Churches, through their clerks, of this decision.

The Deliverance, of course, meant one thing—the point of no return had finally been reached, and the holiness Free Christian Baptists were being compelled to choose between their old Free Christian Baptist traditions and their new obsession with entire sanctification. The executive Deliverance, as one might have expected, was quickly attacked by the forces of holiness, led by Kinghorn, who had shouldered MacDonald aside to become leader of the movement. According to Kinghorn, the Deliverance was a betrayal of Free Christian Baptist principles. "We invite your prayerful consideration and comparison," he argued, "of the plain teaching of *Butler's Theology* and the Holy Scriptures with the last 'Deliverance' of Conference and we think you will be deeply pained to find how widely

'Deliverance' departs from our old and former Standard—*Butler's Theology* and The Bible."[53] Kinghorn was thus attempting to argue that he and his followers were truly orthodox while his opponents had abandoned the old Free Christian Baptist traditions.

After hearing both sides explain, with passion, their views of the Deliverance, the conference finally voted on the seven resolutions. By a surprisingly close vote of 47 to 23, the Deliverance resolutions were accepted, and the executive waited for the Kinghorn group to quit the conference.[54] This they refused to do in 1886 and in 1887. Instead, they continued to try to persuade more Free Christian Baptists and others to accept their view of entire sanctification.

1887–1888

Because of the continuing discord,[55] especially in the Woodstock area, and because the Kinghorn group stubbornly refused to quit the conference, it was decided in October 1887 to compel the holiness advocates to leave. At the annual conference it was resolved

> That in view of the disturbed and divided state of several of our Churches, brought about by new and unscriptural teaching, we believe the time has come when this conference should do more than set forth its views, and should defend and protect the same by making the teaching of "instantaneous entire sanctification" as it has been taught by some of our Ministers of late years, and as this Conference believe, to be unscriptural, a matter of discipline.[56]

Then one year later, at the October 1888 conference held at Blissville, the Free Christian Baptist denomination applied its "discipline" to its "schismatical preachers." The first to be removed from the recognized list of ministers of the conference was Coy of the Main Street Free Christian Baptist Church in Woodstock. He had stubbornly refused "to desist from co-operating with the 'Holiness Convention.'"[57]

---

53. Ibid., 29.
54. Britten, "History of the Reformed Baptist Alliance," 16.
55. *Messenger and Visitor*, 6 July 1887.
56. FCBC, *Minutes* (1887), 47.
57. Ibid. (1888), 188.

Then the conference expelled five other ministers who continued to support Coy and the central importance of instantaneous entire sanctification. These men were Kinghorn, MacDonald, Colpitts, Hartley, and Trafton, most of whom had been converted to the holiness cause in 1882 at Hartt's Woodstock crusade. By a vote of 55 to 6, the Elder's Conference resolved that "this Conference, in heartfelt sorrow, and in the spirit of brotherly kindness, and in the spirit of denominational loyalty, in doing the only thing that now seems to us possible, and just to all our cherished interests, declare that this Elder's Conference is not in sympathy with, and cannot longer fellowship as Ministers of this Conference, brethren who teach or preach the doctrine of 'Instantaneous Entire Sanctification.'"[58]

Church and denominational schisms are always accompanied by myriad manifestations of unchristian behavior as personal bitterness and animus are directed at former friends and associates. Within a few weeks of the October conference, all members of Free Christian Baptist churches who continued to support the purged six ministers found themselves "disfellowshipped."[59] Families were split; close friendships were permanently fractured, and the holiness Free Christian Baptists were driven from their former churches. For a time, it is interesting to note "the only place" they "could worship with freedom was in the Salvation Army."[60] And this Salvationist connection throughout the 1880s, especially in the St. John River Valley region, would be of considerable importance to the holiness Baptists.

On October 20, five days after the conference decisions disfellowshipping the six ministers, a group of dissidents, led by MacDonald, met in Woodstock to plan a general meeting of all Baptist "holiness supporters." The six were joined by three other ministers, A. Kenney, H. H. Cosman, and Wiggins. It decided to issue a general invitation to all interested Free Christian Baptists, not only from New Brunswick, but also from Nova Scotia and neighboring Maine, to attend an organizational meeting in Woodstock on November 1. Some seventy-five people attended, including Aaron Kinney, from south-

58. Ibid., 47–49.
59. *King's Highway*, 30 November 1928.
60. Ibid., 15 February 1913.

western Nova Scotia, who had recently been expelled by the Free Christian Baptist Church of Nova Scotia. He was a man without a movement and consequently felt it necessary to associate himself with the much larger group of New Brunswick dissidents. There were also three ministers from Maine, including Aaron Hartt, whose license to preach had been withdrawn by the Free Christian Baptist Conference in 1884.

After a great deal of debate it was unanimously agreed that it was imperative to organize a new Baptist denomination "that would teach and promote the holiness doctrine."[61] It was also unanimously agreed that the following six propositions would undergird the new denomination, which was to be called the Reformed Baptist Denomination of the Dominion of Canada.

1. That the church polity be Congregational.
2. That we believe the whole Bible to be the Word of God and of supreme authority in interpreting human creeds and opinions and judging human conduct. In other words, we accept the Word of God—the Holy Bible—as our ground of faith and practice.
3. That we believe the Bible teaches the doctrine of the Trinity in Unity.
4. That the denomination be Arminian in doctrine.
5. That the denomination be open communion.
6. That the doctrine of Holiness be especially emphasized, both in our Declaration of Faith and Church Covenant.[62]

Committees were formed to draw up a Declaration of Faith and Church Covenant.[63]

What is particularly striking with the six propositions is that apart from the last one, they carefully reflect the original Free Christian Baptist principles of the early 1830s. Here indeed was an attempt to tap into the primitivism reservoir to be found near the surface of Maritime religious culture. Forces of Free Christ Baptist continuity were of course more than matched by the force of significant change represented by the heavy emphasis on "the doctrine of holiness." The

61. Mullen, "Organization of Reformed Baptists," 13.
62. *History of the Organization*, 12–13.
63. Ibid., 13.

Reformed Baptists tried to have it both ways. Like so many other similar groups, however, they found themselves falling between the Maritime past and the American future.

1889 and Beyond

In their Declaration of Faith, officially adopted in 1889, the Reformed Baptists devoted more space and attention to sanctification than to any other issue. Section 12 of the Declaration began,

> Sanctification denotes the consecration or setting apart for the service of God (Jon xvii, 19); also an act of Divine grace whereby we are made holy, or freed from sin; or cleansed from moral corruption or pollution (1 Thess. v, 23); and is applied to things and places as well as character.
>
> This state is variously expressed in the Scriptures as "Holiness," "Sanctification," "Purity," "Perfection," "Fulness of God," etc.
>
> These expressions mean that participation of the Divine nature which excludes all original depravity or inbred sin from the heart and fills it with perfect love.[64]

Then after over a page and a half devoted to a scriptural justification of entire sanctification as a *second* work of grace after conversion, the section ends with a brief paragraph: "It is divinely imparted, not imputed (Rom. viii, 1–4); and instantaneously received by faith in the atonement (Acts xv, 9) subsequent to regeneration (1 Jno. iii, 7–10), and attested by the Holy Spirit (1 Cor. ii, 12)."[65]

According to section 22, the final section, only two ordinances of the gospel were to be practiced by the Reformed Baptists: "The Lord's Supper" and "the immersion of believers in water in the name of the Father, the Son, and the Holy Spirit."[66]

The new "Reformed Baptist Covenant," apart from clause 8, also owed a great deal to Free Christian Baptist practice. Clause 8 stressed that all Reformed Baptists were to "agree to press on to perfection and not to rest until we have received the baptism of the Holy

64. Ibid., 66.
65. Ibid., 68.
66. Ibid., 74.

Spirit to cleanse us from all sin through the blood of Jesus Christ our Lord."[67]

They were also to avoid "all vain extravagance and sinful conformity to the world . . . theaters, circuses, dances, gambling," and they were "to refrain from all unchaste and profane conversation, all foolish talking and jesting which are not befitting, vain disputing about words and things which engender strife, disregarding promises and not fulfilling engagements, tattling and backbiting, spending time idly, vain and unnecessary worldly conversation on the Lord's Day."[68] "Holiness" was thus to be sought and then practiced in everyday life.

When the Reformed Baptists met in June 1889 at Woodstock, New Brunswick, there were twelve ministers in the alliance—ten pastored churches in New Brunswick, Hartt was from Maine, and Kinney was from Port Maitland, Nova Scotia, near Yarmouth. During the following decades, the Reformed Baptists would grow very little in their area of original strength, the St. John River Valley and the Bay of Fundy Islands and southwestern Nova Scotia. Some growth, however, would take place in southwestern New Brunswick and northeastern Nova Scotia, largely because of the evangelistic campaigns of L. J. King, an ardent anti-Catholic evangelist, as well as in northern and eastern Maine.

The Reformed Baptists were never able to make noteworthy inroads into Maritime religious life. Until their transformation in 1966 into Wesleyans, they remained a largely inward-looking, defensive sect. The decision to publish *The King's Highway* in 1890 probably strengthened a sense of Reformed Baptist insularity and collective morbid introspection. The founding in 1945 of the Holiness Bible Institute in Woodstock (renamed Bethany College in 1947 and moved to Yarmouth in 1948 and later to Sussex) did little to pump badly needed energy into a largely moribund denomination.

Since 1966, the Wesleyans in the Maritimes have shown steady growth—from 1,633 members to 3,608 in 1989.[69] Most of the expansion has taken place in the larger urban areas, notably Moncton,

67. Ibid., 78.
68. Ibid., 77.
69. Atlantic District of the Wesleyan Church Annual District Conference, *Journal* (1989), 74–77.

where the Wesleyans have been remarkably successful in attracting new members. But like other Maritime Protestant denominations, the Wesleyans are experiencing a significant hemorrhaging of members from their rural churches, once their major area of strength. Since 1966 the American connection has without question energized the Reformed Baptists, but at the cost perhaps of jettisoning their rich nineteenth-century Allinite Baptist traditions.

Conclusion

Did the bitter schism of the late 1880s, which created the Reformed Baptists, strengthen or weaken the holiness movement in the Maritime Provinces? It may be argued that the Reformed Baptists probably did both. On the one hand, the new denomination provided the organizational structure for all those who believed in and who wished to practice entire sanctification. They could worship in the beauty of holiness with like-minded Christians who had sacrificed so much during the Baptists' religious civil war of the 1880s. On the other hand, there is some evidence to suggest that the Reformed Baptists actually weakened the holiness movement in the Maritimes. In the polarizing situation immediately before and after 1888, holiness supporters who first and foremost were Regular Baptists and Free Christian Baptists found themselves pulling back from the movement. Not eager to alienate their friends and families, and repelled by the hubris and discord sown by the Reformed Baptists, they internalized their holiness enthusiasm, and many would soon afterward unceremoniously marginalize it in terms of their Christian belief structures.

When the United Baptist Convention of the Maritime Provinces came into being in 1905 and 1906, there was no emphasis placed on the holiness tradition, and especially that of the Free Christian Baptists. It was as though both the Calvinists and the Free Christian Baptists wanted to blot from their collective memory the events of the 1880s. In the process of trying to accomplish this end, however, they cut from the heart of their tradition (i.e., the Allinite-Garrettson legacy) a unique Maritime version of New Light holiness.

12

Conservative Evangelicalism in the Twentieth-Century "West"

British Columbia and the United States

Robert K. Burkinshaw

British Columbia, Canada's most westerly province, is rightly reputed to be a secular lotus land, the materialistic and recreation-oriented "California of Canada," rather than a stronghold of Christian orthodoxy and evangelical activity. Yet, by Canadian standards, the variety and strength of evangelical activity in the province is actually quite considerable. Overall conservative Protestant numerical growth in the province was stronger between 1921 and 1981 than anywhere else in Canada. The evangelical population exceeded that of Alberta, often called Canada's Bible Belt, in number by the 1970s and rivaled it proportionate to population in 1981.[1]

---

1. Compiled from denominational reports and the *1981 Census of Canada*, 1:92–912, table 1. See also the table "Christianity: Affiliation and Participation" in Tom Sinclair-Faulkner, "Christianity," *Canadian Encyclopedia* (Edmonton, 1985).

Much remains to be learned about the history of conservative evangelicalism in British Columbia, but enough is known to attempt to draw comparisons with its larger, more famous American counterpart. Some similarities between the two exist, and many evidences of direct influence from the south may be cited. However, it is clear that American influences and characteristics were not prevalent within British Columbian evangelicalism to the same extent that they were in the neighboring province of Alberta.

Alberta is most often cited as an example of great similarities, and direct linkages, with American evangelicalism. This is not surprising, considering that by 1911 fully 22 percent of the Albertans had come from the United States. That influx continued for several years; by the 1920s it was estimated that up to 50 percent of the farmers in southern Alberta were American in origin.[2] A number of developments in conservative evangelicalism in the province provide clear evidence of American influences. For example, L. E. Maxwell, founding principal of Prairie Bible Institute in 1922 and its dominant personality for over sixty years, was from Kansas and likely retained his American citizenship all his life.[3] Radio preaching by American evangelists also played a remarkable role in shaping evangelicalism in Alberta. Preaching on stations in Calgary and Edmonton, the American preachers reportedly reached audiences of up to 500,000, most of them in Alberta, and sparked significant evangelical growth from the late 1930s until after World War II.[4]

2. Howard Palmer, with Tamara Palmer, *Alberta: A New History* (Edmonton, 1990), 83.

3. David R. Elliott, "Studies in Canadian Fundamentalism: 1870–1970" (Ph.D. diss., University of British Columbia, Vancouver, 1989), 272. Prairie Bible Institute, which eventually became one of the largest Bible schools in the world, exerted a powerful influence in the province of Alberta and throughout the Prairie Provinces and into the hinterlands of British Columbia by providing trained workers for much of the early evangelical groups. Among these were the Christian and Missionary Alliance, the Evangelical Free, the Associated Gospel, and independent churches and home mission organizations (Donald Goertz, "The Development of a Bible Belt: The Socio-Religious Interaction in Alberta between 1926 and 1938" [M.C.S. thesis, Regent College, Vancouver, 1980], 220–32).

4. The evangelists were J. D. Carlson, O. Lowry, and Sawtell. Their reported audiences may have been somewhat exaggerated, but their message sparked a major revival in Alberta and western Saskatchewan from 1938 through the war years. The Christian and Missionary Alliance, Evangelical Free, Church of the Nazarene, and independent churches experienced very significant growth as a result (Goertz, "Development of a Bible Belt," 209–24; and W. E. Mann, *Sect, Cult, and Church in Alberta* [Toronto, 1955], 118–27).

By way of contrast, British Columbia received by far the highest number of British immigrants of any province. Vancouver has been described as a city with a strikingly British ambiance in the era before World War I.[5] Victoria has always been perceived as an Anglophile's outpost of Empire. Approximately one-third of all residents were recent British immigrants; the proportion of American immigrants in British Columbia was considerably less than half that in Alberta in 1911.[6] It is thus understandable that the influences on conservative evangelicalism were often British rather than American.

Because of such influences, the contrasts between British Columbian and American evangelicals are significant. Some of these differences include the relatively late beginnings of conservative evangelical reaction to liberalism in British Columbia and the differences in tone, stance, orientation, and origins of the various conservative subgroups.

Organized conservative resistance to liberalism came late in British Columbia, when compared with that in the western United States. Not until 1917 did some conservatives in the province make a major issue of modernism in the denominations and begin organizing their own, alternative institutions. Before that time there was certainly an awareness of changes in theology in certain quarters, but no specific institutional action, whether denominational or interdenominational, was organized to counteract it. There is no evidence that British Columbian Methodists supported Albert Carman and his fellow conservative evangelicals from Ontario and Manitoba in their unsuccessful attempts to check theological innovation in the denomination's colleges before and during 1910.[7] The Baptist Convention of British Columbia contained a wide diversity of theological positions, including liberals and militant conservatives, but no evidence of convention-wide controversy before World War I has been found. The convention was not connected to the Baptist Union of Quebec and Ontario and

5. Jean Barman, *The West beyond the West* (Vancouver, 1991), 139–40.
6. Canadian Department of the Interior, *Atlas of Canada* (Ottawa, 1915), 94.
7. Accounts of the controversy are found in Margaret Prang, *N. W. Rowell: Ontario Nationalists* (Toronto, 1975), 78–88; and Tom Sinclair-Faulkner, "Theory Divided from Practice: The Introduction of the Higher Criticism into Canadian Protestant Seminaries," Canadian Society of Church History, *Papers*, 1979, 49–69. The Victoria-based *Western Methodist Recorder* was highly supportive of the decision of the national conference, held that year in Victoria, to refrain from restraining faculty in the denomination's seminaries. See *Western Methodist Recorder*, vol. 11, no. 15 (September 1910): 8.

did not participate in protests within that body in 1910 over charges of liberalism at McMaster University in Hamilton.[8] At the local level, however, strong Social Gospel preaching from the pulpit did cause a serious division in one Vancouver congregation in 1915.[9]

Among the Presbyterians in British Columbia, as in Canada as a whole, a liberal-conservative division was simply one aspect of the larger question of organic union with the Methodists and Congregationalists. One important reason for the resistance to union by theologically conservative Presbyterians was their antipathy toward what they saw as the liberal impulse behind the unionists. However, the motivations for both those resisting and those supporting union were many and complex, thus reducing the potential for the type of direct confrontation over liberal versus conservative theology that occurred among the Northern Presbyterians in the United States.[10]

By way of contrast, conservative institutional developments took place much earlier in the western United States. The Bible Institute of Los Angeles was founded in 1908, and Northwestern Bible and Missionary Training School in Minneapolis in 1902. In Seattle, Mark Matthews of First Presbyterian Church was waging a conservative campaign against Union Theological Seminary for years prior to World War I.[11]

There are several explanations for the lack of open controversy before 1917 in British Columbia. An important factor was the relatively low population, which reduced the likelihood of institutional growth and organization. The population of the whole province was 178,000

8. Clark H. Pinnock, "The Modernist Impulse at McMaster University, 1887–1927," in *Baptists in Canada: Search for Identity amidst Diversity*, ed. J. Zeman (Burlington, Ont., 1980), 193–208.

9. G. Pousett, "A History of the Convention of Baptist Churches of British Columbia" (M.Th. thesis, Vancouver School of Theology, Vancouver, 1982), 172–74; J. Richards, *Baptists in British Columbia: A Struggle to Maintain Sectarianism* (Vancouver, 1977), 60–63; and interview with Mrs. I. Frith, Vancouver, 12 March 1980.

10. N. Keith Clifford's *The Resistance to Church Union in Canada, 1904–1939* (Vancouver, 1985) is the best exploration of the motivations for and against the union movement. While he carefully outlines the liberal motivation behind the unionist movement, it must be noted that a direct one-to-one correspondence between theological liberalism and church union did not exist. For example, Principal Daniel Fraser of Presbyterian College, Montreal, was a liberal who rejected union because the basis of union was too orthodox.

11. Lisa S. Nolland, "The Uniqueness of Mark Matthews, Fundamentalist: A Study of His Social Concerns" (M.C.S. thesis, Regent College, Vancouver, 1984), 53–54.

in 1901, only one-third of Washington State's 518,000 in 1900, a small fraction of the 2,400,000 in the American Pacific Coast states, and a minuscule fraction of the 10,440,000 in the West North Central States.[12] British Columbia's largest city, Vancouver, contained only 27,000 people in 1901, one-third of Seattle's population and an even smaller fraction of that in Portland, Los Angeles, and, especially, San Francisco.[13]

New residents were pouring in, however, and the provincial population more than doubled to 392,000 in the next decade, while Vancouver's quadrupled to 100,000. By far the largest group of new residents were immigrants from the British Isles; this point needs to be stressed. A massive wave of immigration began shortly before 1900, and by 1911, an incredible 56 percent of the city's population had been born outside of Canada, twice the proportion of foreign-born in Seattle and many times that of California.[14] The effort and time required from the new settlers to establish themselves and the enormous amount of energy and resources expended by the various denominations simply to keep up with such a staggering influx of newcomers diverted attention away from rumblings of theological discontent heard elsewhere in North America.

Another important factor was the small proportion of conservative Protestants in the population, as compared with that in the United States. Certainly the heavy immigration from Britain, where evangelicals were a minority, helped account for the smaller proportion.[15] The Anglican Church, which gained the most from the British immigration, was the largest in the province. The influence of conservative Anglican theologian W. H. Griffith Thomas of Wycliffe College, Tor-

12. Bureau of the Census, *Historical Statistics of the United States—Colonial Times to 1957: A Statistical Abstract Supplement* (Washington, D.C., 1961), 12–13. The seven West North Central states are Minnesota, Iowa, Missouri, North Dakota, South Dakota, Nebraska, and Kansas.

13. Norbert Macdonald, "A Critical Growth Cycle in Vancouver," *BC Studies*, no. 17 (Spring 1973): 28.

14. Compiled from Norbert Macdonald, "Population Growth and Change in Seattle and Vancouver, 1880–1960," in *Historical Essays on British Columbia*, ed. J. Friesen and H. K. Ralson (Toronto, 1976), 208–9.

15. For example, see Randle Manwaring, *From Controversy to Co-existence: Evangelicals in the Church of England, 1914–1980* (Cambridge, 1980), 1–17; and David Bebbington, *Evangelicalism in Modern Britain: A History from the 1730s to the 1980s* (Grand Rapids, 1992), 141–43.

onto, was felt in the establishment of the Low Church Anglican theological college in Vancouver in 1910, but the nonevangelical wing within the province clearly was dominant.[16] Large numbers of the Presbyterian Church, the second largest Protestant body in British Columbia, also were newcomers from the British Isles. The generally liberal orientation of Presbyterianism was indicated in 1925 when 77 percent of its membership joined the United Church.[17] Revivalistic evangelicalism had never been an important characteristic of Methodism in British Columbia, and liberalism was clearly the pervasive tone.[18] Baptists, theologically mixed but mostly conservative, composed only approximately 4 percent of the provincial population in 1911, and the homogeneously conservative Plymouth Brethren and Salvation Army together accounted for less than 1 percent.[19] For the most part, the prevalent liberalism was not extremely radical, but sympathy with the new methods of biblical study and the Social Gospel was very widespread.[20]

16. Bishop Latimer Hall, Minutes of Council and Minutes of Trustees, 1909–12, Anglican Archives, Vancouver School of Theology, Vancouver; Neale Adams, *Living Stones: A Centennial History of Christ Church Cathedral, 1889–1989* (Vancouver, 1989), 38–39.

17. Runnalls, *It's God's Country* (n.p., 1974), 204; and Mervyn E. Kennedy, "The History of Presbyterianism in British Columbia, 1861–1935" (M.A. thesis, University of British Columbia, Vancouver, 1938), 131, 148.

18. Runnalls, *It's God's Country*, 85, 88–89, 132; Bob Stewart, "The United Church of Canada in British Columbia," in *Circle of Voices: A History of the Religious Communities of British Columbia* (Lantzeville, B.C., 1989), 201. In addition the *Western Methodist Recorder* 2–11 (1900–10) makes this clear.

19. *1951 Census of Canada*, vol. 10, table 36.

20. Sheila P. Mosher, "The Social Gospel in British Columbia" (M.A. thesis, University of Victoria, Victoria, 1974). The very recent and derivative nature of most of Protestantism in British Columbia makes it difficult to compare it with its manifestations in other parts of Canada, but the descriptions of Moir, Van Die, and Gauvreau seem to apply in the province. Both J. S. Moir and Marguerite Van Die describe the generally cautious, accommodating, and moderate approach of Canadian scholars such as Nathaniel Burwash and J. F. McCurdy (John S. Moir, *A History of Biblical Studies in Canada: A Sense of Proportion* [Chico, Calif., 1982]; and Marguerite Van Die, *An Evangelical Mind: Nathanael Burwash and the Methodist Tradition in Canada, 1839–1918* [Montreal and Kingston, 1989]). Michael Gauvreau stresses that, until 1905, the critical acceptance of evolutionary and higher critical ideas within Canadian Methodist and Presbyterian seminaries was seen by most, even those described as conservative, as preserving the essentials of nineteenth-century evangelicalism. He argues that "English-Canadian evangelicals were not plagued by the widening gulf between religious modernists and antimodernists" (*The Evangelical Century: College and Creed in English Canada from the Great Revival to the Great Depression* [Montreal and Kingston, 1991], 11).

Because of their minority position in British Columbia society, and in the British society from which so many had come, evangelicals were not used to playing the same dominant role that George Marsden notes American evangelicals played in shaping their culture. Therefore Canadian evangelicals did not as readily experience the sense of loss of respectability and influence that their American counterparts did when nonevangelical values came to dominate the American culture. Canadians did not respond with the same urgency born of "insider aspirations" as did a number of American fundamentalists.[21] Only at the height of World War I did they begin to respond with something like the zeal evident in American fundamentalists to charges of modernist influence. Even then, however, they developed nothing like Mark Matthews's campaign in Seattle for "a righteous America" or W. B. Riley's anti-evolution crusade in Minnesota or other fundamentalist causes in the United States aimed at directly changing the society.[22]

However, a dramatic, high-profile conservative-liberal clash did develop in Vancouver in 1917, and immediately afterward conservative evangelicals began to develop their own alternate conservative institutions. An extended evangelistic campaign in the late spring and early summer of that year sparked a bitter, public polarization of Vancouver's (and to a much lesser extent, Victoria's) Protestants into liberal and conservative camps.[23] Preaching for a period of nine weeks before overflow crowds sometimes exceeding five thousand, American evangelist French E. Oliver, a Presbyterian affiliated with the Bible Institute of Los Angeles, bluntly and scathingly castigated the majority of the city's clergy. He hurled epithets such as "theological degenerates," "little puppets in the pulpit," and "ecclesiastical buz-

---

21. George Marsden, "Fundamentalism as an American Phenomenon," in *Fundamentalism and American Culture: The Shaping of Twentieth-Century Evangelicalism, 1870–1925* (New York, 1980), 221–28; and idem, "Defining American Fundamentalism," in *The Fundamentalist Phenomenon: A View from Within; a Response from Without*, ed. Norman J. Cohen (Grand Rapids, 1990), 22–37.

22. C. Allyn Russell, *Voices of American Fundamentalism* (Philadelphia, 1976), 93–95; and Nolland, "Uniqueness of Mark Matthews," 54.

23. A well-attended but much less controversial campaign was held in Victoria a month after the Vancouver campaign. For a more complete description of the Oliver campaigns and the controversy surrounding it, see Robert Burkinshaw, "Conservative Protestantism and the Modernist Challenge in Vancouver, 1917–1927," *BC Studies*, no. 85 (Spring 1990): 24–44.

zards" at liberal ministers. Many of the city's more liberal clergy responded with bitter attacks of their own, and the theological controversy raged publicly from the city's pulpits and in its secular press and served to polarize much of the Protestant community.[24]

The Vancouver Ministerial Association had refused to sponsor Oliver, citing his antipathy to modern scholarship, but a group calling itself the Vancouver Evangelistic Movement (VEM) brought him to the city. It was composed of Baptists, Presbyterians, Anglicans, and Plymouth Brethren laymen and clergy who had begun organizing in late 1916 for the purpose of countering the growing secularism in the city and liberalism within the churches. They were concerned that the work of evangelism had almost been eclipsed by a particularly heavy political and Social Gospel emphasis in Vancouver pulpits since 1915, when the city's Protestant ministers had taken a leading role in the province's politics.[25] As one member of the VEM explained, "The need of 'regeneration' or better still the old-fashioned term, 'conversion,' was seldom heard, from very few pulpits was emphasis laid upon the need of men to flee from wrath to come. Very few urged the people with all the powers at their command 'Be ye reconciled to God.' Therefore it was time for the rank and file to move."[26]

Acute wartime tensions in Vancouver contributed greatly to the response to Oliver's campaign in the city. Indeed the tension in Vancouver may have been even higher than in most American cities because of the fervent support in the city for the British cause and because of the conscription crisis raging in Canada throughout the duration of Oliver's campaign. The evangelist and his supporters made much of the argument, used elsewhere by conservatives such as W. H. Griffith

24. R. W. Sharpe, VEM chairman, to Rev. A. E. Cooke, president of Ministerial Association, 7 May 1917; and Rev. A. E. Cooke, Vancouver Ministerial Association Correspondence files, United Church Archives, Vancouver School of Theology, Vancouver; letter to the editor, *Vancouver Daily World*, 14 July 1917, 11; and Vancouver Evangelistic Movement handbill, "A Statement of Christian Faith" (1917).

25. The 1916 provincial election was fought around charges of corruption against the Conservative government of Richard McBridge. The Ministerial Union of the Lower Mainland of British Columbia had launched its own investigation and published a blistering attack in a pamphlet entitled *The Crisis in British Columbia: An Appeal for Investigation* (Vancouver, 1915). Its publication and a province-wide speaking tour by the president of the Ministerial Union created a political sensation and helped sweep the government out of power in the election of 1916.

26. F. Berry, letter to the editor, *Vancouver Daily World*, 19 July 1917, 6.

Thomas, that modernist theology had originated in Germany and had weakened Christian faith and morals in that country to the extent that German militarism could develop there unhindered.[27] Oliver lamented that so many clergy had swallowed "David Strauss and his war-soaked theology, the same theology which forced war upon the world."[28] In a prominently advertised sermon entitled "German Infidelity and German Sympathizers," his supporter J. L. Campbell of First Baptist Church claimed that "a large placard with the words 'made in Germany' printed upon it might be hung over the door of some of our colleges and seminaries and churches."[29] Such arguments had a telling impact on the passionately pro-British public of Vancouver.

Stimulated by the polarization and the several thousand new converts resulting from the evangelistic campaign, conservative evangelicals began the process of laying the institutional foundations of their own, separate version of Protestantism. The existence of liberalism was not news to most, but the highly publicized nature of the charges, the urgency imparted by the wartime setting, and the very public and derisive opposition of many of the mainline Protestant clergy to the whole campaign galvanized many conservatives into organizing institutional alternatives to the mainline denominations.

In the first decade following 1917, three discernible, though not always entirely separate, conservative subgroups emerged: (1) mainline conservatives, (2) militant or separatist Baptists, and (3) Pentecostalism. In addition, two conservative groups already existing in the province, the Plymouth Brethren and the Salvation Army, continued to grow in the urban areas. The Plymouth Brethren, in particular, were stimulated by the Oliver campaign and grew significantly thereafter.

It must be noted that these did not remain the only significant evangelical subgroups in British Columbia. Ongoing immigration resulted in the addition of a number of other groups. Beginning in 1928, migration from the Prairie Provinces brought numbers of Mennonites into the province, particularly to the Fraser Valley near Vancou-

27. See Marsden's account of the development of the argument in *Fundamentalism and American Culture*, 143–53.
28. *Victoria Daily Times*, 1 October 1917, 8.
29. *Vancouver Daily World*, 7 July 1917, 3.

ver. By the 1950s one of the largest concentrations in North America of the strongly evangelical Mennonite Brethren resided in the province. Also by that time the Christian and Missionary Alliance, the Christian Reformed Church, the Evangelical Free Church, the North American Baptist Conference, and the Baptist General Conference were beginning to make some inroads.[30] Nevertheless, the three groups emerging after 1917 were the dominant evangelical groups in British Columbia at least until mid-century and remained highly influential thereafter. Their similarities and differences with their American counterparts are particularly noteworthy.

Mainline Conservatives

Perhaps the most significant differences between British Columbian conservatives and those in the Northwest United States were to be found among conservatives remaining within the mainline Protestant denominations. Largely Presbyterian, Anglican, and Baptist, with a few Methodists, they remained within the major Protestant denominations, even though they were seriously concerned with the theological direction in which the groups were heading. Their response to liberal inroads was characterized by moderation, inclusiveness, and a reluctance to denounce modernists in a militant manner. In this they were more like the British conservative evangelicals described by David Bebbington than the geographically closer American fundamentalists.[31]

The majority of the conservatives in the province were in the major denominations before 1917, and the mainline conservatives formed the largest and most important of the conservative subgroups for several decades thereafter. The case of British Columbia confirms John Stackhouse's argument that the most significant evangelical institutions were more closely connected with the conservatives in the mainline denominations before mid-century than with those in the smaller, sectarian or separatist churches.[32] Between 1917 and the late

30. Burkinshaw, "Strangers and Pilgrims in Lotus Land: Conservative Protestantism in British Columbia" (Ph.D. diss., University of British Columbia, Vancouver, 1988), 209–18, 234–52, 268–97.

31. Bebbington, *Evangelicalism in Modern Britain*, 220–26.

32. John G. Stackhouse, Jr., "Proclaiming the Word: Canadian Evangelicalism since the First World War" (Ph.D. diss., University of Chicago, 1987).

1920s the mainline conservatives in British Columbia established an important network of institutions that encompassed a Bible institute, foreign missions, church planting, and home missions (city, rural, and frontier), child evangelism, and university student work.[33] In the first few decades the Vancouver Bible Training School and the China Inland Mission were the most important of these. Later, the InterVarsity Christian Fellowship and, after 1968, Regent College played more central roles for these mainline conservatives.

There was not a complete separation between the mainline conservatives and those in more sectarian groups. Many of the latter were involved in some way in supporting the various organizations, especially in the first years before there were virtually any other alternatives. In particular, some of the most "open" of Vancouver's large number of Plymouth Brethren cooperated in the Bible institute, in various evangelistic endeavors, and in the Inter-Varsity Christian Fellowship at the University of British Columbia.

The most significant mainline conservative institution for several decades in British Columbia, the Vancouver Bible Training School (VBTS), was the first Bible institute in western Canada. It was established in 1918, four years before the better-known Prairie Bible Institute in Alberta was founded. Its principal from 1918 to 1944 was Walter Ellis, an Anglican serving a Presbyterian congregation, and between 1944 and 1952 Joseph E. Harris, a minister of the mainline Baptist Convention of British Columbia, served as principal. Its governing council, part-time faculty, and student body were composed of Presbyterians, Baptists, Anglicans, Plymouth Brethren, and a few from some smaller religious groups. The school did not grow as large as several Bible schools on the prairies later became; its com-

---

33. The other organizations established by mainline conservatives in the province included the Girls' Corner Club, an evangelistic outreach to young women working in downtown Vancouver established in 1917; the Shantyman's Christian Association, expanding from eastern Canada in 1919 with the backing of local evangelicals to work with loggers, fishermen, and miners in outlying areas of the province; the British Columbia Evangelical Mission, organized locally in 1923 to begin churches and Sunday schools in the outlying areas of greater Vancouver and the Fraser Valley; the Inter-Varsity Christian Fellowship, originally founded in 1926 at the University of British Columbia as the Student Christian Fundamentalist Society; and the British Columbia Sunday School Mission, organized in 1929 to reach children in the most isolated regions of the province. For a fuller description of these organizations, see Burkinshaw, "Strangers and Pilgrims," 111–33, 230–34.

bined full- and part-time enrollments never quite reached one hundred in the 1920s and exceeded that figure only a few times in the 1930s and 1940s.[34] The growth of its full-time student body was hindered by the fact that, unlike many American schools that began to train prospective ministers after 1915, it did not intend to train men for ordination.[35] Indeed, with a few exceptions, the mainline churches in its constituency would not have accepted a candidate with only Bible institute training. Instead, as the designation "Training School" had been understood to signify for several decades, the school sought to train male and female workers for the foreign and home missions field, children's workers, pastors' assistants, and lay leaders.[36]

Nevertheless, VBTS played a central role, to use Joel Carpenter's apt expression, as the "regional coordinating center" of many of the province's evangelicals, especially those in the mainline denominations.[37] Ellis in particular, and many of the school's council members and part-time faculty, played crucial leadership roles in the other organizations of the interlocking conservative network. Between 1918 and 1953 a total of 154 of its students entered some kind of Christian ministry in a full-time capacity, or married someone who did. Quite a large proportion of those went overseas as missionaries, particularly with the China Inland Mission, but many also worked in the local conservative network of organizations and churches.[38]

The importance of VBTS to its constituency was considerably enhanced by its sponsorship of Keswick "deeper life" conferences, missions conferences, and public lectures. Especially important were Ellis's regular weekly evening lectures for Sunday school teachers, in which he presented a conservative interpretation of the lesson of the

34. VBTS, Council Minutes, Principal's Reports, 1918–55.

35. Ibid., 17 May 1918; and Virginia L. Brereton, *Training God's Army: The American Bible School, 1880–1940* (Bloomington, Ind., 1990), 82–83.

36. In its sixty-one-year history the school was variously known as the Vancouver Bible Training School, the Vancouver Bible School, then Vancouver Bible Institute, and, finally, while under the auspices of the Baptist General Conference, Vancouver Bible College. For the sake of simplicity, the designation VBTS is used throughout this chapter. Brereton, *Training God's Army*, 55–77, traces the background of the religious training schools.

37. Joel Carpenter, "Fundamentalist Institutions and the Rise of Evangelical Protestantism, 1929–1942," *Church History* (March 1980), 67.

38. Mrs. A. E. Ellis to G. Carlson, 10 January 1964 (copy in author's papers).

week in the International Uniform Lesson series. Upward of 150 Sunday school teachers and leaders from a broad cross-section of city churches regularly crowded into the VBTS auditorium for the popular lectures.[39]

The China Inland Mission (CIM), one of the world's largest and most influential interdenominational mission societies, composed the original foreign missions component of the mainline conservative network. Vancouver, "the gateway to the Orient," played a key support role in the CIM's operations. In the early twentieth century the mission was maintaining approximately one thousand missionaries in the interior of China, and Vancouver was their Pacific port of entry and embarkation.[40] Consequently hundreds of missionaries from Britain, Europe, Canada, and the United States passed through the city each year. In 1917 members of the VEM helped the mission acquire a large house on the west side of the city to accommodate such personnel and to provide facilities for an orientation program for missionary recruits from the western part of the continent.[41] The house gave the mission a stronger presence in Vancouver and made it possible for traveling missionaries to remain longer in the city.

Not only did the CIM receive a great deal of support in Vancouver, it contributed considerably to the character and strength of interdenominational evangelicalism in the city. Its personnel frequently preached in city churches and thus raised the awareness of overseas missions. The mission's stress on the most broadly based cooperation possible within the spectrum of evangelicalism at the same time that it was endeavoring to keep liberalism out of the mission fields provided a model for many Vancouver evangelicals.[42]

The common roots of the CIM missionaries and the Vancouver mainline evangelicals in the major British denominations and in Keswick holiness teachings strengthened evangelical cooperation in

39. For a discussion of the International Uniform Lesson series, see Gerald E. Knoff, *The World Sunday School Movement* (New York, 1979), 2, 35, 41, 64–68, 103.

40. J. Hudson Taylor, *A Retrospect* (Philadelphia, ca. 1910), inside cover.

41. VBTS, Council Minutes, 1918–1949, and Ellis interview, 11 and 22 January 1982.

42. Marsden, *Fundamentalism and American Culture*, 97; Ernest R. Sandeen, *Roots of Fundamentalism: British and American Millenarianism, 1800–1930* (Chicago, 1970), 250; and interview with L. Street, Vancouver, 9 February 1982. Mr. Street was in China with the China Inland Mission for many years before 1949.

the city.[43] The ties were strongest between the CIM and VBTS. When constructing its own facilities in 1923, the school chose a site less than a block from the mission's house. The first president of the council of VBTS was also a member of the CIM's North American Council, while the local director of the CIM served for a time as vice-president of the school's council and as a part-time lecturer.[44] The close relationship between the two institutions and the steady stream of missionaries as guest lecturers and inspirational speakers was a strong stimulant to the school and its students; Ellis was also a great booster of the mission. Both before emigrating to Canada and after his graduation, he had seriously considered going to China as a missionary. Although unable to do so, he maintained a strong interest in foreign missions in general, and China in particular. Understandably, then, along with other members of the VEM, he was eager to help establish the CIM's regional headquarters in Vancouver in 1917. He sat on its local council for many years and strongly encouraged his students to serve in China with the CIM.[45]

Despite the outburst of vitriolic controversy surrounding the Oliver campaign, which had helped to trigger their institution-building efforts, the mainline conservatives were not characterized by the contentious and combative tone and the dispensationalist and exclusivist stance that characterized much of American fundamentalism, especially from the end of the war through the 1920s.[46] Instead their concerns centered largely on Bible training for young people, cultivating and promoting personal holiness of the Keswick variety, and engaging actively in evangelism at home and overseas. High priority was given to the evangelism and training of youth by means of several

43. Anglicans, Presbyterians, Methodists, and Baptists predominated among the missionaries. J. Hudson Taylor was very closely associated with the Keswick movement and, in many respects, embodied its teachings (Marsden, *Fundamentalism and American Culture*, 97).

44. Walter Ellis, *In Memoriam, Robert Watt Sharpe* (Vancouver, 1925); VBTS, Council Minutes, 1918–30.

45. Winnifred Francis, *Rev. Walter Ellis, M.A., B.D.: A Memorial, a Tribute* (Vancouver, 1945), 5–6; Ellis to Carlson, 10 January 1964 (see n. 38); and interview with Miss Norma Cuthbertson, Vancouver, 11 February 1982.

46. Marsden emphasizes the militancy of American fundamentalism in the period. In her recent study, Brereton takes issue with Marsden on that point and emphasizes that fundamentalists associated with the Bible schools were not particularly militant (*Training God's Army*, 165–70).

children's evangelistic and Sunday school missions and the Bible training school and university student work. That focus would seem to indicate, as Bebbington suggests was the case with British conservatives, that the winning of "the next generation for the truth" was more important than denouncing the present generation's defections from the truth.[47]

The mainline conservative characteristics are best illustrated in Walter Ellis, for nearly three decades the central figure of the province's mainline conservative community. He made his best-known contribution while serving in the dual capacity as principal of the VBTS from its founding in 1918 until his death in 1944 and as minister of Fairview Presbyterian Church from 1926 until 1944. In addition, he played key roles in the establishment of a number of interdenominational organizations in the city. More than any other person, he was the hub of the interlocking network of organizations. Not only was he an influential and active member of a number of boards of evangelistic organizations, he recruited, trained, and provided moral support for many of the necessary workers.

Ellis was born and raised in England but received his postsecondary education in Toronto. Born in 1883 in Derbyshire, England, he came to Canada in 1903 as the assistant to the Anglican chaplain of the Barr Colony in Saskatchewan. He spent the next nine years studying in Toronto earning his B.A., his M.A. in Semitics from the University of Toronto, and his B.D. from Wycliffe College. In 1913 he came to Vancouver to serve a one-year locum at St. Mark's Church and the following year joined the faculty of Bishop Latimer Hall, teaching Old Testament, apologetics, and church history.[48]

By the time Ellis arrived in Vancouver he was a strong proponent of Keswick holiness teaching. He had been converted under the ministry of Archdeacon Joynt, one of the speakers at the Keswick conferences, and attended his church most of his teenage years.[49] At Wycliffe College he was profoundly influenced by W. H. Griffith Thomas, one of the foremost exponents of Keswick holiness teaching in North

47. Bebbington, *Evangelicals in Modern Britain*, 225–26.
48. Francis, *Rev. Walter Ellis*, 4–7; Bishop Latimer Hall, Quarterly Reports of Principal Minutes of Council, 1913–1918.
49. Francis, *Rev. Walter Ellis*, 4.

America.[50] In Vancouver, for over a period of nearly twenty years, Ellis, along with representatives of the China Inland Mission, planned "Keswick weeks" aimed at deepening the spiritual life of his students and of other local people.[51] His own teaching and preaching constantly bore Keswick's characteristic traits of a stress on consecration, reliance on the power of the Holy Spirit, personal holiness, daily communion with God, and a life of active service, especially in evangelism and foreign missions.[52]

As was earlier noted, his commitment to evangelism and missions was also long-standing. This commitment to evangelism prompted Ellis to become a key figure in the VEM and then to start the VBTS. Despite deep disappointment at the vituperative nature of the Oliver campaign and some significant ongoing differences in approach with more militant members of the VEM, he led Bible classes organized under its auspices for the new converts resulting from the campaign. During the first year he helped develop those classes into the Vancouver Bible Training School and was appointed its principal.[53]

In many ways Ellis's emphases were much like those of the founders of the earliest American Bible schools in the years well before the heat of the controversies in the period of World War I, and the 1920s heightened the mood of defensiveness and militancy.[54] He did not see his school as competing with the denominational theological colleges. Instead, his purpose of the new school was to train a generation of evangelists. It "aims to furnish a thorough and practical use of the English Bible, and to send forth the workers with an extreme love of souls, and a full realization of the presence and power of the Holy Spirit in their life and service."[55] The primary goal of Bible schools, he stated a year later, was to be "hotbeds of evangelistic action."[56]

50. Ellis Interview, 1 January 1982; and Marsden, *Fundamentalism and American Culture*, 99, 246.

51. VBTS, Council Minutes, 1917–1935.

52. Walter E. Ellis, sermons, 1942–43, notes taken by Norma Cuthbertson in Cuthbertson private papers, Vancouver; Francis, *Rev. Walter Ellis*, 4–17.

53. A. E. Ellis interview, 11 January 1981; and Vancouver Evangelistic Movement, Minutes, 7 August 1917.

54. Brereton, *Training God's Army*, 1–10; and Marsden, *Fundamentalism and American Culture*, 141–84.

55. VBTS, Council Minutes, 17 May 1918.

56. Ibid., 8 March, 1919.

In 1925 he became minister of Fairview Presbyterian Church, a conservative congregation whose members had refused to enter the new United Church of Canada. Seven years earlier the High Church British Columbian bishop dePencier had refused to renew Ellis's ministerial license because of his extensive involvement in an inter-denominational institution. Ellis was loath to leave the Anglican denomination, even though unable to preach within it, but he was persuaded by the need of the theologically compatible Presbyterians and by his own family's need for a larger income than VBTS could provide. The church's membership was strongly supportive of his continuing with his work at the Bible school, which was located only one block from the church's location on the city's west side.[57]

Under his leadership Fairview Presbyterian Church developed into one of the more influential evangelical congregations in the city. It was never very large, growing from 140 members in 1926 to 250 in 1944. It was not extremely wealthy, although its congregation was largely of the respectable middle class.[58] Despite its modest size and wealth, the congregation's influence was far out of proportion to its size. Ellis's emphases helped keep the congregation strongly focused on evangelism and missions, and over the years it contributed a disproportionately high number of its members to full-time ministry and provided a very significant level of financial support to denominational and interdenominational missions.[59]

In several other ways, Ellis helped to shape the contours of main-

57. Ibid.

58. Two-thirds of the members were employed in the professional, managerial, clerical, and business occupations, and most owned their own homes in the somewhat above-average housing-cost districts of Fairview, Kitsilano, and West Point Grey. Fairview Presbyterian Church, Communicant Rolls, 1925–45; Minutes of Session, 1925–45; *Wrigley-Henderson British Columbia Directory*, 1925–45 editions; City of Vancouver, District Lot Assessment Books, 1944, City of Vancouver Archives.

59. From its founding in 1926 until 1981, thirty-one of its members became full-time ministers and missionaries, twenty in the Presbyterian Church and the rest in other denominations and independent missions. (From list, in author's papers, compiled by Mrs. A. E. Ellis, with the assistance from other members of Fairview Presbyterian Church.) Not only did the congregation contribute financially to the Presbyterian mission fund at a higher rate per member than did nearly all other Presbyterian churches in the city, it also supported interdenominational causes heavily through a special missions budget and the individual contributions of its members (*Acts and Proceedings of the General Assembly of the Presbyterian Church in Canada* [1926–44], statistical reports).

line evangelicalism in British Columbia. He was distressed that both sides of the fundamentalist-modernist debate at times pitted scholarship against belief in traditional Christian doctrines in a way that implied the two were necessarily opposed to one another. He had excelled in his graduate work in Semitics at the University of Toronto under J. F. McCurdy, the "father of biblical studies in Canada." McCurdy had indicated his respect for the young Ellis by inviting him to be his associate in the School of Archaeology in Cairo.[60] As a young minister, Ellis had quickly acquired a reputation for preaching thoughtful, scholarly sermons, and in 1916 he gained the respect of the theologically diverse Vancouver Ministerial Association through a well-received paper on the Minor Prophets that he delivered to one of its meetings.[61]

He encouraged rigorous study, asking in a sermon, "Investigate every phase of the universe—have you a greater or lesser appreciation of God the more you understand these things?"[62] Like American conservatives, he accepted the common sense distinction between scientific facts and theories. He wrote for a popular audience, "Sometimes in the enthrallment of their investigations scientists formulate hypotheses to explain or coordinate the facts they have discovered. Sometimes these hypotheses conflict with Scripture, but we must always distinguish between the Scientist's fact and his explanations."[63]

Ellis's ability to deal with modernism in a scholarly manner earned him a reputation among many conservatives as an effective and reliable defender against that threat. His style appealed to many respectable and educated people, both within and without his own congregation. A student from a conservative Presbyterian home, the daughter of a city physician, credited Ellis with helping her rediscover her faith. She described herself as drifting into agnosticism during her university training until she was persuaded by her mother to listen to one of Ellis's public lectures at the Bible school. After listening to him

60. Francis, *Rev. Walter Ellis*, 6. For the importance of McCurdy to biblical studies in Canada, see Moir, *History of Biblical Studies in Canada* (Chico, Calif., 1982), 14–15, 26–28, 38–43.

61. Vancouver General Ministerial Association, Minutes, 4 December 1916.

62. Walter E. Ellis, sermon, 24 April 1943, manuscript notes taken by Norma Cuthbertson, in Cuthbertson private papers, Vancouver.

63. Walter E. Ellis, "My Own Religion Today" (manuscript article intended for publication in the *Vancouver Sun*, ca. 1930), copy in author's papers.

weekly for a length of time, she reflected, "I saw clearly that here was a scholar who knew both sides of the argument. . . . Professor Ellis' scholarship and his expository preaching combined with his gentle culture won my full confidence and I was willing to learn from him."[64]

The militant, combative spirit that characterized much of American fundamentalism was largely absent in British Columbia's mainline conservative community and was abhorred by Ellis. Indeed, if militancy is accepted as the feature that distinguished fundamentalists from other evangelicals, then most of the mainline conservatives would not qualify as fundamentalists because of the lack of militancy in their response to liberalism.[65] The contention surrounding the Oliver campaign greatly distressed Ellis. A summer preaching commitment in Toronto made it impossible for him to be in Vancouver during the actual duration of the evangelistic campaign, but upon his return he let his disappointment with Oliver and some of the VEM members be known.[66] It is impossible to know if Ellis's presence in the city would have made a difference to the campaign, but it is conceivable that he might have been able to play a conciliatory role. As it was, in the heated atmosphere after the campaign, he was clearly identified with the conservatives in their defense against further inroads of liberal theology. At the same time, however, his concern that a strong stand for conservative theology should not be associated with invective marked the beginning of a widening chasm between himself and the more militant conservatives, or fundamentalists, in the city.[67] He sometimes referred to his position as "being caught between two fires," with liberalism on the left and militant conservatives on the right.[68]

64. Isobel Kuhn, *By Searching: My Journey through Doubt into Faith* (Chicago, 1959), 24–25.

65. Marsden, "Defining American Fundamentalism," 22–23. It should be noted in this context that Brereton places considerable stress on the moderating influence of the Bible school leaders in the United States, rather than on their militancy (*Training God's Army*, 139–41, 165–70).

66. A. E. Ellis interview, 11 January, 1982. Mrs. Ellis was married to Walter in 1918 but had already been engaged to him in early 1917.

67. VBTS, Council Minutes, 1918–25. The minutes of 8 March 1919, in particular, allude to such a division.

68. A. E. Ellis interview, 11 January 1982. The experience of being a conservative, yet criticized for a lack of militancy, bore similarities to those of American conservatives such as the Baptist J. C. Massee and the Presbyterian Clarence E. Macartney. See C. Allyn Russell, *Voices of American Fundamentalism* (Philadelphia, 1976), 107–34, 190–211.

Like his counterparts in the American Bible schools, Ellis was careful not to meddle in the affairs of denominations being rent by controversy.[69] However, he found the separatist tendency quite distressing and once remarked that he viewed it as "an unhealthy assertion of personal independence" that could only lead to more splits and "eventual wreckage."[70] For their part, separatist Baptists found the inclusiveness of his approach unacceptable; after 1927 almost all of the many Baptists attending the school were from the mainline convention.

Ellis sought to steer clear of needless disputes by stressing the need for considerable breadth on contentious questions. He worked particularly hard to keep the Bible school free from the narrowness that he believed characterized many such institutions in the United States. The academic calendar of VBTS promised that "no sectarian nor merely denominational tenets will be taught in the classes." When the school was under pressure to give up some of that breadth soon after its founding, Ellis argued in his report to its council: "The Bible schools must enlist the sympathy of Christians on the widest lines consistent with the truth. For us this means that we should make friends to ourselves of members of all the Churches who will sympathetically cooperate. So far as possible we should give them a voice in our affairs; at the same time we must zealously guard the matters of our faith which we hold as fundamental."[71]

Rigid views of eschatology, in particular, caused Ellis and VBTS the most difficulty. The Vancouver school was remarkably different from the great majority of American Bible schools in that Ellis did not believe the role of VBTS was to serve as "a primary vehicle for the dissemination of dispensationalism."[72] When James M. Gray, dean of the Moody Bible Institute, attempted in the spring of 1919 to persuade the Bible institutes in North America to adopt a common creedal subscription that included dispensationalist statements, Ellis entered into correspondence with him, forcefully arguing against the adop-

69. Brereton, *Training God's Army*, 139–41.

70. Walter E. Ellis, sermon, 13 June 1943, manuscript notes taken by Norma Cuthbertson, copy in Cuthbertson private papers, Vancouver.

71. VBTS, Principal's Report, Council Minutes, 8 March 1919.

72. Brereton, *Training God's Army*, 20.

tion of a narrow statement.[73] The VBTS council agreed with him and formally declined endorsing the proposed statement.[74]

Such refusals to adopt dispensationalism made VBTS, and Ellis, suspect in the eyes of some fundamentalists. In 1930 the council was informed that Prairie Bible Institute of Three Hills, Alberta, was spreading a rumor that VBTS held a postmillennial position—a view associated in the minds of many conservatives of the period with liberalism.[75] Locally, dispensationalists put such pressure on the school to give up its broad eschatological stance that Ellis at times felt almost as besieged by fellow conservatives as by modernists.[76]

Ellis's own eschatological view was premillennialism, but he held to a historicist, rather than a dispensationalist, version. He stressed the figurative rather than the literal interpretation of apocalyptic literature and found the dispensationalist approach made the Bible into a "grotesque study book."[77] He was very concerned, however, that his own strongly held views not become divisive and was able to work closely and amicably over long periods with some dispensationalist supporters of VBTS.[78]

Ellis was greatly influenced in his insistence on tolerance of eschatological differences by John McNicol, principal of Canada's oldest Bible school, Toronto Bible College. Under McNicol, that school gained a reputation quite different from that of many Bible schools in the United States and, later, in the Canadian prairies. It was theologically conservative but allowed for considerable breadth in eschatological and ecclesiastical questions and gained the support of evangelicals in a variety of mainline denominations.[79] Ellis was a close

73. Sandeen, *Roots of Fundamentalism*, 244.
74. VBTS, Council Minutes, 11 April 1919 and 29 December 1919.
75. Ibid., 2 May 1930.
76. Ellis Interview, 11 January 1982.
77. Walter E. Ellis sermon series, April and May 1942, manuscript notes taken by Norma Cuthbertson. For more complete discussion of the historicist premillennial position, see Sandeen, *Roots of Fundamentalism*, 36–39.
78. W. J. Scott, North Vancouver, to W., 27 December 1933, in VBTS, Council Minutes, 3 January 1934.
79. Warren Charlton, "Dr. John McNicol and Toronto Bible College," Canadian Society of Presbyterian History, *Papers*, 1977, 38–57. The earlier history of Toronto Bible College is told in Ron Sawatsky, "Ellmore Harris: Canadian Baptist Extraordinaire" (unpublished graduate paper, University of Toronto, 1980). Stackhouse, "Proclaiming the Word," 51, lists Toronto Bible

friend of McNicol, and he closely modeled the new Vancouver school after the pattern of the older Toronto school.[80] He was invited by Mc-Nicol in 1923 to join his faculty but turned the offer down in favor of continuing to develop VBTS along similar lines.[81]

The two institutions most closely connected with British Columbia's mainline conservatives declined by mid-century. The CIM home in Vancouver closed following the 1949 fall of the Chiang Kaishek regime in China. In 1956 VBTS ceased functioning as an interdenominational school, and its assets and charter were passed to a newer group in the province, the Baptist General Conference. A variety of factors, including the death of Ellis in 1944, the closing of China to Western missionaries, increasing demands among the mainline conservatives for a higher level of education than a Bible institute could offer, and competition for the remaining potential students from the larger Bible institutes on the prairies, all contributed to the decline of VBTS as an interdenominational institution primarily serving the mainline conservatives.

However, something of the Ellis influence on the mainline conservatives continued in other evangelical organizations. An evangelical student group at the University of British Columbia (UBC) had formed in 1926 and several years later became a chapter of the Inter-Varsity Christian Fellowship of Canada (IVCF). According to Stackhouse, the IVCF was one of "the three most important institutions that Canadian evangelicals founded in the first half of the twentieth century."[82] It is significant that, although founded directly as a reaction to the strong liberal orientation of the Student Christian Movement, the orientation of the UBC group was not on theological contention but on evangelism and holiness teaching.

The character of the denominationally mixed Vancouver IVCF was very strongly influenced by the early mainline conservative institutions in the city. Walter Ellis consistently offered the group warm

College as one of the "three most important institutions that Canadian evangelicals founded in the first half of the twentieth century, other than foreign mission societies."

80. VBTS, Council Minutes, 17 June 1918 and 9 April 1931.

81. Ibid., 7 May 1923.

82. Stackhouse, "Proclaiming the Word," 100–137. David Phillips, "The History of the Inter-Varsity Christian Fellowship in Western Canada" (M.C.S. thesis, Regent College, Vancouver, 1976), provides a very thorough history of the organization.

encouragement and frequently visited the campus and spoke at its meetings. He and his wife so strongly supported the fledgling student-led group that they purchased a large home near the university gates in order to provide a suitable, off-campus meeting place for it.[83] CIM missionaries, many of whom were Oxford and Cambridge graduates, also frequently visited the campus and provided significant encouragement to the group. These influences were significantly reflected in its orientation. In 1927 the UBC society affiliated itself with the League of Evangelical Students, which had a very strong chapter at the University of Washington in Seattle. That affiliation soon lagged, however, as the American group was oriented to a more rationalistic, or Princetonian, form of fundamentalism compared with the Keswick holiness orientation the Canadian students were stressing in Vancouver. A much more satisfactory relationship was established several years later with the Inter-Varsity Christian Fellowship of Canada, which had strong British ties and was very strongly influenced by the CIM and by Keswick holiness teaching. In years following, the UBC group continued to be encouraged by Ellis and the CIM, and it grew to be the strongest chapter in western Canada during the 1930s. In the postwar period it grew to be the largest religious club on UBC's campus.[84]

The inclusive nature of mainline conservatism was also strongly reflected in Regent College, which was founded in Vancouver in 1968 and by the mid-1980s had become Canada's largest graduate school of theology.[85] The statement of faith adopted by the college's founders did not specify a position on eschatology, and on the question of the nature of the Scriptures it allowed for the range of positions historically found within evangelicalism.[86] In conjunction with several influential British and American Plymouth Brethren, the school was founded by members of Vancouver's and Victoria's large Plymouth Brethren community, one of the strongest concentrations

83. Ellis Interview, 22 January 1982.
84. Phillips, "History of the Inter-Varsity Christian Fellowship in Western Canada," 110, 208–9.
85. Stackhouse, "Proclaiming the Word," 196–210.
86. The statement used by the World Evangelical Fellowship and the Evangelical Fellowship of Canada was adopted (Brian P. Sutherland, "Historical Development" [Paper delivered at the conference "Openness to the Future: A Prelude to Planning," Regent College, Vancouver, 1974]; and Stackhouse, "Proclaiming the Word," 293–343).

of Brethren in North America. Unlike most Plymouth Brethren in North America, the "open" Brethren in British Columbia were not necessarily dispensationalists and were not opposed to higher education. The very recent British roots of most of them, and the very extensive and positive involvement on the part of many in institutions and organizations associated with the mainline conservatives, directly influenced the character of Regent College.

Those among Vancouver's open Brethren who had been most involved in cooperative activities with mainline evangelicals took the lead in founding Regent College. Perhaps the most influential of such involvements was their important role in IVCF,[87] but there were other significant contacts as well. For example, businessman E. Marshall Sheppard, prime mover in Vancouver to launch Regent, had been a close friend and strong supporter in the 1930s and 1940s of Walter Ellis. He had regularly attended Ellis's Thursday night public lectures and attached great value to them, often stating that from those meetings he learned all the theology he knew. As superintendent of the Sunday school of the Mount Pleasant assembly, the largest Brethren congregation in Vancouver at the time, he urged all his teachers to take advantage of the lectures.[88] Also, Kenneth O. Smith, a leading supporter of the school and the secretary of its first board of governors, had been greatly influenced by mainline conservative institutions. His father had been president of the IVCF group at UBC in the 1950s.[89]

In turn, mainline conservatives of the sort who had supported VBTS a generation earlier quickly became involved in Regent. For example, Dr. Ian S. Rennie, a former IVCF staff member and minister of Ellis's former congregation, Fairview Presbyterian, joined the board of governors the first year and two years later was appointed associate professor of church history. Several board and faculty members during the first decade came from the Baptist Union (formerly the Baptist Convention of British Columbia), and evangelical Anglicans from Britain and Australia were welcome as full-time and summer-

87. Phillips, "History of the Inter-Varsity Christian Fellowship in Western Canada," 53–54, 75, 83, 93.

88. Ellis Interview, 11 January 1982; and telephone interview with Ian S. Rennie, Toronto, 19 February 1982.

89. VBTS, Council Minutes, 1940–49; and Sutherland, "Historical Development."

session faculty. Increasing numbers of students came from smaller bodies such as Mennonite, Christian and Missionary Alliance, and Pentecostals, but Baptists consistently formed the largest group in the student body. In 1980 the Baptist Union became officially involved by creating at its Carey Hall a seminary program working in very close cooperation with Regent.[90]

Separatist Baptists

In the only major Baptist split in western Canada, the Baptist Convention of British Columbia divided formally into two denominations in 1927.[91] The split paralleled in many respects that in the Northern Baptist Convention, but it also differed in some significant respects.

Charges of modernist teaching at Brandon College, the denomination's liberal arts and theology school in Manitoba, began circulating in 1919. As was the case in the United States, the militant conservatives in British Columbia were unable to persuade moderate conservatives, the largest group in the convention, to join them in their efforts to purge the denomination of liberalism. In 1925 large numbers of the militant conservatives joined the newly established local chapter of the Baptist Bible Union, and the same year they formed the Missionary Council, their own parallel organization within the convention. The rift continued to widen, and rather than risk expulsion from the convention, they withdrew and formed their own separate denomination in 1927.

There were some significant differences between the experience of American separatist Baptists and those in British Columbia. The new, fundamentalist Convention of Regular Baptist Churches of British Columbia was, proportionate to total Baptist population, much larger than the General Association of Regular Baptists (GARB) in the United States, which attracted only a remnant of the old Baptist

90. Regent College, Registrar's reports, 1972–73 to 1979–80; Baptist Union of Western Canada Regent College, Registrar's reports, 1972–73 to 1979–80; Baptist Union of Western Canada, *Yearbook*, 1979–80; Stackhouse, "Proclaiming the Word," 207; and Burkinshaw, "Strangers and Pilgrims," 326–34.

91. Poussett, "History of the Convention," and Richards, *Baptists in British Columbia*, both recount the schism in some detail.

Bible Union.[92] The new British Columbia denomination attracted
nearly one-half of the former membership of the old convention in
the city of Vancouver and one-third of it in the province as a whole.
By the 1950s it had more congregations than the mainline Baptist
Convention, and by the 1970s it was attracting more people to its
worship services than the older body.[93]

Another important difference from their American counterparts
was the strongly British character of the leadership of the Baptist
fundamentalists in British Columbia. They looked to British Baptist
Charles Spurgeon as their model in separation from any form of theological liberalism.[94] Nine of the sixteen ministers who led the separatist movement in the province were British-born, and only one was
from the United States.[95] No dominant personality within British Columbia emerged as leader, but the British-born T. T. Shields of Toronto played a very significant role. He visited Vancouver frequently
and encouraged the local militant conservatives in their resistance.
His church provided significant financial support for the separatist
Baptists organization in British Columbia, and his *Gospel Witness*
was read widely in the province.[96]

In a rather interesting reversal of the usual view of the American
influence on Canadian fundamentalism, Baptists in the more Ameri-
can-oriented provinces of Alberta and Saskatchewan were much less
inclined to separatist fundamentalism than were their more British-
influenced counterparts in British Columbia. A substantially higher
proportion of the Baptists in the two prairie provinces were born in
the United States than was the case in British Columbia, and a much
larger number of ministers had received their training in the United
States.[97] Yet, only three churches in Alberta affiliated with the sepa-

92. In 1936, approximately three years after the founding of the GARB, it claimed 22,345
members and 84 churches, a minuscule proportion of the Baptist membership and churches in
the states in which it existed (Albert W. Wardin, Jr., *Baptist Atlas* [Nashville, 1980], 27).

93. Burkinshaw, "Strangers and Pilgrims," tables III and IV.

94. *British Columbia Baptist*, 19 November 1925, 2–3.

95. Compiled from G. Pousett, "The History of the Regular Baptists of British Columbia"
(B.D. thesis, McMaster Divinity College, 1956), Appendix E, in conjunction with interviews
with J. B. Richards, Vancouver, 7 December 1979, and D. Hills, Vancouver, 3 January 1980.

96. Pousett, "History of the Convention," 176. Issues of the *Gospel Witness* from the first
half of 1926 give extensive coverage to two such trips in the first six months of that year.

97. *1931 Census of Canada*, vol. 4, table 8.

ratist organization, the Regular Baptist Missionary Fellowship, when it was formed in 1930, and no such division occurred at all in Saskatchewan.[98] The significant difference was a strong liberal impulse among prairie Baptists that emanated from seminaries serving the Northern Baptists: Chicago, Rochester, and Crozer. Most of the Brandon College faculty, and many prairie ministers, had received all or part of their training at one of those three schools.[99] Many British Columbian Baptists, in contrast, viewed the Northern Baptist Convention with great suspicion. The University of Chicago Divinity School, in particular, was feared and loathed as a source of heresy by British Columbian conservatives.[100]

Unlike their counterparts separating from the Northern Baptist Convention, the ministers of the new Convention of Regular Baptists in British Columbia were quite diversified in their views of eschatology and of denominationalism. In their diversity on eschatology, they were similar to conservative evangelical British Baptists such as Graham Scroggie, who refused to allow premillennialism to become a condition of fellowship.[101] Indeed, many British Columbian ministers were increasingly influenced by T. T. Shields, who rejected both dispensationalism and antidenominationalism. By the 1940s, dispensationalism was declining among British Columbian Regular Baptist ministers.[102] In addition, most had long since rejected the more extreme separatist approach that favored forming, at most, a loose fellowship of churches as opposed to building a strong and unified conservative denomination.[103]

Indeed, the Baptist best known in the province for his dispensa-

---

98. J. H. Pickford, "Westbourne Baptist Church" (unpublished ms., undated); and Richards, *Baptists in British Columbia*, 113.

99. S. Sharpe Dore to W. E. Ellis, 16 November 1961, cited in W. E. Ellis, "Baptists and Radical Politics in Western Canada (1920–1950)," in *Baptists in Canada: Search for Identity amidst Diversity*, ed. J. Zeman (Burlington, Ont., 1980), 180; and Baptist Union of Western Canada, *1927 Yearbook* (1927), 171–75.

100. For example, the *Vancouver Daily World*, 7 July 1917, 3; *The Dangerous Peril of Religious Education* (Vancouver, December 1921), cited in Pousett, "History of the Regular Baptists," 49; and A. W. Bennett, *Facts concerning Brandon College*, cited in Richards, *Baptists in British Columbia*, 71.

101. Bebbington, *Evangelicalism in Modern Britain*, 222.

102. Richards, *Baptists in British Columbia*, 113–14, 122–23.

103. Ibid., 100–107.

tionalist and nondenominational separatist views, W. M. Robertson, separated from the "worldliness" associated with the incipient denominationalism of the Regular Baptists in 1928.[104] He had been originally called from Liverpool to Mt. Pleasant Baptist, Vancouver, the flagship church of the new denomination, but left with nearly one-half its membership less than a year after his arrival. In reaction to what he perceived as a trend toward centralization in the new denomination, he founded the ardently dispensationalist and separatist Metropolitan Tabernacle and led it in affiliating with the Independent Fundamental Churches of America.[105]

The Regular Baptists explored relationships with two American bodies. In the 1940s informal meetings began for purposes of fellowship with GARB ministers in nearby Washington State. However, these did not last long largely because of the ministers' strongly dispensationalist orientation and their negative view of denominational structures.[106] In the early 1950s, overtures were made to the British Columbian Regular Baptists to join the Southern Baptist Convention. The aggressive evangelism, growth, and strong denominational identity of the Southern Baptists were appealing to some of the British Columbians, but a number of factors, including the "worldly" sanctioning of the use of tobacco in the American South, the "landmarker" tendencies of the Oregon-Washington Convention, and a surge of Canadian nationalism combined to prevent all but a few British Columbian churches from joining the Southern Baptists.[107] Instead, the British Columbian Regular Baptists began forging closer links with like-minded groups across Canada, especially in Ontario, which culminated in 1965 in the formation of the Fellowship of Evangelical Baptists in Canada in 1965.[108]

104. Ibid., 82, 95, 101.

105. Ibid., and James Wilson *The History of Metropolitan Tabernacle, 1928–1978* (n.p., 1978), 3. Robertson was president of the IFCA from 1945 to 1947.

106. John J. Ruhlman, *A History of Northwest Regular Baptists: The General Association of Regular Baptist Churches in Washington, Oregon, and Idaho, 1939–1975* (Schaumburg, IL, 1976), 279–80; and Richards, *Baptists in British Columbia*, 113–14.

107. *Western Regular Baptist*, January 1954 and July 1955; and Richards, *Baptists in British Columbia*, 114–17; Pousett, "History of the Regular Baptists," 130–33.

108. Kenneth R. Davis, "The Struggle for a United Evangelical Baptist Fellowship, 1953–1965," in *Baptists in Canada: Search for Identity amidst Diversity*, ed. J. Zeman (Burlington, Ont., 1980), 237–65.

Pentecostals

Pentecostalism in British Columbia did not experience any appreciable growth until the 1920s, over a decade later than in other parts of North America. When that growth finally came, it was not, as has been argued in the case of the United States, primarily due to large numbers of members of holiness churches attracted to its experiential emphasis.[109] Indeed, very few holiness churches existed in the province at the time. Instead, much of the growth came from radical fundamentalist Baptists, or "ultrafundamentalists," who were attracted by the apologetic value of Pentecostalism's claim of contemporary miraculous occurrences.[110] Such claims refuted the modernists' denial of the supernatural origins of Christianity, many fundamentalists believed. Much of the support for Charles S. Price's enormously successful evangelistic and healing campaigns in Vancouver and Victoria in 1923, described as the most successful of his long career, came from conservative Baptists.[111] Ministers of the leading Baptist churches in Vancouver fully endorsed the British-born preacher from California, who had recently been converted from liberalism to Pentecostalism (and a conservative doctrinal stance) under the preaching of Aimee Semple McPherson.[112] They appeared prominently on his platform and participated in the anointing and prayers for the sick before overflow crowds exceeding ten thousand.[113] When Price came under severe attack, largely from prominent liberal clergymen, fundamentalist Baptists, most of whom were engaged in the bitter struggle within the convention over

109. For example, see Vinson Synan, *The Holiness-Pentecostal Movement in the United States* (Grand Rapids, 1971), 204–6; and David W. Faupel, "The American Pentecostal Movement: A Bibliographical Essay," in *The Higher Christian Life: A Bibliographical Overview*, ed. Donald W. Dayton (New York, 1985), 69–76. Synan and others downplay the link between Pentecostals and fundamentalists, but Brereton includes Pentecostals in her definition of fundamentalism in *Training God's Army*, 165–70.

110. The term is used by Frank S. Mead, *Handbook of Denominations in the United States* (Nashville, 1970), 162, but rejected by Synan, *Holiness-Pentecostal Movement in the United States*, 204–6.

111. R. M. Riss, "Price, Charles Sydney," in *Dictionary of Pentecostal and Charismatic Movements*, ed. S. M. Burgess and G. B. McGee (Grand Rapids, 1988), 726–77.

112. Charles S. Price, *Story of My Life* (Pasadena, Calif., c. 1935), 23–44.

113. For example, the *Vancouver Daily Province*, 11 May 1923, 3; and 22 May 1923, 14.

charges of liberalism at Brandon College, rallied to his defense.[114] One year later, 1924, when Price returned again, some of the same ministers and churches endorsed him again.[115]

Only when Price began stressing "speaking in tongues" as the evidence of the baptism of the Holy Spirit in the 1924 campaign did he lose the support of most of the fundamentalist leadership. However, hundreds of fundamentalist Baptist members continued their support for his view and made their way into one of the new Pentecostal congregations that sprang up in Vancouver in the immediate aftermath of Price's 1924 campaign. By late 1925 several thousand people had left existing Protestant churches in Vancouver and formed eight new Pentecostal congregations, in addition to swelling the membership of the one congregation and one downtown mission previously in existence.[116] After that, relations between fundamentalist Baptists and Pentecostals became more characteristic of those reported elsewhere in North America, and a strong anti-Pentecostal note began sounding from major fundamentalist Baptist pulpits.[117]

It was too late for such fundamentalists to repair the "damage," however. A strong and vibrant Pentecostal movement had become well established in Vancouver by 1927. From that base the movement, particularly the Pentecostal Assemblies of Canada, spread rapidly into every region of the province. The number of congregations affiliated with the Pentecostal Assemblies alone grew from nine in 1928 to sixty-six in 1941. Drawing upon a pool of young workers converted in the Price meetings, some supported partially by Vancouver churches, it was the first explicitly evangelical group to establish a province-wide network of churches.[118] It is doubtful that such an ac-

114. "Resolution regarding meetings held by Dr. Charles S. Price in Vancouver, B.C., from 6 May to 21 May, inclusive; adopted at a regular meeting of the Baptist Ministerial Association of Greater Vancouver, held on 10 June 1923" (reprinted in Price, *The Great Physician* [Oakland, Calif., 1923], 79–80).

115. For example, Ruth Morton Baptist Church, Minutes of Deacon's Board, 24 March 1924.

116. Donald Klan, "Pentecostal Assemblies of Canada Church Growth in British Columbia from Origins until 1953" (M.C.S. thesis, Regent College, Vancouver, 1979), 69–161, offers a thorough description of these developments.

117. This whole episode is explored in much greater depth in Burkinshaw, "Pentecostalism and Fundamentalism in British Columbia, 1921–1927" *Fides et Historia* 24 (Winter/Spring, 1992): 68–80.

118. Klan, "Pentecostal Assemblies of Canada," 154–84.

complishment would have been possible without the large number of British-oriented fundamentalists who had been drawn to Pentecostalism's new apologetic against modernism in 1923 and 1924.

Conclusion

Like their American counterparts, conservative evangelicals in British Columbia were concerned with the changes a more liberal outlook was bringing to the major Protestant denominations. However, their responses differed in certain important respects from those in the United States. As a minority in a newly settled region, they did not respond as early as did American evangelicals, who had been used to exerting considerable influence in their society. The very recent British origins of many contributed to that easier acceptance of minority status and also contributed to differences in tone and stance.

The mainline conservatives, the largest group and the one most involved in building a conservative institutional network, differed the most. Inclusiveness on doctrinal issues, within certain parameters, and efforts and institutions focusing on evangelism, missions, and personal holiness were more characteristic of them than were militancy, separatism, and dispensationalism. Most of these differences can be explained by the strong British influences—whether resulting from direct immigration or mediated via Toronto—on the mainline conservatives in Vancouver. They were used to working as a fairly respectable minority within a larger doctrinal and ecclesiastical context and thus did not react with the same fervor motivated by the great sense of loss of cultural dominance experienced by American evangelicals. The prevalence of Keswick teaching among British evangelicals resulted in somewhat less concern for doctrinal precision than for personal piety and service.[119] The emphasis among British Columbia mainline conservatives on students, whether in the VBTS or the IVCF, and on children's evangelism seems to follow the British evangelical pattern of focusing on training a future generation rather than decrying losses in the present. Finally, the central and

---

119. Bebbington, *Evangelicalism in Modern Britain*, 179.

moderating role played by Walter Ellis cannot be downplayed. His influence was much like that of moderate conservative leaders in Britain who, according to Bebbington, held the initiative among conservatives, rather than the fundamentalists.[120]

The separatist Baptists were much more like American fundamentalists in their militant insistence on separation from doctrinal error.
However, under British influences and that of T. T. Shields, they were
much less insistent on dispensationalism than were American fundamentalist Baptists. Pentecostal growth in the province was due more
to the desire of ultrafundamentalists for a dynamic new apologetic
against liberalism than it was to the holiness movement, which was
almost nonexistent in British Columbia.

Of course, these differences were not sufficient to render British
Columbia's evangelicals totally unrecognizable to American conservatives nor to preclude cooperation between the two groups. The differences are significant enough, however, to highlight once again the
need for caution against generalizing from what is known of the
American evangelical experience to that in other English-speaking
areas of the world, even in nearby British Columbia.

120. Ibid., 221–23.

13

Knowing No Borders

Canadian Contributions
to American Fundamentalism

David R. Elliott

In his seminal work *Continental Divide*, American sociologist Seymour Lipset has stated that Canadians have "been less prone to both fundamentalism and evangelicalism," largely because of the strong church-state relationship and institutionalism that has existed in Canada.[1] Where fundamentalist sects have appeared in Canada, they have often been seen as American imports.[2] Canadian sociologist Harry H. Hiller has noted that while Canada has produced some sectarian leaders who established international offices in the United States, their Canadian operations have had a "branch-plant" mentality, taking their direction from American headquarters.[3] While that

1. Seymour Martin Lipset, *Continental Divide: The Values and Institutions of the United States and Canada* (New York, 1990), 16.
2. Reginald W. Bibby, *Fragmented Gods: The Poverty and Potential of Religion in Canada* (Toronto, 1987), 218–19.
3. Harry H. Hiller, "Continentalism and the Third Force in Religion," *Canadian Journal of Sociology* 3, no. 2 (1978): 189.

may now be true, this was not the case between 1870 and 1950, when Canadian fundamentalists had an important role in the shaping of American fundamentalism.

Canadian fundamentalists contributed prominently to the prophetic conferences held at Niagara-on-the-Lake between 1875 and 1900,[4] to *The Fundamentals*, to the World's Christian Fundamentals Association, to the Baptist Bible Union, and to other fundamentalist institutions, magazines, and networks. In this chapter special attention will be given to the careers of A. B. Simpson, W. H. Griffith Thomas, P. W. Philpott, Aimee Semple McPherson, T. T. Shields, Oswald J. Smith, and Perry F. Rockwood, whose fundamentalist ministries recognized no international borders.[5]

A. B. Simpson

Albert Benjamin Simpson (1843–1919) was a mystic who frequently suffered from severe bouts of emotional depression, psychosis, and psychosomatic illness. Out of those experiences, some would say, he created a distinctive theology that shaped his own denomination, the Christian and Missionary Alliance, and influenced many aspects of twentieth-century fundamentalism and evangelicalism, including sectarianism, mystical spirituality, Pentecostalism, foreign missions emphasis, and the Bible school movement.[6]

4. See Larry Dean Pettegrew, "The Historical and Theological Contributions of the Niagara Bible Conference to American Fundamentalism" (Th.D. diss., Dallas Theological Seminary, 1976); and Walter Unger, "'Earnestly Contending for the Faith': The Role of the Niagara Bible Conference in the Emergence of American Fundamentalism, 1875–1900" (Ph.D. diss., Simon Fraser University, 1981).

5. This chapter is a summary of the author's Ph.D. dissertation, "Studies of Eight Canadian Fundamentalists" (University of British Columbia, Vancouver, 1989), which is currently being revised and expanded for publication.

6. The first biography of Simpson was A. E. Thompson's *A. B. Simpson: His Life and Work* (Harrisburg, Penn., 1920), which utilized an autobiographical manuscript written by Simpson and took the style of a hagiography. More critical was A. W. Tozer's *Wingspread: Albert B. Simpson: A Study in Spiritual Altitude* (Harrisburg, Penn., 1943). Tozer had access to Simpson's diary but suppressed important information on Simpson's relationship to Pentecostalism. The centenary of the Christian and Missionary Alliance generated several other studies. See Robert L. Niklaus, John S. Sawin, and Samuel J. Stoesz, *Jesus for All: God at Work in the Christian and Missionary Alliance over One Hundred Years* (Camp Hill, Penn., 1986); and a festschrift edited by David F. Hartzfeld and Charles Nienkirchen, *The Birth of a Vision* (Regina, 1986). These works are of varied historical worth; some of the articles in Hartzfeld and Nienkirchen are of critical value.

As a youth, Simpson experienced a traumatic crisis that caused him to see Christ as his personal savior. This became the first plank in his theology. He went on to be ordained in the Free Presbyterian Church in Hamilton, Ontario. From there Simpson received a call to Louisville, Kentucky, in 1873. Shortly after arriving there, Simpson underwent another emotional crisis. He longed for a deeper spiritual life and sought sanctification, the mystical experience of being made holy. In his search he was highly influenced by a book by W. E. Boardman, one of the founders of the Keswick movement,[7] and another book given to him by a friend. He described the latter book as an "old medieval message."[8] Subsequent research has shown it to have been a collection of writings by the seventeenth-century quietists such as Madam Guyon, Archbishop Fénelon, and Miguel de Molinos, edited by two Quakers.[9] According to Simpson, the central theme of the book was "that God was waiting in the depths of my being to talk to me if I would only get still enough to hear His voice."[10]

From those books and his experiences Simpson came to believe that sanctification was a gift of God, not self-perfectionism. It came about by a consecration or a deliberate separation from sin, "death to self," and a dedication to God.[11] Christ, not the person, became the sanctifier because Christ was now actually living within the body of the Christian.[12] Thus was formed the second plank of Simpson's fourfold gospel: Christ the Sanctifier.

Armed with this new understanding, Simpson was instrumental in arranging a revival campaign conducted in 1875 by D. L. Moody's associates Major Daniel Whittle and the singer/songwriter Philip Bliss. During the revival Simpson added the third plank to his distinctive theology. He became a convinced premillennialist, following the historicist interpretations of H. Grattan Guinness and A. J. Gordon, who viewed the papacy as the Antichrist and Islam as the False Prophet.

7. Niklaus, Sawin, and Stoesz, *Jesus for All*, 7, 277.

8. A. B Simpson, *The Holy Spirit; or, Power from On High* (Harrisburg, Penn., 1895), 1.160–62.

9. See Dwayne Ratzlaff, "An Old Medieval Message: A Turning Point in the Life of A. B. Simpson," in *The Birth of a Vision*, ed. David F. Hartzfeld and Charles Nienkirchen (Regina, 1986), 165–72. The book was possibly entitled: *Spiritual Progress*. See Hannah Whitall Smith, *The Unselfishness of God and How I Discovered It* (New York, 1903), 232.

10. Simpson, *Holy Spirit*, 1:161.

11. A. B. Simpson, *The Four-Fold Gospel* (Harrisburg, Penn., 1887), 27–46.

12. Thompson, *Simpson*, 66–71.

Like Guinness, Simpson also attempted to set dates for the return of Christ, which he felt was imminent. Simpson mixed in some aspects of dispensationalism, such as the pretribulation rapture, but then he added another twist. He taught a partial rapture based on the parable of the ten virgins (Matt. 25:1–13). Only those Christians who had experienced the baptism of the Holy Spirit (another term he used for sanctification) would be spirited out of the world. The rest of the Christian community would have to experience the tribulation, which he did not restrict to seven years.[13]

Simpson's new theology and his revivalistic methods caused conflict between himself and his Presbyterian elders. It apparently resulted in the presbytery demanding his resignation in November 1879.[14] Simpson left Kentucky for New York City, where he accepted the pulpit of Thirteenth Street Presbyterian Church.

In New York City disputes soon occurred when Simpson tried to impose his own vision of holiness and evangelism upon the congregation. Under considerable stress, he suffered another complete physical and nervous breakdown. Again he feared he was on the verge of death.[15]

In order to get help Simpson tried a number of quack cures but only became worse.[16] In August 1881, while visiting a vacation spot at Old Orchard, Maine, Simpson attended faith healing meetings being conducted by Dr. Charles Cullis. Simpson came to believe that healing was part of the atonement of Christ. Christ died not only for one's sin, but also for one's various sicknesses.

After praying, Simpson claimed he was miraculously healed of heart disease. To prove his healing to himself, he went out and climbed a nearby mountain.[17] Thus, divine healing became the fourth plank in his distinctive theology. His fourfold gospel was Jesus as Savior, Sanctifier, Healer, and Coming King.[18]

---

13. Simpson, *Holy Spirit*, 2:29–36. For a further discussion of Simpson's eschatology, see Franklin Arthur Pyles, "The Missionary Eschatology of A. B. Simpson," in *The Birth of a Vision*, ed. David F. Hartzfeld and Charles Nienkirchen (Regina, 1986), 29–47.

14. See *Alliance Witness*, 4 March 1987, 30.

15. Thompson, *Simpson*, 74.

16. Niklaus, Sawin, and Stoesz, *Jesus for All*, 39.

17. A. B. Simpson, *The Gospel of Healing* (Harrisburg, Penn., 1915), 161–69.

18. Simpson, *Four-Fold Gospel*, 47–67. For Simpson's belief that healing was connected to the atonement, see his *How to Receive Divine Healing* (Harrisburg, Penn., ca. 1885), 2–3.

When Simpson returned to New York City, divine healing became the new emphasis in his preaching. Next he came to reject infant baptism, and in October 1881 he was himself immersed by a Baptist minister.[19] Because he now refused to perform any more infant baptisms and because of his views on divine healing, the presbytery would not allow him to conduct any more worship and Communion services.[20] Simpson resigned from the church in November 1881 and from the Presbyterian denomination altogether.

That same month he established an independent ministry called the Gospel Tabernacle, where he could present his fourfold gospel to all classes of society. He started with seven people, and the seven soon became seventy and more.

Simpson gained a reputation as a faith healer, although he preferred the term "divine healing," since he believed that the healing did not depend upon the faith of the seeker but rather that it was a product of sanctification. He wrote, "We are healed by the life of Christ in our body. It is a tender union with Him; nearer than the bond of connubial oneness; so near that the very life of His veins is transfused into ours. That is divine healing."[21]

Simpson's Gospel Tabernacle stressed the importance of foreign missions. This was related to Simpson's eschatology because he believed that the return of Christ would be hastened if the world was evangelized.[22] Simpson's rejection of the established denominations and their efforts was further demonstrated in 1882, when he started another illustrated foreign missions magazine to promote the independent "faith" missions. In 1883 he organized the Missionary Union for the Evangelization of the World, and several months later he opened the Missionary Training College in New York City to train missionaries for home and foreign missions. It was modeled after similar institutions that H. Grattan Guinness had established in London and a short-lived one that Dr. Cullis had started in Boston several years earlier.[23] Simpson's college, which was later moved to Nyack,

---

19. Thompson, *Simpson*, 85–86; Niklaus, Sawin, and Stoesz, *Jesus for All*, 43–44.
20. Niklaus, Sawin, and Stoesz, *Jesus for All*, 45.
21. Simpson, *Four-Fold Gospel*, 61.
22. Ibid., 92–93; Thompson, *Simpson*, 111.
23. See W. H. Daniels, ed., *Dr. Cullis and His Work: Twenty Years of Blessing in Answer to Prayer* (Boston, 1885), 359.

New York, became the model for many of the Bible colleges and Bible institutes that soon dotted the landscape of North America.

As Simpson's fame spread, he began to address holiness and healing conferences in Britain, Canada, and across the eastern and midwestern United States. By 1886 he was holding his own conferences at Old Orchard, Maine. Those who spoke at his meetings represented the core of the Keswick faith mission and premillennial leadership, many of whom shaped twentieth-century evangelicalism and fundamentalism: Andrew Murray, H. Grattan Guinness, F. B. Meyer, J. Hudson Taylor, A. J. Gordon, A. T. Pierson, R. A. Torrey, George F. Pentecost, D. L. Moody, Major Whittle, James A. Brookes, W. E. Blackstone, C. I. Scofield, Nathaniel West, James M. Gray, Charles A. Blanchard, J. Wilbur Chapman, A. C. Dixon, William Bell Riley, Charles G. Trumbull, Phoebe Palmer, and Frances E. Willard.[24]

After 1887 Simpson organized branches of his Christian Alliance across the United States and Canada. The first organizational meeting in Canada was held in Hamilton in 1889, but Toronto soon became the headquarters. William H. Howland, the first president of the Alliance in Canada, was a noted social and civic reformer who served two terms as mayor of Toronto (1886–88).[25] Howland became a vice-president of Simpson's international organization in New York City.

Simpson had a marked effect on the development of the Pentecostal movement. Charles F. Parham, who helped to shape the Pentecostal movement at Topeka, Kansas, had been influenced by Simpson.[26] Quite a number of Alliance members were favorable to the Pentecostal practice of "speaking in tongues." In his 1907 diary entries Simpson himself struggled with the issue. While in Hamilton celebrating the anniversary of his ordination there forty-two years before, he made a curious entry in his diary: "Asked God to accept my offering and ordain me anew. The Spirit came with a baptism of holy laughter for an hour or more and I am waiting for all He has yet to give and

24. Thompson, *Simpson*, 110.

25. Howland's career has been treated in Desmond Morton, *Mayor Howland, the Citizen's Candidate* (Toronto, 1973); and Ron Sawatsky, "William Holmes Howland," in *Dictionary of Canadian Biography*, vol. 12 (Toronto, 1990), 453–55.

26. Charles Nienkirchen, "A. B. Simpson: Forerunner and Critic of the Pentecostal Movement," in *The Birth of a Vision*, ed. David F. Hartzfeld and Charles Nienkirchen (Regina, 1986), 126.

manifest."[27] Five years later Simpson was still seeking to speak in tongues, but it had not happened.

Because Simpson was open to the Pentecostals' definition of speaking in tongues, it quickly spread throughout his movement. However, he was opposed to the attitude within Pentecostalism that claimed speaking in tongues as a prerequisite for all Spirit-filled Christians.[28] As a result, a number of ministers and congregations of the alliance withdrew and joined the Assemblies of God or other Pentecostal groups.[29]

Although Simpson died before the major battles of the modernist-fundamentalist controversy occurred, by 1911 he was showing the militancy and separatism that later characterized fundamentalism. In his book *The Old Faith and the New Gospels* (1911), he spoke out strongly against the theory of evolution,[30] social Darwinism, biblical criticism, and theological liberalism. He denounced the existing schools, colleges, and seminaries and suggested the creation of new educational institutions. Simpson also attacked modernism and religious syncretism among the denominational foreign missionaries and called for the diversion of funds to the independent missionary societies.

Premillennial pessimism came to dominate Simpson's thought, and he moved away from his earlier interest in Christian social work. Of the evangelical social workers studied by Norris Magnuson, Simpson became the most reactionary and exemplified the "great reversal" in evangelical social attitudes.[31] Simpson attacked socialism and linked it with modernist theology.[32]

When A. B. Simpson died in 1919, he left behind him a legacy of 101 published books, consisting of biographies and collections of ser-

27. Simpson's diary, 12 September 1907; copy in Archives of the Canadian Theological Seminary, Regina.

28. Lindsay Reynolds, *Footprints: The Beginnings of the Christian and Missionary Alliance in Canada* (Beaverlodge, Alta.: 1981), 567, citing the *Christian and Missionary Alliance*, April 1910, 78.

29. Nienkirchen, "A. B. Simpson," 126–30.

30. Simpson, *The Old Faith and the New Gospels* (New York, 1911), 12–14. Simpson accepted Darwin's view of natural selection as being operative in nature but maintained the special creation of humans.

31. Norris Magnuson, *Salvation in the Slums: Evangelical Social Work, 1865–1920* (Metuchen, N.J., 1977).

32. Simpson, *Old Faith and New Gospels*, 63–65, 119–32.

mons, commentaries, and hymnbooks, which the Christian and Missionary Alliance continues to reprint.[33] He composed about 181 hymns of varied quality which played a great role in the worship services of the new denomination. Most of their themes dealt with his views on sanctification, foreign missions, and the second coming.[34]

While Simpson created his own distinctive theology, he was not doctrinaire about it within his international organizations. Quite a bit of latitude on eschatology, divine healing, and speaking in tongues was allowed. While his theological distinctives on those matters would have alienated him from some proto-fundamentalists, his views did have a great impact upon Pentecostalism, the faith missions movement, and a number of Canadian and American fundamentalists such as Smith, Philpott, Aimee Semple McPherson, and L. E. Maxwell.[35]

W. H. Griffith Thomas

Anglicans have not generally been known for their role in North American fundamentalism, but William Henry Griffith Thomas (1861–1924) definitely played a leading role. Thomas was born in England and was trained as an Anglican priest. Between 1910 and 1919 he was a professor of Old Testament and Systematic Theology at the low-Anglican Wycliffe College in Toronto.

Thomas was one of a number of Canadian fundamentalists and conservative evangelicals who contributed to *The Fundamentals*. In the first part of his article on Old Testament criticism, Thomas argued for the legitimacy of higher criticism. But he would limit biblical criticism by claiming that Jesus, through the incarnation, experienced no limitation of knowledge and had complete omniscience, and therefore all the passing statements Jesus made on Hebrew history and

33. See John Savin, "Publications of Albert B. Simpson," in *The Birth of a Vision*, ed. David F. Hartzfeld and Charles Nienkirchen (Regina, 1986), 279–303.

34. Eugene Rivard, "Rediscovering the Music of A. B. Simpson," in *The Birth of a Vision*, ed. David F. Hartzfeld and Charles Nienkirchen (Regina, 1986), 75–105.

35. L. E. Maxwell and Prairie Bible Institute at Three Hills, Alberta, have not been included in this chapter because Maxwell was born and trained in Kansas.

Scripture had to be completely authoritative.[36] Thomas wrote many important theological works on Anglican liturgy,[37] pastoral theology, homiletics,[38] and dogmatics,[39] as well as devotional commentaries and popular theology. The latter works reflect his increasing dispensationalism and emphasis on Keswick holiness, which came to shape much of fundamentalist thought.[40] He frequently contributed to the *Sunday School Times, Moody Monthly,* and *Bibliotheca Sacra.*[41]

In 1919 Thomas was forced to resign from Wycliffe College. There had been personality clashes as well as increasing accusations that he was neglecting his teaching duties and denominational responsibilities by teaching at Toronto Bible College, by going on interdenominational speaking tours, and by writing extensively for non-Anglican publications. He was also unhappy with his salary and his living arrangements.[42] His relationship with Wycliffe College was so poisoned that his name was never mentioned in the 1927 official history of the college.[43]

In May of 1919 Thomas was the chairman of the resolutions committee of the World Conference on Christian Fundamentals in Philadelphia, which attracted about six thousand delegates. The published proceedings contained a strident condemnation of "the Great Apostasy . . . spreading like a plague throughout Christendom."[44]

36. W. H. Griffith Thomas, "Old Testament Criticism and New Testament Christianity," in A. C. Dixon et al., *The Fundamentals* (Chicago, 1910–15), 8:5–26. Thomas's deductive Christology was also exemplified in his *Christianity Is Christ* (London, 1909).

37. W. H. Griffith Thomas, *"A Sacrament of our Redemption": An Enquiry into the Meaning of the Lord's Supper in the New Testament and the Church of England* (London, 1903).

38. W. H. Griffith Thomas, *The Work of the Ministry* (London, ca. 1910).

39. Three of Thomas's books on dogmatics are *The Holy Spirit of God* (London, 1913), *The Catholic Faith: A Manual of Instruction for Members of the Church of England* (London, 1920), and *The Principles of Theology: An Introduction of the Thirty-Nine Articles* (London, 1930).

40. For his views on holiness, see W. H. Griffith Thomas, *Grace and Power: Some Aspects of the Spiritual Life* (London, 1916), and *The Christian Life and How to Live It* (Chicago, 1919).

41. For an obituary of Thomas, see Dyson Hague, "Dr. W. H. Griffith Thomas," *Moody Monthly* (August 1924): 596–97. For other aspects of Thomas's career, see E. W. Kennedy, "W. H. Griffith Thomas," in *Dictionary of Christianity in America*, ed. Daniel G. Reid (Downers Grove, Ill., 1990), 1172.

42. See the Minutes of Wycliffe College Council, Wycliffe College Archives, Toronto, for the complaints against Thomas and the tabled correspondence between Thomas and the council.

43. *The Jubilee Volume of Wycliffe College, 1877–1927* (Toronto, 1927).

44. *God Hath Spoken: Twenty-five Addresses at the World Conference on Christian Fundamentals, May 25–June 1, 1919* (Philadelphia, 1919), 7.

Thomas's resolutions report reflected a garrison mentality, condemning the seminaries and recent decisions of the YMCA and placing faith in the Bible school movement as a way of fighting modernism.[45]

Thomas moved on to Moody Bible Institute. While he was there, he supported T. T. Shields in his campaign against the publication *Canadian Baptist* and against McMaster University and its "modernism."[46] In 1920 Thomas and C. G. Trumbull, the editor of the *Sunday School Times*, toured mission stations in the Orient. Thomas found what he felt was too much emphasis on education and too little on evangelism. He also complained that much of the education was directed along modernistic lines and was religiously syncretistic. In response he helped organize the Bible Union of China, which sought to drive out modernism.[47] When the American liberal Baptist preacher Harry Emerson Fosdick observed the actions of the fundamentalists in China, he was led to preach his famous sermon, "Shall the Fundamentalists Win?"[48] That sermon launched the modernist-fundamentalist war.

Thomas continued his fight against modernism and negative higher criticism.[49] He died in 1924, just as he was about to become one of the founding faculty members of Dallas Theological Seminary along with a fellow Canadian, the Reverend A. B. Winchester of Knox Presbyterian Church in Toronto.

P. W. Philpott

Another Canadian preacher, Peter Wiley Philpott (1865–1957), a former blacksmith, forged many of the links in the network of funda-

45. Ibid., 12–13, 16–17.
46. W. H. Griffith Thomas to T. T. Shields, 12 November 1919, Shields Papers, Jarvis St. Baptist Church, Toronto.
47. W. H. Griffith Thomas, "The Fundamentals in China," *Moody Monthly* (May 1921): 389–91, and "Modernism in China," *Princeton Theological Review* 19 (October 1921): 630–71. For Thomas's role in the Bible Union, see William R. Hutchison, *Errand to the World: American Protestant Thought and Foreign Missions* (Chicago, 1987), 128–45.
48. Harry Emerson Fosdick, "Shall the Fundamentalists Win?" 21 May 1922, copy in T. T. Shields Papers. See also Fosdick, *The Living of These Days* (New York, 1956), 135–36, 144–46.
49. W. H. Griffith Thomas, "Dr. Jowett and Criticism," *Moody Monthly* (May 1923): 419–21; "A Higher Critic Backs Water," ibid. (August 1923): 561–62; "What D. L. Moody Believed and Taught, and How He Taught It," ibid (November 1923): 101–6.

mentalism. His ministry, which covered more than seven decades, started with the Salvation Army in Ontario and extended throughout North America while he held pastorates in fundamentalist churches in Hamilton, Chicago, Los Angeles, and Toronto. He was also in heavy demand as a revival and conference speaker across the continent.[50]

After leaving the Salvation Army in 1892, Philpott was ordained by Simpson's Christian Missionary Alliance. After serving that new denomination in Canada, he organized an independent gospel mission in Hamilton that later became the headquarters for his new denomination, the Associated Gospel Churches.

As the modernist-fundamentalist controversy was developing, Philpott took the fundamentalist position. In 1919 he was one of the speakers at the World Conference of Christian Fundamentals in Philadelphia. In his presentation he suggested that higher critics of the Bible should be treated like little boys who were trying to throw mud at the moon. They should be ignored.[51] Stressing the importance of conversionism and Keswick-style holiness, he was suspicious of any theology that placed too much stress on human reason.[52]

Philpott's influence was widened in 1922 when he became minister of Moody Tabernacle in Chicago, which was a center for fundamentalism and Keswick holiness. When Philpott took over, the building was in much disrepair and still had sawdust-covered dirt floors. Feeling that the building was a disgrace to Moody's name, Philpott launched a building scheme to create a memorial to Moody. With a massive fund-raising campaign and an expenditure of a million dollars, the congregation constructed a huge brick Romanesque-style building modeled after the Hagia Sophia and seating over four thousand people.[53] Moody Memorial Church was opened in November 1925, and for the next months the building was the scene of evangelistic campaigns conducted by R. A. Torrey and Billy Sunday.[54]

---

50. This study has made use of the Philpott Papers held by Philpott's granddaughter, Lynn Butler, in St. Catharines, Ontario. The papers include diaries, correspondence, press clippings, scrapbooks, other memorabilia, and two family histories written by Philpott's children.

51. P. W. Philpott, "The Witness of Human Experience to the Inspiration of the Word," in *God Hath Spoken* (Philadelphia, 1919), 109.

52. Ibid., 113–14.

53. P. W. Philpott, "'What Mean These Stones?' A Memorial Sermon," reproduced in Robert G. Flood, *The Story of Moody Church: A Light in the City* (Chicago, 1985), 71–76.

54. Flood, *Story of Moody Church*, 25.

Philpott was an active member of the World's Christian Fundamentals Association. In 1925 he, along with Shields, Riley, J. Frank Norris, and others, signed a manifesto that read:

The time has come when Fundamentalists and Modernists should no longer remain in the same fold, for how can two walk together except they be agreed? Therefore we call upon all Fundamentalists of all denominations to possess their souls with holy boldness and challenge every false teacher, whether he be professor in a denominational school or state school; whether he be editor of a religious publication or the secretary of a denominational board; and whether he be pastor in a pulpit in the homeland or a missionary on the foreign field.[55]

Philpott held a high place of honor within fundamentalism, and in recognition of his construction of Moody Memorial Church, he was awarded an honorary D.D. by nearby Wheaton College in 1925 and made a board member of that institution.[56] In 1929 Philpott announced his resignation from Moody Memorial Church. He left primarily for health reasons. Before he left Moody Church, Philpott was able to hand-pick his successor, Harry A. Ironside (1876–1951), another self-taught evangelist who had been born in Canada and whose religious background had been in the Salvation Army and the Plymouth Brethren.

From Chicago Philpott went to Los Angeles, where he became minister of the Church of the Open Door, which was housed in the Bible Institute of Los Angeles.[57] These organizations had recently purged from their staff Dr. John M. MacInnis and G. Campbell Morgan, who were not hard-line fundamentalists.[58]

In spite of his connections with most of the militant fundamentalists, Philpott's preaching tended to be more conciliatory. His sermons were simple evangelistic messages with an emphasis upon holy living.

At the end of 1931 Philpott resigned from the Church of the Open Door because of tensions there, but he seems to have picked as his

55. *Gospel Witness*, 18 June 1925.
56. Flood, *Story of Moody Church*, 25.
57. *Los Angeles Times*, 5 October 1929.
58. *Moody Monthly* (June 1929).

successor Louis T. Talbot, who had been the minister at Philpott Tabernacle in Hamilton, Ontario, since 1929.[59]

Philpott was by this time sixty-seven years of age. He went into semiretirement but remained active in evangelistic work. He returned to Canada but continued to travel to the United States to speak at conferences for Moody Bible Institute. During the winter of 1939 and 1940 he was again in Los Angeles at the Church of the Open Door.[60] From 1945 to 1947 the Philpotts spent much of their time on the West Coast, while he preached in Vancouver, Seattle, and Los Angeles.

Philpott, with his fatherly demeanor, personal integrity, and conciliatory spirit, no doubt influenced by the Keswick movement, was able to work with a great diversity of fundamentalists, including Charles Templeton, Simpson, Shields, Ironside, Maxwell, Smith, and Talbot. Through his dealings with so many diverse characters, Philpott helped extend the holiness and fundamentalist network across North America with its Bible schools, missionary conferences, and evangelistic campaigns.

Aimee Semple McPherson

Many of the characteristics of American fundamentalism after 1925—a pronounced anti-intellectualism, apocalypticism, sectarianism, Pentecostalism, skillful use of radio, religious drama, and advertising, the building of religious empires around one's personality, and the resulting power struggles—found their expression in the life and career of Aimee Semple McPherson, the founder of the International Church of the Foursquare Gospel. In many ways she became a model for other religious celebrities of the period. Her dramatic publicity stunts, her sexual scandals, and her legal battles made her one of the most famous women in North America, rivaling even the Hollywood starlets.

Aimee Kennedy was born near Ingersoll, Ontario, in 1890, into a dysfunctional family; she was torn between her mother's member-

59. Ibid. (December 1931).

60. P. W. Philpott to Stuart Philpott, 5 December 1939; and Jessie Philpott to Stuart Philpott, 3 February 1940.

ship in the Salvation Army and her father's Methodism. In 1907 she married Robert Semple, a Pentecostal evangelist, who took her to China in 1910, where they began missionary work. He died there soon afterward from malaria, and Aimee returned to North America destitute and with a small baby.

While conducting religious services in Chicago, she married Harold McPherson, but the marriage did not work out. Again pregnant, she fluctuated between depression and her obsession to be an evangelist. After the birth of her son, she took her children and left her husband, returning to Canada, where she began revival meetings in Mount Forest, Ontario.

When Harold McPherson located his wife at Mount Forest, he found her a transformed personality; all traces of depression had vanished. Aimee claimed that he was converted under her ministry there. Harold joined her revival campaign, and during the next two years Aimee and Harold held meetings in American cities along the Atlantic seaboard, with Harold being responsible for raising the big-top tent she used in her meetings. In Florida Harold became dissatisfied with the itinerant life. Aimee deserted him again, this time for good.

Aimee was soon joined by her mother, who became her assistant. Together with the two children and a secretary, they traveled by car through the southern states conducting meetings among white and black congregations. As they traveled westward, Aimee may have been the first woman to drive a car across the United States. By 1919 they had reached Los Angeles.

Wanting to have a permanent home for herself and the children, Aimee chose Los Angeles as her base of operations. Leaving her mother in charge of the children, she set off on a revival and faith-healing campaign through the northern states and Canada. The Winnipeg press billed Aimee as "the female Billy Sunday."[61] She made news when she visited Winnipeg's nightclubs and the famous brothels on Annabella Street, where she prayed with the inhabitants.[62] In Montreal she had large crowds. After her crusades in Canada, Aimee concentrated her attention on the southwestern states, holding meetings in Denver, Dallas, San Jose, Oakland, and San Diego.

61. *Winnipeg Free Press*, 31 January 1920.
62. *Winnipeg Tribune*, 23 February 1920.

During her crusades around the United States and Canada, Aimee had been talking about her plans to build a great religious edifice in Los Angeles. In January of 1923 Aimee opened Angelus Temple, situated on Glendale Boulevard between Echo Lake and Sunset Boulevard. She had personally designed and supervised the construction of the 5,300-seat, theater-style, domed auditorium, which cost about one million dollars.[63] There she preached her foursquare gospel, which was quite similar to Simpson's fourfold gospel and was no doubt influenced by it.

Fundamentalists such as William Jennings Bryan and L. W. Munhall, a Methodist Episcopal minister who was the vice-president of the International Fundamentalist Association, were happy to work with Aimee and appear on her platform.[64] Oswald J. Smith from the Alliance Tabernacle in Toronto also beat a path to her door and was favorably impressed.[65]

Charles S. Price, a modernist Congregationalist minister from California, was converted in her meetings and soon took the faith-healing message through Canada, where he had once lived.[66] Another minister who was influenced by both Price and McPherson was Henry B. Taylor, who was serving a Methodist church in Vancouver, British Columbia. He soon opened Pyramid Temple there, which combined the foursquare gospel and British-Israelism.[67]

Aimee regarded herself as a Canadian and made repeated trips to her native country. While conducting a revival in Calgary in 1935, she spoke favorably of William Aberhart's Social Credit movement and believed that the church should be involved in political life.[68]

Theologically Aimee considered herself a fundamentalist. In her *Bridal Call* magazine she thundered in Billy Sundayish terms against modernistic seminaries and formal church services. She advertised

63. Aimee Semple McPherson, *This Is That* (Los Angeles, 1923), 528–48.
64. *Bridal Call*, November 1924. See also L. W. Munhall to T. T. Shields, 29 August 1925, Shields Papers.
65. *Bridal Call*, May 1925.
66. Charles S. Price, *And Signs Followed: The Story of Charles S. Price*, rev. ed. (Plainfield, N.J., 1972). See also McPherson, *This Is That*, 442–51.
67. Henry B. Taylor, *See What God Hath Wrought! Personal Experiences of Evangelist Henry B. Taylor and the Origin and Growth of the Work of the Pyramid Temple* (Vancouver, 1925).
68. *Alberta Social Credit Chronicle*, 15 November 1935.

herself as a fundamentalist in 1934, when she debated Charles Lee Smith, the president of the American Association for the Advancement of Atheism.[69]

Aimee Semple McPherson was the first fundamentalist to join evangelism and show business. She was a talented organizer and actress who outshone her silver screen contemporaries. Men were attracted by her sex appeal. Women followed her fashions and saw her as a liberated woman. Her platform presence was powerful, and she used the radio effectively. In 1931 she began experimenting with television.[70] In spite of her tragic personal life and endless scandals, thousands followed her. Many others remembered her more for her generous social service activities.

T. T. Shields

One of the most militant fundamentalists in North America between 1920 and 1955 was the Reverend T. T. Shields (1873–1955), the British-born minister of Jarvis Street Baptist Church in Toronto.[71] By the end of the First World War, Shields became known as a staunch fundamentalist. During the war he had been able to fulfill his childhood ambition of speaking in Spurgeon's Tabernacle in London. He filled the pulpit for several months there during the absence of the current minister, the American fundamentalist A. C. Dixon, who had edited *The Fundamentals*.[72]

Shields's alignment with the growing fundamentalist movement was strengthened in January 1920, when he hosted meetings in Toronto's Massey Hall that featured Dixon, William Bell Riley, and J. C. Massee, who were leaders in the American fundamentalist net-

69. Aimee Semple McPherson, ed., *There Is a God: Debate between Aimee Semple McPherson and Charles Lee Smith* (Los Angeles, [ca. 1934]).

70. *Bridal Call*, January 1932.

71. The definitive biography of Shields has yet to be written. A hagiographic study has been done by Leslie K. Tarr, *Shields of Canada* (Grand Rapids, 1967). The best theological study of Shields is Mark Parent, "The Christology of T. T. Shields: The Irony of Fundamentalism" (Ph.D. diss., McGill University, 1991). Shields's papers, housed at Jarvis Street Baptist Church, Toronto, contain a mine of information on fundamentalism because Shields corresponded with all of the major participants in the North American fundamentalist network.

72. *Gospel Witness*, 17 April 1930; for Dixon's career, see Brenda M. Meehan, "A. C. Dixon: An Early Fundamentalist," *Foundations* 10 (1967): 50–63.

work.[73] During the summer months of 1921 Shields had John Roach Straton, a prominent fundamentalist from New York City, hold revival services at Jarvis Street Baptist Church.

In 1922 Shields founded the *Gospel Witness*, a weekly magazine to further the cause of fundamentalism because the pages of the *Canadian Baptist* were becoming closed to him. The journal reproduced his sermons and important correspondence. Eventually it reached a weekly circulation of thirty thousand copies, which were distributed across North America and other parts of the world.

In May 1923 Shields's influence increased when he was elected as first president of the Baptist Bible Union of North America, a group of militant fundamentalist Baptists whose object was to purge modernism from all Baptist churches, colleges, seminaries, and missionary organizations.[74] In his presidential address given in Kansas City, Shields declared a holy war on modernism, which he believed to be a satanic conspiracy. Military language was sprinkled throughout his speech. "It is a war which has superhuman powers behind it; it is a war which has behind it all the resourcefulness of the Pit."[75]

As president of the Baptist Bible Union, Shields meddled in the affairs of the Southern and Northern Baptists. When the Southern Baptists held their convention, Shields organized a rump convention of fundamentalists several days before in the same city in order to plan strategy to oppose modernism within that denomination. His religious imperialism caused hard feelings even among some fundamentalists.[76] Shields reported the proceedings of both conferences in the pages of the *Gospel Witness* and often resorted to character assassination of not only the liberals but the moderates.

Shields used the same disruptive tactics against the Northern Baptist Convention and tried to have delegates from Park Avenue Baptist Church in New York City excluded from the convention. That church, which had recently hired Harry Emerson Fosdick, practiced open membership.[77] When the fundamentalists were not successful

73. *Toronto Globe*, 3 January 1920.

74. *Gospel Witness*, 21 June 1923.

75. T. T. Shields, "A Holy War," ibid.

76. J. C. Massee to T. T. Shields, 12 November 1923; and Shields to Massee, 29 November 1923, Shields Papers.

77. *Gospel Witness*, 28 May 1925.

in excluding the liberals, Shields denounced the Northern Baptist Convention as the "religious department of the Standard Oil Company" because John D. Rockefeller, Jr., had been a supporter of Fosdick and the liberal theological school at the University of Chicago.[78] Shields's influence in the United States was also extended when he supplied the pulpit of the Church of the Open Door in Los Angeles during July 1925.

Shields and the Baptist Bible Union next decided to boycott the missionary activities of the Southern, Northern, and Canadian Baptist conventions and organized their own missionary society, which would support only fundamentalist missionaries. In 1927, after Shields no longer had a direct hand in the affairs of McMaster University, which he failed to capture, he turned his attention southward. Des Moines University, a Baptist institution in Iowa, was in deep financial trouble, and Shields, on behalf of the Baptist Bible Union of North America, purchased it and tried to turn it into a bastion for fundamentalism.[79] Shields became president of the board of trustees and acting president of the university. Forced resignations were required of those faculty members who would not sign the creed of the Baptist Bible Union. According to Shields there would be "no teaching of evolution, no teaching of higher criticism of the Bible, and no one will be permitted to teach in any department whose teaching would deny the divine inspiration and infallibility of the Bible as the Word of God."[80] At the same time Shields was also involved in restructuring the Bible Institute of Los Angeles (Biola). Shields wanted to get rid of the entire board of directors and faculty, but his activities at Biola were soon cut short by problems back in Des Moines.[81]

Shields's association with Des Moines University lasted less than two years; it was forced to close because of a series of fiascoes.[82] Students became angry when Shields shut down their fraternities and

78. T. T. Shields, "Shall the Northern Baptists Convention Remain the Religious Department of the Standard Oil Co.?" *Gospel Witness*, 9 July 1925.

79. T. T. Shields, "The Baptist Bible Union University of Des Moines," *Gospel Witness*, 16 June 1927.

80. Ibid., 7.

81. T. T. Shields to Charles E. Fuller, 25 May 1929; Fuller to Shields, 24 June 1929; Shields to Fuller, 1 July 1929, Shields Papers.

82. See George S. May, "Des Moines University and Dr. T. T. Shields," *Iowa Journal of History* 54, no. 3 (1956): 193–232.

sororities, stopped their dances, and required daily chapel attendance. His pro-British anti-Americanism also angered the students; he had opposed their Independence Day celebrations. Some of the new faculty members, unhappy with Shields's dictatorial control, also resigned during the first year. He also canceled Sunday church services, which were held in the chapel on Sunday, and in its place created a Regular Baptist Church.[83] Moreover, he removed the university from the Iowa Baptist Convention.

For the first year Shields commuted from Toronto on a weekly basis until a president could be found. In 1928 Shields hired H. C. Wayman, who had been president of William Jewell College in Missouri. When Shields announced a complete reorganization of the university, which called for faculty cuts and the closing of the professional departments of pharmacy and engineering, Wayman objected.[84] Soon Wayman reported rumors that Shields, a married man, had been having an affair with Miss Edith Rebman, his representative on the campus and the secretary of the Baptist Bible Union.

William Bell Riley had seen enough himself of the relationship between Shields and Rebman that he believed the rumors. He suggested that Rebman be fired and that Shields should resign after the controversy had blown over.[85] A hasty meeting of some members of the executive of the Baptist Bible Union was called. Shields claimed that he and Miss Rebman had been cleared, but the organization and the wider fundamentalist network quickly disintegrated. Within days Riley resigned from the Baptist organization and also removed Shields from the board of the World's Christian Fundamentals Association, which Riley headed.[86]

Shields refused to resign from his position at the university; he pressed ahead and fired Wayman and the entire faculty. The students rioted, the administration building was wrecked, and Shields and his

83. *Gospel Witness*, 12 January 1928.

84. Ibid., 27 June 1929.

85. William Bell Riley to Dr. H. C. Wayman, 8 May and 10 May 1929, copies in Shields Papers. See also T. T. Shields to Riley, 4 April 1930, Shields Papers. In the letter to Shields, Riley states, "The basis of my conviction in the Des Moines matter is not at all that of hearsay, but what I myself saw and grieved and feared for some years." Riley to Shields, 10 April 1930, Shields Papers.

86. William Bell Riley to T. T. Shields, 13 May 1929; and William Bell Riley to Miss Violet Stoakley, 24 May 1929, Shields Papers.

party had to be taken into protective custody by the police.[87] That fall Des Moines University closed its doors.

Shields's place in the American fundamentalist movement was severely weakened by the Des Moines debacle. Shields became very bitter and lashed out at his former colleagues. Riley summed up Shields's character as follows: "The attitude you have maintained through your entire course in Canada and in the States [is], 'consent to my will, and you are all right; brook it and you are blasted, if it is within my power.'"[88]

Shields also now openly rejected the dispensational views of most of the American fundamentalists. Commenting on their use of the Scofield Reference Bible, he said, "I have found ... a great many Scoffieldits [sic] who seem to be more sure of the inspiration of Dr. Scoffield's [sic] notes than they are of the Book itself. I believe the whole principle of binding up notes of that sort with the Word of God is vicious."[89]

In 1930 Shields began radio broadcasting on CKGW, a powerful station near Toronto that could be heard across the continent. Through those broadcasts and his *Gospel Witness* he continued to influence the American fundamentalist movement. His denunciations of dispensationalism furthered the rise of amillennialism in some evangelical circles.[90]

In 1938 Carl McIntyre, a Presbyterian renegade from New Jersey, sought out Shields.[91] In 1948 they formed the International Council of Christian Churches to oppose the World Council of Churches. Just as Shields had organized rump conventions to disrupt the Baptist conventions, they did the same with the meetings of the World Council of Churches. They accused it of modernism and of being soft on Roman Catholicism and communism.

McIntyre was one of few fundamentalists with whom Shields fellowshipped. Shields's seminary granted McIntyre an honorary doctorate in 1950,[92] and McIntyre preached at Shields's funeral in 1955.

87. T. T. Shields, "Des Moines University Riots," *Gospel Witness*, 23 May 1929.
88. W. B. Riley to T. T. Shields, 10 April 1930, Shields Papers.
89. See the *Gospel Witness*, 15 May 1930.
90. T. T. Shields to Philip Mauro, 9 March 1932, Shields Papers.
91. Carl McIntyre to T. T. Shields, 16 June 1938, Shields Papers.
92. G. A. Adams, ed., *By Grace to His Glory* (Toronto, 1987), 119.

Shield's successor, H. C. Slade, had a continued influence on American fundamentalism by being a board member of Bob Jones University.[93]

Oswald J. Smith

Another Toronto fundamentalist was Oswald J. Smith (1889–1986), who gained an international reputation among fundamentalists as an evangelist, promoter of foreign missions, author, and hymn writer.[94] During his eight decades of active ministry Smith helped create what Marsden has called "the evangelical denomination," with its Keswick holiness and foreign missions emphasis.

On graduating from Toronto Bible College in 1912, Smith attended McCormick Theological Seminary in Chicago. Much of his time was spent at Moody Tabernacle, where Paul Rader was the minister. Smith also took part in Billy Sunday's campaign. He was impressed with Sunday's style and wrestled within himself whether to become an evangelist or to pursue his goal of becoming a foreign missionary.

After graduating, Smith returned to Canada and worked for a brief time with the Presbyterian Church in Canada. Then he was with the Plymouth Brethren, the Shantymen, and the Christian and Missionary Alliance. Smith found his position of alliance superintendent unfulfilling, and when he could not return to the Alliance Tabernacle in Toronto, he headed south. For about a month he occupied Paul Rader's pulpit in Chicago. From Chicago Smith traveled to Los Angeles, where he began an alliance church known as the Gospel Tabernacle in April 1927.[95]

Smith was an unashamed self-promoter. His newspaper advertisements in Los Angeles read:

Hear Rev. Oswald J. Smith, of Toronto, Author-Evangelist, the man who so successfully filled the pulpit for PAUL RADER in his great Chicago Tabernacle. Mr. Smith, who founded the Toronto Tabernacle, seating

93. Ibid., 33.
94. For some of the biographies of Oswald J. Smith, see J. Edwin Orr, *Always Abounding: An Intimate Sketch of Dr. Oswald J. Smith* (London, n.d.); Douglas Hall, *Not Made for Defeat: The Authorized Biography of Oswald J. Smith* (Grand Rapids, 1969); and Lois Neely, *Fire in His Bones: The Official Biography of Oswald J. Smith* (Wheaton, Ill., 1982).
95. *Los Angeles Times*, 9 April 1927.

2,300, has travelled extensively in Europe and America, in Evangelistic work. He has written nearly a dozen books, of which almost 100,000 copies have been issued. . . . The magnetism and masterly message of Oswald Smith will grip you. His addresses on Prophecy have stirred multiplied thousands. He will give a series of messages on the subject IS THE ANTICHRIST AT HAND?[96]

As much as Smith tried, he could not make the headway he wanted in Los Angeles and came to realize that his move to California had been a mistake; he longed for Toronto. On his way back to Toronto, Smith teamed up with Rader and became the Canadian director of Rader's new organization, the World-Wide Christian Couriers. He also became the editor-at-large for Gerald Winrod's *Defender Magazine*, based in Kansas.

Smith settled in Toronto and created what became Peoples Church, which became the headquarters for his international ministry. He maintained an active ministry in the United States and was a frequent speaker at fundamentalist institutions in the United States, including Moody Bible Institute, the Bible Institute of Los Angeles, Angelus Temple,[97] Asbury Seminary, Bob Jones University, and Houghton College. The last three institutions gave him honorary doctorates in 1936, 1940, and 1946 respectively.[98]

Smith was not a militant fundamentalist, even though he was part of the fundamentalist network. He left others, such as Riley, Shields, and Winrod, to fight the battles.

In assessing his life's work, Smith claimed that his writing was his greatest ministry.[99] He wrote about 35 books, which were translated into 128 languages. He had also published over 1,200 poems, of which over 100 were turned into hymns and gospel songs. Over six million copies of his books were sold or given away.[100] Smith viewed the distribution of his books as an important way to spread the gospel, even though they were filled with personal anecdotes and had little theological substance.

96. Ibid., 28 May 1927.
97. *Foursquare Magazine*, April 1954 and March 1955.
98. Oswald J. Smith, *The Story of My Life* (Burlington, Ont.,1983), 123.
99. Oswald J. Smith, *The Cry of the World* (London, 1959), 57.
100. *Peoples Magazine* (Spring 1986).

Oswald J. Smith preached his last sermon at Peoples Church in December 1981. He died at the age of ninety-six in January 1986. His funeral service was conducted by Billy Graham,[101] who described Smith as "the greatest combination pastor, hymnwriter, missionary statesman, and evangelist of our time."[102] Several years earlier Graham had said of him: "Oswald Smith has been a legend in his time. He stands tall in the nations of the earth. No other man I know has the drive, determination, or the singleness of mind to serve God. My whole life and ministry have been touched and directed by Oswald J. Smith. I wanted to do the same as he has done as long as I have breath."[103]

Oswald J. Smith's ministry, which spanned most of the twentieth century, placed him in the center of fundamentalism and emerging evangelicalism. He had worked with the greats of fundamentalism, including McPherson, Rader, Winrod, Riley, Philpott, and Bob Jones, Sr. Shields, however, considered Smith a fraudulent showman and denounced him in very strong language.[104]

In his activities Smith was autocratic and was not able to work within a denominational framework. Instead he built his own autocratic church and influenced the next generation of evangelists, who established their own religious empires and were answerable to no one but themselves. Peoples Church became one of the largest churches in Canada and a model for the emerging megachurches. Billy Graham claimed that Smith's "beloved Peoples Church of Toronto has set a pattern for what a successful church and pastor ought to be."[105] If anything, Smith helped create the shallowness of so much of late twentieth-century fundamentalism, which has favored quantity over quality. Religious entertainment replaced worship, and the "gospel" accordingly often lacked theological depth and a social emphasis.[106]

101. Neely, *Fire in His Bones*, 257.
102. *Faith Today* (March/April 1986).
103. Neely, "The Last Interview," *Peoples Magazine* (August 1987).
104. See T. T. Shields to Rev. B. A. Whitten, 21 November 1931; and Shields to Dr. Albert G. Johnson, 23 January 1939, Shields Papers.
105. *Peoples Magazine* (third quarter, 1960).
106. See Carl F. H. Henry, *The Uneasy Social Conscience of Fundamentalism* (Grand Rapids, 1948); Edward J. Carnell, *The Case for Orthodox Theology* (London, 1959); and Thomas Howard, *Evangelical Is Not Enough* (Nashville, 1984).

Perry F. Rockwood

One of the most separatist and hard-line fundamentalists in North America is Perry F. Rockwood (1917–), a "radio pastor" based in Halifax, Nova Scotia. Rockwood remains the only Canadian fundamentalist who has a vast radio audience in the United States.

In 1947 Rockwood was defrocked by the Presbyterian Church after he charged his denomination with modernism and cooperation with Roman Catholicism.[107] With the help of Shields, Rockwood created an independent Peoples Church in Truro, Nova Scotia.[108]

Rockwood soon began radio broadcasting. In 1953 he extended his radio work to the United States and opened a branch office in Boston. Today his daily Peoples Gospel Hour and prophetic broadcasts are taped in Halifax and carried on Canadian and American radio stations from coast to coast. His broadcasts are also heard in Europe and Africa.[109] In Halifax he also operates a small Bible Missionary Church attached to his radio ministry headquarters.

Rockwood's theology can be described as baptistic, dispensational, and devoted to personal holiness. He has been influenced by the writings of Ironside and the faculty of Dallas Theological Seminary.[110] However, Rockwood has become so rigid and separatist that he fellowships with hardly anyone now. He even turned against the ultrafundamentalist Bob Jones University because it used versions of the Bible other than the King James Version.[111] He has no use for any form of Pentecostalism, new evangelicalism, or ecumenism and is especially condemnatory of Roman Catholicism. His bookstore carries salacious anti–Roman Catholic literature by Father Chinquay and Alberto Rivera.

A major part of Rockwood's ministry is the distribution of tracts and pamphlets, mostly written by himself, which thunder against ver-

---

107. Perry F. Rockwood, *Triumph in God: The Life Story of Radio Pastor Perry F. Rockwood* (Halifax, n.d.), 14–40.

108. *Gospel Witness*, 24 April 1947 and 22 April 1948.

109. Peoples Gospel Hour radio log, January 1992.

110. Interview with Perry F. Rockwood, Halifax, 2 January 1992.

111. Perry F. Rockwood, *Official Position of Bob Jones University* (Halifax, n.d.). For his attitudes on other versions, see Perry F. Rockwood, ed. *God's Inspired Preserved Bible: King James Version* (Halifax, n.d.) and *A Review of the NIV and NASV of the Bible* (Halifax, n.d.).

sions of the Bible other than the King James, moderism, ecumenism, charismatics, all television watching,[112] disco dancing, women wearing slacks, unisex fashions,[113] homosexuality, false cults, and so on. While Rockwood may not have had much influence over the official fundamentalist movement, his narrow, separatist views are popular enough at the grass-roots level to generate enough offerings—by one estimate, approximately $3 million annually[114]—to keep his daily radio broadcasts on the air.

Conclusion

We have much more to learn about Canadian fundamentalism. It has had a much richer history than has often been assumed and stated by Lipset, although it never greatly influenced the national culture of Canada. From the above examples it is quite evident that Canadian fundamentalists have had a tremendous impact on American fundamentalism and evangelicalism during the past century; they moved back and forth across the border as if it did not exist.

Fundamentalist theology did not fit well into the Canadian religious ethos, which, as Michael Gauvreau has noted, did not have a marked history of speculative theology or doctrinal controversies other than over church-state relations.[115] Premillennial fundamentalism was also at odds with the "national gospel" of the mainline churches, which had a postmillennial vision.[116] In spite of the empire building and the divisiveness of many Canadian fundamentalists, their insistence on the importance of theology was a prophetic message to the Canadian churches, which had often confused nationalism with Christianity.[117]

112. Perry F. Rockwood, *Believers and Television* (Halifax, n.d.).

113. Perry F. Rockwood, ed., *Modern Trends—Scriptural?* (Halifax, n.d.).

114. Estimate made by Rockwood's estranged son, Rev. Paul Rockwood, interview 23 February 1992. This figure is probably far too high.

115. Michael Gauvreau, *The Evangelical Century: College and Creed in English Canada from the Great Revival to the Great Depression* (Montreal and Kingston, 1991), 11.

116. See William H. Magney, "The Methodist Church and the National Gospel, 1884–1914," *The Bulletin* 20 (1968): 3–95; and Phyllis D. Airhart, *Serving the Present Age: Revivalism, Progressivism, and the Methodist Tradition in Canada* (Montreal and Kingston, 1992).

117. For the nationalistic thrust of mainline Canadian churches, see N. K. Clifford, "His Dominion: A Vision in Crisis," *Studies in Religion* 2, no. 4 (1973): 315–26.

The impact of Canadian fundamentalism on the American religious scene was stronger than its influence on the Canadian churches because of the freer cultural and religious atmosphere in the United States. Canadian fundamentalists such as Simpson, Philpott, Shields, and Smith were organizers and active participants in the American fundamentalist conferences, institutions, and networks. Most were contributors to the major fundamentalist journals such as the *Moody Monthly* and the *Sunday School Times*, and their books were published and marketed by American and British publishers. In the United States Simpson and McPherson organized their own denominations, the Christian and Missionary Alliance and the Foursquare Gospel Church, which they reimported into Canada before they expanded overseas. Philpott, Shields, Smith, and Rockwood, while they often ministered in the United States, kept their headquarters in Canada. American fundamentalists welcomed these Canadian fundamentalists, regarding them as fellow true-believers.

14

More Than a Hyphen

Twentieth-Century Canadian Evangelicalism in Anglo-American Context

John G. Stackhouse, Jr.

It is scarcely self-effacement, but rather common sense, that leads a Canadian to affirm that much of Anglophone Canadian culture flows out of the intermingling of British and American currents. The same can fairly be said of Canadian evangelicalism in the twentieth century.[1] Important evangelical institutions in Canada, for instance, originated in Great Britain or in the United States, or at least self-consciously resembled predecessors in those countries. Inter-Varsity Christian Fellowship began in Britain as the Inter-Varsity Fellowship broke away from the still-earlier Student Christian Movement in the

1. This chapter arises out of several other research projects, some of the results of which are cited below. I am glad to acknowledge support for these ventures from the following agencies: the Canadian Studies Program of the Canadian Embassy to the United States, Washington, D.C.; the Social Sciences and Humanities Research Council of Canada; the Institute for the Study of American Evangelicals; and the Abilene Foundation.

first quarter of the century, and Campus Crusade for Christ, Young Life, and the Navigators all came from the United States. Evangelical Bible schools, seminaries, and liberal arts universities all were inspired by—and in some cases patterned closely after—British or American counterparts. Canadian missions, most notably the large Sudan Interior Mission, followed the lead of the China Inland Mission of England (now Overseas Missionary Fellowship), with many Canadians in fact serving in the latter mission through the years. And the idea of the Evangelical Fellowship of Canada (EFC) seems to have been prompted by Canadian experience in the National Association of Evangelicals in the United States.[2]

Furthermore, British and especially American educational institutions have trained many Canadian evangelical leaders. London Bible College, St. John's College, Nottingham, and Tyndale House, Cambridge, are all places that Canadians have attended. Much more so have Wheaton College and Graduate School, Moody Bible Institute, Dallas Theological Seminary, Trinity Evangelical Divinity School, and Fuller Theological Seminary shaped pastors, professors, and parachurch leaders for service north of the border. And prominent British and American speakers and authors have influenced Canadian evangelicalism in person and through various mass media: from preachers like the Welshman Martyn Lloyd-Jones and Englishman John Stott to Americans Billy Graham and A. W. Tozer; from British authors like J. I. Packer and F. F. Bruce to Americans Carl Henry and Francis Schaeffer; from the publishing houses of InterVarsity Press in both countries and the Grand Rapids cluster in the United States to the wide variety of American televangelism broadcast across Canada.

To stop here, however, and view Canadian evangelicalism simply as the confluence of these two currents would be to stop short. For one thing, there has been cultural influence the other way, even if much less, leading to a very disproportionate, but still definite, balance of trade. Canadian individuals and institutions have made significant contributions to the larger evangelical community. American

2. For a comparison of the Evangelical Fellowship of Canada and the National Association of Evangelicals, see John G. Stackhouse, Jr., "The National Association of Evangelicals, the Evangelical Fellowship of Canada, and the Limits of Evangelical Cooperation," paper in the possession of the author.

and British Christians alike will recognize missionary statesmen Rowland Bingham (founder of the Sudan Interior Mission) and Oswald Smith; theological scholars Clark Pinnock, Richard Longenecker, John Warwick Montgomery, D. A. Carson, and Ronald Sider; and even several members of Billy Graham's own "All-American" team: fellow evangelist and brother-in-law Leighton Ford, soloist George Beverly Shea, and pianist Tedd Smith.[3] In terms of institutions, one can note that InterVarsity Christian Fellowship in the United States originally came south from Canada. A significant number of Americans trained at Canada's Prairie Bible Institute and Regent College. And American and British Christians helped to swell the ranks of the Sudan Interior Mission, making it the largest "faith mission" in the world in the 1950s.[4]

For a second thing, Canadian evangelicalism in the twentieth century has demonstrated a character that is different from, if clearly also related to, its British and American counterparts.[5] What follows sets out some of the key components of this broader characterization of Canadian evangelicalism.

3. Indeed, Steve Bruce begins his account of "crusades and conversion" in Britain by describing a crusade held by Canadian Barry Moore in Belfast (*Firm in the Faith* [Brookfield, Vt., 1984], 95–98).

4. The following skillfully trace some of these interconnections: Robert K. Burkinshaw, "Strangers and Pilgrims in Lotus Land: Conservative Protestantism in British Columbia, 1917–1981" (Ph.D. diss., University of British Columbia, Vancouver, 1988); Brian Alexander McKenzie, "Fundamentalism, Christian Unity, and Premillennialism in the Thought of Rowland Victor Bingham (1872–1942): A Study of Anti-Modernism in Canada" (Ph.D. diss., Toronto School of Theology, 1985); and Ronald George Sawatsky, "Looking for That Blessed Hope: The Roots of Fundamentalism in Canada, 1878–1914" (Ph.D. diss., University of Toronto, 1985).

5. For broad characterizations of twentieth-century evangelicalism in Britain, see especially D. W. Bebbington, *Evangelicalism in Modern Britain: A History from the 1730s to the 1980s* (London, 1989; Grand Rapids, 1992); and Bruce, *Firm in the Faith*. For the Anglicans, the most important members of the British cast, see Kenneth Hylson-Smith, *Evangelicals in the Church of England, 1734–1984* (Edinburgh, 1988); and Randle Manwaring, *From Controversy to Co-Existence: Evangelicals in the Church of England, 1914–1980* (Cambridge, 1985). There was an explosion of literature on American evangelicalism in the 1970s, 1980s, and early 1990s. Important introductions are the following: Donald W. Dayton and Robert K. Johnston, eds., *The Variety of American Evangelicalism* (Knoxville, 1991); George Marsden, ed., *Evangelicalism and Modern America* (Grand Rapids, 1984); and idem, *Understanding Fundamentalism and Evangelicalism* (Grand Rapids, 1991). Splendid bibliographical guides are the following: Edith L. Blumhofer and Joel A. Carpenter, *Twentieth-Century Evangelicalism: A Guide to the Sources* (New York, 1990); and Leonard I. Sweet, "The Evangelical Tradition in America," in *The Evangelical Tradition in America*, ed. Sweet (Macon, 1984), 1–86.

Canadian evangelicals in the twentieth century, like Protestants in the sixteenth and seventeenth centuries, continued to disagree about baptism and the doctrine of the church, about the character of Christ's presence in the Lord's Supper, about predestination and human freedom, and about church polity. These, and other areas that have divided Christians, still divided evangelicals into denominations. But most Canadian evangelicals in the twentieth century recognized areas of agreement that they saw together to be more crucial than the disagreements that had utterly divided Christians in the past. While they maintained faithfulness to the distinctives that denominated them, nevertheless these Christians joined together in faithfulness to shared beliefs and concerns.[6]

In the first place, Canadian evangelicals held to a common core of doctrine. Most of the institutions they supported insisted that those involved with them—or at least those in leadership and in some cases everyone—agree on a set of beliefs that set out the essence of evangelical Christianity. And these various statements in fact agree with each other remarkably. Indeed, the statement of the World Evangelical Fellowship, adopted directly by two of the most prominent of

6. At the risk of obfuscating further a widely recognized semantic problem, one might see the Canadian Christians who cooperated across denominational lines—those generally in view here—as at least implicitly committed to the idea or even ideology of "evangelical*ism*." Thus they might be termed "evangelical*ists*." Others, however, who were not so committed saw other issues as primary also or instead, and so would not have joined up with such a coalition. In particular, those denominations of strong denominational*ism*, who tended to see everything about the denomination as important, would have had trouble compromising *anything* in order to cooperate. These nonjoiners, then, who would nonetheless have shared those basic evangelical doctrines and concerns with others, would be seen as generic evangelicals per se, members of the set one might call (with apologies to C. S. Lewis) "mere evangelicality."

Making thus a distinction between the more generic "evangelicalism" ("mere evangelicality") and the particular conviction of "transdenominational evangelicalism" ("evangelical*ism*") might be valid enough, but there is no obvious nomenclature to distinguish persons belonging to the one group from those in the other. One could use the standard term "evangelical" for the former, inclusive group and "transdenominational evangelical" for those identified with "evangelicalism" in this special sense, but the latter term might inaccurately misrepresent evangelicals who nonetheless maintained denominational identities. Indeed, the term "nondenominational" should be reserved for instances in which denominational differences are eroded or even explicitly resisted, and the term "interdenominational" reserved for instances of official cooperation among denominations. One could resort instead to a neologism, "evangelicalist," for this more narrowly defined group, but its unfamiliarity might engender its own confusions. This chapter, then, focuses on transdenominational evangelicalism, with the hope that the context will make clear the particular instances when the larger sense of "evangelical" is meant.

these institutions, namely, Regent College and the Evangelical Fellowship of Canada, serves as a generic statement of Canadian evangelical belief:

1. The Holy Scriptures as originally given by God, divinely inspired, infallible, entirely trustworthy; and the only supreme authority in all matters of faith and conduct.
2. One God, eternally existent in three Persons, Father, Son and Holy Spirit.
3. Our Lord Jesus Christ, God manifest in the flesh, His virgin birth, His sinless human life, His divine miracles, His bodily resurrection, His ascension, His mediatorial work, and His personal return in power and glory.
4. The salvation of lost and sinful man through the shed blood of the Lord Jesus Christ by faith apart from works, and regeneration by the Holy Spirit.
5. The Holy Spirit by whose indwelling the believer is enabled to live a holy life to witness and work for the Lord Jesus Christ.
6. The unity of the Spirit of all true believers, the Church, the Body of Christ.
7. The resurrection of both the saved and the lost; they that are saved unto the resurrection of life, and they that are lost unto the resurrection of damnation.[7]

Evangelicals did not all precisely agree on this statement, as respective statements of faith of each of the institutions they support make clear. For instance, some preferred to use the word "inerrancy" in articulating the doctrine of Scripture, seeing it as a bulwark against creeping liberalism; others preferred *not* to use it, seeing it as a shibboleth that served only to divide evangelicals from each other.[8] But the disagreement among Canadian evangelicals over this matter was slight indeed; Canadian evangelical institutions generally set out very high doctrines of Scripture, and these statements could

7. *The Evangelical Fellowship of Canada* (N.p., [1986]), n.p. On the World Evangelical Fellowship, see David M. Howard, *The Dream That Would Not Die: The Birth and Growth of the World Evangelical Fellowship, 1846–1986* (Exeter, 1986).

8. See the discussion on the differences between Trinity Western University and Regent College in the conclusion to John G. Stackhouse, Jr., *Canadian Evangelicalism in the Twentieth Century: An Introduction to Its Character* (Toronto, 1993).

be contained by the phrases above, even as some would use different language.

The remaining clauses of the statement aroused little controversy among most Canadian evangelicals. To be sure, dispensationalists disagreed with Christian Reformed believers over the nature of the millennium and therefore over the exact character of Christ's "personal return in power and glory," but all agreed on the statement as written.[9] Nazarenes differed with Pentecostals, and both groups disagreed with Presbyterians when they went beyond the language of the statement to describe more fully the nature of the work of the Holy Spirit as it "indwells" believers, "enabling" them to live holy lives, but again all agreed with what *was* said therein. And while the conceptions of church polity among Canadian evangelicals ran the gamut from episcopal to congregational and qualifications for church membership from simple profession of conversion to completion of a full catechetical program, all agreed that the essential characteristics of a member of the universal church were true belief and unity in the Holy Spirit. Canadian evangelicals, then, continued to disagree about matters they saw to be important enough to justify the continuance of denominations. But it is crucial to see here again that evangelicals from each of these traditions were content to leave these disagreements for certain forums, certain times; in other contexts, they were glad to work together on this sort of doctrinal basis.

Why this set of beliefs united Canadian evangelicals and not others, however, can be explained best in terms of other concerns that these Christians held in common. Canadian evangelicals shared with evangelicals of other countries characteristic concern not only for correct doctrine but also for warm-hearted and disciplined piety and for energetic missions. And the particular doctrines emphasized by transdenominational groups square with these concerns. If a group of Christians understands the nature of Christian identity as involv-

9. Prairie Bible Institute and Trinity Western University had premillennialism in their statements of faith. But considerable evidence suggests that this was not a crucial doctrine among even these evangelicals. Prairie's magazines devoted little attention to this doctrine relative to that afforded concerns common to all evangelicals. The recognition and support Prairie and Trinity Western gave to other evangelical groups who did not hold to this view also indicates that it was not a crucial conviction for them (see the pertinent chapters in Stackhouse, "Canadian Evangelicalism").

ing belief in a basic doctrine ("by faith alone through grace alone") and a heartfelt commitment to the person of Christ; if they emphasize increasing holiness in the life of faith; and if they see the task of the church as primarily to evangelize the unconverted, then they will emphasize those doctrines that have to do with the basic nature of God, the salvific work of Christ, the regenerating and sanctifying work of the Holy Spirit, and the outcome entailed by one's response to these things. And they will stress the foundation for these particular beliefs, which they believe is the Bible alone. These are the doctrines of the evangelical statements.[10]

Another concern, however, underlay these statements of faith. Such creeds emerge in response to particular, historical circumstances. The nature of evangelicalism's central concerns, just described, is one set of circumstances informing these statements of belief. But the rise and spread of new theologies in the Canadian church since the beginning of this century seems also to have influenced these statements, since virtually all of the ideas they contain have been challenged or denied by one strand or another of modern theology. This interpretation also agrees with the fact that many of the institutions of Canadian evangelicalism were founded as alternatives to organizations that, in the view of the evangelicals, had been compromised and diverted by new theologies (usually categorized by evangelicals simply as "liberal") in other directions. Denominational seminaries that no longer taught evangelical truth but presented or even advocated alternatives, student organizations that no longer sought to evangelize but rather to seek only this-worldly justice, universities that no longer encouraged Christian belief but rather hired and defended its attackers, ecumenical organizations that paid lip service to evangelical concerns while watering down the truth and neglecting missions—all of these, as seen through evangelical eyes, demanded new schools, new student groups, new fellowships. To provide backbones to these new groups, statements of faith

10. Regent College, for one, recognized this pattern, as it introduced its statement of faith in this way: "We accept wholeheartedly the revelation of God given in the Scriptures of the Old and New Testaments and confess the faith therein set forth and summarized in such historic statements of the Christian Church as the Apostles' Creed and the Nicene Creed. We here explicitly assert doctrines that they regard as crucial to the understanding and proclamation of the Gospel and to practical Christian living" (*1989–90 Catalogue*, 8; author's files).

per se were seen to be necessary, and statements of these doctrines in particular, to fortify these evangelical organizations against those ideas that had compromised the others.[11]

The third consideration that explains these statements is evangelical consciousness of Roman Catholicism. In Canada, which has areas of such strong Roman Catholic dominance, the distinctness of evangelicalism has lain not only in its commitment to orthodoxy, personal piety, and missions, and not only in its differences from new theologies, but also in its strong Protestantism. Evangelical magazines, like Prairie Bible Institute's *Prairie Overcomer*, spoke for many in their repudiation of Roman Catholicism. The Canadian Protestant League, founded by fundamentalist Baptist pastor T. T. Shields at the time of the Second World War, drew support during its brief flourishing across the denominational and even theological spectrum and involved prominent evangelicals. And Inter-Varsity Christian Fellowship, which contained elements quite favorable to Roman Catholicism, especially since the openness of Vatican II and the rise of the charismatic movement, which shared many concerns with evangelicals, yet decided to adopt the International Fellowship of Evangelical Students' statement of faith in the early 1980s, which made it more explicit than ever it was a Protestant organization. (Indeed, most evangelical statements dealt with the matter directly, and usually right at the beginning, as they posited the singular authority of the Bible, quite clearly implying evangelicalism's basic disagreement with the Roman Catholic understanding of the relationship of Scripture, tradition, and teaching office.)

If these concerns together outline one dimension of the mainstream of Canadian evangelicalism as it flowed through the twentieth century, so does the participation of evangelicals from a variety of denominations trace another. Many were from small, uniformly evan-

11. Particularly germane here are the following studies: D. C. Masters, *Protestant Church Colleges in Canada* (Toronto, 1966); idem, "The Rise of Liberalism in Canadian Protestant Churches," *Canadian Catholic Historical Association Study Sessions* (1969), 27–39; John S. Moir, *A History of Biblical Studies in Canada: A Sense of Proportion* (Chico, Calif., 1982); Marguerite Van Die, *An Evangelical Mind: Nathanael Burwash and the Methodist Tradition in Canada, 1839–1918* (Montreal and Kingston, 1989); and Michael Gauvreau, *The Evangelical Century: College and Creed in English Canada from the Great Revival to the Great Depression* (Montreal and Kingston, 1991).

gelical groups, like Baptists, Christian Brethren, and the Christian and Missionary Alliance. But evangelicals from the large Anglican and especially Presbyterian communions figured importantly in the story as well. The smaller groups did, however, emerge into greater prominence as the century progressed, and Mennonites and Pentecostals began to rival or surpass the Anglicans, Presbyterians, and Brethren in numbers and influence.[12]

It is not strictly true, then, that evangelicalism through the century increasingly withdrew from the mainline denominations per se, much less that evangelicalism was made up merely of sectarian groups in the traditional sense of the term,[13] since Presbyterians, Anglicans, and mainline Baptists continued to support the movement. But several related observations are in order. The first is that the United Church of Canada, Canada's largest Protestant denomination and an ecumenical amalgam of traditions founded in 1925, never was well represented among Canadian evangelicals, and certainly not in proportion to the numbers on its rolls. As several historians have detailed, however, this reflects the decline of evangelical concerns within this communion, a decline manifest earlier among the Methodists, Congregationalists, and Presbyterians who made it up, and a decline increased since the 1960s.[14] There were evangelicals within

12. The significance of Anglicans and Brethren in evangelicalism was similar in Canada and Britain versus their relatively small place in the American story, although they remained proportionately the most influential in the British case. The growing presence of Pentecostalism since the 1960s was a common story in all three countries. Only in Canada were the Mennonites a quite significant factor in evangelicalism, reflecting the larger proportion of Mennonites in the Canadian population versus those of the other two countries.

13. This latter idea is evident, however, in H. H. Walsh's book *The Christian Church in Canada* (Toronto, 1956), chap. 20, "Persistence of Sect Movements"; in the work of S. D. Clark (e.g., a church-sect typology—with evangelicals represented exclusively by sects—underlies his influential *Church and Sect in Canada* [Toronto, 1948]); and in Hans Mol's later study of religion in Canada, which speaks of evangelicals only as they are represented by "new movements" (e.g., Pentecostalism) and does not discuss the crucial category "evangelicalism" at all (*Faith and Fragility: Religion and Identity in Canada* [Burlington, Ont., 1985]).

14. Neil Semple, "The Decline of Revival in Nineteenth Century, Central-Canadian Methodism: The Extraordinary Means of Grace," *Canadian Methodist Historical Society Papers* 2 (N.p., n.d.); Harry Manning, "Changes in Evangelism within the Methodist Church in Canada during the Time of Carman and Chown, 1884–1925: A Study of the Causes for the Shifts in Evangelism" (Th.M. thesis, Toronto School of Theology, 1975); Twila F. Buttimer, "'Great Expectations': The Maritime Methodist Church and Church Union, 1925" (M.A. thesis, University of New Brunswick, 1980); Randolph C. Chalmers and John W. Grant, "The United Church of Canada:

this church, and a movement of them intent on renewal began to sound evangelical notes in the 1960s, but the general direction of the denomination throughout the century was away from those things that united evangelicals.

A different case is that of Canadian Lutherans. Many of these shared the concern of Canadian evangelicals for orthodoxy, piety, and mission, even if the traditional evangelical imperative of *personal* evangelism was uncommon among them. But these Lutherans, notably those affiliated with the American Missouri Synod known as the Lutheran Church–Canada, like their American counterparts, kept to themselves in ethnic and denominational enclaves and so did not join the larger movement.[15]

A somewhat similar situation obtained in the Atlantic Provinces. The influence of evangelical Protestantism was strong in many parts of this region, seen in the relatively large numbers of Salvationists and Pentecostals in Newfoundland, Baptists in Nova Scotia and New Brunswick, and Scottish Presbyterians in northern Nova Scotia and elsewhere. But the cultural separation of this region from the rest of the country, well known in other contexts in Canada, shows up here again in the limited number of links with the transdenominational and transitional movement elsewhere.[16] The denominational isola-

---

Its Way of Experiencing and Expressing the Ultimate Reality and Meaning," *Ultimate Reality and Meaning* 1 (1978): 100–14; John Webster Grant, "The United Church and Its Heritage in Evangelism," *Touchstone* 1 (October 1983): 6–13; N. K. Clifford, "The United Church of Canada and Doctrinal Confession," *Touchstone* 2 (May 1984): 6–21; Michael Gauvreau, "History and Faith: A Study of Aspects of Presbyterian and Methodist Thought in Canada, 1820–1940" (Ph.D. diss., University of Toronto, 1985); idem, "War, Culture, and the Problem of Religious Certainty: Methodist and Presbyterian Church Colleges, 1914–1930," *Journal of the Canadian Church Historical Society* 29 (April 1987): 12–31; idem, *Evangelical Century*; Phyllis D. Airhart, *Serving the Present Age* (Montreal and Kingston, 1992) and Van Die, *Evangelical Mind*.

15. See George O. Evenson, *Adventuring for Christ: The Story of the Evangelical Lutheran Church of Canada* (Calgary, 1974). A more recent discussion of the different accents and alliances of North American Lutherans versus evangelicals is Bryan V. Hillis, "The Evangel and Evangelicalism: A Lutheran Perspective" (Paper delivered at the Canadian Evangelical Theological Association, University of Prince Edward Island, Charlottetown, 6 June 1992).

16. The slowly growing presence of IVCF in Atlantic Canada and the increasing involvement of leaders from Atlantic Baptist College and Acadia Divinity College with the national network of evangelicals, notably with the Evangelical Fellowship of Canada, perhaps reflected a sea change among at least some evangelicals in Atlantic Canada by the 1980s. The refusal of the United Baptist Convention of the Atlantic Provinces in 1989 to join the EFC, however, indicated yet some widespread hesitancy about joining the national transdenominational move-

tion typical of the region meant that evangelicals in this area did not start significant transdenominational movements of their own.

A final observation in this regard is that evangelicals indeed felt increasingly alienated from the *leadership* and *institutions* of all three of the mainline Protestant groups, whether United Church, Anglican, or Presbyterian. Many evangelicals saw a prevalence of liberal or neo-orthodox theology and destructive biblical criticism in the seminaries, preoccupation with politics and ideology among denominational leaders, and neglect of evangelism both home and abroad. So the century witnessed evangelicals, including many from within these denominations, sponsoring alternative organizations that represented evangelical concerns.

With this developing sense of separateness from the leadership of the large denominations and the forming of these alternative institutions, evangelicals became conscious of themselves as a network of like-minded individuals and organizations. That all of the institutions shared basic similarities—similar doctrine, similar concern for piety and evangelism—is quite clear. What remains is to delineate the historical connections between them.

This task, however, is made difficult by two facts. In the first place, the formal links among the institutions were relatively few. There were informal links among the institutions, though, which increased to an overwhelming number through the century. Only representative examples can be presented here of the hundreds easily documented from the records. In the first half-century since World War 1, evangelical institutions had little contact with each other over distance. Inter-Varsity Christian Fellowship and Toronto Bible College naturally had interlocking boards of directors even then, for example, but they had little direct contact with Prairie Bible Institute, whose board was drawn from local supporters well into the late 1980s. They were yet connected, however, by several indirect links. In the first place, Christians of certain denominations, notably the Baptists and the Christian and Missionary Alliance, supported all three institutions. In the second place, evangelical leaders and organizations contributed to them. Rowland V. Bingham, for instance, sat on the board of Toronto Bible

---

ment per se. (It should be noted in this respect, however, that the small Atlantic Canada Association of Free Will Baptists was in fact a member of the EFC.)

College and was an early supporter of Inter-Varsity Christian Fellowship. And his Sudan Interior Mission sent missionary speakers frequently to Prairie, in turn receiving for some decades the largest amounts of money given through Prairie each year for foreign missions. Moreover, Prairie's President L. E. Maxwell himself was invited to address Inter-Varsity groups in Ontario and to speak at IVCF's first triennial missions conference in Toronto. And third, certain American and British evangelical institutions and individuals provided Canadian evangelicals with a certain amount of commonality as they shared in the influence of these foreign resources.[17]

For all this, however, the relationships among evangelicals remained loose and informal for the most part. Subgroups of evangelicals generally continued to support their own institutions, even as they were grateful for the success of the projects of their fellow evangelicals. Canadian evangelicals also continued to disagree about political strategies (e.g., all-or-nothing vs. piecemeal reform in the abortion struggle), about mission priorities (e.g., evangelistic projects vs. academic consultations), about ecumenical relationships (e.g., links between charismatic Protestants and Roman Catholics), and about issues facing the whole church (e.g., the public ministry of women).[18] Finally, the increasing size and prominence of charismatic and especially Pentecostal churches in a network that included dispensationalists and certain kinds of Reformed whose theologies normally had no room for postapostolic charismatic experience per se, and of Asian, French-Canadian, and other ethnic churches in a network dominated by Anglo-Canadians, challenged evangelicalism with more cultural plurality than it had ever experienced before.[19]

By the late 1980s, that is, evangelicals in Canada had not been welded into a coherent movement by strong leadership, influential national institutions, or compelling issues. Instead, the vast geogra-

17. One thinks of the ironic parallel of George Whitefield, the visiting English preacher, helping to weld together the thirteen colonies in the generation before the American Revolution.

18. This is evident in the pages of the two main national periodicals sponsored by evangelicals: the EFC's *Faith Today* and the independent *ChristianWeek*. On the last issue, see Shirley Bentall, "The Experience of Women in Canadian Evangelicalism," *Ecumenism* 85 (March 1987): 17–19; and John G. Stackhouse, Jr., "Women in Public Ministry in Twentieth-Century Canadian and American Evangelicalism: Five Models," in *Studies in Religion/Sciences religieuses* 17 (Fall 1988): 471–85.

phy of Canada, the influence of and allegiance to regionally prominent leaders and institutions, or different dispositions even toward concerns common to all evangelicals separated them into definite subgroups only loosely linked to make up the larger evangelical fellowship. Indeed, the very word "fellowship," used by Canadian evangelicals to describe the two institutions that did the most to bring them together— Inter-Varsity Christian Fellowship and the Evangelical Fellowship of Canada—perhaps best denotes this relationship of distinct elements united by limited, if crucial, common concerns and engaging in limited, but regular and substantial, common activity.[20]

In the second place, for all of the connections between them, differences remained between two distinct forms of Canadian evangelicalism. The first sort supported Ontario Bible College (and Toronto Bible College before it) and Regent College and dominated the central leadership of both Inter-Varsity Christian Fellowship and the Evangelical Fellowship of Canada. This first kind, which I have called "churchish," was centered in urban southern Ontario, especially Toronto; in Vancouver; and in urban, English-speaking Quebec, especially Montreal.[21]

19. The presence of notable Pentecostal leaders in the EFC—from Harry Faught in the earliest days to Brian Stiller in the 1980s—did not reflect the prominence of Pentecostals per se in similar evangelical institutions until well into the 1970s. Ontario Bible College and Theological Seminary and Regent College both were notable in their addressing of the needs of both Pentecostal and Asian churches in the 1980s as they offered courses directed specifically to their interests.

The charismatic movement and Pentecostalism have received much more scholarly scrutiny in Britain and especially the United States than it has in Canada. For sources examining the Canadian scene, see the bibliographical essay following John G. Stackhouse, Jr., "The Protestant Experience in Canada since 1945," in *The Canadian Protestant Experience, 1760–1990*, ed. George A. Rawlyk (Burlington, Ont., 1990), 246–47 and 250–51.

20. A brief account of these developments is John G. Stackhouse, Jr., "The Emergence of a Fellowship: Canadian Evangelicalism in the Twentieth Century," *Church History* 60 (June 1991): 247–62.

21. The original meanings of the terms "church" and "sect," as formulated by Ernest Troeltsch (1865–1923) in a Europe of state churches, do not apply exactly to the twentieth-century Canadian situation, in which there were no established churches and dissenting sects. By derivation, however, the terms have come to denote something like this. A *church* is a denomination that enjoys status in the culture, participates in the culture, and indeed manifests something of a proprietary interest in the culture. It includes many whose allegiance is only nominal and typically comprises a variety of views and practices (remnant of the "territorial church" idea) as part of its stature as a broadly "accepted" and "accepting" denomination. A *sect*, in contrast, enjoys no status in the culture but rather consciously separates itself from the culture. It is made up only of "believers," those who consciously join it and who maintain its intellectual

The counterpart, the second sort of Canadian evangelicalism, which I have called "sectish," supported most of the prairie Bible schools and Trinity Western University, among other institutions. While present across Canada, it was most noticeable on the prairies and in their extension-by-emigration, the lower Fraser River valley of British Columbia, home to Trinity Western University.

The first kind—described by some as conservative evangelicals—drew support and leadership from evangelicals among the Presbyterians, the Anglicans, and the mainline or Federation Baptists, as well as from smaller evangelical groups; the second—a little more fundamentalistic in tone and strategy—drew from the smaller, uniformly evangelical denominations almost exclusively, including sometimes the separatist heirs of the Baptist fundamentalists, the Fellowship Baptists.[22] The first type was strongest in urban areas of long-standing British immigration, notably Toronto and Vancouver; the second was strongest in rural areas of more recent American and European immigration. The first actively engaged contemporary culture and scholarship, including biblical and theological studies and placed a premium upon leaders with education respected by society at large; the second manifested much more caution toward, and even suspicion of or outright hostility toward, modern ideas and sought leaders with training from "safe" schools over those from prestigious ones. The first declared its fundamental belief in the unique authority and divine inspiration of Scripture; the second insisted on the use of the word "inerrancy" or its verbal equivalents in the same context and sometimes suspected the first of compromising or helping to compromise this doctrine.[23] The first refused to make anything more than

---

and behavioral discipline.I have modified these terms, then, to suit the different evangelical *mentalités* herein described and to underscore that these identify dispositions with social ramifications that yet are contained within one broad "fellowship"—rather than using "churchly" and "sectarian," which might perpetuate the idea that these two groups are divided always into clearly separate institutions.

22. For an example of the ambivalence of Fellowship Baptists regarding cooperation with other groups, see Charles A. Tipp, "Objections to Unity," in *One Church, Two Nations?* ed. Philip LeBlanc and Arnold Edinborough (Don Mills, Ont., 1968), 54–68.

23. See, for example, the editorials to this effect by Ted S. Rendall in the *Prairie Overcomer* 51 (September 1978): 482–83 and (November 1978): 601–2. The difference between the two types of evangelicalism again is one of tone, of insistence that the common agreement on the absolute authority and trustworthiness of the Scriptures must not be minimized.

a belief in Christ's literal second coming an article of common faith; the second preferred an articulated premillennialism.[24] The first believed in the practice of personal holiness but left the application up to the individual; the second was more comfortable with a clear code, and in particular forbade alcohol and dancing from the life of the Christian.

These characterizations, to be sure, form two poles of a continuum along which Canadian evangelicals would have been individually located. Nevertheless, most, it may be argued, would have been clustered at one end or the other, since the institution they sponsored tended to manifest one type or the other. And the geographic-demographic referents in particular should not be pressed too far. The more important point is that there were in Canada two distinct kinds of evangelical dispositions, two *mentalités*, rather than that they were dominant in distinct geographic and demographic areas. Both dispositions were represented, albeit in various proportions, across Canada. Metropolitan areas especially, and Toronto and Vancouver in particular, were home to both types, as were some regionally prominent organizations, such as Ontario Bible College in Toronto and Trinity Western University in British Columbia, and especially national groups like Inter-Varsity Christian Fellowship and the Evangelical Fellowship of Canada.

This difference, although real enough, should not be exaggerated, however. It certainly did not keep these two communities from recognizing essential kinship in each other, a recognition that extended not only to involvement in common projects, like the Evangelical Fellowship of Canada, but also to direct links among leaders and programs. More broadly yet, these two kinds of evangelicalism not only shared the qualities outlined above, but they also evolved in similar ways. Both increasingly articulated a broad understanding of Christian vocation. And both demonstrated a concern to affect society in a number of ways, not merely in evangelism. They stood together

24. While premillennialism remained a vital force in sections of American evangelicalism, David Bebbington reports that in Britain "by the 1970s it was ceasing to be a feature even of the Brethren [who] had popularized it." Many conservative Evangelicals, while adhering to the belief in a personal second coming guarded by the IVF [Inter-Varsity Fellowship] basis of faith, moved more or less unconsciously to an amillennial view" (Bebbington, *Evangelicalism in Modern Britain*, 264).

even as differences remained. Finally, it perhaps should be underscored that differences among Canadian evangelicals over everything from gender roles to political philosophy could never be reduced to just two positions coordinate with these two mind-sets, since evangelicals characteristically held a variety of views on most subjects; those who might line up together on one issue might well disagree on another.[25]

The character of Canadian evangelicalism in the twentieth century—indeed, the very propriety of using the term as if there were such a thing as a distinctly *Canadian* evangelicalism as opposed to a generic evangelicalism within Canadian society—can be thrown into relief by a brief comparison with evangelicalism in Britain and the United States.[26]

For all the links among British, Canadian, and American evangelicalism, the Canadian variant was not a matter simply of British colonial residues or American "branch plants." The institutions that have been central in the life of Canadian evangelicalism in the twentieth century have been, without exception, indigenous Canadian products. However much they benefited from British or American initiative (e.g., British initiative in the drawing together of student groups into IVCF; the American model of Moody Bible Institute for Prairie Bible Institute [PBI]; the American Evangelical Free Church denominational support for Trinity Western University [TWU], especially in its early days) or from leaders from either place (e.g., American founding presidents L. E. Maxwell of PBI and Calvin Hanson of TWU; Englishman James Houston and Americans Carl Armerding and Ward

25. To select just two examples: Ward Gasque and James Packer, professors together at Regent College in the 1980s, each identified publicly with an evangelical organization at odds with the other one over gender roles in home and church ("Christians for Biblical Equality" and the "Council for Biblical Manhood and Womanhood" respectively); and (also in the 1980s) Clark Pinnock of McMaster Divinity College and George Rawlyk of Queen's University, both members of the Baptist Convention of Ontario and Quebec and both important evangelical scholars, publicly defended radically different ideologies, with Pinnock on the side of democratic capitalism, and Rawlyk democratic socialism.

26. See the following pioneering essays: Ernest R. Sandeen, *The Roots of Fundamentalism: British and American Millenarianism, 1800–1930* (Grand Rapids, 1978; orig. 1970); George Marsden, "Fundamentalism as an American Phenomenon: A Comparison with English Evangelicalism," *Church History* 46 (1977): 215–32, and Harry H. Hiller, "Continentalism and the Third Force in Religion," *Canadian Journal of Sociology* 3 (1978): 183–207.

Gasque of Regent), the institutions were founded and funded and staffed almost entirely by Canadians.[27] Moreover, they reflected the typically Canadian denominational representation in evangelicalism: stronger representation from pluralistic, mainstream churches than was the case in the United States,[28] but also stronger representation from a wider mix of groups (such as the Pentecostal, Mennonite, holiness, and Dutch Reformed) than was the British pattern of dominance by Evangelical Anglicans and a relatively few Nonconformist denominations.[29] In this regard, furthermore, Canadian evangelicalism was more varied than the British counterpart but less spectacularly varied than the American; Canadian culture refused to produce the number and degree of colorful individual leaders, groups, and institutions that were all too typical of American evangelicalism.[30]

Instead, Canadian evangelicalism, like Canadian Anglophone culture in general, tended toward the norm, tended toward homogeneity. Twentieth-century evangelicalism, furthermore, manifested this trait in a manner unparalleled in Canadian religious history. In previous centuries, the two main styles of evangelicalism had been evident, but in different movements (like the Salvation Army vs. evangelical Anglicans) or in the same movement at different times (like Methodism in the eighteenth and nineteenth centuries). In the second half of the twentieth century, however, Canadian evangelicalism

27. Regent College, with its penchant for hiring American or British professors with "household names" over lesser-known Canadians, seems to be a conspicuous exception in this respect. Yet Regent in fact reflected the pattern in many other Canadian evangelical institutions as they gladly hired non-Canadians who fit best the particular professional and confessional requirements of a job—whether local pastor or seminary professor—over Canadians who did not seem to fit them so well. Some would argue that this pattern, in itself, is quintessentially Anglo-Canadian! It does not gainsay the other marks of indigenousness noted in what follows.

28. The National Association of Evangelicals, for instance, excluded denominations that wished to maintain membership also in the National Council of Churches and thus was dominated from the beginning by smaller, uniformly evangelical denominations; the Evangelical Fellowship of Canada had no such proscription and welcomed much more leadership from a wider range of denominations (see Stackhouse, "The National Association of Evangelicals").

29. One important British variety is not similarly represented in Canada, namely, the house church movement; see Bebbington, *Evangelicalism in Modern Britain*, 230–31; and Bruce, *Firm in the Faith*, 43.

30. For vivid examples, see Randall Balmer, *Mine Eyes Have Seen the Glory: A Journey into the Evangelical Subculture in America* (New York, 1989); Dayton and Johnston, *The Variety of American Evangelicalism*; and Richard Quebedeaux, *The Young Evangelicals* (New York, 1974).

had broadened in its concerns but also coalesced into at least a loose network of institutions that incorporated moderate versions of both *mentalités*. In fact, the new fellowship of evangelicalism adopted a cultural stance that moved beyond the former alternatives of "outsider" and "insider" toward that of an important group within a pluralized society, one participant among many others in the shaping of Canadian culture.[31]

This remarkable confluence of Canadian evangelicalism took place as Canadian culture steadily became less influenced by traditional Christianity. Those evangelicals who once had been more comfortable in that larger culture began to set up alternative institutions to those they saw to have been deeply compromised, and in this they began to resemble more their sectish siblings. In turn, the more sectish evangelicals, perhaps because of a rise in social and economic standing, perhaps because of the erosion of the mainline alternative, which had seemed to them the proprietor of contemporary culture, and perhaps because of a new sensitivity to the needs of Canada in the post-Victorian religious situation, began to open up to a wider vision of ministry. This led them to improve their educational institutions and join with other evangelicals in projects of cultural influence beyond the evangelistic. So Canadian evangelicalism became at once more unified and more prominent precisely as the old "Christian Canada" fragmented.[32] Indeed, observers wondered if British Columbia was a bellwether of Canadian society in this regard as it has been in others. By 1990 it not only included the largest proportion of those who claimed "no religion" in all of Canada, but it also included the largest and fastest growing proportion of evangelical churches as well—a proportion that outstripped both the Roman Catholic and the United churches.[33] Canadian evangelicals, then,

31. Particularly apposite examples were the establishment in 1991 of the Task Force on Canada's Future by the Evangelical Fellowship of Canada (see Aileen Van Ginkel, ed., *Shaping a Christian Vision for Canada: Discussion Papers on Canada's Future* [Markham, Ont., 1992]) and a set of "citizens' forums" on the national constitutional debate sponsored across Canada by the Citizens for Public Justice (a ginger group arising out of the Christian Reformed community).

32. This argument is sustained at greater length in the author's "Protestant Experience in Canada since 1945," 198–252.

33. See the several articles devoted to this in *Christian Week* 4 (20 November 1990), and especially the piece by Robert Burkinshaw, "Flourishing in a Secular Lotus Land," 8–11.

were reacting against certain modern trends and forces, to be sure, but they also were responding to those challenges in new ways and with some success.

It is important in this regard to note, therefore, that fundamentalism played a smaller part in Canadian evangelicalism, as it did in Britain, versus the importance of that school in American Christianity.[34] Canadians, like their British counterparts, became more and more concerned about the general drift of their culture away from traditional Christianity and responded to that drift in various ways, but they did so generally without the militancy and the sense of loss of cultural authority typical of much of American evangelicalism affected by the fundamentalist heritage.[35] (In fact, the only communities to experience a genuine fundamentalist-modernist schism were the Baptists of Ontario and British Columbia.)[36] Most Canadian and British evangelicals, that is, tended either to avoid the larger culture or to seek to influence it as one important viewpoint among many, rather than harking back to a golden age of "Christian America" in hopes of regaining cultural dominance (although it could be argued that Canada and Britain were, at certain times in their histories, as

34. David Bebbington claims that it is "quite mistaken to hold (as it has sometimes been held) that Britain escaped a Fundamentalist controversy." The remainder of his discussion of the conflicts during the interwar years, however, bears out his judgment that the trauma was much more contained, much less dramatic and significant, than in the United States. "It seems clear," he concludes, "that organised Fundamentalism in Britain was a weak force," putting it graphically: "Fundamentalist controversies did exist in Britain, but they were storms in a teacup when compared with the blizzards of invective that swept contemporary America" (*Evangelicalism in Modern Britain*, 182, 224, 227; cf. Marsden, "Fundamentalism as an American Phenomenon"). On the insignificance of fundamentalism in Canada, see G. A. Rawlyk, *Champions of the Truth: Fundamentalism, Modernism, and the Maritime Baptists* (Montreal and Kingston, 1990); and part 1 of Stackhouse, *Canadian Evangelicalism*.

35. This characterization of American fundamentalism relies chiefly upon George M. Marsden, *Fundamentalism and American Culture: The Shaping of Twentieth-Century Evangelicalism, 1870–1925* (New York, 1980). A small gesture symbolizes the distancing of the mainstream of Canadian evangelicalism from fundamentalism. The Executive Committee of the Evangelical Fellowship of Canada discussed a proposal entitled "Expansion of [the] Evangelical Fellowship of Canada" in 1966 and deliberately deleted terms like "campaign," "enlist," and "militant" from the draft (Minutes of 29 September 1966).

36. For the Baptist stories, see the sources listed in Philip G. A. Griffin-Allwood et al., eds., *Baptists in Canada, 1760–1990: A Bibliography of Selected Printed Resources in English* (Hantsport, N.S., 1989). The Presbyterians also divided in the mid-1920s, but they divided instead over the issue of joining the United Church of Canada; see N. Keith Clifford, *The Resistance to Church Union in Canada, 1904–1939* (Vancouver, 1985).

"Christian" as America had ever been). Indeed, such political movements as there were in Canada to "recall" Canada to a Christian heritage, such as Ken Campbell's "Renaissance International" movement or the Christian Heritage party, remained on the fringes of evangelicalism itself, let alone of the society as a whole.[37]

Michael Gauvreau, at a different level, has suggested that there might be a significant "relationship between a missing tradition of systematic theology [in nineteenth-century Canadian evangelicalism] and the failure of a militant fundamentalist movement to find a congenial home in Canada."[38] Certainly Canadian evangelicals in the twentieth century were slow to institutionalize any substantial concern for advanced theology as they founded such centers as Regent College and Ontario Theological Seminary or the Christian Reformed Institute for Christian Studies and Mennonite Conrad Grebel College only since the 1960s. Of these, only the Institute for Christian Studies was established with philosophical and theological scholarship primarily in mind.[39] The very nature of transdenominational evangelicalism, furthermore, militates against elaborate theological sophistication and precision, as it seeks only the minimal theological ground upon which to proclaim the gospel. Evangelicalism, that is, is concerned only for theological essentials in its drive to evangelize the world and foster spiritual vitality. This spirit of pragmatic compromise is nicely in line with the Anglophone Canadian temper in general, then, so it is not surprising to see fundamentalism less important in Canadian evangelicalism than elsewhere. Canadian evangelicalism manifested a corresponding weakness, though, in that it had no strong surge of theological scholarship after World War II to compare with those in the United States or Great Britain.[40]

37. Cf. Steve Bruce's observation that "unlike the American fundamentalists, . . . few English evangelical leaders offer clear political direction to their followers" (*Firm in the Faith*, 176). To be sure, the EFC itself could use rhetoric like this, but it was used in the service of this or that specific lobbying effort, rather than to advance a particular and comprehensive political option.

38. Gauvreau, *Evangelical Century*, 12.

39. See John G. Stackhouse, Jr., "Respectfully Submitted for American Consideration: Canadian Options in Christian Higher Education," *Faculty Dialogue*, no. 17 (Spring 1992): 51–71.

40. For the United States and Britain, see Mark A. Noll, *Between Faith and Criticism: Evangelicals, Scholarship, and the Bible in America* (San Francisco, 1986), 62–214; One might note in this regard that even in Britain and America it was primarily first-order *biblical*

In these respects, therefore, as well as in the basic convictions that marked the whole evangelical tradition, Canadian transdenominational evangelicalism manifested a "mainstream" in the twentieth century: a more varied stream than the British, and yet a much more coherent, if also much smaller, fellowship than the American.

Several themes in this comparison between evangelicalism in Canada and counterparts in the United States and Britain, finally, come together in a consideration of the temporal dimension. It has been a commonplace among Canadian pundits and scholars that Anglophone Canada has become steadily more American and correspondingly less British in the twentieth century. This examination of one aspect of Anglophone Canadian culture, however, might retard the easy adoption of that popular thesis. Evangelicalism itself in Canada has resembled the British in the ways outlined and in further respects as well. Perhaps most significantly, the convergence of Canadian evangelicalism into a "fellowship" or "network" with an identity divergent from the leadership of the major Protestant denominations appeared institutionally in the 1960s, even as its roots went back further. This paralleled the British case, as the National Evangelical Anglican Congress at Keele, "the chief landmark in a postwar Evangelical renaissance," took place in 1967, exactly the same year as the opening of the "Sermons from Science" pavilion in Montreal that marked the public emergence of the Canadian evangelical fellowship.[41] Unlike the polarization in the United States between the two world wars, that is, Canadian and British evangelicals did not coalesce into an alternative network until well after World War II and particularly only as their nations faced the turmoil of the 1960s.

One need not stretch this point and suggest that Canadian evangelicals were more British than American in all respects. In important ways, as we have noted, the American influence surely was stronger. But specific developments in the 1980s and 1990s point up also the increasing sense among Canadian evangelicals of their distinctness from either British or American counterparts. While American mag-

---

scholarship (upon which many evangelicals could agree), not constructive theology and ethics (in which denominational and other differences would necessarily emerge), that flourished.

41. Bebbington, *Evangelicalism in Modern Britain*, 249. For "Sermons from Science," see Stackhouse, *Canadian Evangelicalism*, chap. 6

azines like *Christianity Today* and *Decision* counted Canadians among their subscribers, the EFC's *Faith Today* and the independent biweekly newspaper *ChristianWeek* came into their own in the latter part of the 1980s as distinctly Canadian journals. While Canadians continued to watch American televangelists, they supported even more strongly their Canadian counterparts, notably David Mainse of Toronto and Terry Winter of Vancouver, whose programs were broadcast also in the United States. While Canadian theologians continued to appreciate their debts to British and American sources, the Canadian branch of the Evangelical Theological Society broke off in an amicable split and reconstituted itself as the Canadian Evangelical Theological Association in 1990, citing its concern to pursue a distinctly Canadian agenda. And while relations across the undefended border remained friendly, various Canadian denominations became independent of their larger American counterparts, whether smaller groups like the Free Methodists and the Evangelical Free Church or larger groups like both major denominations of Lutherans. This *chronology*, then, underscores points made earlier about the Canadian evangelical *character*.[42]

With all of these developments, however, Canadian evangelicalism experienced challenges that it had not adequately dealt with by the early 1990s. In the first place, substantial evidence supports the idea that Canadian evangelicalism indeed had become as strong as or stronger than mainline Protestantism in its institutions and the involvement of its constituencies, from theological education to student work, missions, and weekly church attendance. But this was really only half of a perverse "good news, bad news" joke. While evangelicals could rejoice in their newly won status, they confronted a society that had become only more secular as they had become relatively more powerful. Their position vis-à-vis mainline Christianity, that is, had come from losses among the major denominations at least as much as from growth among evangelicals.

In this respect also, Canadian Anglophone culture resembled Britain more than the United States. The pattern of secularization in Can-

---

42. Indeed, one of the quieter signs of growing consciousness of distinctly Canadian evangelicalism was the increased scholarly interest in its history and character, as represented by the publication dates (1980s and 1990s) of a number of the works cited herein.

ada looked more like the British model than the American—and more and more like it as the twentieth century continued. Rather than the American pattern of flourishing religion compartmentalized in the private sphere, Canadian Christianity eroded steadily along British lines.[43] While in 1990 nine in ten Canadians continued to identify with a religious group and the vast majority of them with Protestant or Catholic Christianity, only two in ten attended religious services regularly, and only one-quarter read the Bible or other Scriptures even once a month.[44] This pattern of crumbling Christianity in Canada, with a relatively few denominations dominating the landscape in a highly modernized culture, nicely fits the basic contours of David Martin's "general theory of secularization."[45] It also underscores one challenge that faced evangelicals in Canada as it did in Britain. The gargantuan task of converting to evangelical Christianity a Canadian population mostly secular in orientation confronted evangelicals with the foolishness of any premature triumphalism,[46] especially as some students of evangelicalism were unimpressed with its ability to attract those without significant evangelical background.[47]

The second challenge confronting Canadian evangelicals was to reconsider their tradition of social ministry. Some Canadian evangelical leaders followed the historical paradigm about American evangelicalism in their interpretation of their own history in this regard. They taught that twentieth-century evangelicals in Canada aban-

43. For helpful sketches of "American" and "British" models, see Martin E. Marty, *The Modern Schism: Three Paths to the Secular* (New York, 1969); and Os Guinness, *The Gravedigger File: Papers on the Subversion of the Modern Church* (Downers Grove, Ill., 1983), 107–39.

44. Reported by Reginald W. Bibby in news release no. 11 of "Project Can90," 26 March 1991 (author's files); for a published digest and commentary, see the several articles in *ChristianWeek* 5 (16 April 1991).

45. David Martin, *A General Theory of Secularization* (New York, 1978).

46. Dennis Mackintosh Oliver, "The New Canadian Religious Pluralism" (Paper delivered at the Canadian Society of Church History, Saskatoon, Sask., 1 June 1979).

47. See especially the oeuvre on this question of Reginald W. Bibby, summarized in the pertinent sections of his *Fragmented Gods: The Poverty and Potential of Religion in Canada* (Toronto, 1987). A confirming study is Ken Little et al., "Are the Conservative Churches Reaching Canada?" *His Dominion* 4 (Spring 1977): 12–13. See also Arnell Motz, ed., *Reclaiming a Nation: The Challenge of Re-Evangelizing Canada by the Year 2000* (Richmond, B.C., 1990).

doned their social ministry of the nineteenth century in some sort of
"Great Reversal" because the liberals had taken it over in the name of
the Social Gospel.[48] Perhaps this line of interpretation does not hold
completely for Canada, however, since there was no great split in
Canada along the fundamentalist-modernist lines. Perhaps instead,
twentieth-century evangelicals largely concentrated their energies
elsewhere precisely because they apparently had accomplished their
nineteenth-century goal of a generally Christian public policy of benevolence in certain issues, including Sunday closings, child labor
laws, and Prohibition.[49] Once these specific problems were dealt
with satisfactorily, then, as many of them had been dealt with by 1900
or so, perhaps evangelicals blithely left the driving of the social "bus"
to the government—at least until the 1960s, when there could be no
more illusion of a Christian consensus in Canadian life. Since that
time, then, evangelicals have had to consider taking up again and expanding upon their heritage of social ministry in an age of shrinking
government budgets and the greater fragmentation of cultural consensus on matters of public policy.[50]

A third challenge was a perennial one. Despite the news reports
from the United States in the 1970s and 1980s of vast financial empires dominated by television preachers or evangelical entrepre-
neurs, Canadian evangelical institutions perpetually had trouble raising money and staying within budget. Donations typically were small.
Canadian evangelicalism produced few wealthy businesspersons
and no large foundations to underwrite major projects, especially of
a transdenominational sort. What this meant, then, is that projects
among these Christians had to appeal to a broad middle sector, rather
than to the interests of a particular sector of evangelicalism, if they

48. Brian Stiller of the Evangelical Fellowship of Canada is an important example here, as
several publications of the EFC demonstrate, although writings of his in the early 1990s indicate a shift toward the thesis argued here.

49. This questioning owes a debt particularly to the following interpretations: John Webster Grant, *A Profusion of Spires: Religion in Nineteenth-Century Ontario* (Toronto, 1988);
William Westfall, *Two Worlds: The Protestant Culture of Nineteenth-Century Ontario* (Montreal and Kingston, 1989); and those in Rawlyk, ed., *The Canadian Protestant Experience*.

50. This paragraph hardly qualifies as an interpretation per se because too few data are
available about Canadian evangelical social ministry, especially in the twentieth century.
Enough differences from the American pattern of evangelicalism have shown up in this study,
however, to make this question worth further examination.

were to survive, much less thrive. This only confirmed the tendency of Canadian evangelical institutions to "deviate toward the norm." Whether bold ventures not typically supported by evangelicals in the past could fly, therefore, would depend on highly successful leadership among the grass roots, rather than upon the vision of a few well-heeled magnates.[51]

The final challenge confronted Canadian evangelicals as it confronts any group that moves from an outsider or an insider status to that of a participant status, from feeling estranged from or dominant over the culture to taking one's place with others in joint responsibility for the culture.[52] The challenge was to maintain the evangelical commitment to orthodoxy, personal piety, and evangelism even as the mainstream of evangelicalism broadened to include a larger range of theologies, a commitment to social justice, and support of all vocations.[53] As wrong as it has been for Canadian historians and sociologists to see Canadian evangelicalism only in terms of particular sectarian movements or denominations, the basic character of the movement at mid-century was indeed classically sectarian in its growing sense of alienation from the new directions of the major denominations and the culture itself. As evangelicalism began to reengage the culture in the 1960s, then, the second challenge remained: would evangelicals present Canadians with a new synthesis of evangelical convictions about orthodoxy, spiritual experience, and personal evangelism combined with convictions about theological sophistication, cultural responsibility, vocation, and social ministry? Or would "theological sophistication" merely mask theological fuzziness, "cultural responsibility" whitewash the selfishness of just another special interest, "vocation" justify individual greed, and "social ministry" serve as a more culturally acceptable alternative to proselytizing?

51. The social and economic status of Canadian evangelicals through the twentieth century is a virtually unexplored field to date, and a question that clearly would complement those raised in this study. My research into seven prominent Canadian evangelical institutions, however, provides the basis for this assertion (see *Canadian Evangelicalism*).

52. The terminology of "outsider" and "insider" has been used to considerable effect on the American scene in the recent study by R. Laurence Moore, *Religious Outsiders and the Making of Americans* (New York, 1986).

53. This challenge was recognized in part by Ted. S. Rendall of Prairie Bible Institute in "On the Crest of the Wave," *Prairie Overcomer* 51 (September 1978): 486–92.

In sum, Canadian evangelicals (and observers of them) might be pleased to find that, despite the American media stereotypes or the imprints of British evangelicalism, they were distinct, and distinctly like other Canadians. They might also find to their chagrin, however, that they were indeed not all that different from other Canadians.[54]

54. Implicit warnings in this regard are raised in terms of late nineteenth-century Canadian evangelicals by Ramsay Cook, *The Regenerators: Social Criticism in Late Victorian English Canada* (Toronto, 1985); by Gauvreau, *The Evangelical Century*; by A. B. McKillop, *A Disciplined Intelligence: Critical Inquiry and Canadian Thought in the Victorian Era* (Montreal and Kingston, 1979), esp. 205–32; and by Van Die, *Evangelical Mind*. Contemporary criticism in the late twentieth century has come notably from Reginald Bibby, *Fragmented Gods*.

Bibliographic Afterword

An Introductory Guide to the Literature of Comparative Evangelical History

Larry Eskridge

The study of evangelicals—of which this book is but a part—has exploded in the last two decades. Understandably, coming to grips with such a diverse, far-flung movement amid the accelerating output of dissertations, articles, and monographs is no easy chore. What follows will provide a starting point for both the scholar and the interested layperson seeking to gain a basic grounding in evangelicalism and the comparative international dimensions of this remarkably complex religious movement.

For an overview of the development of evangelicalism in specific locales, several general histories provide excellent summaries. For the British context, David Bebbington's *Evangelicalism in Modern Britain: A History for the 1730s to the 1980s* (London, 1989; Grand Rapids, 1992) is a thorough overview that provides particularly good background for understanding the development of missions agencies and other voluntary parachurch organizations that sprang up in Britain and were later duplicated elsewhere. For the United States, Sidney Ahlstrom's massive *Religious History of the American People* (New Haven, Conn., 1972) is probably still the standard one-volume history of American religion. It provides a satisfactory, if not outstanding, analysis of the evangelical dimension of the religious history of the United States. Shorter, but more readable, is Winthrop S. Hudson's *Religion in America* (4th ed., New York, 1987). Martin Marty's multivolume history *Modern American Religion* (vol. 1: *The Irony of It All, 1893–1919;* Vol. 2: *The Noise of Conflict, 1919–1941* [Chicago, 1986–91]), still in progress, is useful for its treatment of events and personalities since the late nineteenth century and is informed by the renaissance of scholarship on things evangelical. Robert T. Handy, *A History of the Churches in the United States and Canada* (New York, 1977), and Mark A. Noll, *A History of Christianity in the United States and Canada* (Grand Rapids, 1992), are two important works that provide an excellent overview of the North American context by looking jointly at the development of Christianity in both the United States and Canada. George A. Rawlyk, ed., *The Canadian Protestant Experience, 1760–1990* (Burlington, Ont., 1990), is a valuable collection of essays that filters Canadian Protestantism through, among other things, a distinctly evangelical prism. Recently a symposium from the United Kingdom has presented a valuable collection of essays on the growth of evangelicalism in several national regions: Keith Robbins, ed., *Protestant Evangelicalism: Britain, Ireland, Germany, and America, c. 1750–c. 1950: Essays in Honour of W. R. Ward* (Oxford, 1990).

The pivotal eighteenth-century revivalistic awakenings were the seedbed for the development of modern evangelicalism, undergirded by a flourishing transatlantic network linking pietistic revivalist groups in Britain and the North American colonies. The first major examination of these connections was by Susan (Durden) O'Brien in a pair of important journal articles: "A Study of the First Evangelical Magazines, 1740–1748," *Journal of Ecclesiastical History* 27 (July 1976): 255–75; and "A Transatlantic Community of Saints: The Great Awakening and the First Evangelical Networks, 1735–1755," *American Historical Review* 91 (October 1986): 811–32. One key facet of O'Brien's work was her success in establishing the importance of the

Celtic fringe, and especially Scotland, in the evolution of evangelicalism. A flurry of recent high-quality scholarship on developments in this region has emerged, including Ned C. Landsman's *Scotland and Its First American Colony, 1683–1765* (Princeton, N.J., 1985) and "Witherspoon and the Problem of Provincial Identity in Scottish Evangelical Culture," in *Scotland and America in the Age of the Enlightenment*, ed. Richard B. Sher and Jeffrey R. Smitten (Princeton, 1990); Marilyn J. Westerkamp, *Triumph of the Laity: Scots-Irish Piety and the Great Awakening, 1625–1760* (New York, 1988); Leigh Eric Schmidt, *Holy Fairs: Scottish Communions and American Revivals in the Early Modern Period* (Princeton, N.J., 1989); Michael J. Crawford, *Seasons of Grace: Colonial New England's Revival Tradition in Its British Context* (New York, 1991); and David Hempton and Myrtle Hill, *Evangelical Protestantism in Ulster Society, 1740–1890* (New York, 1992). Of particular interest because of its emphasis on the Continental roots of the awakening is William R. Ward, *The Protestant Evangelical Awakening* (New York, 1992).

The Great Awakening, which profoundly shaped eighteenth-century North American religious life, has been examined in a number of important books. Among the best are Edwin Scott Gaustad's *Great Awakening in New England* (New York, 1957); Alan Heimert's influential *Religion and the American Mind: From the Great Awakening to the American Revolution* (Cambridge, Mass., 1966); George A. Rawlyk, *Ravished by the Spirit: Religious Revivals, Baptists, and Henry Alline* (Montreal and Kingston, 1984); and Harry S. Stout, *The New England Soul: Preaching and Religious Culture in Colonial New England* (New York, 1986), which goes into Puritan backgrounds as well as the period of the Awakening.

Undoubtedly the three pivotal figures in this period, especially within the transatlantic revivalist network, were Jonathan Edwards, George Whitefield, and John Wesley. Their influence has been sensitively traced in recent years. Nathan O. Hatch and Harry S. Stout, eds., *Jonathan Edwards and the American Experience* (New York, 1988), furnishes a solid overview of the state of current Edwardsean studies. Stout's recent *Divine Dramatist: George Whitefield and the Rise of Modern Evangelicalism* (Grand Rapids, 1991) is a provocative and highly readable analysis of Whitefield's style and rhetoric that supplements Arnold A. Dallimore's earlier, meticulous—if somewhat uncritical—two-volume biography *George Whitefield: The Life and Times of the Great Evangelist* (London, 1970). Unfortunately, the definitive Wesley biography has yet to be written, but Henry D. Rack's *Reasonable Enthusiast: John Wesley and the Rise of Methodism* (Philadelphia, 1989) provides a thoroughly serviceable, if at times overly detailed, examination of this complex figure. For a somewhat different picture of Wesley and for an illuminating look at what the rise of evangelicalism meant for women, see Paul Wesley Chilcote's *John Wesley and the Women Preachers of Early Methodism* (Metuchen, N.J., 1991).

The story of evangelicalism in the nineteenth century was in many ways one of growth, achievement, and—in the United States—cultural hegemony. Several books stand out as particularly important for understanding this period. Nathan Hatch's *Democratization of American Christianity* (New Haven, Conn., 1989) explores the seminal role that evangelicalism played in creating American culture in the early national period. For an important treatment of the British scene, Ian Bradley's *Call to Seriousness: The Evangelical Impact on the Victorians* (New York, 1976) sketches the way in which evangelical sensibilities colored middle-class life and thought. John Wolffe's book *The Protestant Crusade in Great Britain, 1829–1860* (New York, 1991) provides additional insights into evangelicals' attempts to dominate their society and the anti-Catholic tack such efforts frequently took. The continuing development of cross-Atlantic influences—with an eye to the evolution of voluntary agencies and formalized revivalism—is explored in Richard Carwardine's pioneering *Transatlantic Revivalism: Popular Evangelicalism in Britain and America, 1790–1865* (Westport, Conn., 1978).

Regional and racial developments in the South were a central aspect of the story of American evangelicalism in this period. There has been much good work done on these topics, which provides a needed counterpoint to the sometimes imperious lily-white Yankeeness that dominates mainstream interpretations of the North American evangelical scene. Solid comparative examinations of evangelicalism on both sides of the Mason-Dixon line include Samuel S. Hill's *The South and the North in American Religion* (Athens, Ga., 1980) and Richard Carwardine's *Evangelicals and Politics in Antebellum America* (New Haven, Conn., 1993). For understanding the origins of antebellum southern evangelicalism, John B. Boles's *Great Revival, 1787–1805: The Origins of the Southern Evangelical Mind* (Lexington, Ky., 1975) and Donald G. Mathews's *Religion in the Old South* (Chicago, 1977) are foundational. The premier examination of the early development of African-American Christianity is Albert Raboteau's *Slave Religion: The "Invisible" Institution in the Antebellum South* (New York, 1978), although Eugene Genovese's exhaustive, Marxist-oriented study *Roll, Jordan, Roll: The World the Slaves Made* (New York, 1974) is an invaluable study. For the period after the Civil War, Ted Owenby's *Subduing Satan: Religion, Recreation, and Manhood in the Rural South, 1865–1920* (Chapel Hill, N.C., 1990) provides an excellent treatment of the evolution of white southern evangelicalism in the late nineteenth and early twentieth centuries and its ever-increasing dominance of southern society. William E. Montgomery's recent *Under Their Own Vine and Fig Tree: The African-American Church in the South, 1865–1900* (Baton Rouge, 1993) is an important examination of black Christians' adjustment to freedom, Reconstruction, and Jim Crow.

D. L. Moody was truly *the* international evangelical presence in the mid to late nineteenth century. Surprisingly, Moody has received little direct attention in the outpouring of evangelical historiography since the publication of Stanley Gundry's *Love Them In: The Proclamation Theology of D. L. Moody* (Chicago, 1976). The best biographical examination of his life is still James F. Findlay's *Dwight L. Moody: American Evangelist, 1837–1899* (Chicago, 1969).

By the late nineteenth century evangelical confidence was being shaken by scientific, intellectual, and theological developments that ultimately issued in a crisis in evangelicalism and—again most forcefully in America—the fundamentalist-modernist controversy. The genesis of these difficulties is ably mapped out in James Turner, *Without God, Without Creed* (Baltimore, 1985). Likewise, William R. Hutchison's *Modernist Impulse in American Protestantism* (Cambridge, Mass., 1976) examines the rise of the liberal wing of American Protestantism that set out to accommodate Christianity to the spirit of the times. The reaction against these developments—fundamentalism—is explored in Ernest R. Sandeen, *The Roots of Fundamentalism: British and American Millenarianism, 1800–1930* (Chicago, 1970), and George Marsden's monumental *Fundamentalism*

*and American Culture: The Shaping of Twentieth-Century Evan-
gelicalism, 1870–1925* (New York, 1980). Marsden's article "Fundamentalism as an American Phenomenon: A Comparison with English
Evangelicalism," *Church History* 46 (1977): 215–32, is a valuable
early comparative study. Other insights into the evangelical movement are contained in the various articles and essays of the premier
biographer of the movement, C. Allyn Russell. His *Voices of American Fundamentalism: Seven Biographical Studies* (Philadelphia,
1976) is still the most sophisticated examination of several important
fundamentalist figures. Additionally, his essay "Thomas Todhunter
Shields: Canadian Fundamentalist," *Foundations* 24 (January–
March 1981): 15–31, is a perceptive examination of the Canadian fundamentalist context, as is George Rawlyk's *Champions of the Truth:
Fundamentalism, Modernism, and the Maritime Baptists* (Montreal and Kingston, 1990).

The period since the 1920s has produced a small number of comparative works that elaborate on the evolution of the traditional
trans-Atlantic connections. Steve Bruce's *Firm in the Faith* (Brook-
field, Vt., 1984) is a compelling look at militant fundamentalists in
Northern Ireland, Scotland, and their American ties. On a more irenic
subject, Keith and Gladys Hunt's in-house examination of the American wing of the Inter-Varsity movement, *For Christ and the University: The Story of InterVarsity Christian Fellowship of the U.S.A.,
1940–1990* (Downers Grove, Ill., 1991), also provides some information about British and Canadian backgrounds and developments.

While there is a shortage of comparative works, several excellent
books on specific subjects and personalities during this period provide a valuable background for general trends since the fundamentalist controversy. For the United States, Joel Carpenter, *Revive Us
Again: The Recovery of American Fundamentalism, 1930–1950*
(forthcoming), provides the definitive look at the rise of the funda-
mentalist/evangelical armada that stormed into the era after World
War II. George Marsden's *Reforming Fundamentalism: Fuller Seminary and the New Evangelicalism* (Grand Rapids, 1987) is one of
those rare institutional histories that sheds great light on a wider
movement—in this case, neo-evangelicalism. One of the important
developments in recent years, the emergence of the heavily funda-
mentalist/evangelical "religious right," is ably dissected in Steve

Bruce's *Rise and Fall of the New Christian Right: Conservative Protestant Politics in America, 1978–1988* (Oxford, 1988).

No one person has played a more important role in postwar evangelicalism on the international level than North Carolina's William Franklin "Billy" Graham. William Martin's recent *Prophet with Honor: The Billy Graham Story* (New York, 1991) will be the definitive biography for years to come. However, the work of Graham's authorized biographer—Briton John Pollock—in *Billy Graham, Evangelist to the World: An Authorized Biography of the Decisive Years* (San Francisco, 1979) and *To All the Nations: The Billy Graham Story* (San Francisco, 1985) particularly emphasizes the international dimension of Graham's career with an eye to his missions in the United Kingdom and Australia.

Graham's globe-trotting is but one evidence of how the postwar period has also seen the rise of a truly global evangelicalism that is no longer largely limited to the English-speaking world. *Earthen Vessels: American Evangelicals and Foreign Missions, 1880–1980* (Grand Rapids, 1990), edited by Joel Carpenter and Wilbert Shenk, is a good collection of essays that explore the role that missions has played in the development. David Barrett's *Encyclopedia of World Christianity: A Comparative Study of Churches and Religions in the Modern World*, A.D. *1900–2000* (New York, 1982), although dated, is still a gold mine of information for understanding the worldwide growth of evangelical movements.

Central to the explosion of evangelicalism in the non-English-speaking world has been the spread of Pentecostalism as a kind of "world evangelicalism." Robert Mapes Anderson, *Vision of the Disinherited: The Making of American Pentecostalism* (New York, 1979), provides an authoritative, if thoroughly secular, view of the origins of the movement. Edith L. Blumhofer's *Restoring the Faith: The Assemblies of God, Pentecostalism, and American Culture* (Urbana, Ill., 1993) is a more balanced monograph that uses one denomination as a lens through which she examines the broader movement. The premier biography of a Pentecostal leader is David Edwin Harrell's tour de force *Oral Roberts: An American Life* (Bloomington, Ind., 1985). On the international level, Walter Hollenweger, *The Pentecostals: The Charismatic Movement in the Churches* (1969; U.S. ed., Minneapolis, 1972) is a massive, if now dated, survey of worldwide

Pentecostalism. The spread of Pentecostalism and the threat of an evangelical "takeover" in certain parts of Latin America has recently produced two important books that provide intriguing insights into the penetration of evangelical—particularly American evangelical—Protestantism in a Third World context: David Stoll, *Is Latin America Turning Protestant? The Politics of Evangelical Growth* (Berkeley, Calif., 1990); and David Martin, *Tongues of Fire: The Explosion of Protestantism in Latin America* (New York, 1990). Despite its title, Martin's book also contains some of the most intriguing analysis to date of the dynamics of evangelical movements in the English-speaking world and in Asia.

One of the handiest outworkings of the evangelical information explosion has been a number of fine reference volumes and bibliographies. Edith L. Blumhofer and Joel A. Carpenter, eds., *Twentieth-Century Evangelicalism: A Guide to the Sources* (New York, 1990), is the best of the bibliographies dealing with the North American context. It provides not only annotated entries but contextual essays, descriptions of library and archival resources, and information on evangelical publishers and periodicals. Other valuable reference works include Stanley M. Burgess and Gary B. McGee, eds., *Dictionary of Pentecostal and Charismatic Movements* (Grand Rapids, 1988); Samuel S. Hill, ed., *Encyclopedia of Religion in the South* (Macon, Ga., 1984); and Daniel G. Reid et al., eds., *Dictionary of Christianity in America* (Downers Grove, Ill., 1990). While these volumes are almost exclusively American in purview, a biographical dictionary of Australian evangelicals (Stuart Piggin and Brian Dickey, eds.) is in preparation, and the forthcoming *Blackwell's Encyclopedia of Evangelical Biography* (Donald Lewis, ed.) will be truly international in scope.

This survey of the emerging terrain of evangelical historiography cannot, of course, be exhaustive. Perhaps most encouraging is that the scholarly work covered within—and numerous articles and books that cannot be noted here—are but the beginnings of a long-term quest for a historical understanding of evangelicalism worldwide. Interest continues to grow in this enterprise, and a growing contingent of academics, many of them with evangelical sympathies, are shedding new light on movements, forces, and individuals that have hitherto been largely neglected. Moreover, links between evangelical scholars have been forged in recent years that not only promise a better understanding of evangelical movements but, ironically, mirror the processes by which evangelicalism has emerged as an international Christian movement. We can only hope that these attempts to comprehend the evangelical past flourish with a vigor that matches the movement itself.

Index